INFORMER
The Wars of Men

Copyright * 2020 Rhoan Flowers

All rights reserved. Except as permitted under (U.S Copyright Act of 1976), or (Canadian Copyright Act of 2012), no part of this publication may be reproduced, distributed, or transmitted in any form or by any means, or stored in a database or retrieval system, without the prior written permission of the publisher.

ISBN: 978-1-9991642-3-2
ISBN: 978-1-9991642-7-0
ISBN: 978-1-9991642-6-3

Library and Archives of Canada

The
Street Author

Introduction

Throughout humans' existence, people have treasured their loyal friends, whom they considered in many cases, to be more like family. The world of organized crime topped all other categories, for which it was necessary to work with trustworthy associates. Even the most vicious killers needed unbiased comrades for them to continue breathing, therefore, when Kevin reconnected with Kadeem, the gangster knew, he was then equipped to defeat his enemies.

The biker crew, which became Kevin nemesis, was governed by a cult of billionaires, who used the bikers' brawn and unethical problem-solving methods, to rule the illegal drug markets, intimidate opposers, and assassinate whosoever defied their orders. The cult members, who were already wealthy beyond imagination, sought money, power, and the ability to implement laws; therefore, they were heavily invested in politics, and used government officials to achieve their directives.

Throughout this city of corruption, murders, extortion, bribery, drug trafficking, theft, prostitution, racism, racketeering, rape, money laundering, and lies, the two warring factions fought over control. Following years of confrontations with numerous comrades lost, the rebellious immigrant and the Canadian biker boss, agreed to meet for a decisive battle, where the winner would legislate how business was conducted across the entire city, from that time forth.

Part 1

Maxwell Bishop could hardly conceal his anxiety as he stormed up the staircase towards the third floor of Building G; at the El Greco Tropical Resort. The sun had been blasphemous throughout the day, but with the shades of evening came a mild tropical breeze. Jamaica's land temperature during the latter part of the year was divinely soothing, as was the payment with which Maxwell expected. He shouted adieu to a hotel groundskeeper on the second floor, before weaseling his way up the final flight of stairs. There was a scruffy-looking hotel employee standing at the top of the stairs, whom Maxwell felt conflicted about bothering. Maxwell asked the employee for directions; yet harbored the thought that the man appeared slightly out of character.

Suite D-316 was almost to the end of the corridor, thus Maxwell used his few seconds before reaching the door, to assess and properly groom himself. Before knocking, however, Maxwell noticed that his left shoelace was untied and bent over to correct the problem, which landed him a Luger 9mm nozzle to the rear of his head. With the weapon pressed against Maxwell's temple, a separate hand came through the mist of air between he and the door; and knocked.

A bass-toned voice whispered from behind him, "If you breathe anything but you name, me a splatter your morrow all over the front door! You feel me, my youth?"

By then, a Latin accent sounded behind the door, demanding the visitor's name. Maxwell barely conjured up the strength to announce himself, after first swallowing a huge lump of saliva, that had crept up the back of his throat. The sudden jolt of terror that shook Maxwell's very foundation had him clenching his ass tight in an attempt to avoid defecating on himself.

The visitor exclaimed, "Bishop! It's me, Maxwell!"

With the clack of the door lock came a huge, size fifteen boot that smashed the door into the small frame man on the opposite end. Before anyone could protectively maneuver themselves, Maxwell was tossed into the condominium head over heels, and went crashing against the center table. Both robbers then quickly rushed into the condo, locked the door behind them and held everyone frozen at gunpoint.

The taller of the two intruders threatened, "Nobody move, nobody get hurt, seen!"

The sole person inside the room, whose mannerisms were those of someone important, exclaimed, "What's the fucking meaning of this? This is disrespectful! How dare you barge into my suite?"

"Th-th-th-this ie-ie-is a-a-a fu-fu-fu-fucking st-st-st-stick-up," said the shorter man is his stammering lingo.

The boss, who'd settled back into his seat, asked, "What the fuck did he just say?"

"Him just say we accept all credit cards, jewelry, and money. Or, in layman's terms, fill up me blood-clatt bag," translated the taller man of the two robbers.

The sixth man inside the room asked, "You fools have any idea who y'all trying to rip off?"

"An-an-an-any bo-bo-body a-a-a-ask yu-yu-you an-any ti-ti-thing," argued the stuttering bandit?

The five-foot-six Spanish bodyguard fired back, "What!?"

"Just keep you blood-clatt shut, before somebody put a bullet inna it," warned the young thief! "Stamma, me a go check out the rest of the place. Just keep everybody covered till me come back!"

With the taller of the two robbers away checking each individual room for additional victims, Stamma remained in place and surveyed the entire room. "The guard left in place is that scruffy-looking worker", thought Maxwell to himself as he slowly regained consciousness. He immediately turned to the person he'd come to meet and began apologizing profusely.

"Mr. Lopez, sir, I have absolutely nothing to do with this robbery! I'm sorry, I didn't notice them coming up the stairs, and I'm sorry I brought them into you place, but them did go kill me boss!"

"You would be a fool to bring anyone here to rob me! Obviously, these men have no idea who I am, or they would tuck their tails between their legs and run out of here like the chumps they are," stated Mr. Lopez!

The initial guard who attended the door was bloodied and wobbly. The man rolled over onto his back and attempted to sit up, before he was forced back to the ground by a sturdy boot to the left temple. Instead of further aggravating his intruders, the guard simply wiped the blood from his eyes and remained tranquil on the floor. After reasserting their dominance, Stamma hollered at his partner to ensure his safety.

"Ki-Ki-Killa," Stamma shouted!
"Everything is everything Stamma," advised his partner, who then rejoined the party. "Now! Weah the money deah big man? A the money we come for, so give it up before things start get ugly in here!?"
"Ki-Killa, se-se-see t-t-them ha-ha-have a-a-a bre-bre-bre-briefcase o-o-over de-de-there s-s-so," pointed out Stamma.
"All right, before all that, tie up them blood-clatt before someone start feel like a hero," said Killa.

At that point, Stamma removed his backpack from his back, unzipped it, and removed a few pieces of rope and a roll of duct tape. The bleeding guard, who was the closest, was the first in restraints. At session's end, the man resembled a calf that had been hog-tied by a cowboy in a Rodeo. The second of the two guards leapt to his feet and began immediately protesting. Having committed similar offenses in the past, the guard assumed they were being prepped for execution, via bullets to the back of the head.

"You fucking puta-maricons, ain't gonna execute me like some fucking butcher slaying cattle! Fuck them guns, I take you fuckers with or without them guns," threatened the guard!

"A what you feel like," Killa demanded?

"Boom", sounded an explosion that raised the severity of the situation!

Killa's Taurus G3 9mm Luger, exploded and struck the guard directly in the kneecap, which forced him back onto the floor achingly. The impact of the bullet blasted out the guard's knee, as Stamma ran over to him and immediately gagged him, before flipping him on his stomach and hog-tying him, despite the injured knee. The big boss, who wished for no added injury to befall his mates, immediately tossed the briefcase Stamma spoke of at his antagonists.

"If anybody else in here feels like Superman, let me know? If not, shut the fuck up and we'll be gone as soon as we get paid for all this work! We understand each other?"

The young thugs bound each of their captives securely, before they turned their attention to the briefcase "Ching-ching," exclaimed both robbers as their faces lit up like Christmas trees, the instant they saw the briefcase's contents! The briefcase contained more U.S. dead presidents on paper than they had ever seen. As Killa went about maintaining order, his partner began transferring their newly acquired wealth into the backpack he had brought.

The sound of the condominium's telephone startled Stamma, who immediately grabbed for his pistol and looked around confused. Killa signaled him to continue his task, as he peeked through the windows for uninvited guests. Once he was satisfied there were no law enforcement officials sent to investigate, Killa walked over to the phone and paused, then picked up the receiver and answered.

"Do-do-don't a-a-a-answer th-th-the f-f-f-phone, Ki-Ki-Killa," Stamma instructed!

Again, Killa signaled him to proceed with his task, as he placed the receiver to his ear. Mimicking their captives' Spanish accents Killa responded. "Si, can I help you?"

"Hello, sir! Excuse me, but we received several complaints from other guests who reported hearing some sort of banging from your unit. We're just checking to make sure that everything is fine with you guys, and if you guys could please offer our other guests the same quiet courtesy, they do you, it would be greatly appreciated," stated an employee!?

"Si señorita, excuse us! There will be no more noise. Thank you!"

With that, both thugs finalized their dealings and casually exited the condo. The thugs waked to the Plaza and showed the guard their fake identification, that gained them entry when they arrived. They then took an elevator from the top floor down to street level, where they hopped into a taxi, that brought them to the Gully Market. With the sidewalks crammed with vendors seeking sales for their items, Stamma stopped and purchased some vegetables and fruits for his grandmother, who raised him. Both Gully thugs chewed on sugar cane, as they made their way home through the rough Gully streets.

The ghetto known as Canterbury was home to both bandits, who were educated young men that could not find proper employment, due to their place of residence. The community mainly ran along King Street, but could also be accessed from Upper King Street, Seaview Avenue and Bottom Gully. Residents of the community, had to cross bridges over the infamous storm drainage canal called Gully, to enter the neighborhood, which was only accessible by foot. There were no streets built in Canterbury, therefore, the many pathways that led through the community, made it resemble a mystical maze across the hillside. With an undisclosed number of illegal firearms and ruthless thugs who terrorized the area, even the local police were terrified to enter one of Jamaica's toughest neighborhoods.

On the edge of Canterbury was a wooden shack convenience store that belonged to Hatchet. Hatchet was considered the Gully don, because of his interactions in the daily affairs of the poor and needy; plus, his influence over the tough headed youths. The Don would prepare large meals for himself and everyone in need, as his daily contribution to ensure the hungry children were fed. The many personalities of Hatchet were known throughout; yet the locals loved him, and revered him, especially because he maintained order. Hatched controlled the only ghetto business that remained open after 7:00 PM, simply because other vendors feared the turbulence brought on by nightfall. The Gully don was the face of hope, as well as that of despair, considering he operated the underground sales of armaments and drugs, which he mainly sold outside his poor neighborhood.

Stamma and Killa arrived moments after the evening meal was served, to find a slew of thugs and others eating their proper fill. Hatchet was, as usual, behind the counter of his store, but, paused his food-demolishment to serve a client. As soon as the returning thugs walked into the store, Hatchet directed them to come around to the rear door of his establishment.

"Onnou want two flour," Hatchet demanded?

Killer greedily answered, "But of course Iah!"

"See two plates right there! The food over there in the pot," Hatchet directed.

Killa and Stamma were intelligent enough to maintain their poise and composure around the kennel of wolves, knowing there were those within the group, who were vindictive and conniving motherfuckers. The thought of there being a hundred thousand U.S. dollars in the knapsack on Stamma's back, would be motivation enough for anyone to attempt something sooner or later. Thus, both Stamma and Killa collected their food and joined Hatchet behind the counter, during which they all demolished their portions and discussed the ordeal.

The Gully don had a hand in every major business affair to translate from Bottom Gully to the edge of Canterbury. Hence, a portion of every gross intake by Gully soldiers had to be paid to the, "Feed the Community Fund." While many assumed and would argue that Hatchet provided such nutritious meals from his honest earnings at the store, the thugs who stole, hustled and handled his illegal dealings knew otherwise. Stamma donated five thousand to the "Feed the Community Fund" before paying Hatchet another five hundred for the 9mm he negotiated on consignment.

"So, Killa, you a go pan the move with Justin and Stamma them later," Hatchet asked?

"Nah man, me noh greedy, me nice for today," Killa exclaimed!

"Congratulations, mi buoy! You just purchase you first toy," Hatchet declared!

Stamma tapped the weapon attached to his waist and let off a huge grin, before an embarrassing burp shot from his mouth. Killa broke out in laughter as his accomplice covered his mouth and mumbled, "Excuse me!" After dinner, the thugs individually rolled their separate Marijuana joints, as music bounced from the jukebox in Hatchet's grocery. The successful bandits bought a round of beers for everyone present and drank a few themselves, however, they paid the bill with Jamaican currency to avoid brandishing the foreign dollars they stole. Killa and Stamma eventually left and continued their journey toward home, along a pathway that had a hell-forsaking climb. The terrain up the hill was rocky and dangerous, yet the thugs trotted up as if it wasn't of any consequence.

On their way up the pathway lined by sheets of rusted zinc and torn down fences, Stamma's cellular sounded with his uncle on the other line. Stamma's Uncle Rev was the orchestrator of the theft, although he hadn't the testicular fortitude to physically rob someone at gunpoint. Rev was a closeted homosexual who occasionally slept with Maxwell Bishop. The idea for the heist was originally devised by Maxwell, who was of the upper-class district, with zero ties to the thugs of the ghetto. Hence, Maxwell decided against proceeding with the plot, that he had braggingly brought to Rev's attention.

"Didn't I tell you fucking dummies not to hurt anybody? What kind of shit is shooting out a man's knee? What if security or the police did come by to check on what was going on? You idiots probably would be giving me up now! You know something? Make sure my cut reach me within the hour!" Rev threatened.

Killa knew Stamma was a little scaredy-cat when it came to his uncle, who at one time was the only person financially assisting their grandmother. Rev was twenty-four years older than Stamma and grew up on the Gully side, before relocating in fear of what would happen to him should anyone around the neighborhood discovered his sexual preferences. What may had been considered rumors prior to Rev moving away soon became fact, as the ex-Canterbury native moved in with a man in the West Green community. After listening to Stamma stutter to get a word in during their conversation, Killa grabbed the phone from him and spoke candidly.

"If you feel entitled to a dime you have to come get it pussyhole! A can't bad man you a call and a demand things!? We naw pay you a cent batty buoy, go suck you man an go way," Killa garnished!

"That's why I don't deal with hood rats! You want to fuck with me? Let's see how you like me sending some of my bad batty buoy police friends after your ass? I go make sure say you get yours, because me go get mine one way or the other!" Rev commented.

"You a go get yours; one fat shot inna you blood-clatt the next time mi see you!" Killa threatened, before disconnecting the call.

Slightly after their antagonists had departed, the two guards shuffled themselves across the floor to each other, where they untied each other's ropes, before setting everyone else free. The injured guard moaned and groaned as his fellow companion rushed him a towel filled with ice cubes. While the guard attended to his mate, Maxwell continuously apologized for the mishap that transpired.

"Mister Lopez sir, not many people here in Jamaica get the opportunity that you gave me; and I can never repay your kindness! I'll do my best to find those fucking lowlifes who take you money, but whatever I can do to make this right, please let me know?"

Ernesto responded, "Listen to me, my friend. If you have anything to do with this robbery, I will find out, and then you will be no more! Until then, I need you to find me a doctor to come treat my assistant, and as for our original deal, I'll have someone here by tomorrow with the agreed payment! Now, find me a doctor to come and help my friend? I suggest you go, and hurry! I don't want him to lose his leg."

Ernesto was a drug smuggler whose operations extended from South America to the Great White North. Following the seizure of nearly ten metric-tons of cocaine by the DEA, Ernesto decided to open a new pipeline that would flow through the Caribbean and back into the United States. The trip to Jamaica was the first leg of Ernesto's travels, and he planned to implant similar routes through Haiti and Cuba. The sensitivity of the journey was one that demanded secrecy, which was Ernesto's reasoning for demanding a private physician. With several different agencies such as the DEA and ATF breathing down his neck, Ernesto knew the grave implication any such report would bring, especially it being a gunshot wound.

Within two hours, Maxwell had returned with a qualified physician, who was a fifty years old doctor that practiced medicine around the Rose Hall District. The doctor was a roots man who asked little and behaved as if the gunshot wound was a regular fracture. Serious injuries to tourists on vacation islands are expected to be reported, hence, the government officials from whom Ernesto hid his business affairs, would be pervy to that information. Ernesto walked over to the physician as he performed his duties and spoke candidly with him, considering his immediate financial status.

"This man works for me; but I'm afraid to say that I won't have your exact fees until the bank opens in the morning. If you could please take my Rolex watch as a temporary payment, I will pay you in full once the bank opens in the morning, and you can then, still keep the watch," negotiated Ernesto.

The doctor, who was by then simply bandaging the guard's leg after repairing and cleaning the wound, looked up at the watch and was stunned at the gesture. It was an eighty-five-thousand-dollar watch, with lavish diamond studs throughout the center point. The doctor nonchalantly accepted the deal without hesitation. Ernesto charged a bottle of Petron Tequila to his suite, before making an overseas call to his assistant in Florida, in order to arrange the replacement of the funds. After the drug kingpin got through with his phone dealings, the men inside the suite drank the night away as if nothing faulty had occurred. The next day, Ernesto made good on his promises, as he paid the doctor in full and awarded Maxwell a second briefcase filled with loot.

Part 2

Kevin Walsh left Jamaica at the tender age of thirteen, to reside with his single mother in West Palm Beach, Florida. Tragedy soon struck his family with the untimely death of his mother, after Kevin's third year in the United States. The death of his mother at the hand of some would-be bank robber, attempting to empty her cash register, sparked a flame under Kevin that blazed throughout the remainder of his natural life. After discovering that, due to technicalities in the case, the murderer received only thirty-six months of imprisonment, Kevin decided to judge for himself the man who killed his beloved mother.

Kevin lined up calendars for the next three years and kept a constant check on the prisoner, through the prison's online services. To ensure he remained up to date in his personal pursuit of justice, Kevin visited the prison website at least five times every week. Once Kevin found out that his mother's murderer was awarded early release some nine months before his scheduled date, he knew the time had come to settle the score.

After more than two years in Broward County State Prison, Hector Dominguez walked out a free man. With a slew of his cohorts at hand to greet him at the entrance, Kevin watched his first opportunity slip agonizingly away, as he had planned on slaughtering Hector once he stepped foot from protective custody. Kevin trailed his intended target and his thuggish friends, who joked and played around inside their vehicles for the duration of the journey.

With his heart pounding nervously, to calm himself the unsuspected pursuer toked heavily on his Marijuana Joint, and temporarily focused on a photo of his mother to keep him motivated. There was blood in his eyes and revenge in his thoughts, as he trailed the killer's entourage back to their hood in South Miami Beach. By the time they arrived in Little Haiti, Miami, Kevin had thoroughly demolished his Marijuana joint, which helped to intensify his fiery glowing eyes. The vengeance-thirsty Jamaican followed the eccentric partiers into the heart of their gang turf, where he fearlessly drove through sections of the city, which most residents avoided.

The young hard head scoped out the scene, parked his vehicle across the street from the ongoing party, and left the engine running, with the doors locked and the remote attached to his belt buckle. The roads throughout the neighborhood were filled with obvious gangbangers, residents enjoying the evening calm, and children playing throughout. Kevin watched as his intended target walked over to the house, where they had an ongoing barbeque, and more of Hector's associates. Casually dressed in jeans, a marina white T-shirt, track shoes, and a backpack on his back, Kevin walked directly across to the festivities and unveiled a pair of Springfield Armory nickel-plated 9mm pistols.

With both eyes plastered on the man who had murdered his mother, Kevin began shooting everyone that stood between himself and Hector. However, Kevin's earlier, inaccurate assessment of how many people were inside the three-bedroom house, soon hindered the promise he had made to his deceased mother. The welcoming festivities quickly turned from celebrative to survival mode, but members of the community were quite capable of defending their turf. The gang of Cuban thugs were, as Kevin had expected, fully armed to the teeth, and after his initial scare wore thin, a shoot-out between he and his antagonist arose. Before a single shot was returned at Kevin, three thugs laid dead, with a fourth screaming at the top of his lungs that, "I've been shot"!

Hector quickly ducked from Kevin's vision, narrowly escaping the shells fired at him. However, once the Cuban mob began laying down cover fire, Kevin was forced to rethink his attack. As the revenge-seeking Jamaican scurried back to his vehicle, four thugs from half a block down the road began racing towards him, with bullets from their 9mm pistols striking everything except their target. By then, the entire street had nearly emptied, as residents who'd grown accustomed to the violence fled for their dear lives. Kevin kept his head lowered and popped up as he reached his car door, to force the four charging thugs to rethink their intentions. One of the five shots Kevin blasted at them, struck one man in the chest and forced the others to rethink their actions. Kevin then hammered a few bullets at the front door from which armed assailants were emerging, as the regrouped thugs sought the head of the lone intruder, who had bravely attacked the core of their Cuban movement.

Unknown to Kevin was the fact that there had been two individuals stationed inside a Jeep, Trail Blazer SUV, a few meters up the street constructing a small surveillance on the mob. The two men, who sat and watched Kevin in action were impressed at the method with which he over-powered the ruthless bunch of thugs. They were even more surprised at the amount of respect awarded Kevin, who, even as he departed, had each member of Hector's entourage tucked tightly behind some protective shielding. As Kevin departed the scene, the men inside their Trail Blazer truck pulled out thereafter and gave pursuit at a modest distance.

Kevin cruised northbound along Interstate-95 and drove into Broward County. As he exited the highway, he took notice of the Chevy SUV in his rearview mirror, yet, continued on to positively confirm his suspicions. The heated maniac drove down Commercial Boulevard, then continued to his friend's house in Tamarack. Kevin parked his vehicle in his friend's driveway and walked up to the single-story house, located at 439 Eastern Drive. Following a soft knock on the door, an incredibly huge man appeared on the other side, peeked through a side window, then opened the door and allowed Kevin entry.

The Trail Blazer's occupants drove up to the house and parked across the street, which brought their motives into question. Inside the house, Kevin quickly debriefed his friend Swarty on his retaliation mission, before he advised him of the Trail Blazer. The two friends snuck to a bedroom window where Kevin pointed out the vehicle, before he crawled beneath the bed and withdrew a huge duffle bag. Swarty was initially ecstatic to hear Kevin could have avenged his mother's murder; but was none too thrilled about the Chevy truck and its unwanted occupants outside his house. Kevin had already derived at his solution to the problem, which was why he chose to drive to Swarty's dwelling. The huge, six-foot-four, four-hundred and seventy-pounds man blocked the door entrance and stopped Kevin from leaving the room.

"Brethren, don't tell me say you make police follow you back to my place," Swarty argued?

"Police or not they're about to get fucked; because them chose the wrong day to follow me," Kevin answered!

"So, what you plan on doing to make sure them don't come back here?"

"Watch and see!"

The young maniac, after being granted passage through the doorway, tossed the duffle bag and its contents over his shoulder and headed through the main entrance. Seconds before Kevin exited, Swarty realized what he was about to do and dashed into the kitchen. Kevin walked through the front door and began heading in the Chevy's direction. Midway across the street, the petulant Jamaican unveiled the duffle bag's contents, which immediately brought the Trail Blazer's occupants out their vehicle, with their hands held high.

Swarty dashed into the kitchen and grabbed his sawed-off pump rifle from inside the oven. The huge man, who was remarkably light a-foot, ran through the rear door and unnoticeably crept his way around to the blind side of the Trail Blazer. As Kevin got prepared to empty an entire banana clips from his AK-47 into the vehicle, the driver leapt from the cabin in a surrendering posture, with an explanation.

"Please, please, don't kill me! We only wish to talk to you, my friend!"

Before Kevin could inquire about their intentions, Swarty's voice could be heard lashing instructions in the distant. The big man had his pump action pressed against the passenger's head, while ordering him "to exit to vehicle and get his face in the dirt".

"You have five seconds to spark my interest," declared Kevin!

"Our boss says he thinks we have the same problem, and he wants to negotiate with you," advised the driver.

With both men face down onto the asphalt, Kevin pondered over whether or not to execute them. As he weighed his options, a Mercedes Benz Maybach luxury car turned the corner down the road and began moving towards the scuffle. "Who the hell could be so stupid", thought Kevin to himself as the vehicle continued advancing. With his foot centered in the middle of the driver's back and his weapon now pointed at the Mercedes, the vehicle came to a halt. Kevin's finger tickled the trigger of his weapon, as he adjusted himself for combat. As the rear passenger window rolled down, Kevin prepared to dive for the turf while unloading his first clip, should the occupants be unfriendly.

"Hello! My name is Ernesto, and I believe we can greatly benefit each other if we have a talk. My men obviously didn't lie about your survival skills, so please, please join me," suggested the lone passenger who stuck his head out the window to speak.

"That would be my boss." the man beneath Kevin's foot exclaimed!

After they allowed the men to their feet, Kevin collected the duffle bag and placed the weapon back inside. To avoid any unforeseen mishaps, the young thug returned the weapon from which it was taken, then rearmed himself with the dynamic duo he used to light up the Cubans in Miami.

Kevin asked Swarty, "You a come for the ride?"

"Right now, me vex how you didn't call me from morning and let me in on the ruckus that you caused in Miami. If you think mi go miss another minute a this, you mad! I'll drive in the back of the Balzer with these two, but if you don't exit the Benz when we get where we going, these goons don't exit the Blazer either!" warned Swarty, as he hopped into the Trailblazer carrying his shotgun.

Swarty eased back and looked daintily around inside the Trailblazer with his weapon lying across his lap. It didn't take the airy fat man long to jolt his demands; as he immediately ordered, they change radio stations to Hot 96 for jams to roll to. Following his demands, however, Swarty took time out to apologize for the rough treatment he and Kevin had inflicted on the guards. The Spanish-American men, thereafter, emphasized their fascination with Kevin, whom they'd had the fortune of watching perform.

Kevin was in the process of being introduced to the finer aspects of life. After meeting his true host, Kevin was made aware of the real reason he was sought out. Both Ernesto Lopez and he had a common interest in achieving Hector Dominguez' death, but the drug lord also so the benefits in having such a talent on his team. Unlike Kevin, Ernesto had done business with the Cuban gang and witnessed first-hand their treachery. For Ernesto, it was pure business, thus his conversation was a means of convincing Kevin to join his organization.

Ernesto instructed the chauffeur to drive them home, which was a thirty-eight minutes trip that ended in an upper-class neighborhood in Miami. Any doubts that existed about Ernesto's financial status were immediately discarded, after viewing his luxurious two-million-dollar home, with priceless artifacts. Kevin would spend the next few hours in the kind graces of his host, as they discussed business and futuristic ideas. Over the course of their discussions, Ernesto revealed his original plot to simply hire Kevin and have him execute Hector Dominguez, until he arrived on scene and found his men held at gunpoint. Incidentally, once Ernesto and Kevin spoke, the drug boss realized his intellect and reasoning capability above all, thus they came to terms with the expectation of maintaining a solid business repour.

Once a few shots of Cognac crept into the bloodstreams of the newly federated members and their hosts, Kevin discovered the real history behind Hector and Ernesto, as the boss shared his story.

"Life has blessed me, because I came from the gutter. I was born in a poor village in Columbia, to hardworking farmers. When I was three years old, men from the drug cartel came to my village in search of workers to cultivate their cocaine. They shot and killed my father and took my sister, mother, and me into their work camps to work as slaves cultivating their drugs. I'll never forget the sight of my mother and sister, who were beaten and forced to work in the nude, as they packaged the cocaine outside in the labs. The worst was having to watch the guards, rape and molest my mother and sister as they pleased. They would simply enter our lockups and molest the ladies they desired right in front of their friends and families. Many people lost hope as well as their lives, but there were those, like my mother, who, despite our situation, decided to educate the children around the camp. Even an education, like many other things, had to be taught in secrecy, because had the guards, who were themselves dumb bush people, found out about it, it would be the end of that.

"I grew up tending the Pappy Crops, because even as a child I was forced to do physical labor, or else there was no food for me. They worked me when I was a child like they did the grown men seven times my age. Every day, my hands and legs bled from picking the Pappy and walking barefoot through the fields. My temper boiled to the point where, I knew if I ever get into a physical confrontation with anyone, I was going to kill them and suffer the consequences. Still, through all that, I studied the daily chemistry of the guards and their superiors, along with the smugglers and business preps who were buying, paying, or collecting. In a world far beyond the comprehension of most civilized humans, Hector's father was one of the kids who became my friend when honestly, I didn't need anyone.

"A month after my thirteenth birthday, on a foggy Saturday morning, I awoke to the sounds of machine gun fire, which was mainly being fired down from overhead by patrolling helicopters. The guards did their best to hold their own, but in the end, nearly everyone was killed, except for a few workers who fell to the ground and prayed to be rescued. I ran to find my mother and sister, but found my sister holding Mama's body, who had been shot by one of the guards. As for me, I had learned the great distance to which men would go to harvest this plant, that financed the camp I'd lived in, the army protecting it, and the elaborate, lavish lifestyle lived by the cartels, who rarely visit the plantation.

"While those slaves who had been broken over the years awaited their savior, I moved to the only logical place I believed worth investigating, which was General Gustav's quarters. Hector's father, Raphael, was smart enough to follow me, because we found more money and cocaine than we could carry. I ran away from that horrible place as a man, which I became in my young years, and I never looked back! We found our way into the city, where we sold the drugs, then I bought documents and travelled here, to this great country, where I've built my empire from the same product I'd sworn to hate!

"As for Raphael, he remained in Columbia, and we reunited six years later, when I returned to Columbia to negotiate my first trade line. Raphael drove me to the Estrada Cartel estate and introduced me to Senior Estrada, who has since graciously accepted me into his family. I chose to bring Raphael back to the United States, in order for him to be by my side, so I can have someone who I could completely trust. Things were good for the first few years, until Raphael met Hector's mother, Loretta."

Ernesto paused, as he personally reflected over the events that transpired, before indulging in his alcoholic beverage. The story had intrigued Kevin to where his Marijuana joint had lost its' flame, because of his lack of interest therein. However, given a moment of acknowledgment, Kevin soon reignited his joint and puffed away.

"Loretta was the queen of manipulation, and it didn't take her long to convince Raphael that he was worth a whole lot more than I was paying him! In fact, she had him convinced that we should have been partners, because he introduced me to the connect. The next thing I knew, my right-hand man was skimming off the top and planning on ways to overthrow me. Until this day I regret giving that order, but it had gotten to the point where Raphael had conspired with my own enemies, to have me assassinated! Loretta gave birth to young Hector several months later, and had since raised her child to believe, that I killed his father to take over the business. That woman has completely poisoned her son's mind, but after killing his father, I refuse to give the son the same treatment," revealed Ernesto!

"So, what exactly do you want from us," Kevin asked?

"I'd like to offer you and your friend a position working for me," offered Ernesto.

"What kind of a position," Kevin questioned?

"My money collectors have been getting robbed and targeted by those low-life's you attacked. With Hector away, they've been less successful, but I'm sure they're looking to ramp-up their attacks. I need some no-nonsense gunners like you, who will be willing to protect what is mine at all cost. I'll provide you the necessary supplies to get the job done, and if you bring any recruits, they can join the payroll and get properly compensated," Ernesto then motioned his personal assistant over and took an envelope from her! The envelope contained ten thousand dollars in U.S. currency, which was a simple appetizer to tempt Kevin.

"You couldn't hire anybody better than us to do the job," Kevin declared, as he shoved the envelope into a huge jeans pocket!

"Anybody try take your things from now going forward, will get cancelled," lamented Swarty!

"Buena, I trust you'll take care of those hood-rats," Ernesto stated, while nodding his head!

"Without a doubt. Mr. E," Kevin reassured him!

"I'll have Alex here show you the important materials… You go, enjoy yourself, and what's mine is all yours, mi casa es tu casa! Allow me to take care of some minor business and we'll talk later," Ernesto advised.

Ernesto's chief security officer showed Swarty and Kevin to the basement, where they were brought into the weaponry chamber, to properly acquaint themselves with the armory. The newcomers to Ernesto's cartel were amazed at the selection of various weapons, displayed across the walls throughout the room. Kevin felt anxious at the chance to fire several weapons he had only dreamed of, thus, he excitedly leapt onto Swarty's back and pounded his fist across the big man's chest.

Swarty felt confident he'd made the right choice to accompany his friend, as his face lit up the instant, they entered the armory. Within two minutes of entering, the big man fell in love with a .357 Magnum he saw, thus, he tucked the weapon into his waistband, and placed a box of bullets in his pocket. Both men were elated to join Ernesto's organization for the chance to earn a paycheck, considering they were both unemployed. They spent another hour learning specifics about the business from Ernesto's guards, before they were driven back to Swarty's residence.

The men returned home to find Swarty's girlfriend, Deloris, who was a professional clothes thief by trade, bargaining the sale of items she'd stolen with prospective buyers she'd invited over. There were three ladies groping through the clothes, that were spread across the living room furniture, like a showcase exhibit.

"Dwayne, how comes you know say, me gone out on the hustle, and you don't even cook the chicken me leave in the sink? We have bills' round here, and I don't see you big ass getting up and paying any of them! I saw Keith down by the Swap Shop and him say the thing ready, so tell you to check him later," quarreled Deloris!

"You get me the shirt," Swarty demanded?

"It's in the bedroom," Deloris responded!

Swarty dipped into his pocket and tossed Deloris a thousand dollars, as he walked by with the huge, pump action rifle at hand. The female crotcher, who was accustomed to verbally assaulting her mate, fell dumbstruck as Swarty passed and returned the weapon to its place of origin. The sight of the life taker in Swarty's hand may have aroused other females' interest, yet Deloris and company behaved as if that was a regular occurrence. In fact, the ladies were more amazed by Swarty's money gesture, than they actually were over the shotgun. As Kevin passed through on his way to the kitchen, Deloris intercepted him and said, "See the shirt me tell you me think would fit you nicely here," before tossing it at their roommate.

"Yeah man, a dat me a talk bout," said Kevin, as he acknowledged Deloris' exquisite sense of style!

Kevin walked directly into the kitchen and collected two Heinekens from the refrigerator, passed one to his friend, then sat around the five-piece dining set. The two friends began assessing their strategies toward ridding their new employer of the pest, he had contracted them to exterminated. Given the personalities of both men, the decision was quickly made to secretly assassinate every careless member found, until the poisons within were nullified. Both friends also found the time to reminisce on the past, as their friendship, which expanded since the death of Kevin's mother, molded them into brothers.

"Tell me how you feel when you see the buoy who killed you mother," Swarty emotionally asked?

"Believe me brethren', it was like all them years of grief and pain was about to subside! Like mi mother spirit could finally rest in peace knowing me pay back the pussyhole who murder her! Me a tell you say me line up the buoy under a kill or be killed vibe, and it's only by the skin of him teeth that him get way! But you see the next time," Kevin barked angrily as he removed his firearm and stared at it!

"I can't forget them cold sweat; you used to wake up in the middle of the night, when you just moved here. Remember I told you one day you will get you chance to settle the score and you see, I was right," Swarty exclaimed!

"Me dream about that moment for years! One time, those cold sweat dreams used to scare the shit out a mi, because all me used to vision was that bitch Hector pumping gunshot inna me! But over time, you convince me that him a go be the one getting bore up with bullets, and that idea you give me kill all them other weird dreams," Kevin remarked!

The next morning, Kevin had information sent to Deloris' e-mail address concerning the prudent members of Hector's gang, who posed a threat to the daily operations of Ernesto's empire. There were three members who orchestrated attacks against Ernesto's affairs during Hector's absence, with most of the service men being foot soldiers. Hector's mates made up the nucleus of a vicious neighborhood gang called, 'The South Hourds', who ruled and dominated the entire southern portion of Carol City. The South Hourds were renowned for expelling radical gangs like The Bloods and Crips from their turf, in order to fully control the illegal activities throughout their hood.

Kevin detailed his idea for disposing of the troublemakers to Ernesto in a phone conversation, to acquire the assistance of all the boss' lower-level workers across Dade County. Once photos of the wanted men were obtained, Kevin casted an (APB) All Persons Bulletin on their whereabouts, to all the available personnel assigned by Ernesto. With multiple eyes across Miami searching for the persons in question, it was only a matter of time before they were spotted.

Day One Assault - 11:20 AM

Swarty and Kevin cruised by seven members of the South Hourd gang, outside a local fajita restaurant, that belonged to the parents of one of the gang members. The gangbangers all sported their green handkerchiefs, which was the gang's insignia color. With Swarty behind the steering wheel of a Honda Accord EX, loaned to the pair by their employer, Kevin instructed his accomplice to circle the block. While circling, Kevin prepared his U.S military issue M16 assault rifle for discharge, as he instructed Swarty on how to properly maneuver the vehicle, during their impending assault.

The Honda Accord turned back onto the road and approached moderately, to avoid scaring the thugs who screened every unfamiliar vehicle that passed by. None of the thugs had any daunting suspicions about the Honda, therefore, after observing the vehicle for a short time, they began ignoring it. As the Honda drew closer to the preoccupied gangbangers,

Kevin popped the nose of his M16 rifle through the window, then began emptying the clip at the unsuspecting thugs. Once the weapon fell silent, every one of the seven intended victims laid lifeless on the ground; as the seventeen-inch tires of the Honda Accord, screeched as it sped away from the crime scene.

Day One Assault - 12:19 AM

The vigilante pair received a phone call from Carlos, who indicated that one of Hector's valued generals, had been spotted in downtown Miami. The thug was transporting his female on errands, as she reveled in one of her pampering expeditions. The assailant had brought his female friend to a manicure/pedicure appointment, she had on Hollywood Boulevard for 10:40 that morning. At that point, however, they were at her second scheduled stop, which was at Leann's Beauty Salon, on Ives Dairy Road. The sought-after culprit received the notifications concerning the slayings of his peers, though no one had any information about who the drive-by shooters were. Hence, the gangbanger protectively armed himself, as he patiently awaited the woman he had been chauffeuring around. The South Hourd general's Acura Legend was parked reversed against the building, in order to clearly view every vehicle that entered the plaza.

Once Swarty and company spotted the Acura, Kevin instructed his driver to park behind the building, as the vehicle's positioning made a frontal attack extremely difficult. At the rear of the building, was a street bum going through the Starbucks Cafe's garbage, in search of food. Kevin instantly thought of a way to safely approach their target, and thus summoned the bum with the offering of spare change. The Jamaican offered the bum twenty dollars for every piece of his clothing, except the soiled underwear, which the man graciously accepted.

With a cardboard sign that read, "Please, any little thing helps," Kevin walked staggeringly up to the Acura Legend and tapped on the driver's window. Kevin startled the thug whose attention was focused on everything ahead of him, hence, the gangbanger grabbed his firearm and aimed at the imposter. The driver initially waved Kevin away, before compassionately deciding to donate a little spare change to the persistent beggar. The South Hourd gangbanger tapped on the automatic window decent button, then turned his head to the armrest console, to collect his intended donation. As soon as the thug turned his head, Kevin withdrew and repeatedly stuck a six-inch knife into the side of his neck, before leaving the gangbanger bloodied and gasping for oxygen.

Day Two Assault - 9:47 PM

There were more questions than answers in the South Hourd's camp, after losing an incredible eleven thugs in less than thirty-six hours. The sole survivor of the horrific tragedies thus far, was a twenty-two-year-old male, who remained in critical condition at the General Hospital in Hollywood. In response to the crisis, Miami police stated they would insert a curfew throughout the neighborhood of South Carol City, which was to go into effect within two days. Until the curfew's insertion, police squad cars increased their patrols around the outer perimeters, and along the main streets of Carol City, while the thugs governed their territory.

Members of the South Hourd held a meeting to decipher who the lone shooter was from the day before, and what his motivation was for attacking them. None of the thugs knew who the shooter was, what his reasons were for attacking them, or if he was after someone specific. The meeting led those who sought answers, further from the truth, as a disagreement in philosophy brought everyone to finger-pointing. The gathering adjourned with confusion, as individual members sought to defend themselves should they get attacked, rather than combining to fend off whatever dangers arose.

Two gangbangers went to the neighborhood's convenience store thereafter, where they sought to purchase sodas and snacks. As they made their way to the store, the armed thugs discussed the manner with which they would mutilate the persons responsible for their dead homies, should they be fortunate to make the capture. A scruffy-looking Jamaican, wearing pins attached to his shirt of Haile I Selassie and Bob Marley; with dreadlocks, a mangled beard, and a prickly moustache, walked into the store and asked the proprietor for a lighter and two packs of Zig Zag rolling papers? Just then, the two debating thugs walked up to the cash register and waited patiently behind the Rastafarian.

The Rasta Man intently watched the thugs behind him, through the glass casing behind the store clerk, and neither man behaved as if they believed he was a threat. Kevin, who was the man beneath the costume, listened as both thugs discussed dismembering him, should they discover who he was. The dreadlocks man paid for his items and collected his change, before moving towards the exit as if he was about to leave. Before exiting, however, the customer turned back to the clerk, as if he had forgotten something, then started blasting humongous holes through the unsuspecting thugs. To protect himself, the clerk dropped behind the counter and stayed there until the gunshots seized. The Rastafarian, despite there being numerous police officers in the vicinity, shoved both pistols into his pockets and walked out the store and disappeared in the darkness.

The report was unofficial, yet investigators began increasing their interest in locating the person or persons responsible for killing an undercover federal agent. United States Marshall Jeffrey Gains was brutally murdered, while seeking to purchase some ordinary items from a convenience store. The deceptive-looking U.S. Marshall had gained the confidence of the local territory thugs, who embraced and initiated him into their flock, after he had lived among them for more than a year. The undercover agent's objective was to infiltrate the gang, which law officials believed would control the valuable South Beach drug trade, sometime in the future.

The crime scene was thoroughly combed for clues, as investigators sought to collect anything which might prove valuable to solving the case. South Hourd members were astonished and embarrassed to uncover they had been socializing with the feds, whose undercover agent had gained their full confidence. The obituary for Agent Gains simply read, "Killed in the line of duty," without any further information about friends or family. Hence, his fellow Marshalls were determined to bring to justice, those responsible for killing the undercover agent.

Third Assault - 6:36 PM

With an APB out on the Rastafarian's photo, captured from the surveillance camera inside the convenience store, as well as a sketched portrait of the vigilante two days prior, scattered throughout the counties of Dade and Broward, Kevin briefed his Spanish mates on a mission, he wanted them to implement. Reports from the streets indicated that terror was widely felt by residents, who, in most cases, kept their children from attending school out of fear they could be harmed.

South Hourd members would regularly come together at the basketball court inside the Ronald Regan Public Park, off 47th Street, for their routine pickup basketball games. The thugs would assemble several teams, and play for bragging rights way into the late hours, until they decided to quit. Due to the implemented curfew, the players had to change the times of their schedule start, to finish before the community got locked down at sunset.

The only unarmed thugs in the park that day were those immediately involved in the game at hand. Apart from the ten basketball players selected for the first game, there was a waiting team, along with a few spectators, some cheer leading girlfriends, and several lookouts. There were never any officers around the basketball court, due to the estranged relationship between the locals and their city protectors. The officers also knew that many of the thugs carried weapons, therefore they could have quite easily defended themselves.

The players started playing at 2:00 PM that afternoon, with the slew of spectators demonstrating their intrigue in the physical play. While everyone shouted and cheered on the players, an old blue 1984 Ford Bronco appeared from nowhere, and smashed through the eastern fencing that surrounded the court. Everyone inside the Bronco wore ski masks to hide their identities, and the license plate had been removed to disguise the vehicle. The driver of the Bronco proceeded to strike and run over everyone in his path, whether they were gangbangers or innocent females. Members of the South Hourd gang who thought they had every angle of attack protected, fired back at the intrusive vehicle, which caught them all off guard.

The loud screams of terrified females were drowned out by the barking of automatic gunfire, as the Bronco's occupants spat bullets at the crowd through every window of the vehicle. Most of those in the park were smart enough to get on the ground, while others paid the ultimate price with their lives. A few intelligent gangsters used protective shields like trees to fend off bullets, before returning gunfire at their attackers. The Ford Bronco sped across the basketball court and ripped through the fencing on the adjacent side, before it bounced back onto the roadway and drove away.

Fourth Assault - 4:08 AM

Hector got increasingly nervous after he received several threatening phone calls, which indicated that he was the main target being sought after. Instead of sharing the information about their attackers with his fellow gangbangers, Hector kept the news to himself and decided to abstain from the public for a while. At 2:00 AM on the fourth day of assaults, two motorbikes sped by Hector's house and sprayed it with bullets.

Moments after the Miami-Dade police and ambulance arrived, two federal agents passed by the scene and had a candid talk with Hector. The revenge-seeking gangster was given a business card by one of the agents, who assured Hector he would one day desire their services, as so many had before him. To calm his nerves, Hector tried everything from alcohol to cocaine, however, he could not fall asleep which caused him to experience insomnia, thus his paranoia level increased. Within hours, every squeaking sound heard throughout the house began startling Hector, who didn't hesitate to utilize the number, as he sought protection no one else could offer. In exchange for his testimony against Ernesto's cartel, the Feds offered to protect and guard Hector, which was an offer he could not refuse.

Three black Chevy Suburban trucks pulled in front Hector Dominguez's home, moments before someone was spotted being protectively ushered from inside, beneath a wool blanket. The person, who was said to be Hector, was placed in the middle SUV, before being driven to the Hoover Federal Building in downtown Miami. Carlos received information from their contact inside the Bureau, who indicated, that Hector had been shaken by the recent killings, and sought protection after receiving a few death threats. For his testimony against Ernesto's organization, federal agents proposed relocation and sanctuary, which Hector wasn't that enthusiastic about. From the Hoover Federal Building, Hector was transferred to a safe house in Key Biscayne, where he was to remain under guard until official documents in the case had been processed.

Part 3

Stamma and two Gully thugs went to the Rose Hall district, in order to rob the home of a prominent businessman, who was abroad on business. The thugs gained access through the skylight, after breaking the glass and climbing down a rope. Once inside the home, the thugs collected jewelry, appliances, and anything valuable enough to bring in a buck. There was a personal safe underneath the businessman's office desk, that the thugs decided to carry along, considering they'd need professional help to open it. The usage of flashlights by the thieves, alerted the neighbor across the street, who had promised to watch over the house in the owner's absence. The neighbor immediately telephoned the police and advised them of a crime in progress, that was developing in one of the most upscale neighborhoods in Montego Bay.

The robbers had tallied the articles desired and were seeking their exit through the rear, when the loud sounds of police sirens echoed down the street. All three robbers sneaked to a front window and peeked out, to find a gang of officers taking up the perimeter around the house. The robbers were all stunned to find their perfect heist detected, thus, the thugs began nervously considering their options.

The nerviest of the three exclaimed, "What the fuck wi go do now? Police boy dem have the whole house surrounded!"

Justin said, "A which one a you set off some alarm or something?"

The nervous thief again argued, "Before you start critique check you self, maybe it was you who set off the alarm!"

"Le-le-let's g-g-g-get o-o-outta h-h-here," Stamma declared!

The thug who was almost in tears reasoned, "And where the fuck do you suggest we go, Stamma?"

"H-h-here, y-y-you dr-dr-drive," Stamma remarked, as he tossed a pair of BMW keys at his accomplice!

"Where you find this? Lord, please let there be a car in the garage!? Fuck them shit deah, right now me just want out," exclaimed the thief, who was beginning to feel claustrophobic with cops all around.

The nervous thug, ran to the door that led to the garage, then quickly jumped behind the steering wheel. Stamma and Justin were sure to carry their work's compensation, in case they were fortunate enough to escape the grasp of the Jamaican law enforcement. The three thugs sat quietly in the dark vehicle before exiting, as they advised each other of important messages they'd like the others to pass on to family members, should they not make it through their ordeal.

Gunshots began ringing out before the officer caught a clear sight of exactly what to shoot at, as the garage door to the two-story house began elevating. The garage door opened and a BMW 335I sped from inside. One of the four police cruisers was parked at the foot of the garage, and the driver of the BMW narrowly missed the cruiser and the officers seeking protection behind it. There was an intense shoot-out between the thugs who were attempting to gain access to the roadway, and the police officers' intent on finalizing the break-and-entry case right there and then. The BMW narrowly missed the collision, but the bullets being exchanged by the thieves and police, made their way into something or someone.

As the BMW swerved from hitting the cruiser, then straightened out to tackle the tough Jamaican roads, Justin, who had been firing his automatic Glock the moment they exited the garage, got shot in the right side of his chest. The young bandit was immediately taken out of contention, before the battle even begun sizzling, as he crouched in pain and gripped tightly onto the wound. There was a lot of blood gushing from the wound, thus, Justin began grabbing at Stamma, while imploring him, 'not to let him die'?

The petty pistol-firing from the thieves, was greatly outmatched by the officers and the huge automatic rifles they carried, which were necessary for patrolling the vicious streets of Jamaica. The golf balls fired by the officers on the scene, pierced the frame of the BMW and made huge holes, as they also blasted out the rear window and the front passenger-side window. The officers all quickly boarded their vehicles and pursued the suspects, who were intent on gaining their freedom at all cost.

The chase ruffled along the Howard Cook Highway, where the fleeing BMW reached over 120 MPH, narrowly missing similar lunatic drivers, who only shifted to the soft shoulder because of the sirens. The driver behind the wheel of the BMW, made a judgment call to avoid going through the busier downtown district, and cut across Top Road over to Albion instead. From there, they could run down the hill into the safe haven of Canterbury, where they knew the officers would hesitate to follow. With their route plotted, the terrified driver kept his head as lowered, as bullets from the police popped holes in the vehicle's windows and flew through the cabin. The threat of dying from his wound scared Justin, who began mercifully pleading to be dropped off at the hospital.

Stamma utilized his opportunities when granted to partially keep the officers at bay, by hammering bullets from both his and Justin's confiscated weapons at them. Their injured comrade had given up and was more concerned with getting medical assistance, but neither Stamma nor the driver had any intentions to surrender. The valiant effort by Stamma, through areas where the narrowness of the road was favorable to say the least, kept the advancing officers from rear-ending the criminals' stolen BMW off the steep and curvy road. Despite the challenging roadways that kept drivers focused, were humongous ditches that were detrimental to the health of any vehicle. Hence, precaution along the route was an important task, performed by both cops and robbers.

Officers from one of the Toyota trucks in pursuit, fired their M16 rifles at the fleeing BMW, which forced Stamma and his operator to duck their heads or have them blown away like the wind. As the BMW started down the steep Cornwall Heights hill, another of the Toyota cruisers' operators became a bit over-zealous and attempted to ram the car awkwardly down the mammoth hillside. Stamma noted the officer's intuitiveness and hammered two bullets from his 9mm at the vehicle, one of which luckily caught the cruiser's left front tire and blew it completely off the rim. The driver of the Toyota police cruiser lost control of the vehicle, as the right tire slammed into a huge pothole, which caused the vehicle to pirouette down the steep hill. As the vehicle rolled down the steep hillside, one of the officers got tossed from the cabin, thus, the forceful impact rendered him motionless. The other officers aboard all died from various injuries, as the cruiser caught fire once it collided. The last pursuing cruiser detached from the chase and attended to the crash victims, while their peers continued the pursuit expecting to apprehend the suspects.

The officers' intensity increased following the crash, and all the preventive measures previously acknowledged were thrown out the window. As the chase went along Albion Road behind the Cornwall College soccer field, which was a long stretch of road with no sidewalk, two friends walking home from a soiree were shot and killed by stray bullets being fired at the evasive BMW. The field report later submitted by the witnessing officer, indicated that the bystanders were shot by the cowardly thieves, who showed no concern for the public's safety.

The thieves turned off Albion Road onto Seaview Avenue, which led to the back hillside of Canterbury. As Stamma responded to the bullets fired at his entourage, his wounded mate grabbed his thigh one last time, in order to beg his allies to not let him die. The stuttering thief turned to his accomplice and honestly advised him that, 'each man was on his own!' Directly after Stamma warned their wounded accomplice of his possible fate, the driver announced he was about to pull over and bail from the vehicle.

The roughnecks within the garrison of Canterbury were renowned 'Bleachers', because they stayed up throughout the nights to secure their borders, and likewise terrorized other neighborhoods. Even the locals who lived within the community, would retreat to their homes and locked their doors once the sun retired each day. Most of the centurions were preparing to return to the sanctity of their homes, when the first loud crash was heard. Without any further warning, the BMW driver pulled the car to the soft shoulder; and slowed down enough to feel the dirt beneath his feet, before he fled the stolen vehicle. Stamma was not to be outdone by the terrified driver, thus, he also leapt from the vehicle and fled the scene with most of his stolen merchandise. The BMW rolled its' way into Mr. Gale's cemented wall, before smashing its' way to a halt. Officers were around the BMW faster than a race car on the Indy Race circuit, as they quickly moved in on the injured thief. Stamma and the getaway driver were blazing down the hillside, when three shots rang out from the point where they'd crashed the BMW. Stamma gazed at the other survivor running alongside him and shook his head in disbelief, as both men contemplated what may have become of their friend.

The intensity of the chase made four officers over-zealous, hence, they gave no second thought as to where they were pursuing their suspects. With weapons at the ready, the officers bolted from their cruiser and followed the fleeing thieves into one of Montego Bay's most infamous killing zones. The robbers expected the pursuing officers to eventually realize the complexity of the situation, and either retreat or call in the more dominant (JDF) Jamaica Defense Force soldiers, to detain their suspects. However, with the death of their peers and an, "apprehend at all cost" mentality, the four gun-slinging constables chased after the escaping thieves.

The terrain was steep, rocky, and dangerous, and presented a grave challenge to users, who could injure themselves from a fall or from some sharp materials, such as razor-edged rocks. At certain points along the trail, were deep ravines where a tumble over the ledge would prove catastrophic to the victim. Stamma and his partner were well aware of such treacherous conditions, as they scurried along while being extremely cautious.

Hatchet and his most trusted confidante were reasoning on matters vital to the security of Canterbury, when the first eruption of bullets exploded. The two thugs, like most of the Gully youths, had been drinking and smoking throughout the night, as they cohesively protected their territories. The shots heard by Stamma and his chauffeur, alerted the Gully don to the existing feud, therefore, Hatchet summoned two others to join their investigative quest.

"Yow Troy and Danny, grab the AK machines and come! Something happening up a Top Road," Hatchet exclaimed, as he removed the safety latch from his 9mm Beretta handgun!

With the gleams of light from a new day dawning, the officers became better equipped to clearly see the evasive criminals. Stamma and his accomplice were a few paces ahead of the gaining officer, who began gearing up to shoot the escaping thugs in the back. There was a stretch along the rusted zinc and rotten wooden fence pathways, where the pass ran straight for nearly fifty feet. As the clearing unfolded, three of the four constables opened fire and luckily struck the chauffeur in the left thigh. The severity of the situation forced Stamma to abandon his second accomplice, thus, he tucked his head and fired two bullets at their antagonists. The chauffeur tumbled forward and strategically rolled onto his back, to give himself a realistic firing position. With luck, the young thug was able to squeeze off a round from his Smith and Weston thirty-two-caliber, which struck the closest constable directly in the groin.

The entire incident occurred so fast, that the robber became overwhelmed by police before he could pull the trigger again. The constable, who got shot in the groin released his SLR rifle, that was strapped to his body and grabbed his private area, before falling to both knees and grunting like a pig. Two of the three constables ceased pursuit, as they stopped to ensure that the breath of life was properly expunged from the chauffeur's body. Stamma began sucking for oxygen and fought to maintain his fast pace, as the same eruption of bullets that befell Justin, sounded over the chauffeur.

With fatigue setting in, Stamma thought it best to evade his pursuer by cutting through Mr. Turner's yard, then descend the twenty-foot storm drainage wall into the 'Gully' system. After a short run through the storm drain, Stamma could exit at one of the areas designated, where the officers would never find him. The problems with his closest and most logical escape route would be Hercules and Sampson, who were Mr. Turner's pair of Doberman pinscher guard dogs. Both dogs were well over three feet tall, with solid muscles, body mass, and a viciousness, that kept bouncing balls from entering the yard and surviving.

As Stamma contemplated his options, bullets from the advancing officer's automatic rifle whizzed by, and bored golf ball-sized holes through the zinc fences on either side. Stray bullets also ripped through the wooden walls of three Canterbury houses along the pathway and narrowly missed the impoverished residents within. Residents of the neighborhood, who had experienced several elections throughout the years, where the entire country was at war during such proceedings, knew to simply crawl beneath their beds or find alternative shelter during shootouts. Many locals, once gunshots erupted in the community, would only pray to Jehovah that the bullet exchanges cease, as they held their loved ones close.

Maw McPurse, who was an elderly grandmother of six, was preparing her morning coffee before she commenced her daily chores. Old age had slowed the once vibrant female, therefore, once she heard the gunshots it was difficult to quickly get down. The seventy-four-year-old grandma had just removed the tea kettle with hot water from her General Electric gas stove, and was in the process of adding the water to her Blue Mountain coffee crystals, when a stray bullet from the altercation struck her in the chest. The bullet killed Maw McPurse instantly, thus she tumbled across the table and sent the teakettle and everything else sailing in whichever direction.

The sound of the loud crash inside his grandmother's kitchen, brought a concerned Dexter in to investigate, after the threat of gunshot had passed. At the sight of his grandmother, Dexter began yelling hysterically, "Somebody killed mi grandmother," before rushing to the cellar, where he dug up a Chinse AK rifle he had buried there. The scorching sun had not properly descended onto the island, yet all throughout the neighborhood, even residents with cement walls, found themselves crawling beneath beds and other protective structures. The sight of parents grabbing their infants and toddlers and shielding them went on from house to house, as the squeezers of the triggers callously shot at each other.

The phrase, "Babylon, Babylon," began echoing down the pathway, as fear invigorated the normally stuttering Stamma to speak with clarity! With the constable gaining ground by the second, Stamma saw no other alternative than to ignore the 'Beware of Dangerous Dogs' sign and go for broke. The evasive thug leapt over the huge fence into Mr. Turner's gladiator dome and sprinted for the Gully ravine. With no dogs initially in sight, Stamma trotted along, confident that he would safely escape. However, confidence quickly shifted to uncertainty, as Sampson bolted from the back of the house and began giving chase. The long strides of the animal made the fatigued bandit seem as if he was running in slow motion, as the Doberman caught him some ten feet before the ravine and grabbed onto his thigh.

"Arr!" The humongous dog growled, as he attempted to yank a chunk of meat from Stamma's leg.

"Ah", Stamma yelled, as he quickly glanced at the gate to see if the constable had him aligned in his sight of fire.

At a point during his escape, where he had absolutely no time to spare, Sampson the guard dog forced Stamma to surrender valuable time attempting to free himself. With the dog attached to his leg, Stamma thought it best to shed the animal by shooting him, and thus began shifting his weapon in the dog's direction. Before Stamma could aim at the animal, the lone constable in pursuit burst into the yard and began unloading his automatic clip at his suspect. The constable shot Stamma five times, with impactful bullets that pitched the crook over the ledge of the Gully ravine. Sampson, who had his teeth sunken into Stamma's thigh, was yanked over the ledge with his victim, but lucky enough to land on top of the suspected thief.

The constable had begun moving toward the ravine to ensure his kill, when the second of the two animals began charging at him from behind the house. Fright influenced the constable to aim his weapon at the charging dog, which obeyed or listened to no one except its owner. The constable shot and killed the dog, before the animal placed him in the same predicament as its partner held Stamma. After killing the Doberman pinscher, the constable veered into the ravine with a sarcastic smirk, knowing he'd avenged his fallen comrades, by abiding by the code of conduct and getting his man.

The law enforcement officer satisfyingly turned from the Gully and immediately froze in amazement, as his mouth fell wide open. The Jamaican constable was face-to-face with Hatchet and his band of marauders, who all despised the police force. The thugs made no suggestions nor demanded anything of the officer, yet instead opened fire at the proud hero and pitched him into the same ravine, he'd cast their ally. As Hatchet and friends moved to the Gully to investigate who else had been touched by the Grim-Reaper, an eruption of bullets began exchanging slightly up the hill toward Seaview Avenue.

"Blood-clatt Hatchet, a Stamma the Babylon Buoy dem murder," Hatchet's closest confidante exclaimed!

"What happen to Justin and Craig?" Hatchet questioned, seconds before the eruption.

Dexter angrily exited his yard and heard Stamma yelling, 'Babylon', as he charged down the hill, while an unrecognized male pronounced, 'the bwoy shoot off mi dick', slightly up the pathway. The grieving grandson who sought revenge for his murdered granny, crept close by the zinc fence and snuck a peek around a corner. One of the three officers after attending to his injured friend, was about to run off and support the officer chasing Stamma. Without direct evidence to support his judgement of guilt, Dexter opened fire at the officers, who were forced to hit the dirt and likewise returned fire.

Hatchet immediately got on his cellular and began calling his soldiers, who were primarily responsible for their border security. These soldiers, who were ordained as the Gully's first line of defense, lived closest to the edges of Canterbury. The Gully don had ensured their ability to adequately defend against any invasion force, by providing his perimeter defense team with cutting edge weaponry. The government would later admit, 'that it had no idea such weapons existed on the island,' following the violent uprising versus the Canterbury thugs.

The constables who remained at the top of the hill, all protectively aligned themselves once the shooting began inside the Gully borders. Two armor-piercing automatic submachine guns, which had been camouflaged and positioned to cleanse the top road of any interference, began chopping up vehicles and everything else within their path. Hatchet had given the order for his defense team to secure the Gully's borders, therefore, their first task was to drive the officers back from their lines.

The onslaught of bullets forced the constables, who had taken up refuge mainly behind their vehicles, to reconsider their mandate. Once it became evident that the vehicles, trees, or whatever structure protected them would not be adequate to save them from the response of the ghetto thugs, constables could be seen abandoning everything, as they raced to safety at the bottom of the hill. A field report was sent into police headquarters by Sergeant Dilot, who described 'the loss of four officers amidst the violent uprising by natives, who sought to protect their own'.

An explosion sounded when fifty-caliber bullets from the thugs' submachine weapon, struck the fuel line of one of the police cruisers. Locals throughout the community knew to expect disruptions to their daily activities, once the levels of violence got excruciatingly high. This meant, the children would have to miss school and their parents work, while they sat around nervously in fear. The entire ghetto fell under Bad Man's Law, considering the armed thugs were the only persons allowed to freely roam about the neighborhood. Even though Hatchet knew their murdered allies were guilty for whatever reason they were chased, he had to show solidarity with the grieving mass, which demanded blood. Honest, law-abiding citizens became prisoners inside their own homes, moreover, those with limited amounts of food reserves, faced the possibility of starvation.

With Seaview Avenue's entrance to Canterbury blocked, Hatchet ordered a gang of thugs "to close King Street to all commuters" as well. Fifteen armed thugs walked up to the main road and began stopping all motorists and pedestrians who attempted to pass. The first vehicle they stopped was a taxi heading into town from Salt Spring, which was loaded to capacity with seven passengers. They dragged everyone from the vehicle and began confiscating their wallets and jewelry, but the lone male passenger aboard decided against surrendering his belongings. Without arguing, one of the Gully thugs shot the man twice with his SIG Sauer P365 handgun, which killed him instantly. The thugs then forced everyone back into the taxi and ordered them to turn back.

The driver of the next vehicle was speeding along and couldn't avoid the traffic disruption, even though the taxi driver attempted to warm him. There were four people aboard the Nissan Sunny, which came to a halt under the threat of armed thugs. The Canterbury misfits ordered everyone from the vehicle and was about to snatch whatever they had in their purses and wallets, when one of the men withdrew a Smith & Wesson 32mm barrel gun. The security guard who wore a jacket over his uniform, began switching the gun from one thug to another and was about to dictate his demands, when another thug shot and killed him from behind. After taking all the other passengers' belongings, the bandits forced them back into their vehicle and turned them around. Rifle fire then erupted, when an approaching motorist noticed the developed blockade from a distance, and quickly spun his vehicle around.

Word quickly spread across the city to avoid that area at all cost, as the thugs robbed everyone they stopped, before forcing them to return from which they came. Instead of clashing with the uprising thugs, officers decided to stop all unaware motorists travelling towards Canterbury, until a decision was made on how to proceed.

Another loud explosion erupted along King Street, after the thugs dragged into the middle of the roadway, an old car frame, a stove, a refrigerator, a ripped and broken-down sofa, two gas tanks and other flammable materials. The bodies of both assassinated victims were thrown onto the pile of rubbish, as some cheered by firing callously in the air. The armed thugs set ablaze the pile of rubbish, by lighting a couple of bottles filled with gasoline, corked with pieces of fabric, and tossing them. With every entrance to the ghetto securely blocked, thugs manned their patrol stations as they prepared for repercussions.

The road blockages at both Seaview Avenue and King Street inconvenienced residents of the Salt Spring area, the Glendevon area, the Albion area, and everyone east of the problem area. Pedestrians and motorists were forced to take alternate routes, which caused massive delays for all commuters. The altercation, in retrospect, caused a grave number of citizens who lived beneath the poverty line to miss days of earnings, which was detrimental towards their survival.

A battalion of soldiers under the command of one Major West, arrived at the Seaview Avenue location at 8:23 AM. The soldiers were called in, as an alternative strike force to the constables, who carried sufficient fire power to tackle vigilantes on the street; yet lacked the physical training to combat ghetto thugs in their jungle environment. The soldiers immediately sealed off the area by implementing their crowd control measures, which saw them back spectators far away from the danger zone. Major West, however, was subdued by orders not to penetrate the borders, until all diplomatic solutions had been exhausted.

At 9:37 AM, a survey helicopter was sent in by the army to report on the ground activities, in order to provide the soldiers more information, should an invasion and extraction mission become necessary. The two-passenger helicopter came over from the south, with a single pilot and an observer aboard. From their initial entry, the observer reported and recorded the position of six border guards, who were all scattered across the entryway, in their camouflaged and articulate hiding spots.

The observer saw the endangered constables, who had been captured by Dexter and other Gully thugs. All three constables were tied to a huge tree and were being beaten by Dexter, while his associates watched and cheered.

As the helicopter swooped down into the midst of the Gully, the observer saw and reported on a few thugs, who carried weaponry so huge they had to transport them about on Ballawoo carts and wheel-borrows. At the sight of someone taking aim with an assault rifle out in the open, the observer caught fright and instructed the pilot 'to take the helicopter to a higher altitude'! As luck would have it, Killa, who had never fired a bazooka rocket launcher, was also taking aim at the intruders' spy copter from underneath an Ackee Tree. Craig, who wanted to shoot down the helicopter, stood in the middle of the pathway and opened fire with his AK-47.

As bullets struck the tail rotor of the helicopter, the observer yelled, "Them a try shoot wi down! Retreat! Retreat! Get the fuck out of here fast!"

Killa had the launcher aimed at the chopper, yet was unaware of the fact, that he needed to select the tracking sensor. As the helicopter crew resorted to exiting the area, Killa released the rocket, which narrowly missed its mark, before crashing and exploding in Country-Man's vegetation garden. Such a remarkable story would have never been believed, had it not been for a JBC News helicopter, which recorded the incident in real time from a far distance. At the sight of a rocket exploding after missing its target on national television, government officials thought it best to utilize their diplomatic policies, in order to quickly bring such a massive standoff to an end.

The MP for the area, Mr. Trevor Balan, contacted Hatchet, who was an important political figure in his gaining an electoral position. Mr. Balan spoke with the Gully don regarding a termination to the conflict, which had the entire city unraveled. The People's National Party had long since controlled the Canterbury region, with legions of thugs stupidly willing to die for the political party's cause. Most of the barrage of weapons, controlled by Hatchet and his thugs, were donated by their favorite MP, as a strategy to maintain control over the people through fear. Hence, like many other MP and Gully dons before them, Hatchet and

Trevor made a much more cohesive team than people were led to believe.

"Hello, Hatchet! What is all this standoff business and hostage holding me hearing about happening over there," Trevor asked?

"Bigger Boss, you know say is like some idiot police run down inna the ghetto and murder off three a mi soldier them! Obviously, them naw go escape! So right now, is like we have the three batty buoy dem tied up on the base," Hatchet replied!

"How much people have been killed so far," Trevor questioned?

"I don't have an exact figure on that right now," Hatchet answered.

"Listen to me before this thing go escalate pass the point of no return! Mi want you see to it that nothing harmful don't happen to them constables, cause right now, them soldier boys only itching to infiltrate Canterbury and kill off you shooters them," Trevor advised!

"Everything depends on how them boys go about dealing with the business. But I wouldn't advise anybody to try running into Canterbury right now," Hatchet responded.

"Another thing, who is Kadeem Kite and Ron Powers? Me get word from some top police executives that them rip off some tourists out at El Greco, and those people want fi them share of the profits!"

Part 4

"Listen, I know everything about this guy's operation, from where he smuggles his drugs to where he distributes the shit. All the undercover investigations you guys do, the stakeouts, the spy intel, will never in a million years produce the info that I got on this guy," boasted the FBI's newest informant!

"Well, you called us, so let's hear what you got on Ernesto Lopez," the agent inside the interrogations room exclaimed?

"Wait a minute, not so fast. I want to hear what you guys are willing to do for me before I start talking? I used to think my gangbanging partners would extend my life span, but right now they got no idea where the hits are coming from. You fellas gotta assure me that this dying epidemic that's hitting the south isn't getting anywhere close to me," Hector argued!

"It all boils down to what your testimony does! Mind you, as a criminal yourself, your word against a prominent businessman like Ernesto Lopez isn't worth squat, but if you got enough goods on him to help us nab him with his hand in the cookie jar, then we'll fix you up nicely with a house and a fresh start somewhere, like Nevada," said the agent.

Hector gazed into the eyes of the two federal agents inside the room, as he inhaled a cloud of cigarette smoke into his lungs. The informant thought there might be an added reward for a smuggler of Ernesto's caliber and proceeded to negotiate his information for more riches.

"So, you guys are trying to tell me that Crime Stoppers or one of those organizations, ain't got some sort of a reward out on this guy," Hector asked?

"Okay, listen up. This is the way most of these affairs usually unfold. The informant in high profile cases like this one, gets our full protection during the proceeding and an honest reward should a stiff conviction result. We're aware of the fact that Mr. Lopez and your father were partners until his untimely death, so you should know a little about their business affairs," answered the senior agent.

"You mean *killed* my dad over jealousy! I was young, but my mother told me the stories, about my father being the one with the true drug connection back home in Columbia, before Ernesto killed him to gain everything. My mom said she vowed after my father's death to never take a dime from that man, no matter how hard times were, and she never did! She advised me to never work for that man and help his empire get bigger! I would have destroyed it myself, but his money and influences make him hard to get a target on," Hector began.

Hector sat and told the federal agents both true and fictitious stories about one of the agency's most sought-after smugglers in the United States. With their recording device capturing every detail of their informant's accounts, the agents questioned and heckled Hector for chinks in his story. Once the agents were satisfied that they had acquired the knowledge they sought, they immediately arranged for their newfound friend, to be transferred to their version of Club Med.

Ernesto was irate to hear that Hector had decided to turn state's evidence, by offering the Feds valuable information about his empire. A complete overhaul in business affairs was immediately implemented, as Ernesto, who always thought safety first, chose prevention rather than having to search for a cure later. The Columbian drug lord sat uncomfortably inside his office among his advisers, contemplating the major effect certain information would bear on his business. During that occasion was the only time Kevin ever witnessed Ernesto unraveled, where he smacked items from his desk and tossed articles across the room.

"I want that putta dead at any cost! Why hasn't our informant inside that federal building located where they're keeping him," Ernesto demanded?

"Only the agents working the case know where he is being kept boss," Filip answered.

"Don't worry, Boss E. I have an idea how to find out where they plan on hiding him," Kevin suggested.

The newest addition to Ernesto's lynch mob, used his cellular phone to contact the operator for the main number to the Hoover Federal Building. Kevin then blocked his number to remain anonymous, as he imitated an informant calling to report valuable information about Ernesto.

"Hello, you've reached Hoover Federal Administration. How may I direct your call?"

"Good afternoon, madam. I would like to speak with the agent in charge of the Ernesto Lopez' case," Kevin responded?

The receptionist asked, "Do you have an extension number, or are you aware of whom you wish to speak to?"

"I'm sorry, Miss. I have no idea who he is, but some agent gave me this number to get in touch with him if I recalled anything," replied Kevin.

"Please hold while I scan through my directory to find the agent, you're interested in talking to," the receptionist said!

"No problem, ma'am," said Kevin.

The lady was off the line for a few minutes, before returning with the desired information.

"Can you recall whether you spoke with Agents Carbonelli or Agent Dunn, sir?"

"I believe it was Agent Dunn," Kevin answered.

"Agent Dunn's extension is 2258. Would you like me to transfer your call?"

"Yes, thank you," Kevin accepted.

The phone rang several times in Kevin's ear, before a mild-toned voice male responded to the call.

"This is Agent Donald Dunn. How may I assist you?"

Kevin remained silent and disconnected the phone link, leaving the agent on the other end repeating his salutations, before he hung up his phone annoyed. The investigating Jamaican used his newfound information to stroll through the pages of the local telephone directory, in search of an address to accompany the name. There wasn't any information about the agent's residence in the telephone directory. However, the agent's name was all Ernesto's hired hands needed to find his information.

Filip contacted an employee at the local telephone company and gave the female the agent's name. Within fifteen minutes, the female phoned back with the information from a confidential file and disclosed what she had learned. The information received led to the living coordinates of one Agent Dunn, who was assigned to the Miami Dade, Federal Bureau of Investigations Office. Ernesto sent his gun hands to uncover the whereabouts of Hector Dominguez, whom he wanted assassinated.

Agent Dunn was a seven-year veteran of the agency, which he joined shortly after returning from serving his country as a soldier in the United States army. It had always been the agent's dream to become a federal agent, and once the army granted him the opportunity, Dunn quickly jumped aboard. His salary from the government granted him a comfortable living, which he enjoyed in his three-bedroom condo, located in Lauderdale Lakes, Florida. Further information about the agent, revealed that he lived with his pregnant fiancée, and she was due to give birth any day.

Hugo Ramirez, who was undoubtedly Ernesto's fiercest warrior, disguised himself as an employee of the Florida Hydro Company and went to Agent Dunn's front door. After the third ring, a fatigued woman, whose belly was so huge she had to turn sideways to reach the narrow door handle, answered the door. Hugo convinced the woman he was doing some sort of water testing, to determine whether or not the water from the tap, was sanitary enough for the forthcoming baby. Once inside the condominium, Hugo withdrew his weapon and pressed it against the woman's temple, before disrespectfully shoving her onto the sofa. The mild-mannered and polite impersonator changed into a vicious beast, who behaved as if the woman wasn't already in a frail position. The nervous female gazed up at her captor, in the event she was put in the position of having to describe him later. However, the silencer attached to the end of the intruder's weapon caught her attention, because she knew he could kill her in an instant, without anybody hearing a sound.

"I want you to telephone your husband and calmly tell him to come home right now," Hugo ordered!

The frightened female, who had to grab hold of her squeamish mouth, nodded her head in agreement and pointed to the phone across the room. The thought of running to another room and sealing the door behind her crossed her mind, but reality quickly sat in, to which she acknowledged the forty-pound weight gain, as well as the little person inside her. Hugo brought back the phone and proved he was in no mood for gimmicks, as he handed her the device and pressed his weapon directly against her stomach.

The pregnant female begged, "Please, anywhere but there? It might accidently go off!"

"Any funny talks when you talk to your husband and it is going to go off!"

"Please! Please!" The woman cried as the phone rang in her ears.

After a couple of rings, the woman's fiancé answered the call and could immediately discern that there was a problem. Agent Dunn was in the process of transferring Hector to a safe house further south in the Florida Keys, where they suspected he would be well guarded and safe from assassinations or threats. The pregnant woman, for the sake of her unborn child, controlled her emotions to the best of her ability, although it was evident she had been crying.

Agent Dunn asked, "Hey, honey, how are you and my little guy doing?"

"Not so good baby. Could you just please come home?"

"I'm just dropping off an informant with the boys. I'll have this thing wrapped up in about half an hour and then I'll head straight home," said the agent.

"Okay, just come home as soon as you can," pleaded the wife before disconnecting the call.

The phone receiver was barely on the base, before a mild knock sounded at the front door. Hugo maintained a close visual and kept his weapon aimed at the female on the sofa, as he walked over and answered the door like he was the head of the household. Kevin and Gustav walked in wearing uniforms similar to Hugo's, to disguise themselves from inquisitive neighbors.

Forty-nine minutes later, the agent pulled into his parking spot and collected his personal items from the car, before climbing the short stairs to his condominium. With a, "Honey, I'm home", the agent unsuspectingly walked into his condo, where a weapon was placed to the back of his head the instant he closed the door.

Kevin threatened, "You see, right now, everything depends on how well you respond to commands! If you fuck with me, I'll kill both you and your little fiancée. You understand me?" Agent Dunn dropped the bag he was holding and raised his hands to illustrate his compliance.

The shades and curtains inside the living room and other areas of the condo were closed, therefore it was dark throughout. There was a table lamp in the corner of Agent Dunn's living room, which came on and lit up the room, revealing the many characters present. The first-person Agent Dunn took notice of was Hugo, who was standing over his fiancée holding a sawed-off shotgun, pointed at her pregnant stomach. There was a black male standing across the room who acted like the enforcer, with a Mack-10 automatic rifle at hand.

The male who held the weapon to Agent Dunn's head, shoved him forward into the abyss, where he tripped and landed facedown onto the carpet. Before Agent Dunn could attempt to reason with his intruders, a huge boot pinned him to the ground, following which the boot owner began searching him. Once the agent had been properly searched, the male dragged him to his feet, then shoved him toward his pregnant woman. The nervous agent fell at the feet of his fiancée and remained on the ground, unsure of what their invaders had in stored.

"Are you guys okay? These bastards, didn't hurt you, did they," Agent Dunn asked?

"No, they haven't honey. I still don't even know what they want!"

Kevin brought a dining chair from the dining room and forced Agent Dunn onto the seat. The agent was handcuffed to the chair with both feet tied, to completely restrict his movements, while his fiancée sobbed uncontrollably. Agent Dunn had investigated Ernesto Lopez for several years; therefore, he knew who Hugo and his associates were. The Federal Agent also had an idea what their intruders were after, as he contemplated methods of withholding private government information, which shouldn't under any circumstances be leaked to the public.

"This afternoon, you and your coworkers transferred one Hector

Dominguez to a safehouse in the Keys. Where exactly is this safehouse located," Kevin demanded, as he commenced his interrogation? "Now, before you answer me, look at my friend over there with his gun pointed at your unborn child! Fuck that bullshit they taught you in the academy! Your first wrong answer, the baby is dead. The second, the mother, and so forth so forth!"

"He is at 157 Old County Road, a half mile off the final Interstate-95 exit. Turn right and drive down on the beach until you come to a blue condo. There are five guards protecting him, but the beauty about where they are is that the bureau can't get reinforcements down to them fast enough, if any problems occur. I've spent a few nights down there working another case, to know it gets pitch dark at nights. If you boys cut off the power, throw on some night goggles and storm the place, you're guaranteed to get him," instructed the agent, as if he was a member of the strike force battlefield strategy committee!

"I appreciate all the info. But what you have against Hector," Kevin asked?

"He is a convicted killer and I hate murderers. Especially the ones who the system allow to slip through the cracks, so they spend very little time in jail and get back out to cause more families grief," Agent Dunn responded!

At Dunn's response, Kevin thought of his mother and compassionately advised his comrades to, "Tie them up and get ready to leave!"

Hugo argued that the information collected may be false, because the agent was not coerced in his opinion, to provide the truth. Kevin refused to debate the fine arguments pointed out by his mate, yet, stuck to his decision and ordered his accomplices out. Before exiting, however, Kevin telephoned Swarty outside in the vehicle, to determine if they could safely leave. Once Kevin turned away from the couple, the soft whispers of bullets being disbursed through a silencer sounded, thus, he spun around to find Hugo had shot both captives, directly in their foreheads.

"Why the fuck did you kill them," Kevin provokingly asked?

"They saw my face; and that's unacceptable," Hugo exclaimed, as he nonchalantly passed Kevin and exited the condo. Later that same night, two SUVs filled with Ernesto's assassins journeyed to the southern-most region of Florida, where their target sat in waiting. Hector had settled in bed after a strenuous evening of swimming, dart-throwing, table tennis, a couple hands of poker, and Chinese takeout for supper, which he shared with his assigned protectors. At 2:20 in the morning, Hector complained that he missed his bed and could not comfortably fall asleep. Hence, one of the agents on duty loaned him his cell phone, for the nervous informant to telephone his girlfriend. During his conversation with the female, the television inside the room went dark, which immediately concerned the informant. Hector sat up in bed and listened through the silence, for any indication that he needed to hide himself underneath the bed or inside the closet. The silence of his bodyguards, most of whom were passed out in different areas around the house, eventually calmed the informant, and he slowly reclined onto the mattress.

After cutting the electricity cable that led to the safehouse, another of Ernesto's men picked the door lock for them to enter the residence. Kevin, Swarty, and eleven of Ernesto gunners coordinated their invasion effort, as they quietly entered the house and veered off toward different regions of the three-story safehouse. There was an LCD surveillance camera mounted in an entrance corner, that captured everyone entering through the front door, and Kevin, Swarty, Hugo, and two others fell prey to the technology.

As instructed by Agent Dunn, Kevin and company wore night goggles that brightened up the darkened interior, as they sought out everybody's location throughout the house. The agent who loaned Hector the telephone, was jerking off to a porno flick inside his room, when his television suddenly went blank. Aggravated that he was unable to complete his mission, the agent abandoned his third-floor room, and blindly felt his way around the dark, as he headed for the basement to check the circuit breaker.

Four of Ernesto's gunners were heading for the third floor, when they came across the agent feeling his way through the dark. The agent was passing the master bedroom suite, occupied by the informant, when he hollered a word of comfort to soothe their security detail. Despite the agent's words of confidence, the terrified informant was not quite assured there wasn't an attack in process.

"Don't worry, Hector! I'm going to check the circuit breaker. It might just be a little trip," the agent said!

The agent felt the rails that led to the bottom of the staircase and took one step down, before the blast from a pump rifle flung him backward. With that single blast, all hell broke loose as gunshots erupted all over the house. Hector frightfully jumped from his bed and felt his way around, while moving toward the closet, which he'd memorized way before the disruption. The informant slid across the sliding door and scurried inside, as the pitter-patters of footsteps sounded in the hallway. With the sounds of men dying throughout the condo, Hector lunged into the closet and closed the door, as panic began setting in.

"Oh my fucking God! Oh fuck! They here," Hector lamented!

His girlfriend who was still on the phone asked, "Who's there? And what's all that banging I hear?"

"Call the cops, baby! Call the cops! It sounds like we under attack," Hector whispered!

"Where do I send them to?"

"Oh, shit! I have no fucking clue where this place is," Hector exclaimed!

"Then you hang up and call the cops so they can trace you, and then call me back," the girlfriend instructed, which was the last time she'd ever talk to Hector.

Ernesto's hitmen's target trembled as he dialed the numbers on the cellular, while the intruders drew closer to the door. The fear of being unarmed and getting found clouded Hector's judgement, hence, he forgot the glow from an activated phone could be seen and neglected to cover the screen. As the intruders burst into the master suite, Hector, who was in the midst of dialing 911, froze, as the men looked around the room. There was faint green light emanating from the closet, which caught one of the intruder's attention. Once the intruders started moving towards the closet, Hector realized his error and slammed the phone shut. The men inside the room simply paused and opened fire at whoever occupied the closet, killing Hector instantly. The intruders identified their target, before moving on to securing the other rooms around the condo.

Ernesto had the best qualified employees under his employment, men and women who would take a bullet for him and were extremely loyal. The guards who protected the perimeter of his house, were ex-service men who had all been highly trained in various killing techniques. Although the grounds around his house were primarily looked after by his personal gardener, even his property caretakers were trained to kill, should intruders have gotten by the guards. After visiting his business associates in Columbia one year, Ernesto gained an admiration for guards wearing camouflage uniforms, therefore he dressed his exterior security as such.

At 6:25 that same morning, an array of police vehicles drove up to Ernesto's huge metal front gate and threatened to break it down, in order to arrest the killers who invaded their federal safehouse. Ernesto's security guards stood between the army of law enforcement personnel and their bread and butter, until legal warrants were provided that stated the officers had permission to enter the private premises. The guards immediately telephoned Mr. Lopez at the main house, to inform him they had done everything in their power to deter the officers, but their warrants were legal and binding. Ernesto jumped from his bed and informed the lovely señorita beside him to alert his ace gunman, as he scurried to prevent an altercation that would definitely end in turmoil.

Ernesto met Agent Carbonelli and his band of law enforcement professionals at the step outside his mansion, where he was handed the warrants for three of his employees. The government agent was sure to advise Ernesto that, 'he would be back to arrest him once proper evidence was obtained, to identify him solely as the man who ordered the hits, against both the safe house in the Keys and the Dunn's family'. Ernesto convinced the agents, who wanted to raid the separate guard house and apprehend the wanted killers, 'to allow him to summon his workers, whom he assured them would not resist arrest'. The U.S. Marshalls, although anguished, agreed to have Ernesto summon his employees, rather than scurry around for licensed armed killers, who had a genuine dislike for law enforcement personnel. As promised, Ernesto who had children on the premises and wanted to prevent a bloodbath, got the three wanted men to surrender to the Marshalls without incident.

Swarty was home in bed with Deloris, when the U.S. Marshalls made a special house call, to exercise their arrest warrant. There were Marshalls breaking in through the windows and doors, which incredibly only disturbed Swarty's lady, who initially thought they were experiencing a tornado. Both Swarty and Deloris slept naked, therefore, she had to scramble for the sheet once it became evident what was occurring. The Marshalls announced themselves as they stormed the house and surrounded the huge, king-sized Posturepedic bed, where Swarty was remarkably still sound asleep, while Deloris shakenly held her hands up. None of the officers could believe that their loud racket, in addition to the horrified screams of Swarty's lady, did not even tickle the wanted man who continued snoring away. One of the Marshalls who wore a black mask with his tactical suit, butted Swarty on the chest with the handle of his AR-15 Assault Rifle, as Swarty spread out across five-eighths of the bed. Swarty gasped and grabbed for his stomach, then groggily opened his eyes, to find he was staring down the barrels of huge muskets. As he wiped the cold from his eyes, he realized they'd been infiltrated by the infidels.

Perspiration poured through Kevin's pores, as his grabbed onto the hips of the mid-sized woman he'd been sexing for nearly an hour and a half. The sexually promiscuous thug thrusted his sledgehammer inside and out the female, as if he was trying to expel the demons from within himself. Following the invaders' successful night's mission that transpired without any causalities, Kevin went to the home of a female he'd had several telephone conversations with. The couple began having sex at 4:36 that morning and were still as heated as the moment they began at 6:03 AM.

At 6:25 AM, Kevin's cellular began ringing constantly, with every call coming from the same number. Kevin glanced over at the phone once to check the unrecognized number, before proceeding with the sexed lesson he'd been teaching. The gangster tossed the female onto her bed and turned her onto her left side, before throwing her right leg over his left shoulder, with her left leg between his thighs. The female, who lived alone, had been moaning and groaning throughout the experience, despite the roughhouse treatment being handed out. As Kevin gently re-entered his partner, her seductive noises sent chills up his spine, thus, he slowly ground his penis into her moist, juicy vagina. The woman, who had been equal to the challenge, grinned on her partner's nine-inch iron, as he again struck her G-spot, which was always the prelude to her climaxing.

"Ah, yeah, right there, baby," moaned the female, as Kevin pondered over the importance of the call, while caressing and admiring the luscious curves of her body.

"How does it feel, baby? You like that," Kevin teased, as he changed gears and increased his intensity, which startled the woman, who didn't believe another gear was possible.

The woman found it fascinating to conceive that someone could perform for such a long duration of time, without the aid of drugs or some sort of ancient remedy. As the well-satisfied female paused the action and sucked on Kevin's penis, she pampered with his testicles and thought about the constant joy such a strudel would bring to her permanent life. The constant interruptions of his cell phone eventually got to Kevin, who finally decided to respond to the caller.

"Hello," Kevin answered!

"Good morning, Señor Kevin! I am sorry for waking you up, but Ernesto asked me to call you, to tell you that the Marshalls are here with a number of warrants. I guess he wants you to keep yourself in a safe place, and he will be in touch with you as soon as possible," explained the woman on the line.

"Thank you," answered Kevin, and he immediately hung up and telephoned Swarty!

Swarty's phone rang with no answer, due to the fact the Marshalls had taken both he and Deloris into custody, for various violations such as weapons and marijuana possession. Kevin called back several times, before the realization of what might have happened to his number one ace sunk in. The wanted gangster laid back on the female's bed and pondered over his situation, as his lover continued stroking his penis while tickling his fancy with her aggressive tongue action.

It inevitably became obvious that something was bothering Kevin, because his erection slowly subsided even though his lover was performing tricks, which would make other men's toes curl, as they cringed tightly like babies in their mother's arms; and ejaculated uncontrollably. The female paused her erotic maneuvers and rolled up underneath Kevin's arm, as he threw his hand around her thick, healthy body.

"That was one of those worrisome phone calls, wasn't it," she asked, as she compassionately sought to help the man who'd been fucking the daylights out of her?

"Yeah, you can say that," Kevin answered.

"Anything you need, just let me know? Illegal or straight," declared the female?

"Listen to you," Kevin joked as he ran his fingers through her lengthy weave. "I just got word that I might be on the Fed's wanted list."

"Then run away to Canada, like my brother did, but don't just sit back and let them catch you and bury your ass in one of those underground federal institutes! Where the only thing you get to do is probably read fucking books and jerk off this amazing dick," exclaimed the woman!

Kevin chuckled and said, "Isn't your brother American? Then how the hell did he sneak into Canada?"

"He just walked across the border somewhere out there between California and British Columbia, where it's like wide-open plains and where it's as easy as walking across a street," the female replied!

Kevin thought about the woman's suggestion as he once again began kissing her neck, while caressing her luscious body which he'd enjoyed and adored. The gangster decided to abandon his worrisome thoughts and leave matters to Jehovah, as he'd always done in times of great tribulations. Should Kevin get caught and receive a zillion years in prison, the knowledge that he'd avenged his mother's death would offer him solitude. However, he hoped the memories of his final moments with a female, would be sufficient enough to stimulate him through his incarceration.

The first round of intercourse left Kevin feeling a bit sticky and uncomfortable, after buckets of perspiration dripped from his anatomy. As the sensation to perform Round Two overwhelmed him, the gangster rose to his feet and brought the female into her shower. Once inside the bath, Kevin opened the sprinkler with warm water overhead, then backed her against the wall and lift her left leg over his arm, before reinserting his recharged penis. Their heated passion, along with the steam from the pipe, soon fogged up the entire bathroom, through which nothing could be seen. The next session of intercourse was even steamier than the first, and ended on the bedroom floor, where they fell asleep in each other's arms.

Part 5

The Canterbury ghetto standoff between the Jamaica Defense Force, or JDF, and the true sufferers of Jamaica, had entered its fourth day with no signs of compromise from either side. Law officials had made it clear, that they wanted their captured officers released unharmed, while Hatchet's bandits threatened to kill them and anyone who tried to rescue them. The ghetto youths of Canterbury implemented strict no-fly zone regulations around their territory, against all "Babylon System" aircrafts, and would shoot at any which violated their airspace.

Soldiers of the JDF took up positions to the southern portion of Canterbury, the northern portion which runs along King Street, and the eastern sections along the Gully Market. For the three days since the standoff began, there had been repeated exchanges of gunfire from both lines against the borders, with some of the island's largest weaponry being exercised to the fullest. With every introduction of powerful weaponry by members of the Jamaica Defense Force, the ghetto youths of Canterbury responded with something humiliatingly heavier.

The community guards were hidden and defended from trenches, behind houses and whatever bullet-resistant objects they could find, while the Jamaican army personnel hid behind their armored vehicles, citizens' vehicles, and trees. The Jamaican army, which could have ended the conflict sooner, by simply carrying out an all-out raid with their huge battalion, was forced to work through diplomacy, to try and save the lives of the two remaining police hostages.

God-fearing and law-abiding citizens who were forced to find protection inside their own homes, were traumatized by the events, thus, must prayed to whatsoever god they served for the shooting to cease, as the death toll slowly rose. Verwin McKenzy, who served as a community defender, was shot trying to race across an opening to get to his friend's position. The decibel level of hurtful cries that emanated from every home, detailed the extent of sorrow experienced by residents, some of whom were forced to spend days with their murdered loved ones. One such constant bawling came from Kim McPurse, who woke up to find her elderly grandmother killed by a stray bullet, that bored through their half-inch wooden walls and struck the old woman in the head. Kim cried like a cow braying for water for nearly two days, as she sat fixated on the final, pleasant stare on her grandma's face.

Over by the Baker family, nine children under the age of thirteen cried for their bellies, as the poor fisherman's family awaited the return of their father, who had sailed to acquire fish to sell and feed his family. Mr. Baker optimistically stayed away the initial night of the conflict and had been unable to return home to feed his children, due to the escalating violence that struck the area. Regardless of the volatile tension, Mr. Baker, after giving considerable thought to his disadvantaged children, attempted to cross the eastern JDF barricade with groceries. The fisherman had to be physically restrained by police officers, who were placed in charge of crowd and traffic control.

For many other families throughout the ordeal, the experience could have only been compared to that of surviving a hurricane, where food rations ran dangerously thin, while the devastation outdoors rambunctiously claimed lives throughout. There were homes with infuriated mothers who had newborn babies, who required formula or milk. Each of these frustrated mothers, would chastise their partners for not doing enough to provide for their hungry children, despite their situations. As a result, domestic violence and depression increased across the community, where residents felt as if they were being held hostage inside their homes.

The Gibson family suffered one of the toughest losses, when Pamela grabbed her three-month-old baby from the rocker, to find that the child had been horribly murdered. Pamela bawled almost as loud as a packed church with rejoicing members, as she cuddled her baby and refused to surrender the corpse. Members of another six households wept and grieved over their deaths and injuries, although they were all still in terrible danger and unsure if they would survive. Because of the unstable situation, survivors always remained close to the floor, and barricaded themselves behind protective objects, such as hardwood furniture, stoves and other objects.

The officers in captivity were handcuffed to a huge Ackee Tree in the center of the community, along the pathway that led toward Seaview Avenue. Within minutes after they were captured, the wounded officer succumbed to his injuries during the thrashing that unfolded. The other two officers were stripped of all their clothing, shoes, and weapons, and could barely be identified, due to the large amounts of dried blood that covered their bodies. Both officers were beaten with fists, batons, gun handles, pipe irons, and kicks, by the judgmental thugs, some of whom threw filthy manure at the lawmen. One of the officers could barely remain conscious, because of an ex-convict who blamed him for mistreatment, and would clobber him the moment he regained consciousness. However severe the administered beatings were, every ghetto thug was cautious to heed the warnings of Hatchet, who ordered that neither man be killed.

Dexter had a younger brother named Jimmy, who most people believed was a bit senile, because he occasionally spoke to himself. Jimmy, despite the whispers of others, had always been obedient to his grandmother, whom he praised for sheltering them, while their mother tried to acquire permanent living status abroad. Their mother planned to file for their landed immigrant status and have them relocate, once she was legally settled.

While Dexter was out with his band of marauders clashing with soldiers, Jimmy stayed home and listened to Pamela a few houses away, screaming her head off. The confused young man sat quietly on the floor, rocking to-and-fro, while he stared blindly at his grandmother's covered corpse. The voices that warped young Jimmy's mind, instructed him 'to fetch his grandma's machete from the kitchen and go forth in search of evil souls'!

Jimmy, despite all the mayhem outdoors, found himself carelessly wandering along a path, as bullets whistled all around him. There was an ongoing shootout between the JDF soldiers and the ghetto warriors, when Jimmy came across the bloodied captives. The instructions given by the voices in his head were very precise, and specifically told him to, 'make mincemeat of the red devil Babylon worshippers'! Jimmy began mutilating the captives, as if the very Bible he'd rendered devotion to, didn't warn against such volatile acts.

The ghetto soldiers who came across the mutilation once the shooting stopped, were surprised to find the ordinarily tranquil Bible student, carving thick slices of steaks from the officers. Dexter had to be summoned to calm down his lunatic sibling, who appeared to have lost all touch with reality, as he nonchalantly hacked away at the deceased officers. Die-hard thugs who had murdered and splattered men's brain matters, either threw up at the sight of Jimmy's insanity, or admitted to the fact that 'they'd never seen anything as gruesome'.

Dexter had to plead with his younger brother for him to release the machete, before consoling his beloved sibling, and then walking him back down the path toward their home. When the Ghetto don got called to the scene, he felt dumbstruck at the sight of the officers, knowing their bargaining tools were nullified. Hatchet, who'd attempted to avoid a full-scale invasion by the Jamaican Defense Forces, simply warned his followers to 'prepare for Judgment Day', as all gloves were removed once the officers ceased breathing.

Almost immediately, Hatchet's cell phone began erupting, as if someone had a hot story to tell. Once the Gully don responded to the caller, his demeanor completely changed, which indicated to others that he was vex. For the first time since the gunshots began, the JDF soldiers' weapons along all fronts were completely silenced, as their troops withdrew from their positions.

"Hello," Hatchet responded, as he stepped away from the bunch of thugs who'd gathered!

The MP questioned, "Didn't I tell you diplomacy was in the works? Is what kind a rass-clatt thing that mi just see on the television news?"

"Is what you a talk bout," Hatchet asked naively?

"The-the-the rass chop thing me just witness, some butcher a chop the police them like them is some cattle or something!"

——·—— "Boss man, me can't discuss them things right now, mi link you later," declared Hatchet, as he disconnected the call! Sergeant West received confirmation from headquarters, to proceed with a tactical operation code named, "Gully Sweep." The military exercise was developed by Jamaica's finest, as one of the most effective means of clearing through a dangerous community. With many of the Gully thugs confused after the soldiers pulled out, and others celebrating their perceived victory, Killa and several others reloaded their weapons in anticipation of the unknown. For thirty-seven agonizing minutes, there was total silence across Canterbury, which had not been witnessed since the standoff began, thus, some residents slowly started exiting their homes.

Without any warning, two gunship army helicopters swooped over the horizon from Seaview Avenue and immediately began destroying the Ghetto frontlines. The humongous fifty-caliber Remington M-250 sub-machine weapons on board the Huey, annihilated the guard posts around Canterbury that hindered the sergeant and his troops from entering. The helicopters' gunners skillfully avoided hitting any houses and demolished the frontline resistance, before moving further into the community where they dropped off troops. Residents who assumed incorrectly, had to race back to the confines of safety, as gunshots resumed in the community.

The invading soldiers tossed ropes from their helicopters and began sliding down, but had to assert cover fire, at the scattering thugs, who sniped off four descending soldiers. The threat of the gunship helicopters persuaded most of the Canterbury rude boys to rethink their strategy and retreat, considering their defenses had been penetrated and shredded. Neither of the Huey Helicopters were permitted to fire their big guns directly inside the community, but the terrifying sounds from them flying overhead worried the thugs.

Sergeant West and his troops had fully invaded the community and were killing more thugs than they arrested, as they slowly swept across the hillside from Seaview Avenue and Upper King Street. The battalion of soldiers erased all oppositions, as they went from yard to yard in search of the guilty gully thugs and weapons. The Canterbury thugs who were arrested, were placed in the custody of the Jamaican police, several of which had alternative motives for transferring the prisoners. Once given the opportunity, these constables would interrogate the prisoners, to find the two thieves accused of robbing the El Greco Resort guest. An injured prisoner who'd been shot in the elbow after attempting to flee capture, was pressured into disclosing Stamma's address, when the interrogating officer jammed a piece of stick into his wound.

Killa, Hatchet, and several of their colleagues surveyed from which direction the true threat emerged, with intentions to gang-rush whichever entrance provided the least resistance. Throughout the five-day stand-off, the borderline between Canterbury and Bottom Gully, experienced the fewest incidents, therefore they decided to escape through that route. The Canterbury thugs were desperate to flee the neighborhood, as the JDF armed forces captured more and more of their territory. With their course plotted, the twenty-eight uncaptured thugs stampeded toward the Bottom Gully border, along the shadows of trees and tall zinc fences. The fleeing warriors aimed to strike the Bottom Gully border like the helicopters did their guard posts, with a thundering force and vengeance to quickly overpowered whichever security detail was in position.

Sergeant West had stationed a dozen soldiers to the border post, with the expectation of local police support, should his troops desired aid. The JDF strategy to deploy soldiers into Canterbury, was meant to reduce the dangers and gain control over the situation quickly. However, there was no contingency plan for the large number of armed thugs attempting to evacuate the zone. Despite the eruption of gunfire, a little over two hundred yards away, the guards along the Bottom Gully border weren't fazed, as they continued idling on duty. There were soldiers playing cards in the middle of the pathway, talking on cellphones, and doing everything, except paying attention to the ongoing crisis.

"Hey Gibbs, like how the sergeant them start the operation, we shouldn't pay more attention to what a gwan," asked a soldier to their ranking officer, who was on his cell phone talking to a female?

"From the time we get stationed here, did you see anybody try test we," argued Commander Gibbs!

"Not really, but."

"Since you so concerned, then stand guard then! But leave the troops them, let them enjoy themself! You don't hear how quiet the hilltop get? Our boys them certainly done round up all the troublemakers!"

Eighty yards before the border, a group of the fleeing thugs separated and took a different pathway. The rude boys ran ahead for about seventy yards, then snuck through a resident's property, back towards the original pathway. When Hatchet and his band of marauders surprisingly opened fire with their massive weaponry, the defenders along the Bottom Gully border were overwhelmed, hence, their unpreparedness proved fatal for several of them. The soldiers were scattered across the entranceway, with some of them kneeling to gamble playing cards, some off alone smoking cigarettes, and others chatting with females on their cellular.

The police constables expected to offer support, abandoned the JDF soldiers once the barrage of gunfire erupted. Some of the soldiers managed to reach their weapons and returned fire at Hatchet and those along the pathway, but they could not atone for the thugs who snuck up behind the fence. The scanty number of civilians outside the endangered zone, all disappeared at the sound of protruding gunfire, while the JDF soldiers who were incapable of holding their post without assistance, surrendered much of their squad.

Five of the soldiers were forced to run for their lives, not having their assigned service rifles with them when the heavily armed Gully thugs unexpectedly attacked. The shootout between both groups was remarkably short, as the Canterbury thugs overpowered the guards and cleared their escape path. Once they had gained control, some of the escaping thugs abandoned their high-powered weapons in the bushes along the pathway, while others found creative ways to carry theirs. The crew of thugs scattered in different directions, many of which found public transports and left the city, while others went to places, they thought they could avoid capture.

Once order was maintained throughout, caring for the elders and youngest became priority. Stamma's grandmother Granny P, believed the constables who came to call on her, were there to ensure she'd safely made it through the ordeal. The constables aided the old lady to her feet and escorted her outside, after which they advised her, 'they were returning to search the house for fugitives and weapons'. The old lady, who'd been trapped for days, walked to her front gate and looked out at the community she'd lived in for nearly eighty years. There were two bodies lying in the bushes about ten feet away, which startled Granny P, who threw her hands over her mouth, and began asking for Stamma and Killa.

Tension mounted quickly, when several locals began demanding, 'where some of the missing thugs were'? Relatives of some of the deceased, began arguing with police officials, as they sought to remove the bodies and transfer them back home. Constables argued that everything needed to be photographed and documented, before it was possible for anything or bodies to be moved, hence the bickering continued.

Gloria, who was one of the hillside's most notorious gossip queens, came walking up the hill with her eyes filled with tears. Unlike news reporters, who were terrified to enter Canterbury and report the story, the gossip queen walked about documenting those who had been killed, injured, or imprisoned, for more explosive substance to her arguments with girlfriends. Gloria was almost at Granny P's gate, when she noticed the two dead bodies across the way in the bushes and went over to investigate.

"Them should put about fifty more shot inna them two over there," Gloria declared, as she walked back to Granny P's gate!

Gloria resembled someone who had just risen from the comforts of her bed, with her hair all wrapped in curlers and rheum still in the corners of her eyes. The gossiper wore a plain white Mickey Mouse T-shirt that highlighted her round braless breasts, some basic yard slippers and her skimpy little Daze Duke shorts, which hypnotized the soldiers, who gave her permission to freely walk about and check out the area, without a police escort.

"Them kill him, Granny P.! Them kill him," Gloria exclaimed!

"Who you talking child? Who them kill," Granny P. asked?

"Is Stamma, Granny!" Gloria declared.

"Lord, God no! No, not mi son," dramatically exclaimed the old lady who tumbled into Gloria's arms. "Not mi grandson, Lord! No!"

Gloria carried Granny P back into her house and entered to find the police ransacking the residence. The ruthless gossiper began chastising the constables, who quickly ran from inside the home as if a skunk had run in.

"Is what all you doing inside the woman's house, after onnou kill off the woman grandson? Everyone a you come out, onnou dirty stinking rotten shit house! If anyone a you plant anything inna the woman house, onnou go live to regret it! Fuck around and see if I don't put a spell pan all a onnou," threatened Gloria!

Killa, Hatchet, and a few others rode a minibus destined for Savlamar, where they could lay low and hide out until the heat settled, before returning to their domain. Hatchet had a backpack filled with money and guns, which he handed to his gun-bag to carry, should they run into a police barricade. The Canterbury don was originally from the Savlamar district, where his mother and grandmother still resided. The thugs who were just moments before involved in one of Montego Bay's most devastating gun shoot-outs, behaved politely and tranquilly as if the incident didn't faze them in the least.

As the minibus neared West Green, which was a small community south of downtown Montego Bay, Killa yelled out, "One stop, Conductor," in an attempt to dismount the vehicle. The minibus, which was packed with adults and children, returning home after a long day at work or school, stopped across the street from the West Gate Mall, where Killa paid the conductor and exited the taxi. The gangster was sure to hail and recognize his friends, to whom he offered no explanation as to his intentions. Killa looked up and down the street, before yanking his Pittsburgh Steelers peak hat down over his forehead and proceeding in the same direction as the minibus.

The West Green housing development was unlike Canterbury ghetto, with children riding about on bicycles, playing in the streets, lived in decent houses, and ate from golden spoons, according to some haters in poorer class areas. The community was built with more durable, concrete houses that stretched out for acres, and were painted with luscious colors, which enhanced the beauty of the landscape. Police patrolled such neighborhoods more often than they would other places like

Glendevon, Salt Spring, Flankers, or Canterbury, even though most of the middle-class citizens owned weapon. Throughout the poorer ghetto sections of the city, it was almost impossible to get the assistance of local law enforcement, who abstained from entering certain volatile areas due to the crime rates.

Killa walked into the West Green community under scanty streetlights, since one in every three or four light bulbs had been smashed out. The Canterbury thug had thought continuously of his deceased friend since the news reached him, and as he wiped a single tear from his left eye, images of Stamma marching alongside him, played visibly inside the movie theatre in his head. The thoughts of him chucking Stamma or Stamma chucking him as they walked brought a temporary smile to the thug's face, although it quickly vanished once he thought about the man he blamed for his friend's death. Killa totally disregarded the fact that Stamma was attempting to escape capture, after shooting his way from a foiled robbery. Hatchet had disclosed the police's interest in acquiring both he and Stamma, which for Killa proved his very suspicions.

The revenge-seeking thug stopped at the neighborhood convenience store on Orchard Road and bought a dozen Red Stripe beers, with the instructions to have them delivered to 20 Violet Lane. Killa then scurried along in advance before the delivery boy arrived, in order to position himself for his grand entrance. The baptized gunman ensured the streets were relatively calm, before jumping the fence at 20 Violet Lane, then hid in the shade provided by the huge Mango trees in the front yard.

Within minutes, a slender kid came riding his bicycle up the road, with the box of beer seated in a trolley attached to the front of the bike. The kid came to the gate and entered the yard, before briskly walking to the house ahead with both hands on the box. Killa ducked down behind a huge column built at the front porch, as the unsuspecting delivery boy went up and knocked the door.

The voice behind the door inquired, "Is who that?"

The delivery boy answered, "Kenny, from the convenience store!"

"What the fuck you want at my door, Kenny?"

"Mi bring the Red Stripe Beer them for you!"

"But mi never order no Red Stripe Beer! Hold on a minute! Let me see if my friend know anything about this delivery," replied the voice behind the door.

The delivery boy argued, "Listen, boss, somebody done pay for them beer yah, so me just go leave them right here, until you decide fi come pick them up! Mi boy, Usain Bolt, about to run a race on the TV, and me not missing it over some beer!"

"What you say? Paid for already?"

The male inside the house caught the tail end of the delivery boy, who quickly mounted his bicycle and rode away. There was, as promised, a six-pack of cold Red Stripe beer on the porch, thus, the occupant fully opened the door to retrieve the alcohol. The insurmountable level of shock that struck the home dweller, once Killa jumped from the shades, would have instantly killed a person who had heart trouble. The man instantly dropped the free beer, once Killa pointed his weapon directly at his forehead, then slowly backed him inside the house.

"Who else inside here," Killa demanded?

The terrified male answered, "Just Reverend, in the shower!"

The room was bright and properly lit, therefore Kadeem could clearly identity the male frozen at the mouth of his weapon, as he used his thumb and yanked back the hammer. Everything became clear, as a terrified Maxwell again lay directly in the sights of his aim. Killa instructed Maxwell 'to lead the way to the bathroom', as he needed to ensure that no surprises popped out from the woodwork. By the appearance of things, it seemed as if Maxwell and his partner were preparing to celebrate an achievement, with the crystal glasses and a bottle of Moet chilling on ice.

From behind the shower curtains, Rev exclaimed, "Maxwell, I told you to get me a glass of that champagne and come join me in this shower!"

Kadeem used his right leg and stumped Maxwell directly into the shower curtain, sending him and everything else collapsing against the wall. Rev immediately became irate as he began cursing Maxwell, blaming him for being such a klutz and causing him to hurt himself. A huge gash opened above Rev's right eye, thus, he grabbed for his wash rag to cover the wound.

"There is no need for all that bickering, so zip it before me have to zip it for you," Killa threatened!

"Oh, my God! Kadeem, I hope you don't think I meant anything I said to you the other day! Mi did just a runoff mi mouth! You know, say sometimes mi talk too much," Rev pleaded, as he removed the curtain that obstructed his view of Kadeem.

"You send police to kill off your own nephew? How you explain something like that," Killa questioned?

Maxwell realized Kadeem was solely out for revenge and started shouting, "Help! Somebody hel---!"

"Bam-bam-bam-bam!" Killa's pistol, silenced Maxwell permanently.

Reverend, who already had blood gushing from his forehead, caught the spillage that ruptured from his partner's wounds. The severity of the situation became apparent, as it was obvious that Kadeem did not visit simply for a chat. Killa then grabbed the person he came to assassinate and booted Rev like a dog into the living room. The naked informant begged for his life along the way, as he received a number of bruises, scrapes, cuts, and internal injuries.

"Kadeem, Kadeem, wait, please don't kill me! I know say the police them a look for you, cause them say is you kill off them friends during the shoot-out! But just wait, listen me out! Mi have an open ticket to Nassau that me can use any time, and you done know, people always say we resemble bad! Just spare mi life and mi give you my travel documents and the ticket? Mi a beg you please, just leave mi tie up and by time you reach Nassau, and safe, them can't do you nothing after that," Reverend begged?

"Where you have the documents them a hide," Kadeem demanded?

"Look inside one of mi bottom dresser drawers! Like how mi a help you leave the country, spare mi life please," Rev responded?

"Go suck yu mother," Killa lamented!

Killa opened fire at Rev, hitting him four times in the chest and once in the mouth, which indicated to whomever found him, that he was an informant. The satisfied gangster retrieved the materials that were being used to bribe him from Rev's bedroom, before quietly slipping out through the rear exit and disappearing.

The morning Star Newspaper's first text under the subheading, "War In Canterbury" read; "Twenty-seven ruthless thugs, one courageous constable, and eight brave JDF soldiers, were the fatalities in Mo-Bay's brutal shoot-out. Two other JDF soldiers taken to hospital with none-life threatening injuries. There were also eight arrests and five severely wounded thugs taken to the hospital with life-threatening injuries, following the city's worst standoff in history." The mentally challenged youth who hacked to death the handcuffed officers, was amongst those murdered by soldiers, who shot him inside his house. Killa had some unfinished business to which he had to attend in the ghetto, and after lounging about his girlfriend's apartment in Bogue for three and a half days, he decided to briefly return to Canterbury.

The entire hillside had been mourning their losses with Nine Night celebrations, as parents and guardians all coordinated their efforts, in remembering their fallen children. Granny P, like many other relatives about the district, had a yard filled with mourners who'd gathered to celebrate her grandson, who was, in all actuality, a very fun-loving individual to those who knew him. All the law enforcement personnel had withdrawn from the area; therefore, the ghetto was back to normal.

Killa snuck back into the community through the Bottom Gully entrance, then retraced his steps to the coordinates where he'd buried his dividends. After ensuring he was not followed, the rude boy dug up the hidden stash that he and Stamma buried, and removed all the proceeds, as if he closed their bank account. With Nine Night celebrations on going for three border security members, Kadeem temporarily joined the mourning festivities and offered up his condolences to parents.

Stamma's family members became Kadeem's over the years, because Granny P had always included him in family affairs. Once he arrived at the house, everyone wanted to hug him and offer kind sentiments knowing how close both thugs were, thus, Killa soon found himself swinging from embrace to embrace. Drunken Uncle Eddie, who had sworn he found God in the bottom of a Wray and Nephew Over-Proof rum bottle, was preaching at the top of his lungs against the use of weapons. The drunk, paused his ceremony to embrace and assured his nephew that, 'he would always be there for him'! Killa made his way inside to Granny P's room, where the elderly mourner was surrounded by female members from her church congregation.

The sight of Kadeem eased the nervous woman's tension, and she outstretched her weakened arm at him. Everyone inside the room sensed their desire for privacy and exited, allowing Granny P to advise her adopted grandson, who was said to be on the police's wanted list, for murders committed and assumed.

"You okay, my boy? Them no hurt you or anything," Granny P. asked?

"No, Mama! Mi fine," Kadeem answered!

"Listen to me! I want you to find a way to go live with your father in Canada. All these years he has not been the best father, but him at least occasionally sent me a dollar to help you. Make something of your life for me, my son, because me can't afford to bury both you and Ron, so promise me you go do whatever it takes to leave this island," Granny P reasoned?

"I promise, Granny P," Kadeem answered, as they both embraced and tightly held each other. Before leaving, the young criminal handed the old woman a brown paper bag with money and told her, 'to only open it after everyone had left'.

Part 6

Kevin stood on his tailor's mantle, while the clothes specialist measured him for a few garments, he was having made. The midweek morning was filled with rain, and it was forecasted to continue throughout the entire week. There had been a slight fog overshadowing the city of Montreal, which cast a dark shadow and made it seem like night. A loud ticking clock against the wall showed the time of day was 10:53 AM, however, Kevin asked his tailor 'if the time was correct'?

The young designer was an immigrant from Jamaica, who had modified his apprenticeship into a rare form, that became admired and adored by many throughout. The young designer, Carlton, had migrated to Canada some seven years prior, in search of what many attempted to achieve. Carlton himself worked with an apprentice from Trinidad, whom he'd taught and groomed since the young man was sixteen. The two had a modest workshop, where they created and sold the multitude of their designs. The front area of the store displayed the many garments available to the public, while the rear was the factory from which the creations were derived.

Kevin's cellular rang frequently as if he ran a major enterprise, though he managed without the use of a proper secretary. His many illegal dealings saw temporary pauses by the tailor, who demanded perfection of himself and waited for the proper moments to proceed. Kevin would respond to requests demanded of him over the phone, by assigning one of his three employees scattered across the city. Whatever the demand, Kevin maintained a constant calculation over the figures, as his supply on demand business thrived.

Following the altercation that landed the majority of Ernesto's gunners behind federal bars, Kevin was smuggled from Florida to elude capture by government officials. There was an ongoing manhunt for the Jamaican rude-boy, whom federal agents wanted to bury as the main enforcer behind the assassinations of federal agents, a federal informant, the fiancée to an agent, and her deceased fetus. Ernesto arranged a limousine ride for his number one problem-solver to be transported to California, where Kevin followed the instructions given to him by his final American fling, and simply walked across an unmanned portion of the Canadian/United States border, into a new country. Kevin was given a Manila envelope, containing an English passport and a document stapled inside identifying him as a foreign student from the United Kingdom, who had transferred to Canada to complete his studies. There was a Canadian driver's license, a private insurance card and an American Express card to accompany the travel documents, along with a separate Manila envelope that was filled with cash. The fugitive from American justice was picked up directly after he crossed the border, by an Indian whom Ernesto befriended in an immigration holding facility, the first time he attempted to enter the United States.

The Canadian native, whom Ernesto asked to guide Kevin through his transition in a new country, where two languages were recognized, was parked along the roadside. The guide had his engine bonnet raised, as if he was experiencing car trouble. The Indian drove an old Ford F-150 truck and quickly rushed Kevin into the vehicle, before advising him 'to buckle down for the long ride to Quebec'.

"I am Eagle Esquada. How was your trip?"

Kevin was about to roll his given name off the tip of his tongue, when he thought about the documents which referred to his new identity.

"I'm Nicholas Henry. Nice to meet you! The trip wasn't bad, but I think I'll fly the next time around," Kevin answered, and both men chuckled.

"How is my old friend doing back home," Eagle inquired?

Both men struck up an arousing conversation, during which Eagle, who lived on the Indian reservation closest to Chateauguay, south of the island of Montreal, gave his perspective on living with the Frenchmen. The Indian did not care much for the Frenchmen, whom he described as two-faced for stealing their land, while they were degraded to live on reservations. Eagle offered Nicholas a place to stay, which he did not exaggerate as the Royal Palace of Winsor, but emphasized, 'was the safest territory in all of Quebec'.

Eagle disclosed to Nicholas, that he lived with both his sons, who were adult males, yet it would be their honor to welcome him despite their cramped quarters. Nicholas graciously refused the offer because he didn't wish to intrude upon anyone's life, on account of his business involvements. The young fugitive had Eagle drop him off around the Notre Dame de Grace area, where he noticed a vacancy sign in the window of a duplex home. The newcomer to Canada went in and had a brief discussion with the proprietor, who showed him the available space, which he rented for a year and paid in advance, collected his keys, and moved right in.

Five months later, Kevin stood on his tailor's mantle as one of the primary cocaine distributors around the metropolitan area of Montreal. The chimes above the front door sounded, and three huge men wearing raincoats walked into the store. Although the water from their coats drenched the entire entryway, it was their massive structures and tattoos which grasped the Trinidadian helper's attention. The three men appeared to be weightlifters with incredibly muscular physiques, who looked intimidating with their biker club's swatch attached to their coats, and tattoos of demonic elements from their faces down. One of the men wore his German riding helmet that had the Rough Riders insignia against the front. Carlton's helper recognized the biker insignia against the man's helmet and wondered 'what business they had inside the store'.

"Welcome to Carlton's Creations, gentlemen! How may I be of service?"

"We looking for Nicholas Henry," answered one of the Frenchmen, who sounded like he had been practicing the question prior to asking.

"Is he expecting you gentlemen?"

The same biker exclaimed, "He talk to us!"

The Trinidadian continued, "But he's a bit tied up, sir. Is he expecting you?"

"Listen, mon amie, we hear Nicholas here from good source! Now get him, or we find him ourselves," demanded the biker wearing the black German style helmet!?

"I'm sorry, I'm sorry, but who do I say wishes to speak with him?"

The conversation transmitting from the front of the store was almost to a scuffle, and Kevin and Carlton caught notice of the loud voices. Kevin's newest identification came with a different name, which was the very person being hailed by the Frenchmen in the lounge. The curious fugitive crept toward Carlton's office door and peeked out at the men asking for him. None of the Caucasian men looked remotely familiar to Kevin, therefore his biggest concern was their identity, considering they knew a lot about his personal information. The majority of those who knew him in this new world, referred to him as Nick, or Nicholas, which were the names he would surrender at introductions. A handful of friends from the motherland were the only true bearers of Kevin's born identity, however, even those who knew him as such would eventually refer to him as Canadians did.

"If these guys were police of some sort, they wouldn't be asking to talk to me. They would kick down the door and send in all types of Swat teams to get me out," thought Kevin to himself, as he pondered whether or not to confront the intruders. "I wonder if they some bounty hunters like them fools on Cops? Couldn't be, or they would be looking for Kevin Walsh instead of Nicholas Henry."

The Trinidadian helper, who had grown scared by the manner of physicality, forced Kevin's hand when he returned to the rear of the store to get him. Kevin, for the first time since being in Canada felt the regret of not carrying a weapon, though he'd never had the need for one since being there. Thoughts of an escape through the rear exit crossed the fugitive's mind, before the Trinidadian professed, 'they were possible bikers from the Rough Riders clan'. At that point, Kevin intriguingly reported to the front of the store, with curiosity being his primary motive.

The spokesperson of the bunch demanded, "You Nicholas?"

"Yeah, what's up, man," Kevin answered?

"Your business dealings, conflicting against my boss, *mon ami*! You do business with no more my boss' clients. No more business for you 'round neighborhood," began the spokesman before Kevin rudely interrupted.

"Wow, wow, wow! What the fuck you just said? What shit bout boss clients you talking about, man," Kevin argued, demanding clarification of what the Frenchman meant?

"You do business no more in NDG, LaSalle, or downtown, understand? We control the major street hustlers, everywhere---," continued the spokesman.

Kevin's thoughts drifted from the words being uttered at him, thus he confusedly misjudged the entire situation. After months in the drug trade, Kevin had never heard of the Rough Riders nor believed any one entity had enough testicular fortitude to dominate the entire industry, therefore, he speculated someone was attempting to clown him. The Jamaican rude boy believed Ernesto was the jackal responsible for the trickery being played on him, hence he began reacting obnoxiously.

"So, where's this pussyhole? Bring him out! Bring him out, so I can tell him to his face, what he can do with my dick in his mouth," Kevin joked!

From nowhere came a right cross that crashed against Kevin's left earlobe, ringing his ear like a church bell. Before Kevin could debate the cause for the punch, a jaw-breaking uppercut landed him flat on his back, from where he could properly admire the tiles on Carlton's ceiling. A multitude of licks began raining from the heavens, which forced Kevin to protect his vital areas by curling up tightly. The three men yanked Kevin off the floor and worked him over properly, with both his hands held securely by his antagonists. Throughout the severe ass-whooping, Kevin was only left to wonder, 'what he could have done to receive such a beating'.

Carlton rushed to his office and quickly dialed 911, before his entire clothing line was destroyed. His assistant, in the meantime, ran into the nozzle of a P-53 Magnum handgun, when he attempted to assist a fellow Caribbean native. Carlton soon suffered the same fate as did his assistant, though he never swayed from voicing his opinion at the transgressions. The tailor pled with the bikers and argued 'the devaluing of his creations should allegations surface of a killing inside his store'. The minority business owner even removed several of his products from the racks and placed them elsewhere, citing 'his children's need for food as the reason for his actions'.

The man who waved the pistol in the faces of Carlton and his assistant, telephoned his boss with an update on what was transpiring. A faint sound from a police cruiser could be heard in the distance, however, Kevin feared he would not be alive when they arrived. Through this entire ordeal, one thing remained constant, and that was the beating being laid on the arrogant Jamaican. The men pounded Kevin with their fists and steel-toed boots, which opened huge lacerations on his face, punctured several lungs, and fractured multiple bones. Kevin was knocked unconscious by one of the many blows to the head, which may had been the reason the beatings slowed considerably. By then, the faint police cruiser sound was roaring in front the garments store, which brought hope that everyone may yet survive.

A pool of blood surrounded Kevin, who lay motionless on the floor. Carlton had expected their unwelcomed visitors to vacate the premises before the cops arrived, yet the men showed no fear, nor did they panic as the sirens whistled out front. Fear and uncertainty began plaguing the captives, who prayed they would not end up in the middle of a gun battle, between their antagonists and the police. Still, with nobody racing for the rear exit, it appeared that some sort of hostage negotiations was forthcoming.

Two uniformed officers soon waltzed in, while engaged in a comical conversation with a third individual. The third individual wore a simple jeans outfit, Avalanche leather boots with Zadik buckles on the sides, a platinum skull ring glistening with diamonds on the right hand, and a quarter cut diamond in each eye. It became obvious that he was the boss, with his platinum cross beside dog tags stringing from a beaded chain, his Ralph Lauren exclusive sunglasses, and several hell-raising tattoos to complement the style. The two officers stood to the side like spectators, while the man walked over to Kevin and knelt beside him.

"Okay, wake the fuck up! I know you can hear me in there; now make sure you listen to me," the man instructed, before slapping Kevin across the face with a backhand! "I can see your eyes; I can see your eyes mon ami! What is it? I speak better English than my boys do, are you smart enough to look at the man who will bury you in an instant? Now, I'm Martain Lafleur, and if I get word that you set up shop anywhere close to my zones, ain't no more warnings, mon ami!"

Carlton and his assistant looked on in total disbelief at what they were witnessing. The two metropolitan officers stood to the side with their arms properly folded, while the bikers continued their rude mischief. As they looked on, the Rough Rider captain became infuriated by the insult suggesting, 'he performed fellatio on Kevin', thus he signaled an officer for something. It wasn't until one of the officers tossed his flashlight to Martain, that Carlton understood the gesture, that brought a closing to the entire incident. The red lights from an ambulance flashed through portions of the window, as Martain caught the flashlight in midair and whacked Kevin across the temple with one continuous motion.

Martain left Kevin as he found him, unconscious and unresponsive with blood gushing from every portion of his anatomy. As he rose to his feet, one of his enforcers tossed a blouse from a hanger at him, in order to cleanse himself of the blood which tarnished his manicure. The weapon that paralyzed Carlton employee had been withdrawn, yet he remained motionless as he stared down at Kevin, with his mouth wide open. The shorter of the two unlawful police officers, radioed in the ambulance technicians, who'd been demanding clearance to enter and treat the injured. Both the officers and bikers saluted each other, as Martain and company made their exit.

The taller of the two officers shouted, "You Carlton, aren't you? Hey, I'm talking to you! You Carlton?"

Carlton looked over at the officers with disgust and nodded his head. The words which threatened, 'he would report the officers' bobbled in his mouth, as terror caused his legs to shake uncontrollably.

"I'll tell you straight, if you wish to continue doing business in Montreal, you'll forget everything you just witnessed and leave it as if you never saw a thing, because if you report us or them, it's your funeral, so remember that," threatened the same officer!

Kevin was taken to the Jewish General Hospital in a coma, and he remained comatose for the next eight months. The doctors at the hospital diagnosed that Kevin suffered massive brain swelling and had to be rushed into surgery the moment he arrived. The prognosis of him surviving was initially faint, and doctors warned he may become a vegetable, but his will to live was compelling. Kevin underwent four separate surgeries thereafter, to repair broken bones and internal organs. The nursing staff, however, became increasingly worried about Kevin, after the first month and a half passed with zero visitors. The hospital contacted the police precinct with their grievance, before the case was reassigned to the original officers, who were instructed to find a next of kin in case he died.

Officers Roger Pilon, a six-foot-three, two-hundred-and-sixty-pound ex-linebacker from Quebec City, and his partner, Guy Trudeau, a five foot nine and one-hundred and seventy-pound ex-cadet, went to Kevin's bachelor pad at 1315 West Broadway Street. While on-route to the apartment, the officers contacted and disclosed their orders to Martain Lafleur, who advised them 'to check for any form of narcotics', which he'd happily dispose of. The officers ignored procedure, which called for them advising the proprietors before engaging in any form of search, and they went directly to acquiring the information ordered.

Kevin occupied the basement apartment of the duplex, with the proprietors residing above him and an unwed couple on the top floor. The inquiring officers tapped on Kevin's front door, before forcing entry into his bachelor's suite, which was unoccupied. Officers Trudeau and Pilon made no subtle gestures to signify the apartment hadn't been searched, as they ravaged through everything during their search. While Trudeau tore apart Kevin's mattress, along with everything else in his bedroom, Pilon tossed produce from the refrigerator to the floor and messed up the room. Kevin had a quarter pound of marijuana in the cooling storage area of his refrigerator, which, after discovery, convinced the officers there was far more to be had.

The loud ruckus coming from the basement was overheard by Mrs. Brittle, who was the senior proprietor. The vibrant, sixty-nine-year-old woman had not seen for some time the kind young man she rented her basement apartment to, and she curiously went to investigate. With her seventy-two-year-old husband terminally ill, Kevin would assist the tender old woman with her groceries and certain chores, whenever possible. Mrs. Brittle admired her young tenant, for understanding her husband's need for peace and tranquility, and for his providing such without prior demand.

Mrs. Helen Brittle was surprised to come across two officers who had sworn to protect and serve, destroying the belongings of a Canadian student. The old woman had never encountered an event as such, during her fifty-odd years of being a landlord. Mrs. Brittle was cognizant of the regulations regarding interactions with public servants; yet did not comprehend why she had not been informed, prior to the officers' raid.

Mrs. Brittle demanded, "What are you gentlemen looking for, and where is Mr. Henry?"

Office Pilon asked, "Is there something we can help you with, madam?"

"Yes, there is! I'm the proprietor of this establishment, and I would like to know why it is I was not informed before you boys kicked in my door," replied Mrs. Brittle?

"We, ah, did attempt to contact you, ma'am, but we received no response," Officer Pilon responded.

"Bullshit. I've been home all day with my sick husband and no one rang the door or telephoned! By the way, where is Mr. Henry," Mrs. Brittle repeated?

"Well, that's why we're here, ma'am. See, Mr. Henry was in an accident, and we're here in search of any documents of health insurance for the doctors," said Officer Pilon.

"If paperwork is what you're looking for and you did this to the man's apartment, I wouldn't like to see what the place would look like if you were searching for drugs!"

The second officer, who'd ignored the conversation between his partner and the proprietor, materialized from the bedroom with a Smith and Weston handgun, which he'd found taped to the bottom of Kevin's nightstand drawer. Officer Trudeau's elation at finding the weapon was quickly dispelled by the proprietor, who knew the officers' corruptive intentions from them not advising her prior to their search. The vibrancy within Mrs. Brittle orchestrated her fury, as she slandered the officers and threatened her intentions to testify against them, should any legal actions be taken against Mr. Henry. With the old woman's constant yelling of "police corruption," it wasn't long before other neighbors began looking through their windows at what was transpiring.

The officers soon became frustrated after confronting the notion that they would be unable to accomplish their mission. Without the proprietor's intrusion on their dealings, the officers had Kevin's coffin sealed. They could have used the evidence collected, to rid Canada and Martain Lafleur of Mr. Henry permanently, by having him deported back to whichsoever country he came from. The officers expected to collect a handsome payment from Martain Lafleur, for somewhat of an exportation job, which would mean victory for their alternate boss.

Officer Trudeau threatened, "Madam, do you realize we could arrest you for obstruction of justice? Now, I suggest you return to your home, before I'm forced to do something I'd really like to do!"

"Arrest me for standing up for my door being knocked down? You boys are not working with a full deck, and I'd appreciate your names and badge numbers before you boys leave," stated Mrs. Brittle?!

With the altercation between Mrs. Brittle and the police getting loud and confrontational, two of her neighbors who were also her bridge game competitors, joined the fight against the corrupt officers. After watching the event unfold through their windows, Madame Francoise and Mrs. McGraves respectively left their humble abodes in support of their neighbor and friend, who sounded as if she was having difficulties with the intrusive offices. All three Caucasian elderly ladies blasted the officers into submission, to the extent where they mounted an immediate retreat and vacated the premises.

Nicholas Henry awoke from his coma to find himself handcuffed to the bed rails. He began looking around the medical room and saw reflections of himself through a mirror on the wall. His hair was long and knotty and looked like it was forming dreadlocks. There were three other individuals soundly asleep with IVs fastened to their veins. The fugitive, attempted to recollect what got him into his present predicament, but found it difficult to remember anything. Nicholas began moderately tampering with the handcuffs, before he started forcibly dragging against them once his freedom couldn't be attained. From looking around, he could tell all three men inside the room were handcuffed, but when his loud racket didn't disturb any of them, he realized they were comatose. Nicholas fought to remember why he was handcuffed, however, the more he tried to drag the depths of his memory, was the more intense he made his headache.

A French nurse soon entered to perform her scheduled examination of the comatose patients; thus, Nicholas began pretending his status hadn't been modified. The lesbian nurse had recently lost her female partner of six years, to a male firefighter assigned to Fire Station 22 outside of Laval, and she felt extremely bitter towards her masculine counterparts. Nicholas was accustomed to people whistling or singing while they worked, but he found the nurse's conversation with herself slightly abnormal. The idea of the nurse asking herself questions wasn't what puzzled Nicholas, but rather the answers she gave in response.

Nicholas peeked through the slits of his eyelids, as the nurse began examining the second male over toward his left. The nurse's emotional grief manifested immensely, once the door closed behind her with no witnesses to testify, as to what transpired. She did much of her duties, which consisted of temperature checks, heart function assessment, and limb assessments, before finishing with a personal examination of her own. The nurse removed a pair of pliers from her white gown, clinched onto the man's genitals, and dragged the patient's privates from his boxers. Throughout the entire process, the nurse continued speaking to herself like a mentally deranged person. As if possessed by some sort of demon, the woman placed the patient's penis between the grip and squeezed with all her might. The maneuver startled Nicholas, who grabbed for his penis as a shocking sensation travelled through him.

The nurse moved on to her second patient, which led Nicholas to wonder, how many penis vice-grip treatments he'd endured since his coma. With no one at liberty to yell or scream for mercy, Nicholas wondered which torture treatment facility he was being housed in. In support of the victimized helpless patients, the recovered fugitive thought it best to expose the cruel nurse, who might have damaged her patients beyond repair. While lying there, Nicholas thought to himself that 'whichsoever facility he was in better have adequate security, because once the handcuffs were off, escape was his only option'. The second patient, like the first, didn't even grimace from the shocking pain that sent lightning bolts screeching down Nicholas' groin.

"I ain't gonna just lay back and let this bitch crush my shit, I got something for your ass bitch," thought Nicholas, as the nurse conversed with herself.

Nicholas allowed the nurse to examine him, while patiently awaiting her grand finale. The touch of a woman's hand on his penis almost spoiled the surprise, as his soldier stood at attention. With his penis fully erected, the lesbian nurse sought to castrate its empowerment, as she reached into her pocket for her pair of pliers.

"What the fuck," Nicholas shouted, as sat straight up like a frozen corpse resurrected to life!

"Ah! Ah! Ah!" The nurse's eyes nearly popped from their sockets, as she grabbed her chest and ran from the room.

The disgruntled nurse soon returned with two other specialists, who all went to work on different sections of Nicholas' body. While the new technicians welcomed the patient back from his coma, the malicious nurse avoided speaking or making eye contact, because of her guilt. The attending doctor allowed his team of physicians to attend to Nicholas' paralyzed limbs, while he examined whether the patient suffered any form of memory loss during his coma. The doctor began with some basic conversational topics and asked Nicholas a series of questions, to check the status of his memory.

"How are you feeling today mon ami," asked the doctor?

The phrase "mon ami" was like turning on a light bulb in Nicholas' head, as flashing images of the beating he endured passed through his mind. With his revival to the world came the return of the immense hurt he'd forgone during his coma status, hence, he quickly demanded pain relievers. Nicholas could not understand the reasons behind the huge glow glistening on the faces of his physicians, though he was indeed happy about being cared for by professionals, without whom he wouldn't have survived his ordeal.

The doctor said, "Hello, I'm Doctor Sung. Could you please give me your entire name?"

"My name," Kevin repeated, while stalling to remember the information he'd used? "Ah, the pain!"

"I think I should inform you that you were in a terrible fight a while ago, and as a result, you have been in a coma for the past eight months.

Nurse, the injection please? Now, before we continue, I'd like to know if you remember your name," explained the doctor.

"Yeah, yeah," whispered Nicholas softly, as he pondered over the news given to him. "I'm Kevin. No, sorry, Doc—Nicholas Henry!"

"Where are you from, Mr. Henry?"

"I'm from England, in the United Kingdom."

"How old are you, and what's your date of birth?"

"I'm twenty-eight, and my birthday is on the twelfth of June."

"Interesting accent you have. It sounds almost Caribbean?"

"My mother was a Jamaican national before moving to the United Kingdom."

"Do you remember your parents' names?"

"Miss Monica Henry and Mr. Pussyhole."

The doctor burst out with laughter. "Interesting description of your father. I take it you guys never got along?"

Nicholas stared at the doctor with a blank stare, before rattling the handcuff attaching his right hand to the bed frame.

"Those we'll get to, once I've finished asking you a few more questions."

"Nah, fuck that, my memory is fine! Now why am I attached to the rails?"

A well-decorated government official walked into the observation room and stood near the foot of the bed. Nicholas could only catch glimpses of the man through the attendants who encircled him, though the high-ranked officer remained out of harm's way. The light green uniform the officer wore was that of the Immigration Bureau, therefore, Nicholas began wondering what information they possessed. It wasn't long before the INS officer debriefed Nicholas on his predicament, and advised him, 'the government had begun processing documents for the immediate deportation of one Nicholas Henry'.

The immigration officer waited for the doctors to award him clearance, before commencing with the task he was sent to accomplish. The gentleman officer was courteous and polite; and didn't want to be the bearer of unpleasant news; but had to inform Nicholas of his impending dilemma. At the termination of his presentation, which he began by first placing the patient under arrest, the immigration officer handed Nicholas documents explaining the reasons for his detainment, along with solid advice on how to proceed in his defense. Nicholas, who had limited use of his limbs, demanded assistance to sit up in bed, as he examined fully the short list of charges against him.

Once everyone had left and everything was settled, Nicholas telephoned Ernesto, who became elated once the operator announced the collect caller. Ernesto had solicited Eagle and his native friends to find his Canadian link following his disappearance, but all their efforts were unsuccessful. However, once Nicholas related his recent legal dilemma, Ernesto again fell into a severe state of depression. With most of the members behind Hector's assassination team serving federal time, the last person Ernesto wanted to join them was Kevin. The drug boss went from jubilation to anguish, then rode a wave of emotions before he finally transformed into the tyrant, they were accustomed to him being. Both men chatted for an hour, with Nicholas disclosing everything he remembered about how he wound up in an immigration medical ward. Ernesto brought him up to date on the trials of all his former gun hands, charged with the murders of multiple U.S. Marshalls, witnesses, and informants.

Later that night, Nicholas fell asleep, fatigued after willing himself to maneuver his aching limbs, despite his handcuffs. The detained fugitive, of whose identity immigration officials were unaware, awoke in the middle of the night from a horrid nightmare. The sudden jolt from his relaxed position, sent a shocking pain down his sacral plexus and forced him to buzz the attending nurse, for pain medication. After swallowing the Motrin pills handed to him, Nicholas laid in bed and thought of the men responsible for nearly paralyzing him; and terrorizing his dreams every time he would close his eyes.

Physiotherapy was the first order of business on Nicholas' agenda, and he willed himself to reclaim the proper use of his body. With minimal use of his body came the news of a preliminary hearing, to justify the government's rationale for warranting deportation proceedings against the accused. The law offices of Bradley and Carter provided Canada's most revered and expensive immigration attorneys, which were retained for Nicholas by Ernesto. The drug boss had also began making legal arrangements in the United States, should deportation be ordered against Kevin. Private Counsel Ian Carter visited with his client that evening and briefed him on how he expected to proceed throughout the hearings, motions he planned on filing, and his honest opinion on Nicholas' chances of seeing the streets of Montreal again. Following the professional's positive assessment, Nicholas became confident his attorney could deliver on his promises, and therefore chose to withhold the information of him being an American fugitive.

The preliminary hearing was brought before Senior Judge Courtney Sylvester, who was a mild-mannered immigrant from Germany. The seventy-six-year-old senior judge was a product of Adolf Hitler's Nazi regime, which imprisoned and tortured Jews during his childhood years. Courtney was rescued by a German woman who pretended he was her child, before fleeing the dreadful tyranny for Canada. The young Jewish boy grew up in a foreign country, which later naturalized him, though his mother withheld his personal history until his fifteenth birthday.

The courtroom was the second domain of justice Nicholas had visited, with the first being the criminal trial of the man who killed his mother. Special assistance was provided for the disabled detainee, who scurried along in a wheelchair due to the slow recovery of his limbs. Once Nicholas was wheeled in, the judge became increasingly interested in finding out why a molested individual who was beaten to within inches of his life, was removed from the streets, detained for months, and brought into his courtroom for deportation proceedings. Judge Sylvester was also curious to know who tried to kill the defendant and if police had anyone in custody.

The documents presented before the judge by the prosecution appeared legitimate, although communications with the United Kingdom immigration services had thus far neglected to substantiate Nicholas' claims. The prosecution argued that Mr. Henry had voluntarily agreed to reconvene his studies in Canada; and should thus be removed for not complying with the arrangements previously agreed upon. Chief Prosecutor Edward D'avinche also stated that the Municipal Police of Montreal believed Mr. Henry a danger to the public, yet provided no substantial evidence except an unfired handgun, that was alleged to have come from the defendant's apartment. Following the government's presentation, Judge Sylvester listened to the defense's arguments, before citing negligence against the prosecution for bad judgment. The judge recounted his personal tales from law school, where he talked about himself refusing to attend school until he'd gained the affections of the woman who would later become his wife.

The judge asked, "What percentage of mobility do you have right now, young man?"

"Sir, I'm in more pain than I've ever known. I'm slowly regaining strength in my legs, but it's going to take some time before I'm a hundred percent," Nicholas answered.

"Do you remember what happened to you?"

"It's kind of a blur right now, but I think in time it will come back to me," Nicholas stated.

"Mind you, should you appear before me after today, and I find out that whatever happened to you had to do with drugs or anything illegal, I will see to it you end up somewhere you don't want to be," the judge threatened.

"Yes, sir," Nicholas answered!

"Understand also that a firearm is a viable reason for me to have you removed from this country, but considering the circumstances under which the weapon was found, and the fact it had never been used, I'll disallow the matter into evidence, because I'd like to see a young man like yourself make something of your life," said the judge!

"I understand, Your Honor," Nicholas answered, as if responding to his guardian.

"I also suggest that since you're in this country to advance your schooling, you immediately enroll into a facility. Education is the key to a solid future, so don't squander your opportunity. Am I understood Mr. Henry," The judge emphasized?

"Defiantly sir," Nicholas sighted!

Without the dramatic events of a trial, Nicholas was released without having to post bond, although he received instructions to enroll in an academic facility immediately, then present valid evidence to the court thereafter.

Part 7

During the flight to Nassau, Kadeem sat beside a beautiful female who proudly wore an engagement ring. The escaping Jamaican was surprised he had made it that far, however, he was more concerned about completing the final leg of his journey. Throughout most of the trip, Kadeem refrained from conversing with the female, to avoid giving her the impression that he was interested. His seat was at the alleyway, therefore each time she went to the restroom, he politely allowed her by.
It wasn't until she dropped her headphones and Kadeem kindly picked them up, that they finally began conversing. The female introduced herself as Christine and declared that she was returning home, following a family visit with her grandparents. Kadeem introduced himself, then told her he was visiting the island for the first time, to experience what the culture was like. From they commenced talking, Kadeem knew he found the perfect dummy assistant, to help him get through Nassau's immigration services.
When Kadeem departed the airplane in Bahamas, at Nassau's, Lynden Pindling International Airport, he was as nervous as an unprepared student walking into a class exam. Having passed through the Jamaican airport checkpoints successfully, the wanted thug tried to remain confident, as he walked towards the immigration screening area. After assisting Christine with the retrieval of her overhead carryon, the female felt somewhat indebted to help Kadeem get situated, thus they walked

alongside each other like a couple. They had struck up a conversation about Nassau, wherein Christine described some of the fun places to go and dangerous areas to avoid. Kadeem was interested in finding out where he could live temporarily in the country and she gave him a few ideas.

They joined one of several long lines and slowly advanced, before they reached the front where Kadeem allowed Christine to go first. Throughout their time waiting in line, Kadeem was very conversational and interactive with Christine, and made sure that the immigration officers took note. The final wave and farewell by Christine, was the convincing delusion Kadeem needed to trick the agent into assuming, that they were traveling together. After the female went through and Kadeem stepped forward, the imposter shouted, "See you outside," to which she turned and smiled.

"Were you both traveling together," enquired the female customs agent?

"Yes ma'am," declared Kadeem, as he slid her his documents and looked around the room!

The custom's officer stared at the picture inside Rev's passport and looked at Kadeem. The resemblance was uncanny, apart from their hair styles and complexion, wherein Rev wore a Mohawk in his passport photo, and Kadeem sported an Afro. As they spoke, the agent's manager walked over and entered her booth. Kadeem's heartrate began racing faster, with him wondering if she might had secretly pressed an alert button.

"Do you have a skin problem, you look darker in this picture," asked the customs agent?

"That was taken before mi bleached mi skin, to get it a little lighter," stated Kadeem, who rubbed his cheek.

"Reason for visiting?"

"Oh, I'm here to meet my fiancée's family and learn more about the culture!"

"How long will you be staying?"

"For two weeks."

"Where will you be staying?"

"I'm supposed to stay by her parent's, but I go rent a place close to the beach in the tourist area."

"Do you know where her folks live?"

"She said they on the south side of the island."
"You have nothing to declare," asked the agent, who looked over the completed Declaration Form?
"Nothing at all ma'am," answered Kadeem, who thought of the books inside his suitcase, which were made up of the stolen U.S currencies, that he taped together!
The custom agent looked through all the documents presented, then picked up her stamp and stamped a page inside the passport.
"Welcome to Nassau Bahamas, Mister Harris, I hope you enjoy your visit," said the agent, who handed him back his documents.
"Thank you, I plan to," responded Kadeem, whose heartrate finally began returning to normal.
The Jamaican went to the baggage claim area and collected his luggage, then walked directly out of the airport without hesitation. It was Kadeem's first time ever on a foreign soil and he had no idea where to go. There was a section filled with taxis, so he went over and spoke with the only Rasta-man conductor he saw.
"I just reach, and I need some brain food to settle mi nerves," stated Kadeem?
"Where you want to go boss? I got exactly what you need, eh" asked the taxi driver!
The conductor grabbed Kadeem's luggage and loaded them into his trunk, while the newly arrived Jamaican climbed into the front seat. Instead of attracting other customers, the driver got in and departed from the taxi stand.
"Is this your first time in Nassau," asked the taxi driver?
"Yah mon," answered Kadeem!
"My name is Floyd, by the way!"
"Nice meeting you man! Them call mi Rev."
"Where in Nassau you going to Rev?"
"I want you to bring mi somewhere close to the beach. Some motel that cater to tourist, where the rates low?"
"You is a yard man, eh?"
"Yah mon! Straight from Mo-Bay!"
"So how much weed you want, eh?"
"Mi will take two-hundred to start."

The driver withdrew a small pouch from his glove compartment and gave Kadeem two plastic bags with Marijuana. The Jamaican paid his driver for the parcels and pushed them into his pocket, as he looked through the windows at the beautiful scenery. Floyd brought him to a four-star inn, where they only served complimentary breakfast. Kadeem took the conductor's information, knowing he would need to use his services from time to time.

The Rasta driver thought the Orange Hill Beach Inn, on Indigo Drive, would be the perfect place for Kadeem to stay. When they arrived, Floyd brought his client's luggage into the lobby area, while Kadeem went up and spoke with the front desk attendant. The inn was near capacity, but the fugitive managed to get a room for two weeks. After assuring that his passenger got adequately taken care of, Floyd said goodbye to his newly acquired client and left the property.

Kadeem went to his room and threw himself on the bed, grabbed the remote control from the night table and turned on the television. The weather outdoors was hot and sweaty like Jamaica's, therefore he laid on the bed and enjoyed the cool air condition. To fully relax his limbs, Kadeem withdrew a bag of Marijuana and rolled himself a joint. The herbs didn't seem as potent as what he was accustomed to back home, but it managed to create a mild buzz, which caused him to gradually fall asleep. When Kadeem awoke it was dark outside, and the news anchor on the television was reading the evening news. He felt his stomach growl and knew he wanted a decent plate of yard food, instead of some experimental Bahamian dish he'd never ate before, so he telephoned Floyd. After freshening up, he went down to wait for Floyd and took a small walk about the compound. There was a bar area near the pool, where several tourists lounged about enjoying the ambiance. As Kadeem looked out at the number of single and paired female couples, versus traditional couples, he thought he was seeing things due to the wide disparity of available pussy. The estimated time of arrival given by his driver had passed, thus, Kadeem walked out to check if Floyd was there.

The Rasta-man was standing by his taxi smoking a cigarette; and his face lit up with a huge grin the instant he saw Kadeem. They both sat inside the taxi, then drove off the property to a more locally operated section of town. Floyd had his radio tuned in to a vibrant Reggae program, which played much of the latest street hits. After noticing that the imposter Rev failed to comment on his stay thus far, Floyd turned and asked, "so, how you like the inn so far, eh?"

"You know say, from mi reach all mi did was sleep," Kadeem responded.

"So, you ain't get the chance to look round yet?"

"I just did for a little bit."

"And? How you feel bout the ladies them there, eh" asked Floyd, who became excited over the thought?

Kadeem finally understood why Floyd chose that specific inn, and thereby chuckled.

"Listen my friend! That place is renowned for horny and desperate foreign women, eh! I have two partners who work there, and them man no stop get pussy and make money as sex slaves," exclaimed Floyd!

"Alright, thanks for the hookup!"

Even though it was incredibly dark outside, Kadeem continued looking through the window with intrigue. They drove to a Jamaican restaurant called 'Yardman Delights', where Floyd parked and both men entered the venue. The local areas of Nassau reminded Kadeem of Jamaica, especially the block on which the restaurant was located. It was as if they had walked into Little Jamaica, where everyone spoke Patois and the aroma of real jerk pan chicken filled the air. The operator of the establishment had a pleasant conversation with Floyd, then Kadeem watched as he interacted with three other customers. As an offspring of Canterbury, Kadeem knew to never trust anyone, but if he was to commute around with Floyd, he had to be sure about the man's character.

Kadeem bought an array of extra items for times of need, such as Potato Puddings, Coconut Cakes, Ginger Beers, Plantain Chips and Patties. They both collected their food and left the restaurant minutes later, instead of sitting down to dine. Floyd drove his client back to the inn, before departing for another call. The fugitive brought his purchases to his room and put away the extra items, before he partook of his Brown Stew Red Snapper Fish, with Rice and Peas, Salad, and Dumplings. The meal was quite enjoyable; therefore, Kadeem gave Floyd added credits.

After supper, Kadeem laid back in bed and smoked as he flicked through the television channels. Floyd's words kept rumbling through his head, hence, eventually he got up and went down to the bar. There were several tourists lounging and drinking about the grounds, but they all seemed committed to their partners. As a result, Kadeem got himself a glass of White Rum, with a pinch of Coconut Water and, went over to a table where he sat and relit his joint.

Moments later, an older woman tapped Kadeem on the shoulder and asked, "if she could join him?" The woman had recently divorced, after thirty-eight years of marriage and looked great for a fifty-eight-year-old grandmother. She introduced herself as Esmeralda, then they sat and chatted for about twenty minutes, during which Kadeem drank two additional rum. In all the young stallion's days of getting women, he had never gotten pussy so quickly, without having to shell out a payment. Within twenty-five minutes of saying hello, Kadeem was inside Esmeralda's suite, with someone who was far more vibrant in bed than her birth certificate would stipulate.

Once the door closed behind Kadeem, Esmeralda transformed into some sort of wild animal, after it had subdued its prey. Esmeralda backed him against the door and started stripping all his clothing. The older woman, whose body felt remarkably fit despite her age, started kissing Kadeem's earlobes and, kept him frozen against the door, as she travelled downwards. The entire sequences of events felt like a childhood dream, where a young boy made sexual advancements against his teacher, and succeeded, thus, the fugitive pinched himself to make sure he wasn't dreaming. Kadeem looked down at the golden color of his Caucasian partner's blond hair, while she did things to him with her mouth that he'd never experienced. They eventually began having sex from the front door entrance, where Esmeralda professed her desire to be treated like a 'slut'! As requested, Kadeem obliged by going through his repertoire of sexual techniques, which were fueled by the glasses of White Rum.

Whatever deranged sexual fantasy Esmerelda wished Kadeem might fulfill was surpassed, as the young stallion made her orgasm for a record number of times. Their sexual entanglement went from the front door to the shower, where they bathed each other while Esmeralda rode Kadeem. They exited the shower soaked and stopped at the sink, where Kadeem mounted her onto the vanity, with both her legs draped over his arms. Esmeralda reinserted her lover's hardened staff and grabbed him around the neck, as she exhaled a pleasurable moan. The steam from their heated passion fogged up the entire bathroom, wherein they became drenched, as if they had just stepped from under the shower.

Esmeralda felt as if she was floating on clouds, when Kadeem swooped her up again and brought her onto the bed. As their intimate encounter continued, the sexually satisfied female realized she had never reached her ultimate climax point with her ex, hence, she felt a bit of regret not leaving him years before. To reignite the scorching flames, Esmeralda grabbed hold of her lover's penis and began orally stroking it, before she threw herself back onto the bed and surrendered her body. Following all the hair dragging, the breasts nibbling, and the harsh treatments given by Kadeem, he cocked up Esmeralda on the edge of the bed and, began slapping her buttocks as he penetrated her. The young bull rode much of the night away, before he left the older woman lying in bed giggly and feeling like a teenage girl.

The next day, Kadeem again travelled into town with Floyd, who brought him to acquire a local cellular phone. Floyd brought his new client to the BTC, Cable & Wireless store on Blake Road, where he purchased a Nokia phone and connected the service. They left from the wireless communications store and drove back to the Jamaican restaurant, where they both bought food and left. Kadeem wanted to maintain a low profile and avoided being spotted by anyone who might have known him, so he went directly back to the inn. Even though Kadeem was on a new island without the fears of being in Jamaica, he already felt lonely and bored, as if there was nothing to do that would interest him. To avoid boredom Kadeem asked Floyd about the fun things to do on the island, but his guide simply advised him to 'live like the tourists who visited the beaches and historical sites.'

The rude boy thought Floyd's idea made sense, so he enquired about shuttles to the beach at the front desk. There was a small group of people already scheduled to leave within the hour, so Kadeem got himself on the list to visit his first beach in years, even though he had always lived on an island. One of his main intention once he got the phone was to call his girlfriend and Aunty P back in Jamaica, but Kadeem decided to wait until another time. Cable Beach was one of the closest beaches to the inn and the shuttle ride was there in less than twenty minutes. Most of the guests on the trip were older Caucasian people, yet Kadeem felt

more nervous around them than he did around his cut-throat friends.
The beach was quite relaxing and after swimming a few laps along the stretch of seawater owned by Cable Beach, Kadeem laid back on his preselected blue lawn chair under the boiling sun. "Could I trouble you, to rub some suntan lotion on my back please," asked a female who stood over him, whose face he could barely see because of the glaring sun?
"No problem," responded Kadeem, who sat up and walked behind her to her lawn chair.
"I'm Frederika by the way," declared the female as they reached her spot.
"Hi Frederika, I'm Rev," said Kadeem!
"I know!... You did quite the number on my friend Esmerelda last night, she couldn't even get out of bed to join me this morning," joked Frederika!
Kadeem smiled to himself at the declaration, as he reminisced about the radical sex they had. He took the lotion and placed some between his palms, rubbed it all over his hands and gently applied it.
"Wow, so you can be gentle! Esmerelda barely mentioned that side of you," added Frederika.
Kadeem blushed ever so slightly, yet, said nothing and continued applying the lotion. Frederika requested that he rub her entire back to her feet and was very thankful for the assistance. As he got up to leave Frederika whispered, "I'm in room 108."
Later that evening Kadeem went to the room number provided. After he gently knocked a beautiful younger version of Frederika answered the door.
"Excuse me, seems I have the wrong room," said Kadeem!
"Were you looking for Frederika?"
"Yes, is she here?"
"Sorry, she said she would be right back. But she did tell me to let you come in and wait! I'm her daughter Aliana by the way!"
"OK! I'm Rev," said Kadeem, as he stepped in and they shook hands!
"Would you like a drink?"
"I'll take a Rum and Coke!"
Aliana fixed the drink and gave it to Kadeem, who collected it and walked to the window, where he looked out at the dark scenery.
"Seems like you guys have a great view," said Kadeem, who spun around

to a naked Aliana standing directly behind him.

"Yes, we do! Would you mind if we get started before my mom get back and join us?"

Kadeem's mouth fell wide open, as he stared at the curvy features in front of him. Before he could utter a word, Aliana was unbuckling his pants and trying to extract his tongue from his mouth. "What's wrong with this crazy bitch," thought Kadeem to himself, as she attacked him like the police. Even though the rude boy was highly interested in Aliana, he didn't wish to get embarrassed, so he tried reasoning with her.

"But, your mother, what she go think?"

"Oh, don't worry about my mom, we share everything!"

Within no time Aliana stripped Kadeem of all his clothing and brought him on the bed, where she began kissing him all over. Moments later, when they overheard keys rattling in the lock, Alianna did not pretend to be worried, therefore Kadeem simply relaxed. Frederika walked in and was so excited to see Kadeem there, that she undressed instantly and climbed into bed with them. The experience felt weird at first to Kadeem, but he quickly dismissed the notion of who they were and dealt with them accordingly. By the end of the night both ladies felt graciously satisfied, wherein they requested a second encounter.

The next morning Kadeem went directly to the front desk and booked his room for an additional two weeks. Throughout his existence, he had never gotten as much women or sex proposals, as he did during his stay at the ritzy inn. Recommendations amongst women was his primary meaning of getting pussy, therefore, Kadeem left each of his sex partners unequivocally satisfied. If it was financially possible, Kadeem would permanently reside at the inn, but living the life of a tourist was incredibly expensive.

By the third week, the rude boy found an apartment in an upscale neighborhood and paid for six months' rent in advance. Kadeem refurnished the space with some elegant furniture and transformed it into a palace made for a king, which was the dream of most ghetto youths. The week before moving into his new place, the fugitive bought himself a BMW, 320i, which was a lifelong dream of his. Even though the car meant he had no further need for Floyd, they remained good friends, as Kadeem continued buying his weeds from the dread. There wasn't a single night where Kadeem was not booked for an intercourse session, in fact, for eight days during his stay, he either had sex multiple times or with multiple partners. One morning, a grieving husband who found out "Rev" banged his wife, after he had gotten drunk and passed out, threatened to 'kill him', and had to be subdued by his friends. All the male employees at the Orange Hill Beach Inn were overjoyed when Rev checked out, knowing he was responsible for their decline in business. The name Rev became legend at the inn, whereby females from several countries began vacationing there solely for the opportunity to fuck him.

The first time Kadeem contacted his loved ones back in Jamaica, was after he had moved into his new pad and felt life was back to normal. When he spoke with his girlfriend whom he'd spent most of his final days with before leaving the country, the female felt disrespected and was upset that he waited so long to call. She argued that she thought he had been incarcerated or killed, and thus, gave up hope on their relationship. Kadeem persuaded his Jamaican fling that they would be together again, then promised to migrate her to whichsoever country he resided.

Following that conversation, Kadeem phoned Aunty P who was also upset that he did not call sooner. Despite her displeasure, Aunty P was elated that he had safely fled abroad; then proceeded to divulge all the latest gossip in Canterbury. The old, yet strong and lively woman, told her adopted son about the rumors circling his name. She told him of Rev's murder, which was under investigation, and her plans to pay for the funeral. There was nothing to reveal about Stamma and his funeral arrangements yet, as the police still had his corpse in their possession and were doing their investigation. Aunty P sounded content and optimistic, as she spoke about the neighborhood, which partly changed with the removal of those who were either killed or imprisoned. They spoke for well over two-hours, during which they both laughed and cried, mostly about Stamma, whom they truly missed.

The Jamaican fugitive wished he could lodge most of the stolen U.S currencies in a bank account to keep it safe, but he had no way of verifying how he acquired such a large sum. When he stayed at the inn, the room had its own private security safe, but he couldn't find a trustworthy hiding place inside his apartment. After hours of searching, Rev's imposter found an area under his mattress, where he slit open the material and slid the money inside. As a newcomer to the country, who lived in an up-scale neighborhood and drove a quality automobile, Kadeem felt as if people envied him, so the first protection he purchased was a Ratchet knife.

Floyd had used his connections to get Kadeem the apartment from a friend, without him having to provide the necessary documents or have his credit checked. Rev's new landlord, Nigel Fuaego, was described as a lunatic womanizer, who had two females, which were his crazy wife Elena and a trifling side chick named Crista Degoty. Both ladies used to be the best of friends until Crista started fucking Nigel and had a baby by him. Elena discovered early in their marriage that she could not produce children, yet she refused to leave her husband and let Crista have him. Knowing the web of deception between the three, Floyd warned Rev against messing with either women, should they ever cross paths. With all the warnings, Floyd neglected to mention one important fact, which was the women's undeniable beauty.

The rental Kadeem got was one of several apartments on a beautiful two-story guesthouse, in Skyline Park Subdivision on Lake View Drive. To sustain himself financially and ensure he had a constant income, Kadeem began checking into opening a business. He brought his car to get the windows tinted at 'Fusion Detailing' in Olde Towne Sandy Port, and got the idea to start a rim and tire store from the Chinese owner. Quay Chung not only sparked Kadeem's interest in the business venture, but also provide him with the company in China from whom he acquired his supplies. The aspiring entrepreneur contacted the company and began a business contract, to stoke his store with the necessary products. There were some customs and declaration forms necessary for imports into the country, but Rev had no issues with getting them approved. With his business plans in process, Rev located a store front on W Bay Street, beside the Flying Dutchman Liquor Store and began fixing up for business.

Nigel Fuaego and his wife Elena lived at one of his many houses, located on Hampshire Street. Elena rarely left her house; however, she had a number of personal errands that she ran each week. There were a few pampering appointments (manicure, facials and pedicures), shopping, meals at her favorite restaurants and her favorite exercise class, which she attended three times weekly. To maintain his physic and fitness level, Rev signed up for a private gym he drove by several times on Oak Hill Road. The very first workout session he attended; Elena was exiting the gym as he walked in. Since relocating to Nassau, Rev had been with several mediocre females, but when he saw Elena, he realized there were priceless gems still yet to be discovered. The large and notable diamond ring glistening from her wedded finger, made Rev bite his tongue and refrained from making an advancement. But the Jamaican rough neck could not help but to stand and watch Elena's round derriere, as she strutted her way to her Range Rover Sport.

For the next few days, Rev began going to the gym an hour earlier, in order to catch a glimpse of the stunningly beautiful female. It wasn't until the fourth day before Rev again graced his eyes upon the gorgeous and curvy red bone, whom he could barely keep his eyes off while exercising. Even though the female appeared happily married, Rev monitored her schedule and knew exactly when she attended the gym, hence he rescheduled his workouts accordingly.

Two days after Rev opened his tire and rim store, Crista walked into the establishment shopping for new rims. As a new store owner who invested a lot of money in the business and could not afford a salesperson, Rev made himself the primary salesman. Floyd had an unemployed cousin named Larry who was a mechanic, so Kadeem hired him to assemble and install his customers' orders. Crista was undoubtedly the second hottest chick Kadeem had seen since being in Nassau, but she had her little eight-year-old son with her, so he had to be cautious.

Crista was chatty and flirty and gave up her phone number without much pressure, hence Rev thought she was single. Contrary to most of his visitors thus far, Crista purchased via American Express credit card, a set of four premium rims with tires. The mechanic shop was available and so they brought her Mercedes Benz, C 300 in for the installment. Even though Floyd had warned Rev about Crista, it never dawned on him that the customer was one of the females described to him. Nevertheless, with such intrigue Rev was dialing her phone number before nightfall. They spoke that evening for a short time, during which Crista told him about her baby father, whom she constantly referred to as,

"Dah Dumb Cunt"!

Three days after meeting Crista, Rev brought her for drinks at a tourist bar on West Bay Street at night. They had a few shots of liquor and a couple of beers, before they left and took a walk barefoot along the sandy beach. Crista was rather playful and started running away from Rev, who chased her down and tackled her onto the sand. The two connecting strangers began passionately kissing and rolled about close to the water's edge. Suddenly, Crista stopped, then shoved Rev aside, and stood up as if she was hearing voices.

While blankly staring at the ocean, the gorgeous young lady untied the strings on her shoulders that secured her flowery summer dress, then ran off into the sea. Rev could not believe his eyes and was stunned when he realized Crista was naked, so he quickly undressed but left on his boxers. The water was remarkably warm for that late hour, as they came together and embraced, then continued kissing. When Crista seconds later fell to her knees without warning, Rev thought she had spotted her mate and was hiding, so he started looking ashore. The talented female dragged off his boxer and began giving him oral sex in the ocean.

"What the fuck," thought Kadeem to himself, as he looked around to see if anyone was watching, before returning his attention to Crista!

It was as if she was born with gills instead of nostrils, because Rev could not believe she remained under water for nearly three minutes. Once she came up for oxygen, the young stallion lifted his date handily, as she hugged him around the neck and licked his earlobe. Rev was a bit concerned whether she had drunk too much alcohol, but all the nibbling thus far clouded his thoughts, hence he could only remind himself, "don't come inside this bitch!" The entire experience was spectacular, although he had to keep a look out for thieves and the authorities. At the end of their evening, they walked back to their vehicles and exchanged a small kiss, before they both drove off in separate directions.

Even though Floyd knew that Rev avoided Jamaican party scenes at all cost, he told him about an upcoming reggae concert being held over on Paradise Island in two weeks. The concert would feature some of Jamaica's top reggae artists, none of whom Kadeem had ever seen performed live. To Floyd's surprise, on the morning of the concert, Rev phoned and enquired "what time he planned on attending the event?" There was an important reason why Rev dealt with more foreigners than Jamaicans, but with a new business and the idea of making Nassau his new home, he decided to change his views.

Both Floyd and Rev drove their individual vehicles and met up at the concert, which was held on a private beach, on Paradise Island. To disguise himself, Rev wore a baseball hat with his outfit and pulled it down just above his eyebrows. Paradise Island was a small island next to Nassau, which was accessible by a single bridge. Since Kadeem landed in Nassau, he had heard many claims of the locals love for reggae music. Many radio disc jockeys played reggae, but seeing the large amount of concert attendees, solidified the islanders' claim. There were thousands of people happily walking towards the concert venue and they all appeared eager to rock with the lineup of Jamaican artists.

The show started at 3:30 PM under the boiling sun, with a packed lawn of reggae lovers jamming and rocking to every performer. While ordering at the bar with Floyd, Rev looked around the venue and saw Elena off towards the left side of the rum shack. The adorable female was laughing and enjoying herself with two girlfriends, who were equally as excited. Floyd caught Rev staring at Elena and her girlfriends, however, the stare was brief, after Nigel walked up behind her and grabbed her around the waist.

"The vibes real nice eh? See your landlord and his wife Elena over there! Boy she have some fine ass friends, eh," stated Floyd!

Rev remained silent and acted as if he wasn't intrigued, as he looked at Nigel's thuggish associates then turned away. They collected their liquor and moved to a descent location, which had a clear view of the onstage entertainment, plus Nigel's entourage. The urge to stare at Elena was overwhelming, therefore, Rev would take an occasional peek at her. During one of his glances, both their eyes locked, wherein Elena gave him a heartwarming smile. Fifteen minutes before dusk overtook the island, with the audience totally entranced by Sanchez' performance, Crista and three of her female friends entered the venue and, stood a few feet away from both men. Floyd had no idea that they knew each other, thus he pointed Crista out and lamented, "That's your landlord crazy ass baby mother right there!"

Rev pondered over what Floyd meant by such a statement, but he again remained silent in his own defense. Crista eventually noticed them behind her and walked back and acknowledged Rev with a tender hug, then waved hello to Floyd. Once Crista walked away, Rev could sense the curiosity surging through his companion, so to ease the tension he exclaimed, "Mi sell her a set a rims the other day!"

Despite the reduced lighting and the crowded distance between the parties, Nigel observed the interaction between his child's mother and Rev. Over the next few hours, both Rev and Floyd watched as Crista's crew demolished two bottles of Smirnoff, while they partied deep into the night. The four ladies were fully intoxicated when they made their third trip to the portable toilets at 1:42 AM. After watching Crista and her entourage mercilessly consumed both bottles of liquor, Rev concluded that she was undoubtedly an alcoholic, even though he expected a late-night booty call from her.

At the height of the reggae concert, Crista's crew encountered Elena's two female friends by the toilets. Elena was stationed much closer towards the bar area, engaged in a conversation with a cousin she had ran into. The distance and crowd made it impossible for Elena to see the altercation that developed between her friends and Crista's. Both crews had a longstanding feud, therefore, an argument easily sparked once they came in contact with each other.

"If it ain't Miss Try Trap A Man and har street prostitute bitches," said one of Elena's friends.

"The only prostitutes here is all you hoes," answered one of Crista's girls!

"All you prostitute bitches do is turkey baser the man them sperm who y'all sleep with! Then when y'all end up pregnant, you walk tell people lies, how you and man make plans to create family," said the same female!

"Is not our fault big cocky man damage you whores' reproductive systems, now none a you can't produce fuck all," argued another of Crista's friends!

"Say what you want bitch, but no descent man not marrying none a you stinking crablouse cunts," quarreled the same mouthy female.

As tensions escalated, Crista flung her plastic cups with liquor and ice and struck the chatty female directly in the face. Her friends attacked Elena's and a scuffle ensued, wherein combatants were pulling out weaves, breaking nails throwing punches and kicking like MMA rejects. The scuffle was more comical than serious, giving the females were all too intoxicated to cause any serious injuries. When a portion of the crowd broke to watch the scuffle, Elena thought nothing of it and didn't even move. Many spectators circled the gladiators, who rolled about in the sand heckling each other, before the event's security jumped in and broke it up. Even though Rev didn't see any of the fight as it unfolded, watching the participants get escorted out gave him an indication of what Floyd meant by "crazy ass side chick", though he again said nothing.

Part 8

Chief Prosecutor Edward D'avinche telephoned Martain Lafleur with an immediate update on the case which intrigued the biker leader. Monsieur Martain Lafleur was accustomed to acquiring whatever it was he desired and believed failure to be an utter disgrace. With the power to enter any commercial facility and take whatever he wished, Martain would often engage in large shopping sprees, where everything he acquired was stolen, given with contempt, or taken under serious duress. The underground boss of one of Canada's most notorious gangs, owned and operated two Harley Davidson super bike stores, the shipping dock by the Old Montreal Pier, three Ultramar Gas Stations, and a Provigo Supermarket. Despite all of that, he still found time to extort protection payments from small business owners, managed the largest drug distribution north-east of the U.S. border, export stolen, high-end model vehicles to customers abroad, smuggled guns from Russia that were later sold on the U.S. black market, run an exclusive escort service, and pimped a number of females around the city. In business as well as his personal affairs, Martain was a relentless beast when it came to the acquisition of money. Once any agreement was entered into with the biker boss, any payment made late or short the exact amount, came with consequences that were generally harmful to the client.

Martain shouted, "What the fuck do you mean he's to be released with conditions? I didn't grease your whole division's pockets to have this man left in my country!"

"I'm sorry, Mr. Lafleur, but that's the way things go at times. I presented my case as we discussed and asked that Mr. Henry be deported, but we weren't prepared for the judge to make his ruling at a preliminary hearing," explained Edward D'avinche.

"I thought you said the mere fact that he was arrested and was being held automatically warranted an investigation which comes after the preliminary hearing! So why was this fucker released on my streets, before you got to convince the judge otherwise?"

"Sir, the judge Mr. Henry passed before is the toughest immigration judge on the eastern seaboard. I've worked with him for years and have never once seen him come to such an irrational decision so fast. Personally, I believe it's due to Mr. Henry's physical condition at the moment," stated Edward.

"Do I sound like I'm in the mood for your assumptions? What I want is a fucking refund on my investment," Martain rudely disconnected the phone line!

The biker boss was furious after hanging up the phone and went directly toward his liquor cabinet. Martain toppled two bricks of ice into a glass, and then added a dose of his favorite Jack Daniels whiskey. Without so much as a flinch, Martain downed the glass of liquor, before addressing some of the members of his cabinet around the room.

"I paved the way for this incompetent lawyer, who does nothing, but fuck shit up! Well, I want him fucked up; if he believes he's just going to enjoy my money without me enjoying satisfaction, he's got something else to look forward to! Jean, I want you to pay Mr. D'avinche a visit for me and see to it he spends a little time in the ICU," ordered Martain!

"What's up, mon chum," Martain's second-hand man, Yves Buchard, asked?

Yves and Martain became lifetime friends during Yves' preliminary years at James Lynn High School, where he single-handedly muscled the two goals desired for a victory, during a hockey match against their school's local rival. In the dying seconds of that match, an opponent of the visiting team orchestrated a foul play against Martain, where he illegally ran the defenseman into the boards, fracturing his left shoulder and forcing him to leave the ice. Yves ran to his defenseman's aid, dropping his gloves before knocking down the opponent who'd prematurely began celebrating. After the match, the appreciative gesture landed Martain an anchor support throughout the remainder of his life, and the two became inseparable, though Martain would later become Yves' boss.

Martain answered, "They failed to deport the Englishman."

"So, what's the big issue?" Yves asked.

"I don't know why, but I got a funny feeling about this guy. Something tells me he's not going to just sail away into the wind, like everyone else we've influenced," stated Martain!

Yves joked, "I don't see a problem!"

"See, you don't know the numbers, so you definitely won't see a problem. This guy single-handedly, through the quality of his products, increased sales around NDG by at least 1.5%. Since we've recaptured the people he supplied, business is back up with a modest increase in sales. We got lackadaisical in monitoring our affairs, and that opened the door for this Englishman to move right in, but the door is now closed, and we are going to keep it that way," exclaimed Martain!

"I don't see any man come back, after we teach them lesson," professed the muscle head that landed the first punch at Nicholas!

"You sound like you would prefer working with this guy, instead of escorting him out of town," exclaimed Yves.

"That's not it, mon ami, I would love to have taken his suppliers, you know, to maintain a balance in the business. Instead, I know far less about who this stranger truly is, no relatives of importance, nothing. I promise you, though, he better leave this city, or I want him buried beneath it," insisted Martain!

Nicholas decided to trade the finest rehabilitation equipment available in Montreal, for an ancient Indian treatment process, that was suggested by his friends who took him in. Though only physically capable of maneuvering 78% of his body, Nicholas opted to reject the advice of Caucasians and abandon the facilities of modern medicine, which had thus far played a vital role in his recovery. The knowledge that people aimed to cause him bodily harm, forced Nicholas to rethink his security and put distance between both the Rough Riders, their public servant assistants and himself, once he got released from bondage. The recovering victim recalled peeking through the lids of his swollen eyes and seeing the peace officers standing and watching his assault. To enable himself to heal in a safe place, Nicholas telephoned Eagle and asked, "if he could take him up on his previous offer?"

The Indians, who rescued the wanted Jamaican from the jaws of the Babylon, brought him back to their reservation property, where the rules and regulations ran differently from those of the Frenchman. There was a smuggling arrangement in place between Ernesto and certain patrons of the Kahnawake Indian tribe, who brought the illegal items across their territory from upstate New York into Canada. Through the trafficking system of the Kahnawake people, Ernesto transferred millions of dollars in drugs annually, to augment his enterprise. Hence, the Esquada family, with whom Nicholas stayed during his recovery, had become close acquaintances of Ernesto and his associates.

The Esquada family consisted of Eagle Esquada, a fifty-six-year-old native Indian father to Danny Esquada, thirty years of age, and his younger brother, Kane Esquada, who was twenty-five. The Esquada family survived primarily off their crops, with luscious vegetation produced on their five-acre property. The mother to both of Eagle's sons had died after being struck by a drunk driver some fourteen years prior, leaving him as a single parent to raise both boys. With the help of farming and occasional drug trafficking trips, Eagle earned enough money to offer his children a quality education, though they inevitably followed the path of their father.

Danny Esquada was a mere portrait of his father, with similar features and attributes. The two men walked similarly, had similar posture and physic, and might have been considered twins had it not been for Eagle's grey hairs. Danny was a serious individual, who used to be considered a bully by youths his age, because he would forcibly take whatever he wanted from them. During high school, "The Pitbull," as students would refer to him, fell in love with boxing and quickly became a promising talent among young Canadian athletes. With a record of nine wins, no losses, and a draw, Danny was selected to the 1986 Canadian Olympic Boxing Team, to display his talent and skills.

In his semi-final match against a boxer from Russia, Danny knocked out his opponent with a fierce blow, that broke his right wrist. The adrenalin flow after the match caused Danny to shrug off what he believed was a slight twitch, due to his eagerness to compete in his gold medal match, scheduled for the following day versus the Americans. A slight inflammation occurred around the fractured area, before it was determined that his wrist had been broken. Danny refused to undergo an examination at the hospital to determine the severity of his injury; and argued that they had come too far to disregard all that they had worked for. The boxing coach was initially against the idea for him to compete, but decided against his better judgement, when the Mohawk Indian convinced him otherwise.

At the gold medal match the following evening, Danny fought mainly one-handed and made an adequate showing of himself despite being injured. The American fighter dominated most of the fight, with Danny gaining grounds in the final rounds. With the American back-pedaling in an attempt to survive the final round, Danny faked the right hook and brought a left cross that landed the very moment the final bell rang. The American boxer fell like a log, as his trainers and staff rushed to his side. While Danny jumped in the air believing he'd been victorious, the referee began waving both hands in the air, while rushing toward the judge's table. An array of boos was cast by patrons inside the arena, once it was announced the fight had been awarded to the American fighter, who was then struggling to regain his coordination. Despite the loss, Danny made history for all aboriginal Canadians, who were proud to see him win a silver medal; and celebrated once he returned home.

Kane Esquada was the fragile temperament inside the Esquada house, after the lovely Keisha Esquada passed away. The resemblance between Eagle and Danny had always earned numerous comments, but Kane was the splitting image of his mother. "Mama's Protégé," as he was often called, had carried the memories and sorrows of his deceased mother in the deepest trenches of his heart. Moreover, the graphic pictures of Keisha's body would forever torment his dreams. Kane believed there were spirits sent to collect his mother's soul following her passing, and that those same spirits had in turn cast their interest on him. Like his ancestors before him, Kane was proud of his heritage as Canada's first aboriginal people, yet he abstained from alcohol and drugs with the intent of being alert and prepared for the spirits, he presumed were coming to take his soul.

Following two prior incidents, one where he was stabbed in a racial dispute by an ignorant French skinhead, and a second, where he survived being in a crashed car that was totaled, had Kane convinced he had been marked by spirits. A supernatural consultation with the local healing doctor confirmed Kane's suspicions of spirit integration, however, the doctor also advised him that, "Keisha would never allow demonic spirits to tamper with his wellbeing."

After two weeks of physical endurance with the native people who work hard from sunup until sundown, Nicholas regained one hundred percent of his mobility, and could accomplish normal tasks. With Danny's workout regimen from boxing, daily baths underneath a healing fountain, assisting with the heavy-duty labor around the yard, and his personal aspirations of fully regaining his mobility, Nicholas' body remarkably responded and healed itself. However, his terrifying nightmares that involved his newest nemesis continued to plague his every unconscious moment, awakening him from dreams and causing him to yell out in torment.

The Esquada boys and their house guest would often hike into the hills near their home, where Nicholas and Danny would partake of a marijuana joint, before they began target practice with Eagle's home protection pistols. As their friendship grew, the men became tight in all aspects, to the extent where criticisms were never demoralizing comments, but rather signs of thoughtful admiration. It was during one their getaway hikes that Kane chose to address Nicholas' nightmare issues, a problem with which he was all too familiar. Even though Kane had decided against partaking in the ritual, which Indians had successfully used for centuries to rid themselves of evil torments, he still caringly suggested that Nicholas undergo the spiritual healing, to fully cleanse himself of whatever plagued his dreams.

On the first full moon of the new month, Eagle Esquada's entire household attended the Aboriginal Ceremony of the Ancients, which was a gathering of the community to celebrate life and the memories of past ancestors. The festivities were ongoing and featured natives wearing their porcupine headdresses and colorful costumes, while dancing around a huge bonfire chanting and beating drums. Nicholas had never witnessed a gathering of such force and spirituality, nor had he heard the Ojibwa language, which was the aboriginal tongue, as he and the others joined the circle of Indians surrounding the festivities.

There was over three hundred people in attendance, most of whom formed the huge circle, for the medicine man and performers to dance about freely. The primary performer inside the circle was the tribe's Medicine Doctor, who stood alone inside the circle at the commencement of the event, with his staff that featured the skull of a monkey as the crown headpiece. As the ceremony progressed, various patrons seated among the masses would become engulfed by spirits, fall into trance-like states, and dance about as if freeing themselves from the bondages of the soul. An ancient chalice with carvings of the bear, the fish, and the eagle being passed about, though only certain individuals partook of the ceremonial pipe. The eerie vibes soothed Nicholas' emotional state, as he began clapping along with the masses, even though the effects of the Marijuana joint they enjoyed in the car, had since subsided.

Nicholas received the ceremonial pipe from Kane, who, like always, refrained from confronting his personal demons. Before inhaling the fumes, Nicholas took a moment to admire the pipe, which appeared to be of ancient origins. The Esquada men were seated on either side of Nicholas, to add testament to him as their honored guest, thus, Nicholas looked to Eagle for consent to blaze up the pipe. After a slight nod from Eagle, Nicholas inhaled the toxins, which immediately altered his emotions, and gave him the ability to actually see medians gliding about the atmosphere.

From the huge bonfire shot out the faces of Martain and his goons, while Nicholas envisioned himself fully dressed in native attire. Contrary to his nightmares, the fugitive savagely stalked the men who had injured him, in an outback scenario like a forest. After staring a few other ghosts of his past in the face, Nicholas drew courage from his support system around him and tightly closed his eyes. With his fists clenched tightly, Nicholas travelled back to that horrid day in the tailor's shop, where he received the beating of his life. Anger and frustrated, Nicholas stood over himself as Martain and company whooped his ass, before leaving him to the mercies of God. Nicholas soon awoke with tears in his eyes, and a huge smile glistened on his face, because he knew his fears were of no further consequence.

The joy of an entire night without his recurring nightmares, had Nicholas rejuvenated and charged to tackle anything the following day. The recovered former deportee was up early for strength training with Danny, who was all too accustomed to his daily regimen. As Eagle began his day aimed at feeding his precious livestock, the thought of his boys warming up to anyone but him drew a pleasant smirk to his lips, as he went about his affairs. Later that day, the Esquada boys and Nicholas went to the grocers to purchase a few items for the house, in addition to personal hygiene materials. The muffler on Danny's 1982 Nissan Stanza could be heard bawling from a mile away, as they drove along the bumpy local strips. Nicholas demanded they stopped while passing the Abenaki motorbike store on St. Joseph Boulevard, where they traded in Danny's four-wheel rust bucket for helmets and two-wheel hammers.

Nicholas was elated that the Esquada men, who have proven to be wholesome friends, had taken the time to heal all aspects of his injuries. Eagle was surprised when they returned with three motorbikes and the groceries, however, the kind gesture by their honored guest brought tears to his eyes. At supper, where typically each man retrieved his spoils from the kitchen, before planting himself before the television or whatever activity he had engaged in, Nicholas offered to take the entire family out for a night in the city. Eagle had made prior plans to visit an old friend who had fallen ill, thus, he insisted the younger men have a ball without him.

Later that night, the Esquada brothers and Nicholas fired up their new Kawasaki motorbikes and left the reservation. They swerved through traffic along Boulevard St. Francis and the Pont Mercier Bridge, on route to Interstate-20, which brought them to exit Rue Guy, which they took to St. Catherine Street. The Gentlemen's Desire Nightclub housed some of the finest beauties in the city of Montreal; and catered to their customer's every desire. As the thrill-seekers parked their motorbikes against the sidewalk, they realized there was no need to lock up their property, considering every other bike was left unlocked.

The classic ambiance inside the Gentlemen's Desire Nightclub catered to the heterosexual male's desires, which was a variety of women from different nationalities. Women were all over Nicholas and his partners the moment they walked in through the front door. Kane quickly scooped up the sole colored female amongst the group of ladies, leaving Nicholas thought provoked as he lingered along behind the two brothers. Danny found himself a dynamite redhead with astonishing rare beauty, and an ass that said, "Hold on for a bumpy ride!" The three stripper friends who approached the young lads, forced Nicholas to select the weakest link, who was a young French girl from Thunder Bay named Stacey. Each of the three friends followed behind their lovelies, who wore skimpy lingerie which kept the men enticed. They all chose to sit at a booth table toward the rear of the club, where there was adequate surveillance of the entire floor.

Despite the club's logo, which symbolized the sort of customers they'd rather entertaining, there were very few business suits in the house, and a large number of drunken, loud-mouthed bikers, who gawked at the exotic performers while enjoying themselves. Their rude antics, however, didn't mitigate the fact they were spending a large amount of money, in commemorating the birthday of one of their members. The birthday boy was on stage being mauled by a mob of females, who had successfully ripped off his clothing, before they tied him to the pole and brought out the straps. The beating that left the biker's buttocks redder than the planet Mars, was at its grand finale, as Nicholas and friends made their way to their seats.

"If that's the initiation process to get with you ladies, I'm definitely in," Kane commented!

The colored female responded, "That little act on stage? You ain't seen nothing yet!"

"Listen! I told you the kid has no idea how to talk to the Berries," joked Danny, as he nudged a grin from Nicholas.

"Berries," Nicholas mocked!

An account of everyone's beverage was taken by the waitress, who wore a bunny suit and did it justice. The cigarette smokers at the table all lit up their drugs and began puffing away, while engaging in introductory small talk. Once the drinks arrived and everybody began drinking, Kane came up with an audacious idea, and insisted the females engage in a sexual orgy, which he had never experienced. To his surprise, each of the strippers had secretly fantasized about the others, therefore, they were all in agreement with sexually molesting each other, and getting paid in return.

The onstage entertainment, which featured the young and delectable Electra, was instantly replaced by the beautiful nymphos nibbling on each other. Braziers and thongs were tossed at their private audience, who watched in amazement as two of the strippers placed the first victim atop the table; and tickled her fancy until she squirted like a fire hydrant. The force of the young redhead's orgasm splashed against the booth's backrest and stunned her audience, who had never witnessed such a spectacle. Kane, who chose to sit where he had the best view, had to quickly remove himself from the path of the young redhead's orgasm. The young Mohawk was laughed at by his companions, who found it hilarious to watch him brush specks of orgasm from his shoulder.

The ladies' appetites were gruesome, as they fondled each other for what seemed like an eternity. Their moans and groans soon captured the attentions of other patrons, who wished they'd concocted such a marvelous scheme. As Nicholas and his associates watched with intrigue, they all wished they were in a more private setting, wherein they could have taken full advantage of the females.

Nicholas brought his double shot of cognac and cranberry juice cocktail to his lips, as the manager of the establishment vacated his office to oversee the proceedings. The well-built Caucasian male, walked by Nicholas' dark table and smiled at the guests, who'd put on such an amazing event, that others were watching. The Jamaican looked different with his lengthened dreadlocks; thus, the manager did not recognize him. Over the rim of the glass, Nicholas watched as a true ghost of his past waltzed, right by the table he'd acquired. Terrifying memories from his whoop-ass instantly flashed through his mind, and Nicholas began reminiscing on the number of licks he received from the male who passed before him.

"Who that," Nicholas demanded of one of the ladies?

"Oh, that's Pierre the manager, they call him 'Moose'," stated the red head, who finally came up for oxygen, after licking the colored female's clit for some time.

"Who is the owner?"

"He's never here! I think he runs too many businesses, but that's his clan over there. The all-mighty Rough Riders gang," stated the redhead.

Nicholas wondered if everyone else could hear or feel the pounding of his heart, which intensified the moment he laid eyes on the manager. Without hesitation, Nicholas turned to Danny and said, "Tell me you brought the peace-maker?"

"My brother, I'm Indian, it's against my religion to leave the reservation without it," claimed Danny?

As Nicholas collected Danny's self-protection, he took time out to explain the situation to his amigos, who hated to see proficient pussy go to waste. The itch beneath Nicholas' armor desperately needed scratching, so he handsomely paid the ladies, who insisted they be allowed to finish the procedure. Before departing, however, the young lady who was appointed to Nicholas covertly jotted down her number, then slid it to him with a handshake. Following the brief, mediocre farewell between Nicholas' entourage and the luscious strippers, the men waited for the overzealous females to retire to their changing room, before commencing with their antics.

Nicholas insisted both brothers exit the club and await him by their bikes, as he refused to have any harm befall them. While ushering his instructions, Nicholas casually prepared the weapon he'd acquired beneath the table, by removing the safety and placing a shell in the firing chamber.

"Come on man, there are at least two dozen guys over there. I'm staying to help you just in case bro," Kane declared!

"No way! If anything goes wrong, it's my ass again, though I do appreciate the offer," Nicholas answered!

"You got this," asked Danny, who had grown ever closer to Nicholas while training over the past few weeks?

"Yah mon," joked Nicholas in his Jamaican dialect, as they shook hands!

The three men rose from their table and walked towards the exit, before Nicholas change path and moved towards the bikers' celebration. Even though the biker entourage chose a private area to celebrate, their members were scattered throughout the night club, gaping at the many exotic dancers who pranced around wearing their skimpy outfits. With his liquor in his left hand and a tight grip on the Glock handle in his pocket with his right, Nicholas made his way across the floor toward the VIP Champagne Room, where the honored guests and others lounged.

At the front door, Danny handed Kane the keys to his and Nicholas' Kawasaki's, before instructing his younger brother "to keep the motors running!" The ex-professional boxer remained inside the club and out of sight, while preparing himself to assist in whatever faction possible. Danny watched Nicholas through his peripheral vision, while simultaneously maintaining coverage over the remaining bikers inside the club. The man on a mission walked directly into the Champagne Room and stood behind the waitress, who was in the process of tending to a customer's request.

The birthday boy shouted, "Whoo-hoo! This is the best birthday ever! Yow, Moose man, thanks for everything brother! I think I finally lived out my dreams today. Whoo-hoo!"

The waitress asked, "So, you guys want another bottle of Baileys for the ladies and?"

The birthday boy shouted, "Yahoo!"

Another biker shouted, "Bring two more bottles a Jack Daniels with another two liters of Coke?"

The birthday boy again shouted, "Yahoo!"

"Plus, forty-eight chicken wings with mega fries, jumbo salad, and bread. Was that all," the waitress demanded?

The birthday boy again shouted, "Yahoo!"

The waitress collected the orders and turned to a complete stop, as she bumped into Nicholas. "Oh, I'm sorry, sir!"

Nicholas remained silent at the girl's apology, as he maintained a visual on his target. The darkness throughout the club made it increasingly difficult for Moose or any of his four honored guests inside the Champagne Room, to clearly recognize Nicholas, who was simply out for revenge. The drunken birthday boy mistook Nicholas for an ally and told him to "acquire his own bitches," as he was not about to share any of his prizes. A rotating disco light attached to the ceiling some twenty yards away, cast a reflection that made it possible to visualize Nicholas' features. Moose's mouth fell wide open as he quickly grabbed for his protective weapon, which was shoved into his waistband behind his belt buckle.

The first two shells released by Nicholas were launched unexpectedly at the biker to Moose's left, who had managed to arm himself faster than anyone else inside the Champagne Room. The loud music drowned out the blasts for much of the bikers, who didn't even react to the loud bangs. The blaster was aimed at Moose's chest within the blink of an eye, as the club's manager struggled to remove his weapon from his waistband. In his drunken state, the birthday boy could only manage to toss the females in his lap to the floor, before flinging his hands in the air, signaling that he'd surrendered. With his eyes surveying every motion of the bikers inside the Champagne Room, Nicholas took one step forward, placed his weapon directly on Moose's forehead, and pulled the trigger.

Fear overtook the others, who expected the shooter to assassinate them all, therefore, the biker to the left of the birthday boy tossed the sole female on his lap at Nicholas. The rude boy stumped her to the ground instantly with a firm boot across her face. The man then attempted to run from the room, while yelling "assassination" to alert his friends of their predicament. Once again, Nicholas sounded the Big Thing, which tore away the man's chest cavity as it sent the biker airborne, landing him across the bar, where he tumbled head-over-heels.

Several bouncers began cautiously approaching the demolition area, when Danny observed the bar attendant reach beneath the counter for a high-powered, pump action rifle. In the commotion, that saw innocent customers breaking for the exits, exotic females screaming as if they were in danger, and fellow bikers arming themselves with broken bottles and whatever else they could find, Danny sneaked behind the bar to tackle what appeared to be Nicholas' greatest threat. The waiter was focusing in the direction of the assault, when Danny crept behind him and incapacitated him with a bone-crushing punch to the center of his spine. The bar attendant tossed his weapon back over his head, as he grimaced and grabbed for his back, while crumbling to the floor. Danny snatched the Remington Model 7600 pump rifle from midair and jumped on top the bar with one sole command.

"Get on the fucking floor!"

It was through his altered view of the crowd, that Danny realized there were far more patrons armed, than he had previously calculated. DJ Blaster the disc-jockey, abandoned his post with the music playing, and hid beneath the equipment station, once the shooting erupted. The loud music blanketed the sounds of a 36 Caliber handgun being dispersed at Nicholas from the south-west section of the club, which Danny highlighted by the sparks gashing from the weapon. The Indian aimed his high-powered rifle at the shooter behind a table, and blasted two buck-shots at the biker, who was shooting at his friend. The deed took two attempts, but with the second blast from Danny's Remington Model 7600, the biker was sent smashing against the slot machines inside the club.

The only armed security guard shot at Danny from the office area and narrowly missed him, so the Indian leapt off the bar and returned fire. The two traded several times, before Danny shot the guard in the left arm, yet he refused to surrender. Danny was forced to blast another hole through the biker in charge of security, who could have laid down his firearm and let them leave freely.

Most of the Rough Rider bikers were unarmed or it would have been a bloodbath. Nicholas apologized to the terrified strippers, who had been screaming their heads off after witnessing Moose get executed. The two warriors reunited after Nicholas snatched the birthday boy as hostage, then used him as a protective shield to cross the club's main floor. The vengeance-seeking roughneck kept his gun to the man's head and used the birthday boy as leverage to keep his friends calm, while they made their way to the exit.

"Talk to your boys, before mi have to splatter your brains all over the floor! We all can go home to our families. This got nothing to do with anybody else," Danny repeated to his hostage, thus the birthday boy pleaded with his peers not to retaliate!

The streets were serene, as Nicholas, Danny, and their hostage emerged from the club to find a vacant St. Catherine Street. Kane had punctured the tires of the long lineup of Harley Davidson motorcycles outside the club, which belonged to the Rough Rider bikers inside. He had also knocked the guard left to watch over them unconscious, while seated in a corner.

"Get down on you knees; and tell you boss say him should have killed the Englishman when him had the chance," Nicholas commanded, as he and his allies mounted their bikes and rode away, leaving the birthday boy on his bending knees!

The Aftermath

Eagle was forced to remind his overzealous bunch of misfits that, "they weren't the sole living organisms inside his home" at 2:40 AM, after they had returned from their rowdy escapade, and were still overly excited from what had taken place. Once Eagle returned to bed, the three marauders continued their celebrations with his bottle of Jack Daniels liquor, while sharing a huge marihuana joint constructed by Kane. Nicholas knew and expected their actions would escalate the tension between himself and Martain, although he chose to ignore the seriousness of the situation.

Eagle arose from his chamber the next morning, to find all three men strung out in various sections of his living room. The early bird went on to commence his day, by preparing himself a freshly brewed pot of coffee and reading the local newspaper, which was delivered to his porch every morning, before he began his labor. The subtitle to the newspaper's primary story, which read, "Gangbang in Gangster's Town," was Eagle's first inclination of what his pupils did the night prior, before reading the first two sentences.

"Get your asses up now! Get up, get up," Eagle screamed! He turned on the bright overhead light, then proceeded to slap anyone in arm's reach, from his sons to their honored guest.

The young men all attempted to shield their eyes from the blinding light, before discovering the need for evasive actions against Eagle's unexpected onslaught. Nicholas found himself crouching behind Danny, like a child avoiding being scolded by a parent, as Eagle interrupted their peaceful calm.

"You all think this is funny? Think this fucking shit is funny? I know you all had something to do with this shoot-out!" Eagle exclaimed, while waving about the morning's newspaper. "Any of you have any idea who these people y'all decide to fuck with are?"

"What are you talking about, Pop," asked Danny, who didn't believe their actions would have landed them in an article on the front page of the city's main newspaper?

"Damn it, damn it, damn it! Why, boys? You all could have left it alone! Now that y'all spilled blood, ain't no turning back," stated Eagle as he sat on the edge of the sofa with his face buried into his hands!

Kane grabbed the newspaper and began reading aloud the article about what transpired at the Gentlemen's Desire Nightclub. The reporter who wrote the story appeared bias in his coverage towards the bikers, whom he claimed were all targeted by what he described as, "hired assassins for an alternate cause." The reporter went on to convey that the identities of the assassins were gathered from secret video footage that, the bikers refused to hand over to police, citing internal problem-solving methods of their own. The story also disclosed that the bikers would seek out and administer their brand of justice, described by one member as, "with utter hate and malice."

The tears gushing from Eagle's eyes caused him to choke up, as he lectured his squad on whom they were confronting. From experience, rather than gossip, was the knowledge Eagle had about the gruesome force his boys had engaged. However, with each fallen tear, Danny and Kane, who were only witnessing their teary-eyed father for the second time since birth, understood the magnitude of the shit they'd stepped in.

"You boys are seeking a war you can't win, against an enemy you are not equipped to defeat. These are the people who moved into Canada, saw a nation of proud people living here, and took this bitch over like it was theirs to begin with. They stretch from the government to the lowest form of ghetto species known to Canada. I've seen the bravest of Indians go against these people, only to have the lives of their entire families, as well as their own lives, taken without any form of sympathy. You boys are my life, the only reason I've existed since your mother passed away. See, in my younger days, I was a hell of a rebel, and no one could say a word to me, especially one of those French boys. I used to beat their asses and take their money like they owed me allowance. But one day I met your mother, and she changed my life. She corrupted it so bad I turned pussy over time. Then you boys came along with my old fiery temper, and you take no shit! I never changed that in you boys, because I wanted you to change that in yourselves. I see the same fury burning beneath your skin, Nicholas! You and my boys gotta care for each other to do this right, because the time y'all falter is when it's all over. I'm not about to stand by and have these French fuckers take another thing from me, so this no one alert, no one on guard bullshit ends now. To your feet, boys. Indian combat training is in process. Get up, get dressed, and outside right now!"

Part 9

Rev received a phone call from Aunty P late one night. The old woman could barely get out a word, as she choked up and kept sobbing. For the first few minutes of the call, Rev kept asking "what was the matter," but could not get a solid response? Finally, after encouraging her to calm down, Aunty P began discussing what the issues were.

Earlier that day, she went to view Stamma's body after the investigators wrapped up their investigation and released him to his family. The condition of the body was extremely deplorable, which meant he would have to undergo a closed funeral burial. Aunty P could barely recognize her grandson, whose face was tarnished by a bullet and, the fall Stamma sustained into the Gully storm drainage. The old woman went from the coroner to Madden Funeral Home, where she purchased a casket and made the necessary arrangements for the burial. Throughout their conversation the only time Aunty P giggled, was when she spoke of the handlers at the funeral home, who were surprised when she whipped out the entire amount from her bra. Despite her frustrations, the old woman felt elated that she had the requested amount to bury Stamma. The stress from not laying her grandchild to rest, nearly six months after his death was exhausting and, Aunty P could not wait for the funeral date to arrive.

The citizens of Canterbury celebrated the life of Stamma over the course of their Nine Nights celebration. Aunty P appreciated all the donations and assistance she received from the community, which came together and provided the food and entertainment needed each night. Knowing her neighbors' hardships and strife, Aunty P never expected a dime from any of them, yet she collected a third of what the demand was for a basic funeral. Hatchet and several other thieves who would rather steal Stamma's casket than purchase one, surprised the old woman with donations towards his cause.

Even though Kadeem had left enough money for Stamma's burial, he still wished he was there in the flesh to celebrate the life of his best friend. Aunty P was sure to tell him about the rumors circling of his disappearance and, the numerous times she managed to swivel from such topics. People throughout the community have continuously asked her about him, yet she chose to act naive, as if she had no clue where he had run off to. Due to Aunty P's lack of information sharing, several false stories circulated about Killa, some suggested that he had been murdered and disposed of by police, while others claimed he turned Christian and was serving God, in some smaller community.

It had been nearly a week since they buried Reverend and even though Aunty P was less emotional about him, she still divulged her heartfelt sentiments about his loss. Kadeem wanted to know "why Rev's body got released by the police before Stamma's, if he was murdered after," but the old granny simply reminded him "that they came ghetto." Aunty P was emotionally drained after losing two of her family members only days apart, then having to wait months to bury them. Regardless, she hoped that investigators found the persons responsible for Reverend's murder, because she knew who committed the other. Despite the sorrow and anger expressed by the old woman, Kadeem remained firm behind his decision and never wavered from his retaliation effort, to avenge the loss of his brother from another mother. Rev's killing became the one story he would never speak of again, knowing he was wrong for declining to pay the man who gave them the job opportunity.

Aunty P had no clue how Kadeem got to Nassau, nor did she care to know, as long as he was safe and far away from the treacherous hands of Jamaican law enforcement. There was another very important reason for Aunty P's phone call and, that had to do with Kadeem's father, whom she had finally gotten in touch with. Kadeem father lived in Montreal,

Canada, and had a wife and stepson who neither Aunty P nor Kadeem knew of. The old woman had managed to obtain a phone number, which she gave to the young thug and advised him, 'to make the contact'.

Instead of settling down permanently in the Bahamas, Aunty P preferred if Kadeem was amongst his father in a more developed country. Therefore, she arranged for his father to begin the immigration filing process, to have him become a landed immigrant of Canada. Due to the late hour, Aunty P suggested 'that Kadeem telephoned his father sometime in the morning', as he was eager to hear from him. Contrary to his ex-guardian's opinion, the rude boy felt reluctant to call the man who donated his sperm, so he threw the paper he wrote the number on, onto his center table and went to bed.

The next morning, Kadeem felt like skipping the gym, but that was one of Elena's routine workout days, so he decided to attend. He got there fifteen minutes before she routinely arrived and began his workout in the weights area. When Elena arrived, she would typically go for a run on the treadmill, but that morning she went directly to the weight area. Generally, Rev spied on her from across the gym to avoid being found out, but she came and sat on the bench next to his, which was quite uncomfortable.

"Hello, how are you," Elena stated!

"Oh, Oh! Mi alright thanks! How you doing," stammered Rev?

"I'm fine. You're the owner of that new rims' store, aren't you?"

"This bloodclatt gal a study mi or what?" Rev thought to himself, before he uttered, "Yes I do!"

"Can I pass by later today and get you to order me some new rims?"

"For your Range Rover?"

"Yes!"

"Mi have a unique set of rims right now, I'm sure you will love."

"OK then, I'll pass by after I go by the house and clean up."

"No problem, I'm Rev by the way!"

"Nice to meet you Rev, I'm Elena."

As they gingerly shook hands, Rev smiled and looked over Elena's shoulder, through the huge mirror on the wall. It was as if everybody inside the gym were watching him closely, therefore, he moved and went on a dead weight bench. Even though Rev had always admired the female, he was quite aware that many other men had their eyes on her. As a newcomer to Nassau, he expected a full-fledged disapproval rating from every Bahamian with regards to him getting Elena, thus, he would have to operate covertly.

It was lunch time when Elena reached the rim store and Rev's assistant was away. There were two other male shoppers inside the store when she walked in, hence Rev finished with their order before attending to her. During the time, Elena walked around and looked at the inventory, and appeared fascinated with some of the showcase rims. By the time Rev walked over to her, she was focused on one set to Pirelli Rims that she was sure would look amazing on her vehicle. Even though Elena was sure she had found the perfect set, Rev insisted she followed him to the back, where he showed her a set of Chrome Krown Rims. The showcase rims became an instant memory, as Elena went directly to the register and purchased the new set. They arranged for the installation the following morning, then concluded their business with a firm handshake.

When Elena arrived the next morning, the tires were already on the rims, balanced and ready to be mounted on the vehicle. The luscious female stepped from the Range Rover wearing a simple T-shirt, with a tennis skirt and sneakers. While Larry got started with the installation, Rev showed Elena to his office, where he asked her to wait comfortably until the job got finished. The first thing Elena noticed inside the office was Rev's security monitor system, which highlighted everywhere around and inside the building.

As courtesy, Rev offered his client the option of a cup of coffee, water, a beer or juice, to which she accepted the water. The establishment owner went to the back of the store and collected a bottle of water and returned to his office. When Rev returned, Elena was laying on his desk on her back, wearing only her sneakers and, had cleared everything aside. The rude boy did not need any further invitation, as he closed the door behind himself, dropped his pants and underwear, and went over to her. Rev wished he hadn't made his mechanic assemble the tires prior to Elena's arrival, hence he would have much more time available to enjoy her.

Elena's body felt silky soft yet hard in some areas, as Rev ran his hands down her feet to her thighs, then squeezed her firm derriere and continued up to her round Cantaloupe breasts. The fugitive gripped her and lifted her into his embrace, as their lips came together and collided for the first time. While they passionately kissed, Elena impatiently inserted Rev's penis, as if she came for nothing less. Their entire sexual interaction was hot and fiery, wherein they behaved as if they practiced cannibalism and wanted to devour each other. Throughout their intercourse session, Rev kept an eye on his security monitors and made sure that he watched Larry, who would locate the customer once the job was done.

They were granted eighteen-minutes in total, before Larry came back and advised Elena that "her Range Rover was ready to go." When Larry opened the door and walked into the office, Rev was returning the displaced objects back onto his desk, while Elena was seated behind the desk. The boss collected his client's keys from Larry to stop him from fully entering the office, where he would have observed that she was not yet fully dressed. Elena barely got on her T-shirt and was seated without her skirt and panties, after being forced to dress quickly. The adulterous pair would laugh about nearly getting caught after Larry left, even though they knew it could have been disastrous.

Despite the short timeframe allowed, Elena was pleased with Rev's performance, and claimed 'her husband had never lasted so long, nor had she ever experienced multiple orgasms without him performing oral sex'! The Jamaican rude boy found the comment quite preposterous, considering he was dissatisfied with the short time allowed. Besides gloating about how she felt, Elena suggested that they continued their affair and met up whenever possible. Following their steamy interaction, Rev was eager to see her as often as possible, even though he knew it was only a matter of time before trouble was at his doorstep.

The reports Rev received around town about Nigel, indicated that he was the leader for a group of young millionaires, who made most of their money through scamming, yet were also involved in drug trafficking and money laundering. Rev was careful with whom he spoke about Nigel, once he realized that most of the local either feared or loved him. There were quite a number of people who made their living from Nigel's affairs, therefore he considered everyone suspects and eligible to revert information. After Elena departed, Rev spent the remainder of the day thinking about her proposal, which he had already accepted.

By the time the fugitive reached home that evening, he had given adequate thought to Granny P's suggestion. Nassau had been a delightful country to live, but should there be any unsettling times ahead, Kadeem wanted to ensure he had a backup plan available. Although he went home with the intention to call his father Jeremiah in Canada, he still had not yet dialed the phone an hour later. Kadeem had no clue what to say to his father, therefore he sat staring at the phone for nearly two hours, while he smoked his joint and sipped on his liquor. Eventually he struck up the nerve then picked up the phone and dialed the number given to him by Granny P.

"Hello," responded a humble sounding male over the phone!

"Hello, I'm calling to speak with Jeremiah."

"Is who this Kadeem?"

"Yeah mon, a Kadeem this."

"How you been my big son?"

"Mi alright still, mi live in Nassau right now though."

"What, that's nice man! I spoke with Granny P the other day and she tell me that she want me to carry you up here, to live in Montreal!"

"Mi love Bahamas, but I wouldn't mind moving to Canada."

"Great son, great! There is some information you will need to send me for me to start the INS process, but I can't wait to get you up to Montreal, so we can sit and talk face to face!"

"That sounds good to me!"

"Nice, send me your email address and I'll send you some forms for you to fill out and send back to me?"

The Canadian immigration filing process dominated their conversation, following which they chatted casually about what each man did, and were surprised that they worked in the same field. Kadeem and his father had a delightful talk, even though he didn't say much and was really attempting to gage the sort of person who Jeremiah was. Despite their conversation and the promised documents sent by email, Kadeem was still skeptical about his father's pledges, until he received the official welcoming letter for him to bring to the immigration office. Amongst the many documents that needed signing, was a police criminal history report request, for the applicant to acquire his or her police history, then submit that with the form. Once Kadeem read the form's requirements, he stopped everything he was doing and turned aside from any idea he had of going to Canada.

Rev swore he was out of options until a month later, when he attended the annual Andros Crab Festival, at Queen's Park in Fresh Creek. It was the fugitive's first time at the event, so he accompanied his main brethren Floyd, who knew the island like no other. The primary attraction for which Rev wanted to attend, were the many different crab dishes that were advertised by the organizers, some of which he had never tasted. Floyd and Rev first bought two cups of crab soup and were enjoying the delicacy under a shaded tree, when Crista and two of her female friends walked by with their three children. Crista gave Rev a subtle glance and a smiled, before she called to her son who was running away.

Floyd caught the pleasantries and became suspicious of Rev, whom he assumed was secretly seeing Crista. There were hundreds of people present in the park, with various types of music playing throughout. To Rev the atmosphere felt somewhat like Jamaica, but the people were different from what he was accustomed to. Three white ladies from Germany bought themselves some food and asked, "if they could join the two friends under the tree?" Rev wasn't paying attention as he constructed his marijuana joint, so Floyd politely moved and allowed them to take his place. The moment the Bahamian got up and turned around, he saw his children's mother marching towards him.

"Oh God boy, you ready to move or what?

Rev was moistening the rolling paper's adhesive with his tongue, when he noticed that his companion had become a bit skittish. Floyd was by then looking in every direction to see where he could escape to, as if he was in dire need of rescue. A short five feet something tall female walked up like a Pitbull and stepped directly to Floyd.

"And where the fuck you been? Eh! I know you see me calling your phone for the past two days, and your fucking ass not picking up! But mark my words, Mister Small Dick Kadeen, you better make sure you come by the house with the money this evening, or else I go bring them pickneys to your mother yard, and leave them right at the front gate," threatened the female!

The Ladies from Germany nervously got up and moved, fearing the argument had something to do with them being there. Rev lit his joint and inhaled the fumes, then got up and slowly began walking away from the altercation. "Did she just call Floyd Kadeem," Rev thought to himself?

"Why the fuck you always trying to embarrass me, eh? And how many times I have to tell you, don't use man government name in public, eh? What is wrong with you, didn't I tell you I go fucking pass by when I get the money, eh? Just go bout you business and leave man alone, you understand," fired back Floyd, who then walked towards Rev!?

Contrary to certain differences, Rev realized that when it came to chastise their men, Bahamian women were equally as furious as Jamaicans. Both men walked away from the loudmouth female, who would boldly speak her mind wherever she was. As much as they needed to get away from Floyd's ex, Rev was thankful that she opened her big mouth and mentioned his real name.

"Mi think say Floyd was you real name," declared Rev?

"No man, that's just what everybody always called me since I was a child, eh. My real name is Kadeen Campbell," responded Floyd!

"Wow! You serious?"

"Yeah mon, why you say that, eh? You find Kadeen a female name?"

"No mi brethren! Is because mi real name is Kadeem!"

"Jah know star! No wonder I an I spirit receive the man like that, eh!"

There was a vendor who served roast crab, which was one of the best dishes at the festival. Floyd raved about the food to the extent that Rev joined the short lineup to get himself a plate. The chef had to add coal to the fire and set them ablaze, so he apologized and told his customers, 'it would be a short while', but instead of the line reducing, it only lengthened. As they stood there waiting for the production to start flowing again, Rev felt a peace he had never experienced, without having his gun tucked in his waist.

The two associates were the third people in line, when the food service recommenced. By then the lineup was ridiculous, with everybody expecting to receive their orders. While they waited for the next couple to get served, Elena appeared from nowhere and slipped in line in front of them.

"This line is insane! You guys mind if I slip right in here," asked

Elena.

"Go right ahead," answered Rev, as Elena looked at him with a pleasant smiled.

"No! He can't be! Not Elena and Crista, he couldn't be so stupid and brave! Nigel would kill him! But there is something about the way them look at him. As if them did a daydream about fucking him again! What I wouldn't give for five minutes with either of them," thought Floyd to himself!

"How you do Miss Elena," asked Floyd, but all he got was a slight smirk.

"How your truck feel with the new rims," asked Rev?

"Like a million bucks; and it's so much sexier! I got so much compliments since them put on, everybody want to buy my Range! I even caught my husband trying to steal a drive the other night, so I took my keys and lock them up," said Elena!

"Oh, you sold her some rims, eh," enquired Floyd?

"Rims and tires," answered Rev.

The urge to reach out and grab the voluptuous female was intense, but Rev knew there were always eyes watching, so he behaved like a gentleman. Elena received her meal and thanked both men, before she walked off and disappeared in the crowd.

That same night at 11:44, Crista phoned Rev and requested that, "he come over and spend some time with her?" Her son had fallen asleep and couldn't report her antics to his father, therefore she was free to mingle and unleash her freaky side. By the time Rev arrived it was 12:33 AM, hence, Crista was beyond eager for his rough-house treatment. From the moment Rev stepped through the door, Crista had him draped against the wall as if she was some police officer searching her suspect. The horny female grabbed his T-shirt and threatened to rip it off, until he stopped her and removed it normally.

"This bitch plans to send me home naked or what," wondered Kadeem to himself, as he quickly aided her with removing everything else.

Crista wore a skimpy pink lingerie, which was basically a picture frame that highlighted her masterpiece. The single piece lingerie was made with Snap-On clips beneath the crotch, which allowed for easier access, instead of removing the entire garment. As she began passionately kissing his body, the glass and bottles of liquor atop her center table came into focus.

They had been secretly seeing each other for more than seven months, during which they had been extremely cautious to avoid getting caught. Aside from jeopardizing her son's relationship with his father, Crista and her hustling girlfriends did business with Nigel, therefore there was a lot at stake. Three of her girlfriends worked in the tourism industry and, provided their clients with whatever illegal drugs they requested, which they obtained from Nigel through Crista.

With his undercover lover steaming with desire, Rev lifted Crista off her feet and eased her onto his penis, before he carried her across the hall into her bedroom. The regular workouts had chiseled out the Jamaican like a statue, so Crista couldn't get enough of rubbing her hands all over his body. By the time they reached her king size bed, Crista had already sustained one orgasm and was trembling like a leaf. There was no denying that the lingerie did the female's body justice, as a result, Rev never contemplated taking it off and complimented her repeatedly, 'how fabulous she looked in it'!

Instead of lowering his partner on the bed, Rev sat down and had her ride him for a while. The position also gave him the opportunity to caress her breasts and kiss her luscious lips, which he so wished were permanently his. With Crista grinding on him, while he clutched her tight in his embrace, the female uttered an unexpected phrase that surprised him, "I love you baby!" There were many signs which pointed to Crista's determination to keeping their relationship a secret, so, to avoid jeopardizing what they had he responded, "Mi love you too!" They had wild and sweaty sex until 1:57 AM, following which they laid back in bed and shared a marijuana joint.

Rev and Crista relaxed and chatted until way past 3 O'clock, before the visitor began preparing to leave. Even though Crista had denied that she was still sexually active with Nigel, Rev understood why he would have difficulty parting ways with either female. The fugitive knew much more about the female's involvements with Nigel than he had let on, even the days on which he visited her for sex. It was 3:18 AM when Rev finally exited the house, after a long passionate kiss by the front door. Without a hooded sweatshirt or a baseball cap to conceal his identity, the late-night service provider held his head down and briskly walked to his car. A Mercedes Benz, S 500, drove by as he slipped into his BMW and quickly closed the door.

The driver of the Mercedes was an associate of Nigel, who lived a few houses up the street. Big Zeeks as commonly known, thought the male whose vehicle was parked in Crista's driveway had to be Nigel. Despite the darkness of night, the male seemed to have a lighter complexion that Nigel, who also did not own a BMW. The observer took note of the vehicle, which had tinted windows and featured an exclusive set of Chrome rims. Two nights later, Big Zeeks was heading home at 4:24 AM, when he passed Rev's BMW parked half a block down the street from Crista's house.

For several months during certain hours of the day, Elena began feeling ill, so she went to her doctors and they ran several tests. When those tests results came back negative and Elena was still in distress, her doctor did a pregnancy test, since most of her symptoms were those of a pregnant woman. Each time she visited her doctor she went alone, expecting to hear something minor, considering she was a physically healthy person. Because Elena was always under the impression, she could not get pregnant, the positive pregnancy results nearly caused her to faint. Her doctor was elated for the couple, knowing how long and hard Nigel and Elena had tried to produce a child.

The test results confirmed that Elena was pregnant for nearly five months. With her doctor celebrating the pregnancy and touting Nigel as a hero, Elena had to contend with the notion that the child may not be his. After years of having coitus with her husband, the expecting mother knew wholeheartedly who the child's father was, even though she didn't weigh the consequences. Both Rev and Elena had been covertly meeting at least once weekly, sometimes more often whenever her husband went away. Their engagements were purely sexual, therefore, whenever they met each other they had unprotected sex.

When Elena left the doctor's office that day, instead of phoning her husband, she drove directly to Rev's place of business to tell him the news. The fugitive was excited about the pregnancy regardless the circumstances, even though he was under the impression that she could not be impregnated. Elena had all sorts of crazy thoughts about how they could keep everything as they were, and have Nigel raise the child as his own. The idea initially sounded brilliant, but the more Rev thought about it, was the more absurd it became.

All at once, the excitement behind fucking two women who belonged to the same man, lost the cunning appeal that made it challenging. His reality was that Nigel stood a chance of finding out about their relationship, so he had to begin taking precautions. Without very much options available, Rev contacted Floyd and met up with him for a few drinks after work. The friends went to one of Rev's favorite pubs down by the seacoast, where tourists from several of the beach hotels went for drinks and entertainment. Rev knew that Floyd had developed suspicions that he was fucking both Elena and Crista, so his first order of business was to confess.

Following his confession, Rev proceeded to surrender the entire story about Elena and himself, before he talked about his involvement with Crista. Floyd listened attentively like a child being told a thrilling story, with his excitement levels climbing with each word. They had become such good friends that the Bahamian was sincerely excited for Rev, whom he admitted had fulfilled his greatest fantasy. Sooner or later Rev expected his good fortunes to run out, so he asked Floyd if he could use his identification to have travel documents forged, then smuggled his way to Canada. Even though his Jamaican friend was not initially honest about the affairs, and he understood why, Floyd gave his consent without a second thought.

They purchased a bottle of Vodka before leaving the bar, then drove to Rev's apartment where they collected the invitation letter and a thousand dollars. To assist Rev, Floyd brought him to see a man known as 'Countafit', who was a specialist when it came to making false identification. Countafit was a Caucasian from Switzerland, who lived on Paradise Island with his dog Gerry. Floyd greeted the Swiss with the bottle of Vodka, which was his favorite liquor to drink.

Following the introductions and pleasantries, Floyd explained what they wanted from their host, who had to drink two shots from the bottle, before he did anything. Once the time came to work, Countafit took a picture of Rev with his digital polaroid camera, then placed it on a table to dry. With the picture drying, the specialist applied a chemical to a cloth and erased the last name from the invitation letter, before he replaced it with Floyd's family name. After ensuring that the names on both documents matched, Countafit removed Floyd's photo from his license and filled in the slot with Rev's picture. When the transformations concluded, the invitation letter stated that it was sent to Kadeen Campbell; and the original photo from the license had been exchanged with Rev's.

The professional forgery job appeased the rude boy, who was happy to pay the $1000 cost for the service. While Rev admired the documents, Countafit left and went into another room with Floyd. They were inside the room for about five-minutes debating some issue, before they emerged with a S&W M&P9 2.0 9mm handgun, with an extra clip and bullets. Rev was speechless at the extent that Floyd had gone for him, thus, he hugged him and expressed his heartfelt appreciation.

Floyd had never gotten the urge to leave the island of his birth, so he never saw the need to obtain a passport. To ensure that Rev knew everything necessary for him to acquire the passport, the friends returned to his apartment after they left Countafit's place. They spent the next two hours revising any important data Rev didn't already know about Floyd, until he was equipped to step into the role and convince anyone he was the Bahamian.

The next morning Rev went to the passport office and got his application approved, without the agent suspecting he was an imposter. Floyd was the only person he could confide in; therefore, he phoned his friend immediately and gave him the good news. Contrary to Rev, Floyd's revelation that he had regained a copy of his license from the Department of Motor Vehicles, was not as huge an accomplishment, but the Jamaican expressed his joy nevertheless. Despite his urges to tell both Crista and Elena, Rev decided against doing so and threw aside the cellular, after he finished talking to Floyd.

Nigel walked into Crista's house and closed the door behind himself. His son came racing from his bedroom and leapt into his father's arms.

"Daddy, daddy," yelled the little boy!

"How you doing son? I missed you real bad, eh," stated Nigel!

"I missed you too! Are we still going to Miami next month," asked the little boy?

"For sure my little man, but I have a little thing to discuss with mummy, so go hang out in your room and I go come check you after!"

"OK, but make sure you come see me before you leave!"

"Yeah man, definitely!"

As the little boy ran off to his room, Nigel walked into Crista's bedroom, where she was lying in bed wearing her robe. Nigel closed the door and tossed a small package on the bed, before he began undressing as he made his way across the room towards Crista. The bottle of Smirnoff atop the night table was all the information Nigel needed to know what was inside of Crista's glass. Once he came closer, Crista placed the glass of liquor on the night table and focused her attention on him.

"Is that all the dope," Crista asked?

"Yes, everything," Nigel said!

The female knew all of Nigel's sexual tendencies and preferences. Unlike Rev, who was somewhat of an untamable animal, Nigel was more of an easily handled remote-controlled device. Therefore, Crista understood the precise amount of pressure, that was necessary to make him ejaculate like a faucet. The sexually promiscuous female began giving her son's father oral sex, which usually made him shiver like an epileptic patient going into shock. While Crista appeased Nigel, the adulterer momentarily snapped, then grabbed her around the neck and began strangling her. Instead of fighting back to save her life, the female began laughing, as if she was either drunk or psychotic. Nigel removed a picture from his shirt breast pocket and showed it to Crista.

"You fucking bitch, eh! Whose fucking car is this?"

With his son's mother laughing as if he was crazy, Nigel released her neck, which allowed Crista to speak clearly.

"Oh, please Nigel, we all know you ain't no badman! We all know you ain't no Killer!"

"I may not be the killer but, know this! I don't mind paying them shooters to put boy body underground! Now, who the fuck this car belongs to?"

"Them girls was over here few nights with them boyfriend, so it must a been his car!"

"You see once I speak to them girls, if I find out you lying to me, you better get a job, because I done paying the bills for this place!"

"Come on baby, you know I keep this pussy locked for you alone," Crista said, as she began caressing Nigel penis.

The moment she went back to administering oral sex, Nigel dropped the BMW car picture on the bed and forgot about it. After teasing Nigel just enough to get him sexually charged, Crista stopped and climbed into his favorite doggie position. With Crista positioned on her hands and knees, Nigel began performing fellatio, which was the only sex stimulant with which he surpassed Rev. Knowing that his performance was weaker in every other area, the Bahamian spent more time making Crista squirm and moan, as he licked her vagina areas satisfyingly. Once Nigel made his partner's toes curled with an orgasm, he quickly slid his penis inside her and began jamming away. Crista was accustomed to his record time ejaculations with Nigel; therefore, she knew to enjoy the rides for as short as they lasted.

Three and a half minutes into the sex session, Nigel gripped his partner's hips tightly and said, "Oh lord, I coming, I coming!"

After ejaculating inside his son's mother, Nigel tumbled atop the bed, as if he had just run a marathon. Crista collected some baby wipes from a package inside her nightstand and used it to wipe him clean. Provided with the opportune time, Crista waited until Nigel was relaxed then struck up a conversation.

"Baby, I have something to tell you!"

"What is it now Crista, eh?"

"Nigel, I'm two months pregnant!"

"How the fuck you manage get pregnant too, eh?"

"Don't ask me, is you do it!"

Part 10

"Scour this entire island and make sure these fuckers are on the evening news, or someone is going to take their place in the obituaries tomorrow," Martain warned after watching the surveillance video, from the attack at the night club! "I should have killed that fucking tar baby the first time I saw him! Now I gotta go explain to Moose's little kids why my boy isn't coming home!"

"I'll personally find them. A black man and two Indians won't be hard to spot in Montreal," Yves Buchard assured him!

The word went throughout the city, like the expectations of a first-place finish in the National Hockey League's championship finals, to determine the bearers of the Holy Grail. The Rough Riders considered the attack against members of their coalition forces on home soil a family matter; and disclosed no identity of the intruders to the police. The flamboyant crew of Harley Davidson riders instead plastered the photos of the three wanted men across their website, knowing that a sighting or information on one of the men was imminent. Within a half hour, a member of the biker crew's southern division, who surveyed the photos over the bikers' Internet page, recognized Danny Esquada's photo, after combating him some time prior in the boxing ring. The crewmember who phoned in the information, remembered being knocked out by Danny in the fifth round of their exhibition match, and insisted he be inserted among the assassins chosen for the mission. Martain had the biker escorted to his haven, as the biker boss sought to acquire every bit of information possible about his newest nemesis.

Eagle Esquada was a man who lived for his sons, after the tragic death of the only woman he'd ever truly loved. The elderly father of two had fought against the government of Canada, over the rights of aboriginals throughout his tenure, as the oppression of his people persisted. Eagle had been taught by his forefathers to abstain from the calamities of the world, although his personal losses through life caused him to stray from such righteous teaching. The Esquada family head hated the man he'd become, after vowing at an early age 'to abstain from such a path'. The oppression fighter rarely drank in public, though the same could not be said for him in the privacy of his own home. The spiritual Indian warrior had partaken in countless rebellions against the tyranny of the government, by blocking railway lines, bridges, and highways that passed through Indian reservations, and yet his prized knowledge of the Rough Riders sacrament, scared him most.

Eagle had insisted that Nicholas deal his poison across the river, since the day he smuggled into the country. The proud Native Eagle had always been, caused him to compassionately consider the economic bearings such cosmetic drugs would have on his poor community, who already had nothing to survive on. Nicholas had heeded the requests of Eagle throughout, although his sons weren't as optimistic about the people as their dad. Kane had entered the underground market of substance trafficking with the backings of Nicholas weeks prior, and he fought hard to maintain secrecy from his father. Kane Esquada dealt drugs through his entrusted friends, who did all the physical labor without complaints, after receiving the products on consignments with minor penalties. The financial ruin cocaine would bring to the Indian people, according to Eagle, was eventually introduced to the same people he attempted to protect, by his own flesh and blood.

The three friends had spent most of the morning in the hills, where they practiced with 9mm handguns, did evasive fighting maneuvers, exercised, jogged, and played around with each other. On their way down the mountain, Samuel, whose mother was Eagle's younger sister, rang Kane's cell phone and insisted they meet at once. Kane advised his cousin to meet with him at their regular spot, which was along the trail heading home. The urgency of Samuel's tone bothered all three friends, who unanimously decided to attend the meeting.

"There are some biker guys approaching the local crackheads and, offering them free rocks for information on where to find you guys! They're saying they know that you guys supply the reservation! I assume they're friends of yours," informed Samuel!

"I assure you, cousin, they're no friends of ours," said Kane!

"Well, it's only a matter of time before they get an address. With the free shit they're giving away, someone will give up their mother real soon," said Samuel!

"All right, cousin, I want you to bring me the bag I hid by your mother last week," Kane said?

"By the looks of them guys, I'm already ahead of you, because they didn't seem like they looking for conversation," Samuel exclaimed!

The news of strangers on the reservation swept through the communities like the atomic bomb on Hiroshima. By the time the men returned to Eagle's house, the warrior had already received word of the exact infraction he'd expected. Adam Cardozer ran a local corner store, where a large percentage of the community frequented for supplies. Martain Lafleur, Yves Buchard, and three other goons sought information regarding the exact whereabouts of the three men, who'd disrupted his adult lounge. With a population of three thousand, Martain expected the grocer to have adequate knowledge of the community and the people residing in it.

"Good day to you, sir! I'm looking for the Esquada ranch or home, and I know you can definitely help me," said Martain.

"Who did you say you're looking for," Mr. Cardozer asked?

"Esquada family! Two sons with a black friend of theirs," Martain answered.

The store operator looked the tattooed individual up and down over the rim of his glasses, before denying ever hearing the name Esquada. Martain signaled his goons to man the front door, while he extracted valuable information the only way he knew how. Yves and another biker member walked behind the counter and dragged the fierce shopkeeper from his comfort zone. Both men brought him front and center ahead of Martain, who was in no mood for gimmicks. Mr. Cardozer kicked and fought, knocking over merchandise as the two gangsters brought him to their boss.

"Settle him down, enough of the childish bullshit," Martain ordered!

Yves grabbed the shopkeeper's fax machine/telephone from the counter with both hands and smashed it over the man's head. "You didn't hear the boss say to shut the fuck up," Yves yelled, as the revolting proprietor stopped resisting?!

Martain stepped over the shopkeeper and pressed his right foot against the Indian's neck. The leader of the Rough Riders waited for the proprietor to begin gasping for air, before instructing the man on exactly how they would proceed. Martain advised the proprietor that 'any response apart from the absolute truth would result in the loss of his store, his family, and his own life'. With the penalties provided, the proprietor answered truthfully all questions posed to him, in fear of any retribution should they not succeed. Adam waited for the roars of Harleys to dissipate, before calling and advising Eagle of what transpired between, he and the Rough Rider's captain.

Danny, Kane, and Nicholas returned home to find Eagle making preparations for an attack. The Indian was busy reinforcing and barring windows, creating open areas to shoot through, and setting outdoor traps around the yard, before inspecting and preparing his weapons for battle. Eagle summoned his boys and advised them to prepare for the war he'd advised them of, though he knew they were terribly outnumbered and outgunned.

"I have fought a demon in my dreams since the death of your mother. For years, I've been seeing this huge battle, that I once believed came from the demons in the bottle of alcohol, I slept in every night! But now I know that vision was a true prophecy, for the day of that great battle has come! My sons, I have taught you to embrace death when it comes, and I know that is a trait of your young heart, Nicholas. We are outnumbered against this enemy, who has showed up at our doorstep, but we will not be defeated by this enemy! Such is the prophecy this land and my heart have revealed to me. I know of this enemy, for my ancestors ran them from our lands with their liquor and drugs. There is no sense running from these people, for it will only be a matter of time before they find you. Whatever happens on this day, know we battled like warriors, and never surrender, or you surrender your soul," Eagle said!

"All that is understood, but what is that stuff you mixing up," Nicholas asked?

"Before a warrior enters a battle, it is said that the war paint transforms the normal man into the brave heart desired to accomplish his task. With the war paint, a cheetah becomes a lion and a bear becomes a grizzly bear! I am known as the Dark Eagle, and tonight I shall soar one final time, before I too, join my beautiful wife and the rest of my ancestors," Eagle exclaimed, as he designed his war paint to make him look like an eagle.

Contrary to Eagle, there was no motivational speech given before the Rough Riders ascended on the Indians' property, then moved towards Nicholas and his group of warriors. The bikers trespassed on the property by climbing over the northern fence, which was still a short walk from the house. As nightfall sat in, a haze of darkness caused by the tall trees in the yard, overshadowed the house and made it extremely dark inside the residence. Nicholas and his mates were camped by windows around the house, for a clear view of the entire perimeter. The younger men inside the house, conversed among themselves to combat drowsiness, as the hours grew later.

At 11:49 PM, Kane found himself succumbing to the pressures of fatigue and decided to fetch himself and others a drink from the fridge. As he passed by the corridor that led to the bedrooms, Kane checked the status of his father, who had been camped near the window at the end of the hall. Eagle had vacated his post, taking with him his bow and arrows and an Apache knife, while abandoning his Winchester rifle by the foot of the window. Kane ran to his father's post and looked frantically through the window. There was no sign of his father anywhere in the vicinity, so Kane immediately alerted his companions of the situation.

"Eagle left his post," Kane whispered!

"What do mean? He's gone," Nicholas asked?

"He means Dad saw them coming and decided to take the fight to them, so keep your eyes open. They aren't too far away," Danny exclaimed!

Eagle counted fifty invaders seventy-five feet away from his surveillance tower, high among the branches of a maple tree. The Indian warrior withdrew his first arrow from the sachet around his shoulder and took aim at the last man toiling in the background. The silence of the wind guided the arrow directly into the man's chest and brought him down without a sound, and Eagle reloaded his weapon of choice and continued his assault. Eagle knocked off nine consecutive rear targets, as the invaders sneaked their way closer to his house. Forty feet away from the house, one of Martain's gunners stepped into a bear trap, which snapped its jaws like teeth into the man's leg.

"Ahhh! My fucking leg!"

"Shut him the fuck up, before he tells all the animals where we are," Yves instructed!

A man stopped to assist his comrade, by first placing his hand over the injured man's mouth, to prevent any further outbursts. The assisting medic watched his friends continue on their mission, before attempting to free his comrade's leg from the trap's jaws. The gangster succeeded at removing the contraption from his comrade's leg, and turned to ask about the man's well-being, when he observed an arrow lodged into the back of the man's neck.

The biker quickly turned to warn his friends, and he, too, received an arrow directly through the neck, which knocked him on his back. The injured gunner began checking the grounds around for his weapon, as his friends had completely disappeared. The arrow had lodged itself into the man's throat without disrupting any critical organs, although he was forced to gasp harder in order to fill his lungs with oxygen.

There was in the distance the shadow of a man, hidden among the leaves of a tree, hence the injured gangster raised his Walter PPK automatic weapon into firing position, and took aim at the Monkey Man. The Arrow launching assassin seated in the tree had not lost focus of the gangster, whose eyes widened once he realized he'd already been targeted. The biker frightfully yanked on the trigger repeatedly, before he realized that he'd neglected to remove the safety switch. An arrow lodged directly into the man's right eye, killing him instantly with only the sounds of broken twigs, when his body collided with the ground.

Eagle boldly slammed an arrow that nearly ripped the chest cavity from his target, who was at that moment walking within inches of his allies. The closest man to Eagle's latest victim observed him fall to the ground and, realized a sniper was about the area. The gangster quickly calculated the trajectory from which the arrow came, although the darkness of night made it increasingly difficult to pinpoint the sniper.

"There's someone firing arrows from the tree over there," said the biker, who began pointing directly in the vicinity where Eagle was hiding.

The Mohawk Indian fired his last arrow from his stakeout position, which landed in the belly of the biker, who was attempting to locating the sniper's position. Eagle wrapped his hands around a rope he'd used to hoist himself into the tree and attempted a quick retreat. An avalanche of bullets ripped off the tree limb that offered him protection, and he narrowly escaped the onslaught. A bullet from an intruder's AK-47 ripped through the warrior Indian's shoulder, which was wrapped around the rope for support. Instead of a casual swing from one maple tree to the next, Eagle plummeted awkwardly towards the ground, before breaking his fall and changing his trajectory, so he couldn't be located.

"Whoever he is, I want a few of you to find him and kill him," ordered Martain, who had gone along to ensure the job was done properly.

The remaining bikers continued pressing on toward their target, since Martain would not permit them to get discouraged under any circumstance. A second biker soon screamed out in pain as he, too, experienced the clinching pains caused by another bear trap. The closer Martain's gang of misfits got to the house, the deadlier the traps set by Eagle, to reduce their oncoming foes number. The hand-to-hand tactician shoved his hand beneath his clothing and checked the bullet wound he'd recently received. Eagle placed his ear against the ground to determine the number of assassins in pursuit, as he thought of ways to rid himself of the mini-Delta Force at his heels. He ran down the trail that led to the main roadway, knowing his only chance of ridding himself of his pursuers, would be with the assistance of a grenade trap he'd planted along that trail. The darkness made it difficult to pinpoint the exact burial point, at which he assembled the mechanism for the sabotage. The invader who led the charge against Eagle was getting increasingly closer as the Indian's wound slowed him down drastically. The bikers tracking Eagle opened fire at the fleeing warrior, who was forced to duck low behind the first available tree.

Eagle pretended he'd been struck by a shell from the barrages of bullets being spat at him with the thug's AK-47 and tumbled behind a huge tree. From his knees, the warrior peeked around the side of the tree to catch a glimpse of the gangsters shooting at him. Once a man became visible, Eagle tattooed him with an arrow that propelled the attacking invader back a few paces. The allies of the fallen gangster scattered and dove for the turf, as if their lives depended on it, before erratically scattering bullets at everything in front of them. Eagle had reconvened his track session down the hill, but could not outrun the widely scattered bullets, one of which tore chunks of flesh from his right rib cage. Eagle toppled to the ground as he did the first time he got shot, while the gangsters advanced and maintained their barrage of fire, in case the Indian was up to his old tricks. As they cautiously moved forward, one of the five trailing Rough Riders unknowingly stepped on the grenade trap that Eagle had planted. The blast that erupted sent all five men flying in every direction, as an utter calm fell over that section of the woods.

Nervous tensions affected some the bikers, who realized that several of their colleagues had vanished. A rabbit leapt from some bushes and startled three shooters, who opened fire at the animal without hitting the damn bunny. The premature eruption of gunfire by the three house attackers, gave away their position to Nicholas and the Esquada brothers, and likewise awarded them ample time to formulate an evasive plan. Danny had been taught by the best and used his warrior intellect to decipher what may had happened to his father, through the sounds of explosions in the distance. The young Indian could sense that their foes had been reduced in numbers, hence, their moral must be depleted, considering they went from the hunters to the hunted.

Danny decided to bring the battle to their enemies like Eagle did, while working cohesively with his brother and friend. His objective was to sneak out and flank the enemy while they were engaged in a shootout, then killed them all. The traps that were set by Eagle announced the enemies' approach since, every few feet gained by the enemy produced an injured combatant. Aside from Eagle's infamous bow and arrows, were his bear traps, spiked tree limb traps, that were triggered once an invader unknowingly disrupted the tripwires, as well as a few grenades, which also erupted once triggered. It was completely dark in the wooded area of the Esquada property, so the unprepared bikers could not see any of Eagle's tripwires.

The woods surrounding Eagle's home was already filthy with dead bodies, however, another grenade erupted thirty feet from the house, due to the bikers' persistence. Nicholas watched as the huge ball of fire that plumed into the sky, catapulted four motionless bodies onto Eagle's front lawn. Kane, around that point, opened fire at elements through his viewpoint, as Martain and company began dumping bullets at the house.

"What the fuck? They think we don't have any guns," Nicholas yelled, as he aligned a biker's forehead in the center of his night vision scope?

Hollow point bullets spat from Nicholas' assault rifle, as he sniped off a biker member nearly forty feet away from the house. Kane could be heard running from his assigned position, as he was forced to secure the exit where Eagle was originally stationed. Before the youngest of the Esquada's could reach the window, an intruder entered and began inspecting the room for dwellers. Fright brought Kane to create his first ghost, as his nervous, twitchy trigger finger yanked on the trigger, after the invader surprised him by walking out of the bathroom and directly into his aim. Kane froze for a millisecond after drilling the intruder full of holes, before rushing to the window where he executed two different passersby, who believed the area had been secured.

Dressed in a full camouflage outfit, with his face war-painted in black, Danny laid motionless in front of a log, as a biker rushed in to use the fallen wood stump as a shield against bullets. Eagle had blocked several of the windows around the house with plywood, yet he made sure that those inside had ample shooting pockets available. Rider members had no idea how many Indians they were up against, and thus, avoided rushing the house in case an army awaited.

Danny was so well camouflaged that the biker's closest ally ran by the log and even stepped on his left hand, which forced him to bite his tongue to avoid giving away his location. The biker's ally went and took up aim a few feet from the rear window and began unloading his magazine. The young brave unexpectedly stuck his knife up underneath the chin of the biker behind the log, who was only yards away from his trigger-happy companion. The warrior Indian, although not as skillful as his father, had the training and ability to disfigure foes, therefore, he crept up on the biker to the right, grabbed him around the mouth, and slit his throat, before flinging his knife in the neck of the biker who'd stepped on his hand.

Another of Eagle's deadly traps erupted, when four bikers who took up positions around the outdoor shed, tripped a wire that caused the shed to explode. Eagle had packed canisters with nails, sharp objects, and marbles inside the shed, which, once exploded, sent dangerous debris flying, killing instantly three others who were within close proximity. Martain immediately ordered his declining biker force to shoot up the house and everything within, as the developments thus far infuriated the gangster, who hadn't ceased firing since assuming the single knee plant position behind a tree.

After calling to his friend, who, by all accounts, had been holding his own against Nicholas and whoever was trapped inside the house, the biker who initially led Martain across the Champlain River, realized that his colleague had been killed with the bullet lodged in his cranium. There were booby traps being set off around the house, all of which resulted in the deaths or severe injuries of Rough Riders, attempting to gain an advantage on their targets.

With a decreasing number of bikers, Danny removed one of the deceased gunner's club jacket and bandana, put them on, and began playing opossum, by lying on the ground and screaming for help, as if he been wounded by the enemy. As soon as anyone became naive enough to fall for the trap, the Indian would roll them up while either cutting their throats or stabbing them to death. The biker, who had informed Martain about Danny, sought to get his revenge versus the Indian for years of shame, following his loss to the native. To get at Danny, the biker maneuvered cautiously around to find a less dangerous entrance into the house, when he came across the wounded ally, who was beseeching anyone for help. The biker seeking assistance was the opossum playing Danny, who had borrowed the deceptive attires and cleaned up enough to lure his victims. The darkness assisted the Indian, whose red skin and long porcupine hair would have easily given him away to his foes, and they would have skinned him alive had they caught him. By the time the biker realized his executioner was that close, his neck had been slit wide open, and Danny left him hunched over as if he'd fallen asleep in the middle of the battle.

The concerned Indian was determined to find his father, who had failed to answer to the family's ancient summoning method, which mimicked the calls of the great owl. Before he could set out in search of his father, Danny knew he had to eliminate a few more thugs from the equation, before he ended up alone without neither family nor friend. The junior athlete of the year, at St. Augustine High School on the reservation, loved the javelin event, and he still possessed a rocket of an arm. Danny wasn't seen as he crept around the grounds with precision stealth, while armed with his native knife, an Uzi automatic, and a few wooden spears. As expected, Danny waited until his enemies had sunken into trenches with their attention on those inside the house, before he took advantage of their delinquency, crept up from behind and slit their throats. There were a few bikers whose positioning would provide some difficulties getting to, therefore, Danny tossed spears and slaughtered them from a distance.

"Where the fuck are those idiots I sent around back, to blaze them out front so we can end this cowboys and Indians bullshit? Where's Mystro? Someone tell Mystro to grab few shooters and take the house from the side," Martain instructed!

"Mystro can't be found anywhere, boss! As a matter a fact, a lot of people can't be found anywhere," Yves answered, as he kept his body shielded while bullets tore at the tree that protected him.

Martain began assessing the strength of his troops, which had dwindled dramatically without anyone noticing. Every top-ranked biker Martain summoned had either suffered a tragic accident or was being aided back to safety from the war zone. The massive pressure Martain envisioned unleashing on his antagonists, seemed only a fairy tale dream, as he watched his braves cower behind the protection of trees. A fierce expression fell over the biker boss' face, as he counted over the remaining eight gladiators, of a force once fifty strong. Martain looked around and began wondering if his legion of thugs had cowardly deserted the fight, as he considered their ratio for success. While pondering over the idea, Martian witnessed a spear as it pierced through thin air, before pasting one of his bikers to the tree he used as protection, against the golf balls being fired from the house.

"Fuck! They've had us surrounded all this time and we didn't even know it! Retreat! Let's get the fuck out of here before we all get left here!" Martain yelled, as he headed the pack back toward their vehicles, once he observed the trajectory the spear had taken.

Danny knew they could outsmart the bikers into believing they were a much larger and rugged bunch, before he started through the woods in search of Eagle. The number of deceased bikers scattered throughout the woods, told the tale about who truly cast the decisive blow, that defeated the biker army. Nicholas and Kane scurried out of the house once they noticed their antagonists had retreated. The two friends cautiously swept the dark woods with their automatic weapons, to ensure the bikers had left. Danny eventually walked from among the dark trees with his father's body, at which everyone gathered around the great warrior, praising his spirit for living, before ushering him off to the Great Spirit Realm.

PART 11

Crista telephoned Rev as he walked into his apartment and tossed his keys and mail on a side wall table. There was one specific immigration envelope that interested the rude boy, who ripped it open to view its contents. At the sight of the passport, Rev smiled to himself knowing he at least had the chance to get off the island.

"Hello babes, what a gwan," Rev greeted?

"Hi my love! Well, I finally told Nigel I was pregnant yesterday," Crista said!

"And how him take it?"

"He almost had a heart attack babe! But, with word in the streets that him bitch wife Elena pregnant, him go have to deal with this child too!"

"So, him finally breed him wife?"

"It looks so, but nobody out a road don't think it's his pickney! People have it saying, the bitch fucking somebody at her gym!"

"Huh, you know people always talking nonsense," joked Rev, knowing exactly who the guilty party was!

"I don't business with them! Listen babe, somebody take picture of your car once when you was here, now Nigel claim he go investigate to find out whose car it is, and if we have something going on! I done advise the girls and them what to say if him question them, but just watch yourself, hear me!"

Rev thought about mentioning the passport and his plans to relocate in Canada; but decided against doing so. News that his car was of interest meant that his life could be in danger, therefore, he had to get rid of it. Once he disconnected the call, he went in search of his vehicle's legal documents, then telephoned the BMW dealership where he bought the car. The sales office was closing, so they made an appointment for Rev the following late morning.

By 7:30 AM the next morning, Rev was in the line at the Canadian Embassy Office. Despite the early morning, there were eight people already in line when he arrived, therefore he took his place and waited patiently. It was a long wait and Rev didn't get in to see an agent until 10:21 AM. There were only two unhappy clients out of the eight visa seekers who went before Rev, which made him believe he had an excellent chance of getting approved. None of the applicants ahead of the rude boy had an invitation letter, thus, he didn't have anyone with whom he could compare his chances.

The male agent who summoned Rev into the interview, was being considered as the axe man by the applicants who watched the proceedings that morning, because he was the person who denied the first two individuals. Rev was sure that the agent would see through his false pretense, so he had to conjure up his greatest Bahamian act. Once inside the interview office, Rev became social and interactive, wherein he observed things around the room and used them as his talking points.

"Good morning Mister Campbell, I see that you are here to obtain a Canadian visa! Why do you wish to travel to Canada," Agent Drew Markham asked?

"I ain't seen my dad since I was a little boy, but him send me an invitation letter to come visit him for a while, eh" answered Rev.

"Where in Canada does your father live?"

"Somewhere in Montreal him say."

"Do you have the invitation letter? May I see it please?"

Rev slid the paper across the table to him. "I see you love soccer, what's your favorite team?"

The question caught the agent off guard, and he looked over at his Brazil photo on the wall before answering, "Must be Brazil man," with a slight smirk. "So, how long do you plan on staying in Canada?"

"Not too long at all, eh, maybe two three weeks just to see the place!

My partner and I just opened a tire and rims shop, so I can't be gone too long, eh!"

"Where does your mother live?"

"She live right here in Nassau, eh."

"You have any siblings?"

"No, I was a single child, eh!"

"Do you have any children?"

"Yes, I have four," Rev stated proudly!

"You have any intentions on moving to Canada?"

"Me, no man me don't have time for the cold, eh! I is a true Bahamian and I go dead right here in my country, eh!"

The immigration agent had heard enough, therefore he withdrew his approval stamps from his desk drawer and tattooed the official travel visa inside Floyd's passport.

"Congratulations Mr. Campbell, you may go and visit your father as much as you like, because I just granted you a ten-year visa," the agent declared.

Rev stood up and shook the man's hand firmly, with his heart joyously pounding. Everyone inside the waiting room was surprised when he held up a tightly clinched fist, which indicated his success, on his way from the building. The first person the rude boy phoned once he got in his car was Floyd as expected, therein, they agreed to meet up that evening and celebrate over drinks. The fugitive had a programed travel agent's number in his phone, thus, he contacted them thereafter and purchased a flight ticket to Montreal.

Before returning to his shop, Rev had an appointment to attend. The Jamaican drove to his BMW dealership at Executive Motors Limited on Shirley Street, where he met with Prince his salesman. The car dealer could not believe Rev wanted to trade his car, yet, found a different model with the same color to suit his customer. After a few signatures and plate switches, Rev was able to leave with his new ride and drove directly to his store.

The rims store was open for almost a year at that point and business had allowed for Rev to hire a salesgirl, to open, close periodically, and manage whenever he was absent. When the boss reached the shop, a contractor he hired to repair the pipe that travelled to the men's toilet, had just left for lunch. The contractor had smashed out a fraction of the wall that lead from the garage to the men's room, and Rev was not happy that he was not advised about it prior. In order to complete his diversion plot, Rev made Larry change the factory rims off his new car and added a more glamorous set. With the new BMW sedan ready for its stand-in duties, the vehicle was parked in front the store for everyone to see. Half an hour before the store closed, Big Zeeks, Froggy and Juice-Man drove by and slowed down enough to inspect Rev's car. Once they were satisfied that the car didn't match the one in their photo, they drove away from the area.

That evening when Floyd and Rev met for drinks, they had a splendid old time at Nigel's expense. Floyd could listen to his friend's account of the adulterous wife and cheating side chick for hours and, would not allow Rev to skip a single detail. They celebrated everything, from the passport success to Floyd regaining his license, to the pregnancies that could never be claimed by the biological father. After a while the conversation took on a more serious tone, as Rev sought to find out about Nigel's hired killers, whom he would always turn to whenever he needed people executed.

To advise his friend about the psychotic bunch of deranged killers who would certainly come hunting for him, Floyd began by talking about Boogyman, who was the leader of the crew. They called themselves Bahamas Star Crew and were nearly fifty members deep, so there were a few them who needed mentioning. Floyd had to discuss Regan, who was another crazy member of the gang, Stylo-V, Froggy, Juice Man and Baron. There were other dangerous standouts aside from the killers Floyd mentioned, but he wanted Rev to know specifically about those men. The Rastafarian taxi/tour guide, told his friend everything there was to know about the group, including where to find them on specific days. According to Floyd, even the local police were afraid of the bunch, who were suspects in the murders of at least three island police officers. Both Rev and Floyd left the bar hugging each other like long lost brothers, and walked to their vehicles staggering along the sidewalk, while they sang Bob Marley's, 'Redemption Songs'.

It was nearly 11:45 PM, when Nigel met with Boogyman, Froggy,

Juice Man, Big Zeeks and others at their hangout spot in Rocky Pines, on Palm Breeze Drive. There was a lineup of motorcycles parked at the house, where the gang stored most of their inventory and, spent most of their down time. They had music playing loudly while the thugs either played card games, mingled with the women present or did stunts on their bikes.

Rev was already parked down the street when Nigel arrived and got his Rockstar welcome from the crew's loyalists. The Jamaican had seen some of the Bahamas Star Crew members at different functions he had attended, but he had to mark as many individual faces as he could. From Floyd's descriptions he could tell who was Boogyman, Big Zeeks, Baron and Froggy, though he had some trouble pairing the others with their names. As much as Rev wished he could avoid the conflict, it seemed like an unavoidable collision, hence he had to know who to shoot at on sight.

After eliminating Rev from their list, Boogyman and his associates had a few other BMW owners across the island to check out, before they could provide Nigel with a complete report. The unresolved issue infused the scam artist, who could not knowingly accept that he fathered both females' children. The fertility doctors during his consultation meetings with Elena, have already determined that he could not father a child, unless he stopped the excessive drinking and built up his immune system. Even though Nigel knew there were other existing complications prohibiting Elena from having a child, he still had not yet changed his drinking habits or diet, therefore he felt assured that both females were lying.

One of the crew's female groupies brought Nigel, Baron and Regan three cups with liquor. The female known as Jazzy, was not amongst Crista's immediate circle, but rather the first cousin to one of her good friends. Jazzy handed the men their drinks and started walking away, when Nigel stopped her to ask a few questions.

"Hey Jazzy, I ain't seen you cousin with Crista since that reggae show on the beach, how she doing," Nigel asked?

"Her mother's been sick in and out the hospital, so she been going through a lot," Jazzy said.

"She wasn't hanging out over by Crista few weeks ago?"

"I don't think none a them girls been partying much over the past few months, eh. I last heard, Lorna was visiting family members in Miami, over three months now since she been there!"

Four days later, Rev received a call from Elena, who had been assigned to bed rest by her doctor. It had been almost a month since they last saw each other and even though they messaged each other daily, they still had to take extreme precaution not to get discovered. The first-time expecting mother had an appointment with her doctor and wanted to meet up with Rev afterward, which had been an impossible task with Nigel's constant supervision. Nigel had been monitoring his wife closely since she revealed she was pregnant and, was beginning to accept the idea that he impregnated her. The suspicious husband wanted to accompany his wife to the appointment, but she insisted it was just a minor checkup, hence he did not have to take her.

On the morning of her doctor's appointment, Elena got herself ready and left Nigel in bed pretending he was sleeping. Before leaving, the female applied her favorite red lipstick, instead of her regular clear lip gloss, and spayed herself with a bit of her Coco Chanel Perfume. Moments after she drove away, Crista telephoned Nigel with a contraband order for him to fill, yet advised him in advance that, 'the funds were short'. After disconnecting their call, Nigel sat up in bed thinking to himself, as the lingering scent of perfume slithered by his nose. Elena had complained that the perfume made her nauseous since her pregnancy began, therefore, he didn't think it plausible that she would wear it. With all the deceptions in his relationships as of late, the perception of Elena's guilt, made Nigel get dressed and decided to follow her.

The doctor visit passed quickly, and Elena was delighted that everything was on schedule with the baby. She had received a text message from Rev that stated he had arrived; therefore, she couldn't wait to get out of the doctor's office. The pediatrician's office was located at the hospital, which was always a busy place to maneuver through.

When Nigel reached the hospital, he parked his car three lanes over from Elena's, in a position that allowed him to clearly view the Range Rover. As he sat watching his wobbly wife, slowly exit the building and made her way to her truck, Nigel felt the urge to run out and assist her but, decided against doing so. There was a BMW parked two cars over from Elena's and as she approached the Range Rover, Rev hopped out and walked over to her. They both climbed into the rear of the truck, which surprised Nigel, who couldn't believe his wife was that freaky.

Elena was elegantly dressed in a flowery knee length skirt, without panty and a fitted blouse, that made access quite easy. Despite her huge baby bump and difficulty climbing into the rear of the Range Rover, once she got inside, she became a different woman. Rev was already accustomed to their intimate sessions; therefore, he began undressing himself the instant he climbed into the vehicle. They French kissed like sloppy animals, before Elena climbed over on top of Rev, then began riding him.

Nigel exited his car and crept closer to the Range Rover. The vehicle was rattling as if hurricane type wind was pushing it back and forth, nevertheless, Nigel still doubted what he was witnessing. The deeply tinted windows made it difficult to see inside the truck, but Nigel found an angle from which he could clearly see the interior. At the sight of his wife atop another man, Nigel's mouth fell wide open, before he shamefully hung his head and walked back to his car. Tears of sorrow began draining from his eyes, as he replayed continuously the vision he saw in his head. Without any hesitation, the scarred husband picked up his phone and called Boogyman.

"Hello," Boogyman responded!

Nigel could be heard crying over the phone and couldn't utter a single word for the first few seconds of the conversation.

"Nigel, what happening man? Is who fuck with you," Boogyman questioned?

"I want him dead! I want him dead! I want him dead!" Nigel continued mumbling as he cried like a child.

"Who that Nigel, eh? Just say the word boss-man!"

"I know who's been fucking with my woman and them, eh! And I want him dead no later than today!"

"Just say a name, him already dead?"

"It is that same fucking Jamaican fellow who own the tire and rims shop, eh!"

"What, so how them boys claim it's not his car we looking for?"

"I don't give one fuck, eh! I just want him mash up to where him can't even get a open casket funeral... If I did know any killers in Jamaica, eh, I would pay to make them kill him whole family!"

"That man is a ghost before the day finish! I promise you that, eh!"

The infuriated husband sat and watched the Range Rover rattled in the parking lot, until his wife and her partner finished having intercourse. Neither of them demonstrated any signs of affections out in public, as Rev went directly to his BMW and Elena climbed into the driver's seat and drove away. After his adulterous wife and her sex providing mate departed, Nigel started his vehicle's engine and departed from the hospital.

Nigel brought the package that Crista requested to her house. The Bahamian scam artist had a depressed demeanor, which his side chick had never seen before. His son was by Crista's mother's house; therefore, they had the entire residence to play around if they so choose. Crista was wearing her robe, which was a prerequisite demand, that allow for whatever Nigel desired. From her son's father walked in, the pregnant female could sense that there was a problem, so instead of her regular enticing entrapments, she sat and had a descent chat him.

Instead of the hardened demeanor that Nigel demonstrated to Boogyman, he was far less subdued. For one of the most successful hustlers on the island, Nigel acted like a broken man, who just received the worst news of his life. Crista prepared them both alcoholic drinks, then sat inside her living room on the sofa together. Nigel was incredibly stressed but refrained from saying anything for the first three minutes. Knowing her son's father would need some coercing, Crista pulled him closer to her and placed his head on her shoulder.

"I just now find out who breed Elena!"

"When you told me you didn't know how that bitch get pregnant, you was serious!"

Nigel said nothing and went back into silent mode for a few seconds, before he blurted out.

"Is that fucking Jamaican bastard who own that rims store!"

"You mean the same place I bought my rims," surprisingly asked Crista?

"That's the bastard me talking about! But them Star boys go fix him real soon!"

Crista went into silent mode from then, as her temper soured beneath her skin. Nigel opened up from then and continued with an outpour of emotions, about his unfaithful wife, his riches, and everything else he had done to provide for those closest to him. Even though Nigel continued bickering, Crista's attention abruptly ended, once he mentioned Rev impregnating Elena. By the time Nigel finished, Crista had developed a huge headache and refused to participate in any form of sexual acts. The instant she kicked him out, she got on her phone and dialed Rev, who was at work inside his office.

"How you doing my love," responded Rev?

"So, you been fucking Elena? Then you get her pregnant on top of it!"

"Who tell you that?"

"I can't believe you know how much I hate that bitch, and you fucking her behind my back!"

"But Crista, it's not like that!"

"I just phone to tell you one thing, out of respect as my baby father! But after we finish talking, don't ever call my number again, because whatever we have is done after this, eh! Nigel know about you and Elena, and him already send his Star Crew friend them to come kill you! That's all I called to say! Goodbye, you have a good life," Crista declared, as she disconnected the call!

At 2:33 that afternoon, back at the rims shop, Rev was inside his office looking over some papers. He looked at the security footages around the store and realized that his salesgirl was at the back of the building, taking a smoke break with Larry. As Rev looked at the camera footage in front the store, an old Toyota Corolla pulled up and four masked armed thugs jumped out. Two of the shooters ran into the rims store and cautiously made their way to the back, while the other two ran around to the rear of the building.

Rev grabbed his firearm and held his knife in the other hand, as he exited his office and crept along the wall. The fugitive knelt on one knee and patiently waited until the first masked thug peeked around the corner, at which he stabbed the man directly in the groin. The crippling pain made the assassin yelled out loud, then grabbed for his crotch, hence, Rev held his lowered hands securely, and aimed his 9mm at his associate. The Jamaican thrust three bullets into the assassin's accomplice, then hammered another two bullets into the injured thug.

After disposing of the first two assassins, Rev grabbed one of the man's handgun and ran into the men's bathroom, where he peeked through the opening created by his plumber. The two remaining assassins had his employees kneeling in the middle of the garage, with their weapons aimed at the back of the workers' heads. The gunners inside the garage had assumed their companions completed the mission, but they still wanted confirmation for security purpose. Both men kept yelling for either 'Juice Man or Regan' to respond, until they suspected there was possibly a problem. Rev's primary concern was the safety of his two employees, so he kept an eye on the assassins till they made their next move.

None of the remaining assassins knew of the opening in the wall, or that they were being watched by their intended target. The next two intruders were Stylo and Baron underneath the masks. Neither assassin knew what to do without any response coming from inside the store. They decided to make Baron enter the business and check what was holding up their colleagues, who should have already exited. Stylo nervously kept his gun primarily on Larry, while the salesgirl mumblingly begged for her life. Rev knew he would have to act quickly, so once Baron entered the main building, he waited for Stylo0's to slightly move his weapon away from both hostages.

"Bam-bam-bam," sounded the 9mm Glock-17 that he borrowed, as he shot and killed Stylo!

"Get out of the shop now," Rev ordered his employees, who both got up and ran out the back door!

Baron heard the gunshots and thought Rev walked around the building to the rear, so he came back through the door looking for their assigned target. As Baron ran into the garage, he caught a glimpse of Larry running from the building and fired two shots at him. The last remaining assassin started frantically looking around the garage, yet, overlooked the open slot in the wall, that was against the corner. Rev hid himself from Baron, who removed his mask and started shouting, "Come out you fucking coward!"

Baron started moving towards the rear door and had his back turned to Rev, who stepped from his hiding place and shouted, "See mi right here pussyhole!" The assassin tried to spin around and fire, but the Jamaican lodged three bullets into him and killed him instantly.

The approaching emergency sirens sounded like they were blocks away, so the Jamaican dropped the borrowed firearm inside the garage, ran back into his office and hid his personal firearm in the closet. With the Bahamas Star Crew sending assassins after him, there was no way he could afford to make the police confiscate his firearm, therefore he prepared his alibi and walked out of the store. The salesgirl and Larry were happy to see Rev exit the building; thus, they ran to him and embraced each other. Police and ambulance services arrived thereafter and began attending to the situation, while crowds gathered and watched the developments.

Nigel returned home and walked into the house. Elena was in the kitchen cooking supper, while she watched the evening news. The story involving Rev's rim store had not yet aired, but Nigel felt confident that his wife's adultery partner was dead at that point. Moments later, Nigel walked into the kitchen and took a Heineken Beer from the fridge.

"How was your doctor's appointment this morning?"

"Everything went well, the doctor said the baby seem health and should be coming on time."

"So, how long now you been fucking that Jamaican guy?"

"What, what kind of rubbish is that?"

"I came to the appointment and watched you and this fucking guy! So, don't try tell me some bullshit, eh! I said, how long now you fucking him?"

Elena did not offer a response and paid attention to the food on the stove that she was attending to. Her blatant disregard for the question pissed off Nigel, who smashed his bottle of beer on the floor.

"I said, how long you fucking him?"

With Elena's continued failure to respond, Nigel went over to her and spun her around and slapped her across the face. The pregnant female grabbed her face with one hand and rested her other hand over her stomach. Before Nigel could clobber her again, Elena shouted, "Obviously not as long as you been fucking Crista!"

Nigel's hand froze in midair, as he prepared to slap Elena again. The scam artist slowly backed away, until he backed onto the kitchen counter.

"Put your fucking hand on me again and see what's going to happen to you! Yes, I know about your regular fuck session with that bitch, you telling her to make sure she's never wearing any clothes whenever you come over; and I know about that second bastard child that bitch is carrying! So, before you think about hitting me the next time, think about the money I go get when I kick you out this fucking house!"

"Alright… alright eh. Since you know so much facts, let me give you one fact I don't think you know. Both you and Crista have been fucking the same guy, so it seems you both have the same dead baby father!"

Elena knew that if Nigel said someone was dead, chances were that was true. As she walked to the sink and opened the pipe to fetch water and wash her face, Nigel noticed the news coverage of the rims' shop killings on the television and, proudly began boasting about his hired killers. The expecting first time mother could barely conjure up the strength to look at the television screen, but once she heard the reporter mentioned multiple killings, she quickly turned and watched. As the reporter continued his briefing, they eventually learnt that those killed weren't the store's handlers, but rather four armed men who unknowingly ran into the establishment. Once Nigel heard what occurred, he furiously stormed from the kitchen dialing someone on his cellular, while Elena laughed out loud. The infuriated Bahamian left his house thereafter, without saying goodbye or announcing his destination.

Nigel went back to the Bahamas Star Crew's clubhouse, where the members were angry and demanded blood. Boogyman filled him in, on what had been happening with their hunt for Rev, who was proving to be a valiant opponent. They had sent gunners to the wanted man's apartment searching for him, but nobody had any idea where he had disappeared to. The apartment still had all of Rev's furniture, some of his clothes, his cutlery and dishes, but no signs of him. With several small crews out around the island in search of the Jamaican, one of them saw Floyd downtown buying some food, hence they pulled up on him along the roadside and forced him into a vehicle. Floyd was held at gunpoint and brought to their clubhouse, where they transferred him inside and tied him to a chair.

With the deaths of their colleagues, the crew members first tried to get Floyd to inform them of Rev's whereabouts. When Floyd argued that he only served as a tour guide for the Jamaican, Nigel disagreed and recounted different events where he had spotted them together. To encourage Floyd to surrender whatever information he knew, Boogyman and others claimed he should support his fellow countrymen, instead of some foreigner. Floyd had only known Rev for nearly a year, but he had never known a more trusted friend, therefore, he told his kidnappers 'to suck his dick and go find him themselves'! The mourning crew of misfits began beating Floyd with all sorts of cricket bats, metal pipes, kicks and punches, before they stabbed him multiple times and chopped him all over his body with machetes. They dumped Floyd's body in the dumpster behind Rev's tires and rims store, then poured gasoline over him and sat him ablaze.

The only other place where Rev felt comfortable was the inn where he first stayed, so he rented a room with plans to stay there, until he flew to Canada. Elena telephoned him early the next morning and advised him of what they did to Floyd. The rude boy broke down crying and barely thanked the female, before he disconnected the call. Rev could not consciously board an airplane without doing all he could for Floyd's children, even if his deeds would cost his life. After stopping at a liquor store, Rev drove to see the only person who could help him avenge Floyd's death, although he wasn't sure if he would be welcomed.

Countafit opened his door immediately after seeing the two bottles of Vodka Rev brought. He had also heard about Floyd's tragic killing and was rather angry about the way they massacred his friend's body. Both Countafit and Rev sat and had several shots from one of the bottles, as they toasted to the life of their murdered friend. Rev spent the entire day with Countafit and his dog Gerry, but it wasn't until late that afternoon, before his host brought him into his weapon's room. The idea that someone, would singlehandedly go to such extremes for a friend, enlightened Countafit, who armed Rev with a Russian AK-49, with two extended banana clips. There weren't any charges injected into their arrangement, due to the Swiss' desires for retribution against those who harmed his friend. Before handling the weapon or its accessories, Rev put on a pair of rubber gloves, to avoid leaving any fingerprints. Neither of the magazines were loaded, therefore, the revenge seeker spent the next few minutes stacking both.

During the 6:00 o'clock news coverage, Rev passed out and dreamt about Floyd's tragic demise, then awoke later that night from a nightmare. The Jamaican predator had no idea when he fell asleep, but when he reopened his eyes, Countafit was passed out on the sofa across from him, with Gerry asleep at his feet. There was a digital clock on a table that read 2:40 AM, hence Rev slowly got up and looked around the room. Countafit had packed the weapon and extra accessories into a duffle bag, therefore he collected the bag and exited the residence.

Rev drove to the Bahamas Star Crew clubhouse and parked halfway down the street. Dressed all in black, the rude boy held the AK handle alongside the edge of the opened zipper, while he carried his S&W M&P9 in the other hand. The beginning of the dead-end road was extremely quiet, but as he walked closer to the clubhouse, the noise became increasingly louder. As the fugitive mysteriously moved amongst the shadows, a dog startled him, when the animal ran up against the gate inside its yard; and barked at him. After Rev pointed his 9mm at the dog, collected himself and walked pass the yard, he stopped under the shadows of a huge tree, and waited to see if the dog's bark alerted any of the crew members. There were several Star Crew members out on the road engaged with each other, but only two of them turned to look in the direction of the barking. When neither of the two beer drinkers saw anything, they went back to their conversation.

Once Rev realized that the men didn't see him, he reconvened his slow approach along the side of the road, which didn't have overhead lighting. Three more crew members joined the six, who were already standing in the street joking amongst themselves. Rev could hear music playing, dominos being slammed against a table, and ladies yelling the closer he got to the house. The thugs conversing in the street were a bit intoxicated, therefore they spoke quite loudly. Before launching his attack, Rev ducked behind a parked car along the roadside and fully removed the rifle from the bag. He could overhear some of the crew members boasting about what they did to Floyd and, how he begged for his life before they sat him on fire. With each spoken word, Rev grew increasingly angrier and gripped tighter onto the AK's handle, until he exploded and emerged from behind the vehicle.

The revenge seeker brought the rifle up against his shoulder and began annihilating each person who came into his sight of fire. Froggy was amongst the thugs on the street who tried to pull his weapon, but Rev showed him no more mercy than he did the others. One of the three last thugs to join the street gathering, turned and began racing back towards the house, when their attacker shot him in the back. Those inside the house and on the front lawn couldn't believe what they were witnessing, as they watched their colleagues got massacred.

Even though Rev was incredibly brave, he knew he wasn't superman, so he changed the rifle's magazine and looked to make his escape. Five armed thugs cautiously ran towards the road, however, the retreating shooter hindered them from going onto the street.

"Ka-ka-ka-ka-ka-ka," sounded Rev's AK-49, as he backpedaled towards his car.

The thugs began returning fire and carefully gave chase, but Rev ran to his car and sped away. All the remaining thugs were incredibly angry, as they began grieving their losses. Rev drove to his suite at the inn, where he took a long hot shower, then climbed into bed with his handgun. There was no need for any more bloodshed, and Rev felt justice had been served, although he knew the Star Crew members would not consider things as he did.

By the time he awoke the next morning, the murders were all they spoke about on the news. Rev got dressed and went for breakfast before he left the premises, and drove to Nigel's house, where he parked down the street and watched. Almost forty minutes later the scammer exited his house, climbed into his vehicle and drove away. Once Nigel left, Rev walked up to his front door and rang the bell. When Elena opened the door and saw him standing there, she quickly pulled him inside to avoid anyone seeing him.

"Oh my God you're mad! What are you doing here? Nigel already knows about us and he is going crazy!"

"Run away with mi?"

"What?"

"Run away to Canada with mi?"

"You are mad! Are you forgetting that I am married? It wouldn't be so easy as it seems!"

"I know, but yu don't love Nigel!"

"What makes you so sure? Listen, I have a great life here; and Nigel is going to take care of both your newborn babies! Yes, I also know about Crista, but I don't care. You go off to Canada and be well and have a great life, but I can't go with you!"

They had a passionate kiss before Elena ushered him out through the door. Rev snuck around to her bedroom window and placed two 9mm bullets on the window ledge. The things Elena told him were not what he wished to hear, but he knew she was wise with her decision.

With Floyd's family weighing heavily on his mind, Rev drove to his children's mother's house. As he approached the residence, the only noises he heard from within were those of mournful grievers, yet he still stepped forth and knocked the door. Rev remembered Floyd's woman from the Crab Festival and her likewise. The Jamaican didn't pass by the house to spend much time; therefore, he got directly to the point at the door entrance and gave the female the lease, keys and ownership to his tires and rims store. Having no further use for his BMW, Rev signed over the title and gave her the spare key, with instructions on where and when to pick up the car. For help with the funeral and kids, he gave her an envelope with twenty-five-thousand dollars in cash, which was most of the money he had left. Floyd's children's mother was speechless and didn't know how to thank Rev, but he advised her that "he could never repay his deceased friend for what he had done for him!"

Before going to his next unscheduled stop, Rev snuck by his workplace one final time and used his spare key to enter the building. He locked the door after he entered the store, then pulled his weapon and kept it in hand. For precautionary reasons, the rude boy cautiously moved through interior, as he made his way to his office. The Jamaican activated his security system and used a pen to write down the password and other viable important information for Floyd's lady. There was some important video footage captured from the night the Star Crew members dumped his friend's body, therefore, Rev recorded them and sent them to three recipients. To ensure that no single individual deleted the information, he sent a copy to the ZNS Network Station, another to the police community help services and the third to Crime Stoppers. The videos Rev emailed featured the dozen Star Crew members who transported Floyd's dismantled body to his dumpster, then caught it on fire.

The Jamaican departed thereafter, got into his car and drove back to Countafit's house, where he returned the AK-49 rifle. Even though Countafit loaned Rev the rifle, he knew the vicious killers the lone Jamaican was up against, thus, he never expected him to return successfully. Countafit was beyond proud of what he had done and offered his assistance with whatever Rev wanted in the future. Knowing there would be more retributions for the Star Crew, the Jamaican advised the Swiss to 'watch the evening news', without offering added information. With Rev's flight to Montreal scheduled for the following day, both men shook hands respectful of each other, before the rude boy made his leave.

When Rev reached the inn and settled into his bed, he telephoned Nigel to have a small chat. The instant Nigel learnt he was the caller; the Bahamian became boisterous and began inciting all sorts of threats. Rev's intention was to ensure that he never got out of line with either Elena or Crista, should he assume he was in a more dominant position.

"All you ain't done nothing! You think my fellows and them scared a you? The only thing you did was turn up the pressure them boys go put on you," Nigel warned!

"Everything mi do last night was for mi friend, who them batty-boy killed off! But don't get it twisted, I have no fear of dying, so if mi have to take nine more a them pussyhole with me, so be it!"

"Well, once I pay my money somebody must die, so since you can't kill off an army, is only a matter of time before them murder you motherfucker!"

"Yow, listen me, listen me! I didn't call for all a that! I definitely overstepped mi boundaries when mi sleep with yu woman them, plus get them pregnant, and for that I do apologize! But yu see if it wasn't for Elena last night, mi murder yu bloodclatt while yu a sleep!"

"Your little feeble threats don't scare me man!"

"Yu think a feeble threat? Go inside yu bedroom and look through the bloodclatt window on the ledge, and tell mi what yu see?"

"What the fuck is this dude talking about," thought Nigel to himself, as he cautiously went to his bedroom and snuck close to the window. When the Bahamian saw the bullets sitting on the ledge, he fell dumbstruck.

"Yu see how close mi come to killing yu rass last night pussyhole? Make mi tell yu something, any day yu disrespect Elena or Crista from today, yu not living to see the next day! So, make sure yu take good care of mi youths them, plus them mothers yu get mi!"

"I-I-I-I-I swear, I will cancel the contract and, do everything you say!"

"It look like yu need to go watch the news my youth," Rev stated, before disconnecting the call.

The television inside Rev's suite was on ZNS Evening News and their main story was about Floyd's killing. There were officers making several arrests at the Star Crew's clubhouse, which was already under investigation following the murders of multiple members. The ZNS news station aired much of the video that showed Floyd's body being set on fire, which they warned viewers prior, 'contained graphic scenes!' When questioned about whether Floyd's murder had anything to do with the killings of the Star Crew members at their clubhouse, detectives claimed "they were investigating the matter and had several persons of interest with which to speak."

A knock sounded at the door and Rev turned off the television before attending to it. The Jamaican looked through the peephole and saw a lovely mixed female, whom he had met in the lobby the day prior. The female was a tourist named Myshana from Melbourne, Victoria Australia, who was visiting the island with a girlfriend, therefore the rude boy happily allowed her in. As Myshana walked by Rev, she paused, licked him across his lips with her tongue, then grabbed and squeezed his crotch.

"Lord, have mercy," said Rev, as he closed the door!

The next morning, Rev left the inn and drove himself to the airport. He realized he would have no further use for his cellular in Canada, so he sent two identical text messages to Crista and Elena. In the messages, Rev stated that 'he would always cherish the times they spent together, he loved them dearly and, knew they would take excellent care of his children'. After sending the messages, the rude boy removed the sim card from the phone, turned it off and, left the phone inside the glove compartment. With all his travel documents and plane ticket prepared, Rev passed through each check points and caught his flight on time. When the plane finally departed, the fugitive said a silent prayer, knowing he fortunately survived to move on to another chapter in his life.

Part 12

The heroic actions of Nicholas' Rude Boys bunch spread through the streets of Montreal like tales printed in the newspapers. The most notorious gang in Canada had, long ruled the world of underground crime on the island of Montreal, with their well-known, fierce, vigilance and unyielding tactics in battle. Hence, intrigue and suspense surrounded the man credited for temporarily simmering a gang of misfits, who weren't accustomed to failure. The long-time tailor to Nicholas Henry overheard the account, that transpired while altering an evening jacket for one of his customers. With the feeling of desertion still haunting his every dream, Carlton sought to lessen the burden with which he'd caused himself, by merging two entities of similar mindset and futuristic vision.

The tailor was not a close acquaintance of Brogan Alfonso, who was the voice behind the Defenders of the West Island gang. Carlton knew much of his cabinet and professed confidence in the fact that, he'd stitched his way into their inner midst. Carlton perceived the merger between Nicholas and the Defenders to be a marriage for the ages, yet, postponed his initial phone call to set the wheels in motion. The tailor initially feared something tragic developing in their affairs, where he'd end up bleeding from one group's knife, as they tortured him for information about the other. The topic went unmentioned for another week and a half until, one day, Lester, who was one of the Defenders' most vicious gunmen, walked into the tailor shop. Lester was accompanied by

Scotty, who was a vain individual, who always found a mirror wherever he went to check and make sure his face was decent.

The gangster left his chauffeur in front of the store, entered the tailor's, and went straight to the back, beside a huge standing mirror, that was hoisted against the changing room door. Carlton knew his client lacked patience and demanded his attention the instant he walked in, so he halted sewing and attended to the gunman. Lester never wore off-the-rack clothing from department stores, because he hated the idea of seeing someone else in a piece of clothing identical to what he was wearing. In addition, to avoiding such embarrassment, Lester also demanded loose-fitting clothing to help conceal his weapons.

The main intimidator factor for the Defenders crew, hailed the tailor and his assistant, before he began removing his firearms. Lester took off his jacket and threw it against the back support of a chair. He then proceeded to unbuckle the straps to his double Uzi attachment kit, attached to his back, laid it on the seat of the chair, withdrew two Glock 9mm tucked behind his rear belt, and shoved one in his right side pocket, before laying the other against the Uzis on the chair. Lester began walking toward the measuring platform, before realizing he'd forgotten something in the pockets of the Uzi back mount straps. The gangster collected two magazine clips for his weapon and shoved them in the opposite pocket, before indicating he was ready to proceed with the measurements. The most feared arbitrator in the Defenders crew was never a man of too many words, yet Lester spoke admirably about Nicholas, whom he'd heard of and knew was a friend of Carlton's.

"Do you know that, I only recently found out about that hijacking that happened in here over a year ago," Lester began!

Not knowing what to expect from the conversation, Carlton nodded in response and simply pointed at the area in which the beating occurred.

"Tough thing to happen to a man, especially with others around… But I respect you boys for not getting involved and for leaving people's business alone. Hah, I don't think you'd still be here had you interfered," said Lester.

Carlton sensed a bit of empathy from Lester toward Nicholas, however, he maintained discretion, not knowing if the admiration was an enticing piece of bait, being dangled from a string. The tailor found himself at an impasse, after debating the urge to facilitate an introduction between both teams, only a few days prior.

"Believe me, when I tell you my brethren, Nick is the real McCoy when it comes to getting your type of products! The man mild with a decent temper, and he's a cool youth, who deal with the real business, not the fuckery, if you know what I mean," Carlton described!

"So, you and him really tight like that," Lester asked?

"A few times them white boys run up in here, trash the place, and claim they heard he was in here! A few of them slap me around a couple times and claim I know where he's hiding, but even if I did, they'd never get it out of me," Carlton declared! "Good youth, who believe inna him gun and him God!"

"Apart from our regular business, maybe you would like to make some extra money hooking up some other business for us? I believe my boss could really profit from dealing with this English-man," Lester offered!

"Anything you want, boss, me a listen!"

The Unifying

The idea of Canada's native people killing their white counterparts, was never an issue that sat well with the lawmakers of North America. Thus, those who were knowledgeable of their history, knew for certain there would be serious repercussions following any situation of, a white man dying at the hands of an Indian. Following the slaughtering of forty-two of Martain's Rough Riders, the three remaining combatants gathered up the corpses and loaded them into Eagle's old Chevy truck. It took four trips of twelve corpses to scurry away the lifeless bodies that, Eagle and company left scattered across the woods surrounding their house. The three survivors transported the bodies deep into the woods, dug a massive hole, and dumped the bodies of the fallen Rough Riders within. A ten-gallon jug of gasoline was poured across the bodies, before they were set ablaze like a huge barn fire. The three friends watched the bodies burned, as they individually thought about Eagle's brave sacrifice during the previous night, in addition to their tasks ahead, should they wish to survive.

Without Eagle, the word moral took on less meaning in the life of his youngest son, Kane Esquada, who increased his drug trafficking around the Indian reservation. Kane developed a flock of young soldiers eager to earn their piece of the Canadian pie, which was never freely offered to Indians or immigrants from other countries. The modest drug market around the reservation soon blossomed, as the traffickers' addictive products created more and more customers. Despite soaring profit margins on the reservation, Nicholas' interests in the wealth on the island of Montreal grew, knowing that Eagle would never approve of them degrading his people. It wasn't long before they started paying officials from both the Royal Canadian Mounted Police, and the Native Police Bureau, bribes to ignore their drug operation.

The Indian reservations have always provided stiff competition against the Canadian government, regarding the sales of cheaper generic cigarettes and tobacco, which was impossible for the government to tax. These cigarettes and tobacco were often smuggled across the U.S/Canadian borders and sold in souvenir gift shops, located along the roadsides of provincial streets. Smokers from across the river in Montreal often voyage across the Pont Mercier Bridge, for the cheaper native tobacco and cigarettes, sold in several smoke huts throughout the reservation. Aside from the cheaper non-taxed cigarettes sold, conservative motorists who sought cheaper priced gasoline, would travel to the reservation and saved themselves two or three cents on each liter.

Nicholas' empire had grown from the gutters of the Mohawk tribe, who were members of the Twelve Nations of the Native Council of Canada, thus, it was agreed that the introductions between the Defender's boss and he, take place on Indian soil. The location was kept secret between the two bosses, who knew the high compensation for treacherous espionage, especially one with such high-profile personnel. Both bosses navigated their individual drivers from home to the meeting point, which was underneath the Pont Mercier Bridge, that connected Montreal to Chateauguay.

Nicholas' entourage was modest yet complex. With him were Danny his right-hand shooter, Damian his cousin, and Tank, a new driver who was settling in after his first month of chauffeur duties. In case of any unexpected surprises, Nicholas also had fifteen Indian braves invisibly scattered among patches of tall grass, that ran along some areas off the shores of the river. The venue was perfect for a sit-down conversation, while it offered the patrons a clear view of oncoming traffic, with areas to maneuver should the situation get dangerous.

Nicholas rolled with a light infantry, because he knew he had a few trump cards at his disposal, should he find himself in dire need of rescue. One of Nicholas' precautions involved the blocking of the bridge, where, should an ambush plot be successful, the ambushers would find themselves stuck in traffic at a perilous point on the bridge, before either being struck by missiles from a bazooka, or they would find themselves overwhelmed with bullets. There was the law enforcement factor, where Nicholas would call in the cavalry and have the local law enforcement administered their brand of aggressive punishment. The last option was the smash-mouth method, where Indian braves were summoned and, would charge into battle with their arrows-sailing, rifle-blazing, axe-throwing and, scalp removal tactics, designed to hinder and maim one's opponent.

The Defender's entourage was larger than Nicholas', and they arrived in a Denali and a Tahoe SUV, with two female riders saddled on a pair of Suzuki high-powered motorbikes, which brought their total count to ten. Brogan's feet had hardly touched the soil, before he signaled the female riders to patrol the perimeter while the gentlemen conducted business. Nicholas and Brogan approached each other without any personal guards and embraced, with affections toward each other as if they had known each other for decades. Both businessmen walked freely along the shores of the Champlain River, discussing business proposals, ways to assist each other, and strategies to defend against their nemesis, the Rough Riders.

"My respects finally meeting you Brogan! I sometimes think I roll like the president, but damn, you put us all to shame," Nicholas acknowledged!

"If you've had as many attempts on your life as I have, you'd never chance it with a small motorcade like yours, knowing the vultures are always seeking to attack," Brogan laughed, as the two men respectfully walked alongside each other!

"I heard your family originally emigrated from Italy," Nicholas asked?

"Yeah, over forty-five years now; even changed our nationalities and got sworn in as Canadians! Someone told me you were British, but you sound more like some Jamaican home boys related to my family."

"I'm one hundred percent Jamaican, but for immigration purposes, it is what it is!"

A stiff breeze lifted the Rastafarian's, red, gold and green tam from his head, although he quickly caught it before it got soiled from fluttering to the ground. The ten-inch locks atop Nicholas' head appeared to come alive, with the luscious breeze that blew tranquilly from the river, therefore he shook them freely before remounting his hat.

"These bastards wish to tell us how to live, how to make money, how to do everything! They think because we weren't born here we don't have rights like them. Fuck them! I will live to see the last of them or die trying to make it happen! You fellas brought back the dream, that everybody lives for, but can't get to because of these fucking riders! For us, due to the fact they control the docks and shit, we can't seem to get a shipment in for the past few months, because they keep intercepting our cargo and seizing my fucking drugs," Brogan declared!

"So, with thousands of cargo ships coming in every day, how do they specifically find your shipment," Nicholas asked?

"Changed up everything from the sender, place it's coming from, and no matter what we try they keep finding the shit! I hear you can provide whatever weight your customer's desire. If so, I think we can do a lot of business," Brogan said.

While the bosses discussed business and properly acquainted themselves with each other, Damian and Danny kept a close visual on Nicholas, while ensuring their new allies behaved honorably. The two centurions stood well-armed with fully loaded extension magazines sticking out their AK-47 assault rifles, while their counterparts stood across from them, fully armed and undaunted. The unnecessary tension between the two outfits was soon eradicated by Tank, who emerged from behind his getaway driver position with five marijuana joints, gave two to his partners and handed the rest to their counterparts. The men lit up their joints, smoked and passed them around amongst each other, as the barrier walls slowly disintegrated. Within minutes, the guards' entire postures changed, and they became more relaxed and opened toward each other, while debating which NFL teams were going to be victorious that Sunday. A few serious gamblers inherited their picks from the discussion, which was both heated and passionate by true lovers of the sport.

The argument soon shifted from sports to aspects of business, beginning with the sole dark-colored male amongst the Defenders, establishing a marijuana connection with Tank, whom he claimed "ripped off his dome," with the high-grade hydroponic joints he offered them. Tank was more than willing to engage in dealings, especially after discovering the quantity being sought after. The Indians had the freedom and capability to produce their own cannabis, so most of them grew their own crops. But instead of flourishing the drug trade to the north, they chose to smuggle their high grade across the border into upstate New York, for a larger cash pot. With the U.S. dollar valued more than the Canadian and a higher price demand for exotic hydroponic marijuana in the States versus Quebec, most Indians preferred crossing the well-policed waters of the Outaouais River, rather than transporting elsewhere in the country.

Even Eagle Esquada used to smuggle his marijuana into the U.S, until he caught the federal charge that led to him meeting Ernesto Lopez. Unlike the Indians, who smuggled everything from alcohol to tobacco, Tank, like most of his counterparts, was banned from legally entering America, due to their criminal record in Canada. Therefore, given the fact that the product was widely available on the reservation and, they had friends who grew tons of the product, an arrangement was quickly reached on the price of each shipment, as well as the delivery proceedings.

The two motorbike surveyors, who were instructed to patrol their perimeter, came terribly close to the camouflaged Indians, whom Nicholas posted in the brushes, yet rode by the warriors several times without the slightest inclination that they were present. The female riders atop the Kawasaki iron horses handled the powerful motorcycles quite handily. as they rode about in their tight leather outfits, with their automatic weapons across their laps. After riding by her counterpart while they circled the negotiating businessmen, one of the female riders noticed a gang of men who'd ridden onto the grounds and, positioned themselves by the main entrance. The female surveyor came within thirty feet of the Harley Davidson riders, who'd muffled their tailpipes with silencers, quieting their hogs enough for them to sneak in close to their targets. The female rider dug her heel into the ground as she swung the tail end of the motorbike around, kicking up dark sand as the bike's front end rose high into the air, and screeched off the rear wheel. As the motorbike began accelerating, a couple of clappers sounded in the rear, that tossed the female rider from her saddle, and she took an awful fall to the turf.

"Oh, shit! They got Shanann," the female atop the second Kawasaki, immediately sped toward the nucleus of her team!

The report echoed through a Bluetooth device that Brogan had implanted in his left ear, and he immediately demanded 'whether she was killed or injured'. The female in search of added security couldn't quite elaborate on her partner's status, thus everyone began scattering to find the safest vantage point from where to counter. While the newly adjoined business partners scattered to find structures that would provide adequate defense against oncoming bullets, their unexpected antagonists unblocked their dreadful-sounding mufflers, and revved their motors. The bikers wanted to jolt their opponents' nerves, then used the deafening engine sounds to drown out the gunfire eruptions. Brogan was still interested in knowing the fate of his surveyor, as he received further reports on the estimated amounts of combatants.

There were an estimated forty bikers, hence both bosses withdrew their firearms and retreated to the bridge's huge support pillars, which were the closest protective structures available to them. Nicholas listened to Brogan's concerns over his fallen guard, as he pondered over who exactly among their entourage was the informant who not only led their enemies there, but also had been sabotaging the gang's shipments. While racing to the support pillars beneath the bridge, Brogan, who ran with both his German Luger pistols at hand, moved his hand to his earlobe to adjust his earpiece, when he looked up at the bridge above and realized there was an audience of two watching the developments. Brogan immediately knew that one of the leather jacket-wearing spectators, had to be Martain Lafleur, whom he'd disrespected and called a coward on two separate occasions. The Defender leader was especially shocked by Nicholas, who reached behind his back and removed an Uzi automatic rifle, that was attached by carrying straps, then quickly armed it for combat.

Martain Lafleur rode onto the eastbound section of the Pont Mercier Bridge, and had his bodyguard place orange warning cones around their motorbikes, as if they were having vehicle trouble, which disrupted traffic heading into the city. The biker boss sat atop his Harley Davidson, with a Labatt Blue beer in hand, while his companion joined in after readying the video camcorder for image capturing. The two men soon resembled spectators at the movies, with terrific seats and adequate beverage, well, minus the popcorn.

The bikers revved up their motor engines and stirred up more noise than scare, as the Defenders and Nicholas' entourage prepared for target practice, with the expectation of the targets responding. Martain and his companion expected a slaughterhouse, with the expectance of a few causalities of their own. Knowing their primary viewer was prepared for the action, the bikers charged at both the bosses as well as their trusted companions, with their overwhelm numbers and firepower. The female rider, who was the first to crash her bike, hadn't moved since she hit the ground, thus the attacking bikers rode directly by her, as if they thought she was dead.

The Rough Riders had marked that attack as "the day they rid the earth of their foes," during preliminary toasts where they got insanely intoxicated and heightened each other's morale, before the actual battle. Martain thought his assassins were about to spur an unexpected trap, when Nicholas had multiple contingency plans arranged. The attacking bikers observed that the commanders they sought were separated from their troops, therefore they divided into two parties as they charged at their opponents.

Once the Rough Riders charged blindly into battle, Nicholas' hidden warriors waited until they'd ridden by, before they emerged from their camouflaged positions, pelting wooden spears like javelins and sprucing arrows from their bows. The Indians were excellent archers and javelin throwers; therefore, they removed many bikers from their Hogs with detrimental wounds. The undetected Indians surprised Martain, who fell backwards off his motorbike and was nearly struck by a passing motorist, after he landed extremely close to the lane indication line.

The first wave of arrows and spears dismounted fifteen bikers from their Harleys, before a second wave knocked off another thirteen, and the third wave canceled another eight. The bikers who led the charge had absolutely no idea about the fate of their comrades to the rear, who were falling like raindrops. Rough Riders assassins rode through the convoy created by the Defenders and Nicholas' gun hands, exchanging bullets with their nemesis, as they executed their plan of attack.

The bikers planned on circling their targets, and eliminate them with each pass, however, after the first go around, there weren't many assassins left. Once the dwindled number of bikers who survived the ride-by shoot-out, got to the starting point where they were supposed to turn back and attack again, they realized their numbers had substantially decreased. The initial ten bikers who sat out to eliminate Nicholas and Brogan, had shrunk to two following their preliminary drive-by, so the remaining survivors looked to each other confused about what to do.

One of the riders from the pack of two didn't hesitate for long; and turned his motorbike toward the river and rode directly for it. The other five assassins, then realized that their only exit went through a firing squad and an archery/javelin squad, thus they immediately followed their comrade and sped for the river. Their comrade's plan to swim across the Saint Lawrence River may appeared insane, but after second consideration, it was their only chance of survival. With bullets clapping at their heels by the Defenders, who would rather not have to combat the same bikers in the future, the fleeing Rough Riders struck the river and swam like Olympians, as they attempted to evade their assigned targets. Three other assassins were executed by the Defenders who sought to avenge their fallen ally; hence, they raced to the shoreline and fired a barrage of bullets at the speed swimmers.

Shanann, who was believed to be dead after being knocked unconscious by the hard fall, soon rolled over onto her back and slowly sat up, before she removed her helmet. Her riding partner and others ran to her assistance with excitement, knowing it was a miracle that she survived. The enraged biker boss, who had recorded the entire ordeal, mounted his Harley and quickly returned to the sanctity of the city. It wasn't until Martain had left the scene that Brogan informed Nicholas about him being an overseer during the battle. Nicholas who had implemented means to capture or kill anyone within the surrounding area, was disappointed such information wasn't transferred prior as, he would have awarded Martain a taste of his own medicine.

Part 13

Kadeem waited patiently in line as the immigration officer chastised a young female, who was attempting to enter Canada. The thought that he may have selected the wrong check line went through his mind, as he watched the woman be escorted off to a secret chamber for further harassment. It became evident that the woman was suspected of smuggling contraband into the country, after a questionable package was discovered inside her carry-on luggage. The young female initially behaved as if there were no cause for alarm, before realizing her situation had become dire. Suddenly, prior to entering the interrogation chamber, the woman took off racing for the exit with a slew of agents giving chase. A few minutes later, Kadeem nervously presented himself before the agitated officer, while the female smuggler got returned to the chamber, kicking and screaming while pleading for sympathy.

"Are you a native of Nassau, Mr. Campbell," the immigration officer asked, as she thumbed through the pages of Kadeem's passport?

"Yes, ma'am," Kadeem answered, with his best mimicking of the Nassau dialect.

"Is this your first trip to Canada, sir?"

"Yes, ma'am!"

"What's the reason for your visiting Canada, sir?"

"I've recently rediscovered my long-lost dad, and he live here, so I'm here to visit him, eh."

"Have you anything to declare, such as alcohol or gifts received from other family members?"

"I bought my dad two bottles of rum at the duty-free shop inside the airport, but no gifts from the rest of the family, eh."

"The rum is fine," began the officer, before rudely being interrupted by the screams of the smuggler.

"I'm sorry, but I had to do it for the kids! Them hungry! Please, please, Lord Jesus, help me! Let me go, let me go! Help me, Lord, help me," the female smuggler argued as the INS officers dragged her into the room!

"I tell you, the nerve of some people, eh," Kadeem commented!

"Always think they can sneak one by me and my crew, but don't worry, nothing passes through me! You have a wonderful time in Canada, Mr. Campbell, and I hope to see you again," the INS officer said, before stamping the seal of approval on the fourth page of Kadeem's passport!

Kadeem scurried through the automatic sliding doors that lead to the baggage claims area, with his heart racing from the fear of being discovered. There was a meagre walk to an escalator, which brought everyone to freedom one level down, and Kadeem breathed a huge sigh of relief following his immigration experience. A man resembling the person in a photo he'd carried around for years, began waving to him outside the glass casing, which surrounded the escalator. Kadeem had given the INS worker his correct reason for entering the country, though the documents and evidence of whom he truly was remained confidential.

The two men gingerly hugged each other then, walked toward the luggage area, where according to the information screen, luggage from the Bahamas flight was set to be discharge from conveyer belt number three. The father and son, who hadn't seen each other for nearly eighteen years, were reunited through the kind efforts of Granny P, who continued paving the way for a youngster she help raised. Kadeem spent almost two years in Nassau, where he worked honestly and sought means for a more progressive life. During his time in Nassau, Kadeem remained inconspicuous as possible, thus, he partied little, worked more, and spent some of his time with girlfriends, who visited seldom. However, his long-distant relationship with his Jamaican girlfriend ended, after a man from her district impregnated her and moved her into his house.

Along the journey to Jeremiah's house in Notre-Dame-de-Grace, Kadeem's father plastered him with rules of conduct expected of him, while partaking of his generosity and home. Jeremiah professed to being, a man of God, who attended church regularly and expected such of anyone within his immediate circle. The use of indecent language or any profane speech would not be tolerated, and everyone was expected to work, plus contribute to the continued developments of the household. Schooling was cited as a waste of time by Jeremiah, who believed any goals short of a physical labor trade, were unreachable at Kadeem's age. Jeremiah was himself an auto mechanic specialist, who owned and operated a small garage in the Ville Saint Pierre area.

Jeremiah told Kadeem about his wife of nine years, who was a caretaker for the elderly at a privately-owned facility in Montreal. He also advised his son, that he and his wife were incapable of producing a child; but she had a son from a previous relationship, who attended McGill College. "The audacity of this man" thought Kadeem to himself, before dismissing Jeremiah's prejudiced comment. The scenery through Jeremiah's Toyota Camry window, kept Kadeem's mind isolated on one goal, which was to succeed at whatever task lay ahead.

Jeremiah brought home his long-lost son who would have remained as such, had it not been for the thoughtfulness of Granny P. The old woman who was an inspiration in the lives of Kadeem and his father, had helped with the upbringing of countless other youths around the neighborhood. After dropping his son off at home, Jeremiah who had vehicles to repair left for work.

The auto mechanic advised Kadeem, "The world don't stop rotating because you come a foreign," before scurrying off to his daily hustle!

Kadeem placed his luggage inside a small room in the basement, before taking a tour of Jeremiah's first-floor duplex apartment. There were three bedrooms on the main floor, an attached living room, a bathroom, and the kitchen that, led out to a small backyard. The basement had a single room with one bathroom, and most of the space appeared to be used primarily for mechanical purposes and storage.

The fascination of the outdoors soon cluttered Kadeem's mind against anything else inside the house, as he stood by the window and watched the local traffic pass by. After a few hours of watching television, making a few telephone calls to his cousin, Auntie P, and a few others, Kadeem decided to stretch his legs for a moment and tour the surrounding neighborhood. The dilemma over the front door came into consideration once Kadeem was prepared to exit. However, his belief that a break-in would be improbable by him spending a half hour outdoors, prompted him to follow his instincts.

Kadeem took precise notes on the directions travelled and the names of streets he passed along the way. The cleanliness of the streets, the precision with which the houses were aligned, and the remarkable structures fascinated the Jamaican fugitive, but most importantly, he took time to holler at each luscious female he passed. A student of Concordia University gave him a bit more than conversation, as she found him mysterious enough to surrender her phone number. Kadeem spent a short time with the female as she waited for her bus, before finally deciding to return home before anyone got there before he did.

The front door was closed when Kadeem arrived home, which seemed odd considering he had left it unlatched. From inside the house, came the agitated voice of a female yelling at someone over the phone, as Kadeem reached out for the doorbell. A few seconds of waiting eventually produced a four-foot-eight woman, whose thickness attributed to the fact that; she wasn't shy when it came to demolish a plate of food. The woman looked Kadeem from his Bally shoes up to his face with a despicable stare, before finally stepping to the side to offer him entry.

"Okay, honey, I talk to you later!" The woman said, then disconnected her phone call. "So, you is Jeremiah boy? You look like him! I have a twenty-one-year-old son named Junior who is about your height. Come, come give me a hug! Me is you stepmother, Doherty! You father and I married for years now, and I just finally getting to meet you. You hungry? You must hungry by now! Come! Me fix you a plate of rice and peas and oxtail in the kitchen, you can tell me bout Nassau and the rest of the islands!"

Doherty appeared caring and thoughtful despite Kadeem's expectations, after overhearing her earlier phone conversation. The meal she prepared Kadeem, was arguably the best plate of Jamaican food he'd eaten, since fleeing his homeland some two years prior. Kadeem licked the plate and utensils clean, as he answered his stepmother's questions about the beauty surrounding the places he'd been. A half hour into their conversation, Doherty's son arrived home from school and headed into the kitchen, which was his normal routine. Junior walked by Kadeem and directed his attention to the refrigerator, before his mother sighted the fact that 'there was another person in the room'. The response Junior gave his mother, who suggested that "he introduced himself to his stepbrother", had Kadeem wishing the young man continued on his way, without any formal or semi-formal greeting. Junior's response, which was, "Mother, you always forcing me to do everything," had Kadeem confused about his reason for not wanting an introduction.

"But wait, is a Chi-Chi-man them want to give me for a brother," Kadeem thought to himself, as his homosexual sibling extended his hand for a handshake?

"How you doing," Junior responded, as they gingerly shook hands?

Kadeem and Doherty spoke for a few more minutes, before Jeremiah's Volvo engine sounded in the driveway. Once the vehicle's engine shut off, Doherty hurried from the kitchen and went to her room, without so much as a "You're welcome for the food," to Kadeem. The newcomer to Canada finished eating and was in the process of washing the utensils, when his enraged father entered the house.

"Mi wondering if you a set up thief to come rob mi? You leave my door wide open and gone, God knows where, from God knows how long, for thieves to come clean out my little bit! I go check round to make sure nothing was stolen, and if mi find anything missing you go have to pay for its replacement," Jeremiah declared, before storming from the kitchen!

The rapid change in attitude by Jeremiah bewildered Kadeem, who experienced for the first time his father's furious temperament. Even though the culprit who committed the infraction deterred from arguing the facts, the attitude brought forth by his father angered Kadeem, who stepped out on the back porch for some fresh air to distil his rage. The night's breeze was calm, which suited Kadeem, who mumbled to himself while searching for the ideal spot to linger.

"Mi refuse to have anybody deal with mi like some crotches," Kadeem repeated to himself, as he walked by a familiar odor, which caught his attention. "A the boy junior room that sweet scent a Ganja a come from," wondered Kadeem to himself, as he pulled even closer to the window and sniffed the air? "The boy Junior burn marijuana, sweet! Him better have at a joint for mi!

With his temperament blazing like a furnace from his father's accusations, Kadeem knew the perfect remedy to his ailments would be a little paraphernalia, which he had thought about acquiring during his walk, but had absolutely no idea where to search for it. Kadeem tapped lightly on the glass, yet Junior reacted as if a shotgun had been sounded to begin a race.

"Yeah, what's up, man," Junior asked, but didn't appear intimidated by the fact, he was caught smoking weed.

"Give me a spliff son," Kadeem demanded?

"You smoke weed?"

"I'm from the Caribbean! Not to say that everybody from the Caribbean smokes, but I'm in the percentage that does!"

Kadeem pretended he didn't notice the magazine clippings of several male R&B and rap stars, such as a topless Fifty Cent, Usher, Genuine, and others, posted against his stepbrother's wall. The enraged guest simply collected the .6 grams of marijuana with a piece of cigarette, two sheets of Zig Zag, and a half-book of matches, before retreating to a spot behind a broken-down wooden shack in the backyard. Following years of practice, the rude boy had perfected the art of joint rolling, therefore Kadeem constructed an immaculate cone, which he set ablaze, smoked, then meditated over his present predicament. The promise he'd made to Auntie P eventually subdued his rage, as he looked to the skies at faces, he longed to see and shouted, "Jah Rastafari!"

Even though Kadeem was not yet legally eligible of working in the country due to his visitation status, Jeremiah thought it ridiculous that an able-bodied man spent his days lounging about and insisted he assist him at the mechanic shop. Hence, Kadeem began working on this new land before the twenty-fourth hour struck on his arrival clock.

Jeremiah's Auto Repair was a two-division repair shop, where they repaired engines, transmissions, wheel alignments, brakes, shocks, and so on in one section, while performing frame restoration in the other. There were two employees who worked for Jeremiah, Daren, his fifty-three-year-old body man from Antigua, and their twenty-seven-year-old apprentice from Trinidad, named Alwin.

Kadeem's duties at the shop were simply to assist his father, while Jeremiah disassembled, repaired, and reassembled his customers' vehicles. The men worked long shifts, that went anywhere from twelve to fifteen hours, beginning at 8 AM, until the day's work was done or, slightly before their dysfunctional bodies hit the turf. On Friday evenings and Saturdays, the men would often quit early, to engage in a few games of dominos, over a bottle of rum or selected beer. A small number of acquaintances would gradually pass through, simulating a fun atmosphere where friends enjoyed each other's company, while either gambling for money or pride.

The tasks given to Kadeem offered him the ability to learn a trade, which he grasped faster than most men before him. However, it was only a matter of time, before the escalating tensions between he and his father rose to its boiling point. After receiving a meagre fifty dollars for the first week of which he worked three days, Kadeem withheld his objections with the expectation of a larger payment, once he had completed a full week. Hence, he exhibited the same vigor and intrigue toward his greasy duties and, returned for his second week of physically draining work.

Wages were paid out at the end of each week, and after spending his entire earnings along with a meagre personal sum, on the only product which strengthened him to undergo the calamity which transpired inside the Kites residence on a daily basis, Kadeem expected his pockets fully greased after a long and hard week's work. After only a few days in Jeremiah's household, which saw Kadeem chastised constantly, the Jamaican fugitive sought independence and began thinking toward his objectives. Come payday, Jeremiah's favored employees were attended to first, wherein he complimented his crew of yesteryears on another fine week of service. While his peers' faces glistened, Kadeem opened the white envelope handed him to find a single hundred-dollar bill, without any outcry of gratitude.

"What is this supposed to be," Kadeem demanded of his father?

"Uh, you pay," Jeremiah exclaimed!

"Man, you can't look pan big man and give mi hundred dollar," Kadeem argued disagreeably, as he tossed the bill to the floor.

"Hold on! How much you believe you should get pay? You a forget say is my roof you staying under, is my food you a eat every day from breakfast to you late night snack them! Them calls you make to Jamaica and elsewhere that the bill don't arrive for yet, me make sure me collect for them before anything! If you did have to take the bus to work, you don't think you would have to pay for the ride? You make people even take things out of me house, me have to replace, all those things add up! A what you take this thing for? Foreign a no bed a roses, we all had to pay some dues along the way," fired back Jeremiah!

"You know something? You see if I never learn to hold a higher inner meditation, me tear off you face in here for the disrespect! But I give thanks still, cause after all these years of calling you a crotches, mi finally get the opportunity to see that you is truly one!"

Before Kadeem could properly finish expressing himself, a dismantled Acura TL crept between the huge hangar doors. The vehicle resembled something ordained to the junkyard, after a lengthy tour inside a demolition pit, where patrons crashed into other vehicles until they were immobilized. Everyone's attention diverted from the controversy, which was sparked a few minutes earlier, as the squeaky vehicle that was tattooed with huge bullet holes came to a halt. The three men who occupied the vehicle exited like Brinks security guards, who were employed to secure the banking institutions' deposits, made by various businesses. With two of the men's hands lodged inside their pockets, while the third gripped an artefact beneath his shirts, Kadeem slowly moved towards the tools' table. All three men exhibited a screw face look, like they were served shit for lunch, thus they surveyed the area before entering the garage.

"What's happening, Rass Ijah," Alwin commented, after recognizing one of the men?

"You always telling mi bout your body shop, well, mi finally have some body work for you," responded the Rastafarian!

"Damn, boy, what happen to you sweet ride? Daren, come take a look at this so we can give my friend a quote," alerted Alwin, as they began moving toward the vehicle!

"Oh, God boy! But is pure bullet holes full up this yah car!" Daren commented, as he approached the vehicle.

"Some fools just try spray we with two Uzis up on St. Jacques road a few minutes ago," calmly exclaimed Rass Ijah.

"Wow, and with all these holes in the car, nobody no get shot," Alwin asked?

"Jah guidance alone, my boy," Rass Ijah boasted!

"Look like you go need some engine work too, because something surely busted up something under your hood," declared Jeremiah, who intruded to witness the damage.

"You boys lucky you have a tough car around you," said Daren.

Kadeem had privately made the decision to branch off on his own, despite what may and vowed to have nothing to do with his father, after developing a feeling of being used over the past few weeks. The vexed Jamaican, paid respects to his fellow co-workers before departing, and emphasized the fact he would not be returning. While Kadeem was calculating his next endeavor at the bus stop, Junior, who was on an errand for his mom, pulled over and offered him a lift; although he first had to stop by the garage to collect some funds. Kadeem's frustration was evident, and not fully lashing out against Jeremiah left a discontentment in his heart, though explaining his predicament to Junior managed to slightly ease his anger. Junior offered to chauffeur Kadeem wherever he chose to go, knowing he had a lot of luggage. He also offered his new stepbrother a loan and the use of his documents, in case Kadeem needed to rent an apartment.

To not defer from his pledge, the rude boy refused to exit the vehicle once they returned to the garage and waited until his stepbrother returned. Junior parked on the side of the building and indicated that he would be prompt, therefore Kadeem used his few minutes of solitude to think more on how to resolve his issues. The Jamaican fugitive used Junior's cellular from the cupholder and telephoned his second bright spots thus far in Canada, while he lit and inhaled the toxins from his first love, Mr. Hydroponic. The young lady whom he'd met on his first day out walking, had been his only salvation in this new country, where he had hoped to start a different life. They had gotten intimate once but spoke daily for at least an hour on the phone, which became the replenishing medicine that helped Kadeem with coping. The young college student shared a two-bedroom apartment with her close friend, nevertheless, she eagerly offered Kadeem shelter for as long as he so desired.

The offer proposed by Junior was indeed tempting, but Kadeem knew that his mother would never allow him to do any of the things he promised, therefore, he accepted without further thought, but assured his young lover his stay would be brief. Their telephone conversation then changed, as the thoughts of being constantly in each other's presence, jolted their sexual appetites. Kadeem finally revealed his nickname, 'Killa', which was anointed to him while living in Jamaica as a youngster; in hopes of getting the young lady to refer to him as such during intercourse. The young lady, on the other hand, wanted to know if there was a bit of freakiness hidden somewhere inside Kadeem, where he'd be opened to an occasional ménage-a-trois with her roommate. Kadeem attested to the fact that he'd not be performing any oral stimulations, although he fell silent over the idea of the stimulation being performed on him.

Through his peripheral vision, Kadeem caught sight of someone prancing in the air to land a dropkick on Junior, who was simply retreating with his hands up to protect his face. Two other men turned the corner and tried to entrap Junior, where he would be unable to escape. One of the three attackers threw and landed a straight right punch at Junior, who crashed against the hood of his car and realized he had been cornered, with nowhere to run. Reactively, Kadeem jumped from the passenger side door and flung the first article in his reach at the man closest to him. Sadly, though, there went his phone conversation and Junior's link to the world, as the cell phone smashed against the side of the young man's head.

"You bitches have to do me something, too, if any a you plan fi touch my brother," Kadeem firmly stated, in his native dialect as he pranced into action to even up the score!

The young man quickly armed himself and aimed the weapon at the approaching Kadeem's head, while he swiped away the blood trickling down the side of his head.

"A yu battyman boyfriend this to you rescue? Pussy, say goodbye to you lover," threatened the armed thug, whose eyes lit up in preparation to blast!

One of the bystanders cheered, "Yes, Damian, shoot the blood clatt buoy in him face!"

"No, my brethren, stop, stop, stop," Alwin shouted, after he overheard the disruption while departing for home and nosily went to investigate! "Him is the boss man son who just come from Mobay, name Killa, me beg all you, please let him go?"

"All them batty-boy yah fi get gunshot," stated the bleeding thug, whose index finger massaged the trigger of his 9mm, eager to blast one away!

"I hear you, but him a no battyman," conveyed Alwin!

"My youth, you see how close you come to getting you life took? Watch yourself next time you see bad man a handle him business; you stay out a it see mi! Me should all murder you blood clatt fi buss up mi head, still a levity! You dig," commented the thug, while he slowly lowering his weapon!

"Mi don't forget a man who point him gun in my face, member that," Kadeem stated, as he helped his injured stepbrother into the car!

The young thug joked, "Man, you hear this guy?" He then shoved his weapon into his waistband. "Say thank God I allowed you to continue breathing, bout!"

A Toyota Land Cruiser pulled up as Kadeem placed Junior, who was grimacing for his ribs, in the passenger seat of his Chrysler Neon. The crew of thugs who visited the garage to have their vehicle repaired hopped aboard their limousine, leaving the butt of their jokes in anguish. Alwin, who was genuinely concerned, saw to it that everyone departed peacefully, before he left the compound.

Part 14

The luscious plants and colorful assorted flowers around Stephan D'agaruso's garden were complementary assets to the Chairman of the Rough Riders' eight-million-dollar mansion in St. Lazard, east of Montreal. Martain Lafleur had been an honored representative of the east coast division of mobsters for several years, yet it was through the pioneers of the French province that the biker gang was established.

Monsieur Stephan D'agaruso was considered the Chairman and spokesperson for a secret, illicit group of billionaires, who ruled the underground illegal markets of drugs, alcohol, racketeering, and gambling, while they controlled the legislators of Quebec's legal government like puppets. It was through these eleven giant tycoons that some of the most perilous decisions concerning the Province of Quebec were made, despite the public's belief that their anointed premiers, mayors and public servants were the governing faction. The powerful cult that began with only a handful of billionaires, slowly grew over the centuries to include other billionaires who shared the same ideology as their forefathers.

Martain Lafleur was the only leader in the history of the Rough Riders organization, who rose to prominence through blood relations. The man who gave him the honor was his uncle and, was predominantly known as the Dominator, for changing the culture of the biker club. The Dominator became the organization's fourth-ever leader and reigned nearly forty years, before his tragic death, after a mercenary used a semi-trailer to run him over, on one of his infamous Harley Davidson cruises. Born Yves Guy Lafleur, to prominent French parents who bore three other boys and one lone female, it was discovered that his final command was that his reign be handed down to his favorite nephew, who had always professed his desire to be exactly like his uncle. Martain had his experts scour the wreckage for clues and later found out his uncle had met his demise at the hands of their fiercest enemy, who had always been Brogan Alfonso, leader of the Defenders crew.

Both Stephan D'agaruso and Martain walked freely about the grounds while guards patrolled the surroundings. During Martain's tenor at the helm of the Rough Riders gang, he'd only been summoned to the nest on one other occasion, which was at the time a very nerve-wrecking visit. With slightly more fierceness in his demeanor at this meeting, Martain expected intense scrutiny after the Gazette reported that, 'Nicholas' gun hands had struck another severe blow versus the Rough Riders'.

"Here's another list of people in need of persuasion," Stephan began, as he handed Martain an envelope that contained a piece of paper with seventy-eight names written on it. "This never-ending war between you and these immigrants or whatever they are, needs to come to some finalization! We advised you to come to the table with this ruffian you've been trying to eliminate for over a year now. Because you insisted on burying this adversary of yours, we awarded you additional time to handle your business. However, following these recent losses of yours, we're now compelled more than ever to sit down and come to some business terms with this Nicholas. There are greater matters of importance on the table presently, and in order for us all to continue our tradition of excellence, we simply must fortify peace for the greater good," Stephan advised!

"How does the topic of discussion even come up while strategizing? After all, we've toiled for all these years, and you gentlemen simply want to give a portion of that away. Not while I'm still breathing! It's either that bitch or me, but we'll never be on the same team," Martain argued!

"Nobody expected you to grasp the situation, which is simply the fact that we've watched an annual gross of thirty plus million dollars dissipate to half that amount over a three-year term. We have investors to satisfy and partners to persuade that this bickering will not spill over, into affairs that are more urgent! I don't need remind you of our obligations this time around! The bottom line is this, it's either we read about Mr. Henry in the obituaries, or some sort of arrangements will be made," Stephan instructed!

The eighty-four-year-old Stephan D'agaruso held Martain's arm and used his support to bend forward in order to pick a white rose from its stem. The old tycoon, who rose to power through real estate and several other fraudulent businesses, collected an assortment of colored roses, until he'd gained enough to assemble a bouquet. Both men walked to an exquisite gazebo, that was encased inside an assortment of flowers and pine trees, before sitting and chatting for a few additional minutes. Martain opened the envelope and peeked at the list of names, before he placed it inside his shirt pocket. There were several elections underway across the country, from the selection for a new prime minister to mayoral campaigns, yet, the cult was mainly interested in capturing the race to become Quebec's premier.

"You remind me so much of myself as a young man growing up. Take no shit, deal with matters as they come. Though I can't say I was quite as fierce, I can say I did have a lot of fun with the ladies." The men looked at each other and chuckled for a bit. Martain's cellular began vibrating continuously, although he chose to ignore the caller. "The Martain I know hasn't been around for a while now! When was the last time you rode one of your Harleys? Your uncle lived to feel the wind blow through him while riding, but this war of yours prevents you from having any fun!" Stephan paused and looked at Martain, whom he'd known since he was an infant. The blank stare by Martain supported Stephan's assumptions, though the gangster neglected to comment.

"You see this bouquet of roses? Before I met and married my late wife, I wasn't able to see the beauty in one rose, not to mention a colorful bouquet. Life is always going to be about choices and changes, no matter which corner of the world you live in. There is beauty in everybody, but some people strive to have it all, which is why the most evil and vicious people I know are the ones running the world! People do what they do because of personal gratification or loved ones, nothing else. When was the last time you spoke to your father? I think it's time you start mending some issues in your life. Huh! It's funny, my wife used to always tell me to bring her roses and leave them here after she was gone. I used to tell her, 'Don't hold your breath', but look at me now! Ha, ha!"

Martain thought about everything the Chairman had urged, as he looked through the thick, bulletproof glass of his Hummer H2. The leaves on the trees along the interstate outside were transforming to a beautiful golden color, as the change to autumn caused them to flutter to the ground. His personal bodyguards knew of their boss' furious nature and remained silent during their forty-five-minutes trip to the cottage. The cottage was a two-story bungalow located in Laval, where biker members would often take prisoners slated for torture. The biker boss received a phone call from Andre, who called to relay information about an incident that occurred during the late hours. With his cellular phone pressed against his ear, Martain grew very aggravated at the word of an attack against his drug shipment yard on the South Shore, which resulted in the complete destruction of his hangar, as well as the products it housed. The biker boss began stumping the back of the front passenger seat, as he yelled out Nicholas' and Brogan's names and, 'swore he'd personally put them beneath the dirt'!

"It's like they came to steal the stuff, but once they saw that they couldn't come close because of our fire power, they changed plans! Then they came at us with gasoline and torches and lit up the warehouse! While we were busy waiting for the counterattack, they first lit up the blind side of the building, before moving to the back and right around. We had to shoot our way out of the building to safety, because they intended for us to burn inside with the rest of the shit!" The person on the line paused, before releasing a huge sigh. "With everything going up in smoke, we had to get our asses out of that burning building, so we started shooting our way out, but by time we got to safety behind the huge garbage container to the right of the building, there was like three of us left. Those fuckers were out to destroy everything, though, boss, because even after all that, they still threw two or three bottle bombs into the blaze! I don't know through what exit Gilles snuck out of that abyss, but I'm glad he did, because they weren't planning on leaving any witnesses, either! If Young Buck hadn't snuck around on them and picked a few of them off, we wouldn't be here to say shit! I guess, when they started to run away, the fuckers got in a lucky shot on Young Buck and, hit him in right arm, but with the sirens getting closer, we just hightailed it out of there before the cops showed up! I'm happy though, the kid shot one of them in the knee, who couldn't get away, so---."

"How the fuck did they even get that close to the hangar? You idiots must have been partying when you should've been paying fucking attention," Martain commented!

"No, no, boss, that ain't how it was! We—."

The phone line went dead as Martain slammed his Motorola flip phone shut.

Martain planned to rid the planet of Nicholas and his allies, who, had begun supplying Haitians around areas of L'Acadie and the eastern regions of Montreal. The Rough Rider gang had always provided the Haitians with their controlled substances, yet it was forbidden for any man of dark complexion to ever join their exclusive, all-white club. With his biker soldiers perishing at a disproportionally high rate compared to those of their nemesis, the biker boss coupled with a group of Haitians purely as a temporary strategy, which he perceived was a valiant chess move. Whether Martain sent Caucasian assassins or bikers to terminate his nemesis, they had all failed, thus, his foes would return dismembered portions of their anatomies, to ensure that Martain and future attackers understood the fate that befell them.

A Haitian native, pretending to be of African descent, befriended a young shotta named Bruce, who hustled around the downtown core, as one of Nicholas' representatives. Bruce was amongst friends inside a center town apartment, when he received a phone call from someone who claimed, "To be a friend of Spuggy." The young shotta was within his element, and his existence was purely on a "who-knows-who" basis, therefore, he was initially skeptical of the caller. The Haitian convinced the young hustler, that he was directed to deal with him specifically by Spuggy, who had recently begun serving a bid in Boudreaux Penitentiary.

The mention of the name Spuggy, who hustled alongside the young shotta prior to his arrest, gained the Haitian an introductory meeting. Even though the shotta was still somewhat skeptical about the caller, they met up that same night, after Bruce invited him to his location. When the Haitian arrived, they spoke out on the twenty-eighth-floor balcony, where Bruce dropped a cup of ice over the ledge, to warn his visitor of the cost of disloyalty. To further convince the young shotta he was serious about business, the Haitian ordered five kilos of cocaine and prepaid the dealer, ten thousand dollars in cash. Even after the buyer handed over the money, he offered the shotta a sneak peek into a leather laptop case he carried, that contained the remaining funds. The young shotta collected the money and placed the order into head office, after which he gave the Haitian specific instructions on where to meet, in order to complete the transaction.

The Haitian was early to the meeting spot and brought along one witness. The young shotta, who transported the product from across the native reservation, brought along Priest and a female the young shotta was eager to conclude the day with, inside his two-door Toyota Celica. The limousine-style tinted windows around the vehicle, made it practically impossible to see the female in the rear of the car, as they rode up into a vacant parking lot of Ontario Street east of downtown. The young shotta and Priest hopped out the vehicle with the sales product in a regular plastic bag and their weapons concealed, while the buyer stood beside his Acura TL with a thick and attractive red-boned female to his left. Bruce was almost fixated on the beautiful and sturdy stallion, whom the Haitian brought along to serve as the decoy.

"It is good to see you are a man of honesty," the Haitian declared.

The young shotta answered, "I'm a businessman, baby! I see you brought your bodyguard with you! Hi, how you doing?"

"Hello, hello," acknowledged the female!

The young shotta exclaimed, "Oh, I can smell that money!"

The female, who was in possession of the laptop case with the funds, began handing the young shotta the case, before all hell broke loose. Tires from two SUVs screeched as they raced around the corner, that led into the parking lot. The young shotta and Priest took their eyes off their business associates and began reaching for their weapons, before they were halted by the Haitian and his bitch, both of whom quickly jammed their weapons in the sellers' faces.

"Toss them guns over there nice and easy," the Haitian commanded, to which the young shotta and Priest obeyed their orders.

The SUV trucks were filled with bikers, who all hopped out with baseball bats, pipe irons, and batons, expecting to batter the subdued sellers. The driver of one of the SUVs walked over to Bruce and collected the plastic bag of cocaine, before calling his boss to inform him that they were successful. The female inside Bruce's car hid herself, as a biker looked inside the vehicle, yet was unable to see her. The scared female had to cover her mouth to avoid not screaming, as the bikers all began beating the daylights out of the young shotta and Priest. Both men were beaten to death by the bikers, who sought to send a permanent message to Nicholas and his band of thugs. Once they'd completed disfiguring their foes, the Haitian tossed a biker insignia atop the young shotta before yelling, "Rough Riders forever, bitches!"

The leader of the eastern division of the Rough Riders gang walked in through the cottage door, with two massive humans behind him. It was apparent that Martain had his mind focused elsewhere, as he marched by bikers snorting cocaine, loosely engaged in sexual orgies, drinking liquor and playing video games, without acknowledging any of them, and went directly to the basement. There was an area set up for torture, with blades ranging from scalpels to swords, piercing objects from shanks to spears, chopping weapons from machetes to axes, chains, hooks, and electrical connections for shock treatments. With the walls constructed of thick reinforced concrete, captives inside the dungeon could scream for mercy at the top of their lungs, without even the Almighty hearing them. The stench of decomposed bodies and bloodstains spackled across the walls, would easily make the faint of heart either vomit or pass out unconscious.

"Ivan," Martain exclaimed, raising both his indexes and middle fingers in the air, while sitting only a few paces in front the prisoner!

Ivan was Martain's personal do-boy, and he was the one who constructed Martain's marijuana joints laced with cocaine, his cranberry mixed with Hennessy drink, tended to his banking and handled the accounting. The do-boy brought over a pre-rolled joint and placed it between his boss' lips, before sparking the lighter to set it ablaze. Martain sat quietly intoxicating himself with a poison he'd grown to love, while staring at the young prisoner who'd been knocked unconscious, during the constant servings of punches, kicks, slaps, and more licks.

Martain began thinking about the delicate position in which this unexpectedly lengthy war had placed his affairs, while contemplating measures to retain his governing body's confidence. Over their three years of warfare, both sides had surrendered a large amount of fighters in shoot-outs, fist fights, stabbings, and other conflicts, yet Martain remained the sole gangster lobbying for job approval. The thought of what may become of him should the council vote to terminate the bloodshed through negotiations and diplomacy, left a despicable taste in the back of his throat. Martain began considering mutiny against him, should he fail to bring the disputes between himself and Nicholas to a close.

Apart from the Chairman, Sir Honorable Stephan D'agaruso's, Martain knew very little of the secret society he represented or of its members. Hence, without knowing the members of the governing covenant, it would be impossible to confirm from whom an execution order would come. Death was the only one way out of the club for Martain, unless he made it to retirement and passed on the reigns to a successor. However, his performance was paramount to securing his position, considering the high-ranked billionaires they secretly represented.

"Yow, wake up, bro! Wake up! Get his fucking ass up, Ivan!"

Ivan walked over to the unconscious lad and slapped him across his bloodied face, before scornfully fetching his hand towel to cleanse his hand. "Can't you hear someone talking to you, boy," Ivan lamented?

The young lad, who bled from areas throughout, peeked through the tiny window of visibility left him through his left eye since, the right eye had been totally swollen shut. Immediate flashbacks on his ordeal appeared to frighten the prisoner, who flinched terrifyingly after Ivan pretended he was about to slap him across the face.

Martain said, "Do you have any idea what we do to people here? People have given up their grandmothers in hopes that the pain will stop, once we've begun dislodging body parts. Notice you're not gagged or anything? Believe me, screaming is encouraged down here! In fact, the louder you scream the hornier we get, if you want to get technical! Let's see, just the other night we had your partner Gringo down here. I know you recognize the ring," Martain tossed a ring at the lad! The young man's eye opened wide, as he looked down at the ring that landed in his lap.

"Yeah, I know; the big question is, 'What happened to the rest of good old Gringo?' You damn sure look a lot more worried about what's going to happen to you right now, that's for sure! Tell you what—I'm feeling a little generous today, believe it or not, so I'm going to give you a live scoop about what happened to your friend Gringo, and your possible fate."

Martain used a knife to cut the ropes that bound the lad to the chair, before dragging the prisoner halfway across the room. There was a refrigerator in the left corner of the room, with liquid residue resembling blood on the floor in front of it. The biker boss walked over to the refrigerator and lifted a man's entire leg, from the hip to the sole of the foot, from within, before returning to his captive. The prisoner, who was left on his buttocks, utilized the sole moment of freedom awarded him since his capture, to formulate an attack at the leader of the Rough Riders. With all the strength the young lad could muster, he struggled to stand, with the intention to lunge himself at Martain, but his physical capabilities and mind power were not in sync.

"Sit the fuck down! Did I tell you that you could fucking stand," Martain exclaimed, as he whacked the prisoner across the temple with the body part?

Martain went over to the lad with the semi-frozen leg and pinned the prisoner to the floor with it against his neck. The young man looked up at the biker boss, whose rage mounted following his pathetic attempt at an attack. Fearing that Martain would kill him there and then, the captive began pleading for his life.

"I'm sorry, man! Please, I just, lost my head, for a second! It's back on, straight now! I promise, I'll never try, some bullshit, like that again!"

Martain stepped to the lone door a few paces from the refrigerator and, turned the key already in place, before drawing the thick mahogany door open. There was a steel gate with half-inch-thick bars spaced a few inches apart and a small latched port built in the middle of the gate. The stench that breathed from the room immediately engulfed the entire basement, forcing the lad to cover his nostrils with his hands. Martain opened the latched port built into the gate and tossed the human leg into the chamber.

"You wanna find out what happened to your partner Gringo? That was his right leg, and the majority of him, I guess, has already been crunched up and shit out!" Two scavenging hyenas rushed the meat and fought over it, before they devoured it.

The young prisoner crawled into a corner after witnessing a sight he'd only viewed on television programs like Animal Planet.

"Wha-wha-what the fuck is that?"

"Come say hello to Laverne and Shirley, my babies from Africa," Martain declared.

Ivan laughed aloud after watching the lad scurry for safety, once he saw the hyenas attack the body part, and tore it apart. Even Martain's do-boy refused to advance any further, in fear of the gate accidentally falling open, yet he belittled their captive. "Bitches! I tell you, boss, look at how scared that fool is! They only tough in numbers, trust me!"

"Right about now, we would normally be carving off parts of your anatomy and have you watch, while we feed the meat to my pets. But today I'm on a different program, because I believe that you don't only want to continue living, but you are also a smart man who understands the concept of life," Martain stated!

The young lad began envisioning torcher sessions, where mutilated victims surrendered limbs before they died, possibly by heart attack, while their captors toyed and gamed.

"What you want, me to do, man?"

"Don't get me wrong and believe that this isn't a positive gain for you, because, at the end of all this, there is going to be nothing but wealth for everyone involved with the right crew," Martain paused and closed the mahogany door! "Ivan, get me fifty G's from the safe upstairs! Now, I'm going to give you a down payment on some information work I want you to do for me. I understand you just one of the gun hands, so, I won't demand too much, but cross me and I guarantee, I will feed you to my hyenas," Martain said, as his assistant returned with the funds and dropped it on the bloodied thug!

Part 15

Foh Nuey, the biggest Cambodian cocaine dealer in Verdun, Montreal's southwest, thanked Nicholas for the deal, as he exited with his companion. Nicholas reclined on his leather sofa inside his home office, while his two-and-a-half-years-old son crashed his Tonka toy trucks into each other, on the Persian carpet next to him. Although he monitored his son quite frequently, Nicholas occasionally peeked at the television's newscast for reports on the attack his hijackers launched, against Martain's drug warehouse. Instead of any groundbreaking news, the CTV News Network was instead recognizing the ever-charismatic Monsieur Michel Lafleur, who donated an entire eastern wing to the Jewish General Hospital, for cancer research. The old business tycoon also donated medical equipment and aided with fundraising efforts, that brought in another $1.7 million dollars in contributions.

Michel Lafleur was born in Alberta, Canada, in the early 1930s to a crude oil developer and a romance novelist who taught their children proper respect and family values. Michel, Yves, Christopher, and Lorry Ann, lived royally, as their upper-class parents spoiled them with everything they desired. The senior Monsieur Lafleur suffered a tragic accident before his children's teenage years when, an explosion at one of the refineries he supervised, left eight families without fathers. Mrs. Loraine Lafleur moved her family to Quebec six months later, where she bought a house and changed her occupation to that of a successful realtor. Her children grew with the tenet that guides each of us along the way, into becoming the rebel/goody-two-shoes types of people we each amount to. Michel grew with the gentle grace taught to him by his father, whom he'd so admired, to become the country's most successful realtor and businessman, after his mother entrusted him to head her million-dollar empire upon retirement.

Yves was always a ruthless individual, who squandered money and lived lavishly, while occasionally engaging in slap boxing incidences with officers of the law. At the tender age of nineteen, Bad Boy Yves was inaugurated the president of the Rough Riders Gang, and soon dominated the underworld, as they grew in strength and popularity.

Christopher maintained a childhood fascination for the law, which saw him complete the bar exam and became a powerful lawyer. Loraine got her son employed by Brooks and Clarion, which was the city's premier law firm, before the young stud even received his law degree.

The woman the Canadian Globe and Mail, once referred to as "The Iron Curtain of Quebec," received her heart's desire the fourth time around, with the birth of her only daughter, Lorry Ann. The youngest of her four children was equally spectacular in beauty and brawn, being the only female tossed in the den of lions. Lorry Ann studied fashion locally in Quebec as an aspiring designer, before she moved to Paris where she captured the essence of the fashion world.

The wealth and power attained by Michel over the years had placed him amongst the all-time five wealthiest tycoons in Canada. Business associates and investors convinced the business mogul to enter the 1982 Provincial Election, to become the mayor of Quebec. With soaring popularity ratings and a commanding lead in the polls, news of a scandal was released that brought Michel's political aspirations to a screeching halt. The television program W5, did an exclusive on the violent undertakings of the Rough Riders gang, where they mentioned a ruthless Martain Lafleur, who was said to be the first offspring of the soon-to-be mayor. Despite his claims of having no affiliation with his son, whom he claimed, "disgraced his family," Michel forcibly withdrew from the election and politics altogether.

"That old boy better be happy him don't have any dealings with him son, or else me would surely kidnap him bombo-clatt and use him as bait," Nicholas exclaimed to his son, who simply looked up at his dad with baby drool running down the side of his mouth! "What up? My little shotta want some milk?"

There was a slight knock at the door, and Nicholas looked over his shoulder and waved the young thug inside.

"Yow, Boss Man, me and them boys drive go check the Elder Dread up on Decarie, to collect the parcel a yard weed like you asked. We found a quick park just below the rass place, so we all run inside the building and was about to ring the buzzer! But it seemed like them Haitian boys was driving by and see Damian car. The man them stop and come out in the middle road, and start shoot up the car, luckily nobody never stayed inside! We hear the gunshots them and run out on the boy them, and all shoot one of them in his shoulder, before them jumped in them car and speed away!"

While speaking with his hired gun-hand, Nicholas' cousin hurried by outside the door and went into the bathroom.

"What happened to Damian?" Nicholas demanded, after the young thug scampered by with blood splattered across the left side of his face.

"Oh yeah, the mechanic son, fly to him batty-boy brother's side, and almost tear off Damian face! You know D, always a fuck with people, but the little man take exception and give him a telephone to the dome," commented the thug, with a slight chuckle over the details!

"Don't tell me say him put the man in the hospital; or killed him," Nicholas argued?

"No, boss, everything crisp, after what happen to twitchy fingers Spuggy, man start make sure them a fire them gun for a reason!"

Damian was Nicholas' sole relative in Canada, after his mother moved back to Jamaica to assist her ailing mother, who was alone following the death of her elderly husband. Nicholas' aunt did not want to carry her son back to the islands, where she feared he would get killed or end up in prison. The American fugitive was tasked with teaching Damian how to be an independent adult, but he surpassed his cousin's mother's wishes and taught the young man the different aspects of the hustling game, street smarts, the guerrilla tactics necessary to survive the harsh streets of Montreal, in addition to that polite gibberish his mother demanded. The Kid, as he was referred to by his peers, had a degree in chemistry obtained from the University of Toronto, where he completed his studies before entering the wonderful world of crooks.

"A who mash you up, Pops," Nicholas joked, although he was relieved his overly sensitive cousin hadn't added another charge of battery or assault, to his already lengthy record?

"After me a get ready to put some kicks under this batty boy, him pussy-hole brother Killa attack me from back and buss up my head! My boy Alwin save them momentarily, but me personally go make him trip to Canada the shortest ever," exclaimed Damian, while wiping the dried-up blood from his hair!

"His brother who," Nicholas demanded?

"Some cat they said was, Killa."

Nicholas summoned the maid to attend to the baby, before suggesting they go in search of this vigilante, who was disrespectful enough to harm his sole blood relative in Canada. Although Nicholas neglected to mention it, the refugee/vigilante knew of someone from years passed with the same nickname and, wanted to clarify they weren't the same person. Damian, on the other hand, began celebrating by boasting to his fellow shottas, that his status exempted everyone from laying a finger on him. "Yeah, a boy a go get fuck up now," was the sole sentence reverberated by Damian all the way to the vehicles.

Kane pulled closer to Nicholas as they walked through the long hallway to the front door and began informing him of other business matters which weren't discussed. Kane briefed Nicholas on the loss of their two combatants, who never returned from the detail awarded them, though reports from the sole survivor painted a picture that was not reassuring. Another member of the invading force had to be taken to Nicholas' personal physician, who occasionally administered doctoring far beyond his normal practice, for wounded soldiers of his premier client. The material articles, such as vehicles, guns, and other items, that were lost during the battle were inconsequential to Nicholas, who'd created an empire large enough to sustain losses or combat any rivals.

Two Chevy Suburban XLTs were brought up from the garage and parked in front of the main entrance. The five men who emerged from within the lofty eight-million-dollar mansion, separated as they approached the vehicle. Nicholas, Kane, and Rass Ijah opted for the rear transport, while Damian and Tank hopped into the first SUV. Damian could still be heard bumping his gums over what he believed was about to transpire, once they found the patriots for whom they searched.

"Yow, Bobby, link up you boy and find out where Jeremiah the mechanic live, and get us there ASAP, cause a boy about to get fucked up!" Damian said to the driver, who was already inside the truck.

Doherty arrived home and found Kadeem assembling his personal belongings and snuffed her nose at him, as she proceeded en-route to her bedroom. The lady of the house was quick to dial her husband's cellular phone, in order to inform him of what was transpiring. Jeremiah was elated to find out, his son had decided to no longer remain a burden on him and, instructed his wife. "Make sure that boy no take nothing of mine! And make sure him leave the house key right there, if him think him go sneak back inside my place, him have another thing coming!"

Although she remained silent while occasionally snooping to make sure their precious artefacts around the house weren't stolen, Doherty was especially happy to finally be rid of Kadeem after only a few weeks. She had reservations to evict him once he had procured a work skill, a proper job or within a six months' timeframe, whichever came first. Doherty was in the midst of ensuring her husband's wishes were fulfilled, when she bumped into Junior exiting the bathroom. The darkness around her son's left eye first caught her attention, and she immediately proceeded to demand 'who had injured him'. The idea of Kadeem overhearing him cry to his mommy made Junior shrug her off, by suggesting it occurred accidentally from a basketball to the face. Doherty marched back to her room, convinced Kadeem had something to do with her son's misfortune, as Junior had always been the sort of person to abstain from violent confrontations.

With a slight nudge on her bedroom curtain, Doherty secretly watched as Kadeem loaded his luggage into Junior's car. The thought that she would finally regain full control of her household brought a sarcastic smile to her face, yet as Kadeem returned to the house, Doherty closed the curtains to remain unnoticed. Once Kadeem re-entered the house, his stepmother scampered away from beside the window, as if her interests were elsewhere. Respectfully, Kadeem knocked on her door and asked to have a word with her. The Jamaican fugitive proceeded to thank the "conniving manipulator", he had come to know Doherty as, for allowing him the opportunity to reside amongst them. Doherty listened to Kadeem, while she remained seated at the foot of her bed, before she simply waved goodbye to her houseguest. As her stepson turned to walk away, Doherty advised him that 'should he encounter any problems out in society, it would be best if he avoided involving his father'.

Junior's American racing muffler tip roared, as he fired up the engine and rammed the gear stick into the first gear of his economy-sized vehicle. The four-cylinder engine was about to take off, when the Chevy Suburban with Damian onboard blocked its path. Damian pranced from within the Suburban with his 9mm in his hand and went directly to the driver's side. The agitated thug, who still had sprinkles of dried blood around his earlobes from the cellular to the head, jammed his weapon at Junior's temple and asked, 'if he remembered disrespecting him'?

The moments in time stood still, as the eavesdropping Doherty watched the young thug threatened her only begotten son, who had volunteered to transport Kadeem to his destination. The frantic mother raced to the front door and out into harm's way without a second thought. Nobody could at that moment deter Doherty, from believing that Kadeem was responsible for the black eye she noticed around Junior's left eye earlier, and she began screaming for the release of her son.

"Junior! Junior! Not my son! What did he do to you? Leave him be! He's not a violent person!" Doherty screamed, as the sight of added armed gangsters froze her in her tracks.

"Old lady, I suggest you go back inside your house, because if I start shooting out here everybody dead," declared Tank!

"You, pussy-hole, come out the car right now; and make sure you hold your hands them high, where me can see them," Damian ordered, as the second Suburban pulled up!

Kadeem removed himself from the car while ensuring his hands remained visible. The thought that matters would be reversed if he had a weapon scampered across his mind, as he dreaded the idea of being harmed by such toy soldier type thugs. Damian forgot that he'd already selected a bullet into the firing chamber of his 9mm automatic and, looked like an amateur when he expelled that bullet, by attempting to select another. The slight chuckle toward Damian's mishap by Junior bought him the butt of the gun handle, which intensified the screams of his mother, who was quite aware of the slayings that had gripped the city.

Damian began making his way toward Kadeem, who expected his earlier actions to be repaid in full. The knowledge that her son was out of immediate danger, saw Doherty move slightly toward Junior, before being refrozen by Tank's huge .357 Magnum that readjusted her course. With a tight grip on his gun handle and his gut filled with anger, there was absolutely no telling what Damian was about to do to Kadeem, who stood tall and stared down the infringing thug.

"You never think I was coming back this soon, did you? You go get fucked up right now," Damian stated, two steps from knocking Kadeem's lights out!

"Damian, don't you dare touch that youth," Nicholas shouted with conviction!

As Nicholas emerged from the Chevy SUV, there was absolutely no doubt in the minds of those under persecution that he was the head honcho. The untrimmed facial hair, rounded off by his luscious dread locks that pranced off his shoulders, cast a gloomy shadow over Nicholas' identity, as he removed the dark glasses from his face. Doherty began feeling a bit faintish under the stress of the moment and fell to her knees with her head held high, praying to the Lord for His help in the matter. The vengeful look that covered Damian's face was replaced with confusion, as he halted his actions and took one step back for precaution.

"What you mean, 'don't touch him?' Cous, this the motherfucker that I told you about before," exclaimed Damian!

"Mi say back up away from him," Nicholas repeated!

Even with the slight temporary vote of confidence that nothing harmful was about to happen to them, Kadeem prepared for the worst knowing the volatile nature of gangsters, once they've received motivation and sought to impress others. The mystery man who emerged from the SUV, walked halfway toward Kadeem, before he stopped and waited to see if the Jamaican rude boy would recognize him. Not wanting to totally take his eyes off Damian, who Kadeem perceived as a threat, interfered with his ability to cross-reference Nicholas' features, with those stored in his memory banks. However, to distil the fears developed by those involved, after what Nicholas considered a drastic error in judgment, the American fugitive came forward and ended the tensions.

"Killa, you don't recognize me," Nicholas asked?

"You know this fucker," Damian enquired?

"The man is family, of course mi know him," Nicholas responded, with his face glowing from ear to ear!

The acknowledgment that anyone referring to him as such must be an ally, made Kadeem bring his fully attention to this mystery leader, who brought the entire grudge affair to a close with one phrase. The idea that his boss/cousin had prior dealings with this newcomer who embarrassed him earlier, grieved Damian, who turned and began walking toward the vehicle from which he emerged. Nicholas was mystified by the sight of Killa, whom he'd heard countless war tales about, and like many sceptics, had no idea if he was dead or alive. Having snuck into the country himself, Nicholas understood the sacrifices certain individuals had to make to preserve their lives, especially those who departed from places like Jamaica with detrimental criminal records.

"Bombo-clatt, a lie! Mr. Walsh, is really you that," Kadeem smiled, as he hugged Nicholas following a fist bump and a firm handshake?

"You still a beat-up people years later, I see! My boy, mi did truly sorry to hear 'bout Stamma, but it's good seeing you still," Nicholas exclaimed, initially neglecting to mention his identity change in this new world!

Damian had his hand on the door handle and was about to take a seat, when Nicholas summoned him and had him introduce himself to Kadeem, with an apology. The tension had subsided by the time Damian and Kadeem shook hands, yet the nerves of everyone involved had not fully transformed back to their original state. Once Doherty realized that these were friends of Kadeem, she took her freedom of speech rights to another level, as she began cursing and chastising the gangsters who'd begun concealing their weapons, while they familiarized themselves with each another. Junior, who'd become aggravated by the amount of cheap shots taken against his sexuality preference, ran into the house crying. As Junior trotted by Doherty, sobbing with his hand covering the damaged area of his face, the mental anguish of her son aggravated her further. Kadeem's stepmother began unleashing her sentiments of discontent at the thugs on her property, even though none of them paid any attention to her.

Jeremiah arrived home minutes later to find his wife cursing at the youngsters, who weren't paying attention or heeding a word of her message. Doherty's Christian faith counteracted her Caribbean personality, where on one hand she warned of God's penalties for sinners, while she threatened to summon the police should they not vacate the premises. Kadeem, Nicholas, and the others acted like long-lost partners, who hadn't seen each other in quite some time, hence they lit up pre-rolled marijuana joints and smoked.

Jeremiah wasn't pleased to find the gang of thugs courting in front of his domain. After he received the final report from Doherty, Jeremiah shortened his regular Friday night of drinking and gambling with the boys and, raced home to ensure the nucleus of his household was safe. The gang of "young hipsters," as Jeremiah referred to Kadeem's associates in an earlier conversation, were the very same wasted sperm the mechanic warned against inviting to his house. As such, Jeremiah was quick to confront his son, about the choice of people he perceived Kadeem invited to the house.

"What is all this in front my house, some kind a convention? I want all of you gone from my place right now! I don't want you back in my house, you hear me! Is long time I see that you worthless, and you rather rob people money than work for it. The Bible say whatever you sow, you surely will reap, so you can go out into the world with them evil thoughts and actions. Don't make anybody call my phone! From police to morgue attendant, you make sure you tell them stay far from 6648 Terre Bonne Boulevard. If I did know say you would be such disappointment so soon, me would never agree to Auntie P's suggestion that you come up here. Look at the set of hooligans you want hang around with, for each one of them drug dealers there is a hundred more capable souls on the island of Jamaica, who would represent where them come from, much better than them gun-shooting thugs. The Bible say that, 'he who live by the sword shall die by the sword!' Take that message with you and get the hell off my property, before me go call the police them to come move you up!"

Kadeem remarkably remained tranquil despite the lengthy dose of tongue-lashing he received from Jeremiah, who refrained from heeding the advice of his wife, as she tried to warn him not to agitate the thugs too much. There had been numerous reports of people getting killed for reasons far less ridiculous, and knowing the thugs were armed, Doherty tried to calm her uninformed husband. Thoughts of lashing back at his father provoked Kadeem, who saw in a vision an image of Granny P, who yelled at him 'to never disrespect the hands which fed him!' The young Jamaican exile simply walked over to Junior's Nissan Stanza, removed his luggage and handed them to Nicholas' driver, for him to load them aboard the SUV. The poise and composure shown by Kadeem exemplified the type of warrior Nicholas aspired to have within his cabinet, and he welcomed Kadeem with open arms.

Part 16

Danny translated an account to Nicholas, that was told to him by Crazy Horse, who used to smuggle cocaine to the Inuit people who dwelled in northern Canada, before the {Royal Canadian Mounted Police} snuffed out the operations and closed shop. The account was about his sole nemesis' rise to fame, which wasn't a tale loosely discussed. Nicholas would have had to surrender, been killed, or abandon his quest for revenge against Martain years before, due to the disproportionate number of bikers he and the Esquada's were up against. The suggestion to form an alliance with the Rough Riders' most prudent nemesis was made by Danny and Carlton, who both cited the similar aspirations between Nicholas and a local crew of thugs, known as the Defenders.

Brogan and the Defenders, who were the muscle behind the slaying of the Rough Riders' third crew leader, Yves Lafleur, reached a mutual agreement that saw Nicholas expand his business and work force, by supplying allies who shared their exact cause. The Defenders was made up of a territory of friends from the West Island, who chose to dominate the drug trade throughout their communities, despite the city-wide unwritten law that prohibited anyone but Rough Riders from distributing. There were business arrangements possible with the bikers, who offered members of certain communities the chance to retail to addicts in their neighborhood, but they would have to purchase their products from the Rough Riders. The biker crew took notice of the merger between their enemies, who they still viewed as insignificant, even though both groups had demonstrated a convincing resistance. The years since have, however, strengthened all facets of the merger between Nicholas and the Defenders, although the number of members still slightly favored the Rough Riders.

Martain possessed the power and respect desired by many throughout the city of Montreal, with a status almost celebrity-like. The bad boy of Quebec appeared in several local magazines, which found the flare and danger surrounding the gang boss intriguing. With a popularity rating only overshadowed by that of the Prime Minister's, it was said the underground boss controlled more than simple thugs, since they attributed numerous public assistance employees to the payroll.

The loss at the warehouse was Martain's most significant of the campaign thus far, yet the biker boss was determined to avoid being portrayed by historians, as 'the Rough Rider boss who brought their demise'. Both sides had surrendered many fighters through the years of conflict, but none of the generals ever contemplated throwing in the towel. Their intense battles, which often left deceased bodies across pavements, became a huge influence to some young Canadians, who idolized the gangsters they would hear stories about. Young entrepreneurs who would prefer hustling for themselves, sided with Nicholas and the Defenders, who would provide whatever products they desired through their distribution services across the city.

With the destruction of his warehouse, Martain lost over ten million dollars in illegal narcotics. To recoup some of his losses, the biker boss contacted some public servant employees, who were member of the police bureau, in addition to being private honorary bikers. Martain wanted the officers to raid a few of Nicholas' drug bases and, seized for the biker club whatever narcotics was available. The 25th Police Precinct, which was considered Martain's house by attorneys, administered the most illegal drug raids throughout the downtown core, wherein the substances recovered was seldomly turned in as evidence.

Officers from the 25th Precinct, had sanctioned many criminals in order to confiscate their valuables, and regularly got away with the practice. Even if the victims of these officers realized their rights had been violated, most of the times they would get caught with some form of weapon, which negated their arguments. Many of the workforces at the station were French Quebecois, who were born and bred in Montreal. These officers were childhood friends, schoolmates, church mates, neighbors, summer campers, sports combatants, teammates, and acquaintances, of Martain and the members of his Rough Rider brotherhood. One of the biker crew's annual events was a ride-a-thon that raised money for sick kids at the Children's Hospital, where police officers would join them for a Harley Davidson ride across sections of the town. Through events as such, the bikers kept a good repour with law enforcement officers, who saw them more as compassionate Montrealer's, rather than the monsters they were.

Station 25 was located in Centre Ville, where the junkies, drunks, and prostitutes flocked; the main artery of the city with exhibitionists such as peep shows and stripper bars, while the thieves and hustlers schemed for the almighty dollar. Therefore, information on anything or anyone was always either a bribe or a toke away. Two police cruisers and a patty wagon pulled up in front the La Matador building, on the corner of Peel Street and Du Maisonneuve Boulevard, slightly after dusk. The officers all stormed the building on the credibility of information they received, which implied that Nicholas housed a drug base, on the fifteenth floor of the twenty-story building. The drug base was a private restocking plant for the small-scale independent hustlers, who sold their products along street corners and alleyways throughout the downtown sector.

The security system to the building provided residents the opportunity to scan visitors from the lobby area, before granting anyone access into the building. Apart from the building's security system, Nicholas provided his employees with a steel door that matched the mandatory design of the others on the floor, which was almost impenetrable once residents anchored the steel beam behind it into the floor. The three youngsters on duty that evening fucked up and totally disobeyed the security protocol, when instead of watching the building monitors on the TV, they were busy battling each other on their X-Box Def Jam video game. The worker who completed the last transaction, neglected to reconnect the crossbar that gave the door its immovable backing and, only secured the deadbolt.

The door to apartment #1525 got blown off its hinges, by a group of police conducting a search and seizure without a valid warrant. Seven armed representatives of the law stormed into the apartment waving their high-powered weapons and, barking orders for those inside to "get the fuck on the floor," while stumping residents to the concrete. The pressure applied by police since the destruction of Martain's warehouse had been unyielding, with instructions to intensify their vigilance.

Apartment #1525 was a single-bedroom bachelor suite with a bathroom, kitchen, and everything included. The apartment provided a spectacular view of the surrounding downtown area, which wowed viewers watching from the balcony at night. Nicholas had supplementary spots around town through which he dealt his poison in the French-speaking province, yet none as progressive as that of the La Matador base. One of the three workers inside the apartment that evening had only recently been released from lockup, after being detained for possession of an illegal substance three days prior. The young worker was a twenty-one-year-old felon named Ninja, who had only recently received his second consecutive strike according to the courts of Canada. The knowledge of his lengthy criminal record, along with his recent stroke of misfortune, gave the young thug a catastrophic view of his situation, once the officers stormed the apartment. The urge to escape saw the young thug race to the balcony, where he sought refuge from his tormentors by fleeing the scene. Ninja scaled the protective barrier that encased the balcony, and with the confidence and fierce belief in the agility given him by naming him Ninja, attempted to leap to a neighboring balcony.

The two Caribbean employees who worked with Ninja, later told separate stories about what transpired on the balcony, although neither of them was able to clearly watch the incident unfold. According to one of the workers, Ninja ran out on the balcony and wanted to leap across onto the neighboring balcony. Three officers rushed after him and, he karate kicked the first officer, who almost went over the ledge. Both balconies were eight feet apart, so a substantial lift had to be attained to clear the jump. The worker sighted that Ninja's feet slipped from atop the concrete barrier, while he attempted to balance himself before jumping. The drug dealer told his peers, that the ledge of the barrier was damped from the heavy rains, which fell earlier that day and claimed the incident was an accident.

The drug dealer's partner described a different account, where he claimed that Ninja was pushed off the ledge by one of the intruding officers. The young man stated that one, Officer Stephan Riviera, threatened to kill Ninja the next time he caught him. Officer Riviera was one of the arresting officers who brought Ninja in only days before, but the two were well known to each other.

"Yow, mi watch the whole thing brethren; and is the police boy name Riviera, Ninja did a run from when him ran out on the balcony! But Riviera partner try grab Ninja, and get a rass-clatt karate kick, nearly send him over the railing! That's when the boy, Officer Stephan Riviera push Ninja off the ledge," stated the worker!

The blasphemous pressure applied by the treacherous officers forced one worker over the balcony and left his associates terrified, not knowing whether that would be their demise also. All the squad members wore black masks to conceal their identities, until they had gained control over the situation. With little time to waste, the invading officers began interrogating the workers on the whereabouts of the products, they were convinced had been safely stored away. While two of the intruders questioned the handcuffed workers, their mates tore the entire apartment apart, as they searched everywhere for the products. Ninja's body fell to the rear of the building and landed inside a construction waste container, under the shadows of the gloomy Montreal's night sky. The officers weren't exactly sure if anyone had witnessed the fall, nevertheless, they carried additional disposable firearms to plant as evidence if necessary. The workers attempted to play hardball, not wanting to surrender the drug paraphernalia or currency retrieved from sales, which would defiantly stiffen their punishment whenever they appeared before a judge.

Before long, the police were threatening to throw both workers into the dumpster along with their friend, should they have continued refusing to corporate. The use of excessive force, which was customarily Montreal officers' forte for retrieving information, was withheld following Ninja's tragic accident, in addition to them not having a viable search warrant.

When the officers realized they weren't getting anywhere, they began bargaining with the workers and 'offered their freedom in exchange for the goods and money'. Considering the circumstances, both workers agreed and surrendered the money and illegal drugs, which the invading officers came for. The officers collected the products and quickly exited the apartment, in hopes that their presence in the building and the unlawful activities that occurred, would never be linked to them.

Even though they were successful, some of the officers were not pleased with how the situation unfolded and, wanted to kill the remaining workers. The mediocre celebration of their success was delayed until the officers returned to their vehicles, where they properly inspected the volume of the products seized. They had managed to steal a large amount of cocaine and pills, therefore they high fived each other, on a job well done. Halfway to their next scheduled appointment, the emergency dispatcher began alerting emergency personnel of the "possible suicide". A resident of the building, who went out on her balcony to smoke a cigarette, noticed the body inside the container and phoned the police. While listening to the alarm being raised by the dispatcher, the comrades in arms laughed feverishly, as they mimicked the outcries and survival attempting effort with which Ninja toppled to his death.

***

Words of precaution were given to fellow dealers around the area, by the two hustlers from the La Matador building who were spared. Mad Max was among the first to receive word of the officers' treachery, yet he stubbornly remained the only Alliance dealer who continued conducting usual business. Without the first-class novelties as those provided by quality lodgments such as La Matador, Mad Max began concealing the drugs and money where it was impossible to find, knowing the lack of security at the dump in which he resided. There were two entrance doors into the building and, the inner door had a standard-sized metal frame, which was without the center glass that had been broken out by vandals. The walls along the corridors had strips of wallpaper hanging to the floor, with nearly every other lightbulb blown throughout the building. The 'out of order' elevator had become the primary domain of roaches and insects, and drug addicts were often found strung out in various sections of the six-story building. The superintendent tasked with the maintenance duties, did very little work and instead withered away in liquor and desolation.

Mad Max had been harassed by the blue and white squad numerous times throughout the years and had grown familiar with police policies and procedures. Each time the officers raided his residence, they would assault him and destroyed his belongings to find the drugs. However, news of Ninja's death agonized the usually mild-tempered Rastafarian, who had a very close bond with the deceased hustler. After hiding the materials being sought by the crooked officers, Mad Max uncharacteristically armed himself with his Desert Eagle firearm and waited, in case his drug base was their next target. During their last encounter, the coppers belittled Mad Max when they escorted him from his building wearing only his Sponge Bob brief, hence, coupled with Ninja's death, the hustler decided to take a definitive stance.

The local protectors of the Montreal streets arrived, as advertised, with zero tolerance for Mad Max's temperament. Both sides had prior experiences dealing with each other, so the officers knew the volatile personality they were up against. The position of the hustler's door, which was directly towards the end of the hallway, made it impossible for anyone to approach the base without be seeing. Once the squeaky stairway door or the ding of the elevator door sounded, Max watched through his peephole as the officers moved towards his apartment. None of the officers trusted the dweller, so they positioned themselves on both sides of the door. Once they were prepared, one of the officers knocked and demanded entry, under the pretense that they had a warrant to search the premises.

With tears in his eyes after considering what an eyewitness told him about Ninja's death, Mad Max demanded the officers slide the warrant underneath the door, so that he could fully inspect its authenticity before allowing them entry. There were seven officers aligning the hallway in their tactical riot gear, with guns drawn for precautionary measures, yet only three were positioned closest to the peephole. Mad Max maintained a close watch on his antagonists through the peephole, while he maneuvered his weapon to where he calculated someone being.

"Before I open this door, you boys slide that paper underneath, so I can make sure that warrant legal!"

"Open the fucking door or I'm gonna staple this fucking warrant to your forehead when we get in there," The officer holding the fake warrant threatened!

"Man, y'all don't have any warrant to search my shit! Whenever you bitches come here with one, ain't never no knocking on my shit. The door would a been on the floor by now, motherfucker," Mad Max declared!

"Well, I'm giving you 'til the count of three, before I do kick this shit in," the officer advised!

Mad Max peeked through the peephole at the officers, who were becoming agitated by the dealer's disrespect. Thoughts of the tumble suffered by his friend Ninja, had the hustler procrastinating whether or not to empty the magazine of his Desert Eagle pistol through the wooden door. The tension between Nicholas' Rough Riders, the Defenders, and law officials had escalated over the years, to a point where the trust between ordinary civilians and police had grown frail. Infractions that were once dangerous, yet negotiable, had advanced to catastrophic events that worried the minority group leaders, who sought measures to reunify all parties. Mad Max had himself endured the discriminative pressures of the local police, who brought him along their scenic route one night, before bringing him in for processing. Officers of the twenty-fifth precinct were highly praised for getting suspected offenders to confess in detail their crimes, way before the investigating detective got the opportunity to interrogate. Local criminals, from whom officers sought information, were brought along to the abandoned warehouses and desolate sections of the Old Port, where officers would duct tape thick phone books to their bodies, before clubbing the daylights out of them with their police batons. Hence, false testimonies were given, and disproven confessions signed, by many innocent youths to whom the justice system showed absolutely no remorse.

"You know something? I wish one a you fuckers accidentally do kick in my front door," threatened Mad Max, after noticing the officers were only armed with their 9mm service weapons.

An officer along the hallway thought of using the art of persuasion to convince Mad Max to open the door, by surprising him with a huge bang that would normally frighten the typical resident into opening. With the back of his boot, the young genius kicked the door and disobeyed the dealer's order.

Bullets immediately began raining! The first huge bang saw a veteran in the force drop his firearm and grabbed for his shoulder, as the bullet tore through the strap of his vest and hit his collarbone. The officer fell into shock and began hysterically racing for the exit, once he realized he could not handle his weapon and would possibly be a hazard to his teammates. His remaining unit began their roars of discontentment, as they opened fire through and around the door frame of Mad Max's apartment. The thug on the other end of the barrier was forced to retreat behind his kitchen counter, as bullets slammed into and through the articles inside his apartment.

The officers became tactical in their approach, as they quickly kicked in the door in order to properly identify their target. The dread locks man flew into action, once the front door got kicked in, by first hammering two shells through the doorframe at thin air. One of the bullets fired by Mad Max as he attempted to change his position, blindly struck the left arm of an officer who was peeking into the room. The loud groan by the officer was the thug's first indication that his bullets had contacted skin, and he raced into his bedroom while reloading his pistol. The rumblings like those of thunder roared once more, as the invading forces transformed everything inside the apartment into marshmallow. Had Mad Max not abandoned his place of refuge behind the counter, the onslaught delivered by the forthcoming officers would have surely sealed his fate.

"Mad Max was a psychopath," would be what anyone who'd ever met the man would tell you. Most people considered his hospitalization at the Douglas Mental Institute, where he underwent treatment after confessing to interactions with spirit mediums, as the evidence necessary to cast judgment of his insanity, while others believed he should be incarcerated and removed from civilized society. Whatever possessed Mad Max blessed him with balls the size of Hayden mangos, as he shoved the Desert Eagle pistol into his waistband and muscled the mattress from atop the box-spring. Laying on the box spring was an AK-47 automatic assault rifle, which he grabbed and aimed directly through the bedroom door.

The Rastafarian cranked back the selector of his AK rifle and let bullets fly, as officers were forced to hit the turf or find protective measures. Valiant men who perish defending stupid causes aren't looked upon as heroes, especially after being persecuted by the defenders of the law. Regardless the consequence, Mad Max valiantly charged at the police, who were busy scattering for cover and, peppered them with what seemed like a never-ending arsenal assault, made possible by the extra-long banana clip attached to his weapon.

The summoning of the entire cavalry could be heard transmitting through officers' radios, as the emergency dispatcher convectively alerted others, "Shots fired, shots fired—all available units are instructed to proceed to the 1200 block of Rue Dandurand! Kindly approach with caution!" The dispatcher also summoned ambulances to the scene, after receiving reports of injured officers awaiting medical attention. Within minutes of the call, an astounding twelve cruisers had surrounded the building, and, with reckless abandonment, officers raced into the war zone.

At the center of the controversy was Mad Max standing firm, with his disorderly dog barking while cowering from the brave attempts of the Montreal Police. The officers along the hallway knew their allies were under serious duress, as the only weapon sounding for what seemed like an eternity was that of the assailant. Thus, in order to award their comrades assistance to respond, a few of Montreal's finest kept themselves hidden behind the door column, while they fired in the direction from which the AK-47 sounded.

There were three officers inside the apartment clinging to whatever piece of furniture awarded them protection, as their mentally ill host spat countless gunshots at them. The AK-47 eventually made a loud click, which indicated the magazine had run empty. The officers who were placed in precarious positions, hesitated after the momentary shock, yet seized their opportunity to regain full advantage of the situation. Mad Max was caught attempting to reload his weapon, and two of the three officers inside the room shot him at pivotal points of the body, killing him instantly.

At 3:30 that morning, three members of the Defender crew exited the Pussy Katz Strippers nightclub on Gouin Boulevard in Côte-Vertu, after the birthday celebrations of one of the posse's members. The men laughed and joked with each other as they gossiped about the lusciously females who took their money, while offering them whatever it was they spoke of. Although they behaved like children at an amusement park, the men were cautious in their actions, knowing the terrible inner-city gang warfare their squad was involved with.

The three friends were twenty-six-year-old Jacques Carter of Montreal, twenty-seven-year-old Trevor Balan of Montreal, who was the person celebrating his birthday, and twenty-six-year-old Al Miner of Rigeau, Quebec. The Pussy Katz nightclub was a favorite hangout spot for members of the street gang, who customarily spent a large amount of money on liquor, not to mention the exquisitely shaped women who paraded their sexiness around the club. The birthday boy was properly serenaded by several big booty women, who dragged him on stage and stripped his down to his undies, before proceeding with the festivities planned. Trevor was teased and molested by five women of Caucasian, Asian, and African descent, who performed borderline sexual antics that came close to violating the club's policies. Mr. Balan exited the nightclub a few hours later with a distinctive erection, after having naked women grind on him, while others rubbed their pussies in his face, however, none of their actions involved the actual intercourse session.

The Ford Explorer they drove was in the parking lot, with very few other vehicles around considering the late hour. As the men approached the vehicle, Al, who was anointed the designated driver and the least intoxicated of the bunch, removed his Glock pistol from his waistband, before hopping into the truck. There was a police cruiser travelling south on Côte-Vertu Boulevard, with two officers who yielded, before they continued on their merry way. The gangbangers paid no attention to the local protectors, considering the opposite directions in which the vehicles were travelling. With their hip-hop music blasting, the gangsters cruised west along Gouin Boulevard, en-route to lightening the load inside the vehicle around the surrounding West Island areas.

The police cruiser that drove by the thugs earlier reappeared behind the Ford Explorer at Sources Boulevard and Gouin, before the sirens directed them to pull to the side of the road. Officers Pierce Sauvé and Dwayne Campbell used their vast knowledge of the city to intercept the suspected criminals, who had by no means associated the cruiser on their bumper, with that of the vehicle noticed prior. Al advised his comrades, who'd begun mellowing out from the marijuana joint being passed around, of their immediate dilemma, although both men were too nauseated to give a fuck. In order to defuse the hostilities that would have certainly transpired, Al insisted Trevor assemble all weapons and secure them in the stash compartments.

"Yow, you guys good," Al demanded before stopping the vehicle?

"Yeah, man. What the fuck these fools want now," Jacques replied, sprawled out all over the back seat?

Both Metropolitan officers exited their vehicle and approached the Explorer from separate sides. The officers had removed the strap securing their weapons inside their harnesses, prior to exiting their vehicle and, maintained a hold of their weapons as they approached. Trevor peeked through the passenger-side mirror at the officer making his way toward the truck and developed an uneasy sense from his approach.

"Yow, guys, these cops up to something," Trevor exclaimed!

The officer on the driver's side tapped on the tinted glass with his flashlight and demanded the driver lower the window. Trevor's attention, which was momentarily stolen by the tap on the glass, was focused on the officer who came along the passenger-side, after the officer shone his light directly in the thug's face. The same officer proceeded to motion Trevor to also lower his window, in order to harass the passenger.

"License and registration, please," Officer Campbell demanded of the driver?

"Why you guys pull us over, man," Al asked while handing the officer his documents?

"Have you boys been drinking tonight, Mr. Miner," Officer Campbell demanded, while looking over the documents?

The officer at the passenger door asked, "How many of you guys are packed in here?"

"Three of us, man," Trevor exclaimed!

"How about you? You got any identification," The same officer spun his flashlight at Jacques in the rear seat? The officers, who hadn't noticed any infractions thus far, were elated to see Jacques sprawled out across the rear seat with no seat belt protection.

"Sir, are you aware that not wearing a seat belt is punishable by a fine or jail time?"

"How much alcohol have you consumed tonight, Mr. Miner," Officer Campbell questioned?

"Probably three or four Heinekens," Al answered.

The officers glanced at each other, before demanding the occupants of the vehicle exit their vehicle. It was evident by their tone of voice that their already disgusted attitudes had tightened, and they drew their weapons and removed all occupants from the vehicle. The officers had the men laid out in the street with their hands clasped behind their heads, as they proceeded to search the vehicle. At first, the officers neglected to mention their beliefs, which alluded to the thought that they believed weapons were hidden inside the truck. Following their unproductive preliminary search, the officers returned to their detainees for further questioning.

"Yow, guy, if you trying to get me for a DUI, where's the fucking breathalyzer test," Al asked as the officers ripped through the Explorer?

"Listen to me carefully now. I know you boys got a weapon hidden somewhere inside that truck. It would save us a lot of time if you just tell me where to find it," said Officer Sauvé?

"What the fuck are you talking about, man? What gun? Ain't nobody got any guns around here, but you boys," Jacques answered!

Officer Sauvé casually walked up behind Jacques and stepped directly into the man's groin area. "Is this where you got the fucking gun hidden?" His detainee groaned from the painful infliction.

The streets were barren at said hour of the morning, with motorists seldom passing by. Without a weapon found to administer a proper charge, all detainees would have to be released with only a mediocre ticket, for non-compliance of the seatbelt regulation. The officers were determined to land a case against the three men they felt were guilty, even though they had yet to establish physical evidence. Officer Campbell marched over to Al, kneeled down directly in the center of his back, and jammed his assigned 9mm pistol in the back of his head.

"Yow, this is police brutality, man! What kind a shit is this," Trevor yelled, after witnessing his friends being roughed up?

"Shut the fuck up before I come over there and give you some of the same! Now, you're going to tell me what you did with that gun I saw you pull from your waist before getting into the truck," threatened Officer Campbell?

"I don't know what you're talking about, man! I took my keys from out of my pocket! That's all," Al exclaimed!

"You got five seconds to tell me where that gun is, or I'm going blow your head off and then go find it," Officer Campbell stated!

Trevor listened to Officer Campbell count down from five, before cocking the hammer back on his 9mm, at three. By the time the officer uttered the number two, Trevor who believed his friend was about to be murdered, tackled the officer and knocked him to the ground, before proceeding to land a few punches to the officer's face. Officer Campbell's partner caught sight of the rebellion against his partner and fired two rounds at the mutineer. The overpowered officer pranced to his feet and dusted himself off, as he walked over and retrieved his weapon, which had been knocked away.

Al went berserk after witnessing his friend's murder on his very birthday and, attacked the officer who fired both fatal shots. Officer Campbell had retrieved his weapon by then and blasted brain matter from the attacking man's skull, killing him before he had the chance to harm his partner. The sight of both his friends' corpses brought instant tears to Jacques' eyes, therefore, he remained frozen to the ground, so as not to frustrate his antagonists. The lights went out instantly for Jacques, as both officers realized the serious implications one high witness could make. Officer Sauvé removed his backup weapon from the holster around his ankle, placed it in Al's palm, and fired two shots at their previous position, before they radioed in the call to headquarters.

Part 17

Elected candidate Minister Richard Blanc visited the twenty-fifth police precinct the morning following a rallying of minority leaders, who called for investigations into the recent killings of citizens, who the police alleged were criminals. Minister Blanc was at the helm of the Française Quebecois Party, which was a French-legislated electoral party lobbying for the job to become the premier of the province Quebec. Candidate Blanc was on the verge of touring the province of Quebec, while campaigning heavily to sway voters' confidence, before the upcoming elections. The Française Quebecois Party had existed and operated for over a half a century and, inaugurated two grand representatives to the premier's office throughout its tenure.

News of the aspiring premier's visit brought an array of reporters to the precinct, which had already been placed underneath the microscope from recent events. Chief Arnold Dubois had the briefing room prepared with a podium, in order for the minister to deliver his message, as well as an open question period for journalists. The unofficial poll regarding candidates' favorability among the voters, had Minister Joseph McArthur of the Liberal Party in fourth place with a meagre 6% voters' average. Minister Blanc was in third place with 19.7% behind the reigning elected mayor, Sir Gerald Lavoie of the Party Quebecois, who held a mere two-point margin over David McNeil of the People of Quebec National Party.

Minister Richard Blanc entered the conference room to a huge serenade from well-wishers and admirers, who vowed to support the candidate during the upcoming elections. Chief Arnold Dubois and several well-decorated commanders of the police force, who relished the opportunity to display their stripes and medals, escorted the minister to the podium. Freelance photographers and news reporters seized the moment to capture as many photographs as possible, for that one definite front-page photo that summed up the minister's entire visit. As the aspiring premier shook hands and thanked everyone in attendance on his way to the podium, skeptical voters awaited his vision for creating more jobs and cleansing the city of the turmoil that lurked within.

The dust soon settled, as everyone who cheered for the premier candidate took to his or her assigned seat. A pin drop could have echoed throughout the room, before Sergeant Elgin began the festivities, by first introducing the entire panel on stage. Chief Arnold Dubois soon took to center stage and immediately proceeded to announce the guest speaker, rather than tangle with the blood-seeking reporters, who pranced on issues of police brutality throughout the city.

"Ladies and Gentlemen, Mesdames et Messieurs, presenting the next premier of our lovely province, his Honorable Minister Richard Blanc!"

The audience of eighty-nine applauded for another two minutes, before finally coming to terms with the fact that the guest speaker needed silence to speak. The honored guest speaker stepped to the collection of microphones, which belonged to the different news agencies in attendance. An impatient reporter for the Gazette pounced on the topic regarding recent altercations between police and criminals, where public outcries were against excessive force administered by law officials. Minister Blanc waved off the reporter and her question, by simply swiping his hand over the stilled microphones, and thus, denounced her attempts to convene the question-and-answer period.

"My fellow Quebecois, it's time for a change! When I pick up my newspaper in the morning and it reads, "man pops off at cops", and then I read on to discover that this maniac, had an assault weapon, which he used to injure our assigned protectors, I say it's time for a change! We're currently being governed by a premier, who spends more time in the winter skiing, and more time in the summer hiking mountains, than he does representing the people's best interest. I think our premier's love for mountains should empower him to simply become a hermit! After all, we hardly see him, anyway, so he's practically one already!"

The supporters and police staff in attendance all broke into laughter as Minister Blanc took his first cheap shot at the absent premier.

"Instead of standing alongside our officers today with his support and respect for the valiant job these people do to ensure our safety, Premier Lavoie is having tea with the Guatemalan President. While our streets become infested with the filth that our police force gets scrutinized for battling, your honored premier finds time for a vacation. I'm here, ladies and gentlemen, to offer my continued support to our fine law enforcement officers, who go out and tangle with these thugs, rapists, and murderers, who believe themselves above the law, on a daily basis! The city I once knew and proudly grew up in has changed! Our officers had to change with the times, in order to combat these criminals. Come Election Day, you have to show the rest of Canada, that you also will change, and that begins with a new premier of the modern-day era, who knows exactly what Montrealers and Quebecers need!"

The small crowd rose to their feet and applauded the sentiments of the campaigning minister. Minister Blanc addressed the issues with health care around the province, problems and suggestions for strengthening the schools, ideas for securing new jobs for the people of Quebec, and his personal vision for Quebec's future. Monsieur Blanc harnessed the affluent officers, by suggesting they made their methods of crime fighting stricter and, vowed his continued support toward the work they did. Minister Richard Blanc abstained from the persisting argument about "segregation", which was a mandate supported by a great number of Quebecers and, chose instead to conclude his speech by vowing to reduce taxes and jobless rates around the province, once elected.

"Minister Blanc, sir, how did you manage to acquire the services and support of Joseph McArthur of the Liberals, and when is the grand celebration for the merger scheduled," Sandy Walters of the CTV News reporters asked?

The minister replied, "What did you just say?"

Jim Clarity finally closed his eyes at 1:28 AM, after a trifling day of hard work. The chief handler for Minister Joseph McArthur lived the life of a bachelor, who moonlighted with the classiest of women, while he reserved the pillows on his bed, for the undercover men in his life. The former University of McGill student graduated with top honors in his class and continued on to an exceptional career in politics. His bachelor's degree and tainted lifestyle brought him to the steps of an overachieving visionary, who had become the voice and power behind gay activists across Canada. At 4:36 AM, Jim was awoken by two men seated at the foot of his bed, who had sneaked in without raising his security alarm. The two Caucasian males wore steel-toed boots and blue denim jeans, with leather vests adorning their gang insignias, over plain white T-shirts.

One of the two humongous males said, "We really ain't here to hurt you, but give us a reason and you'll truly end up sorry!"

"What is it you gentlemen want," Jim asked?

"We're just here to show you a movie, that's it," said the same individual.

The other male rose from the foot of the bed, shoved his automatic weapon into his waistband, and removed a DVD disc from his inner vest pocket. The man walked over to the DVD player and placed the disc inside the machine, before snatching the remote from atop the dresser on his way back to the bed. Both men behaved as if they were quite at home, as they made themselves comfortable alongside the nerve-shot assistant.

The man with the remote joked, "No popcorn?"

The other exclaimed, "Just play the fucking movie, you idiot!"

The DVD began with a female expressing her sorrow for something she truly did not wish to do, though she had absolutely no choice in the matter. The lady on the disc was a former adultery partner to the man Jim Clarity idolized and praised, while anointing him to the highest pedestal. The female wept as she proceeded to threaten the minister, instructing him of her intent to take their affair public, should he continue lobbying for the post of premier. The female spoke of occasions where she was forced to perform sexual favors, despite her constant refusal to participate. There was a number of photos depicting both parties, followed by a live sex session between the minister and his mistress.

The minister's assistant argued, "Where did you get this disc? It's not possible! She's lying! She must be lying!"

The man with the remote declared, "The man's got his dick all the way up her asshole and you're arguing it's not authentic?"

Jim Clarity took a moment to gather himself, as the disappointing thoughts surrounding the mortal man, he represented soaked in. Both intruders had mellowed into the graphic scenes transmitting through the television, while their host shied away in disgust and chose not to continue watching. Despite the homeowner's objections, the Rough Riders gang members, as was evident by the patches on their vests, chose to watch the DVD in its entirety, before finalizing their visit.

"Now, before you start throwing a kiddie's tantrum, listen! You're going to instruct your boss to concede like the lady said, but, bring those votes of his over to the French Quebec Party. The good minister has until tomorrow at noon, before our lovely Isabella Coy makes that all-important call to the press. Be sure to advise your boss that he'll be more than welcomed in the nest of the new Quebec premier; and as long as his support remains loyal, that Miss Coy remains invisible! That's your boss' personal copy of his freak show; I don't need to advise you that copies are easily dispersed. Besides, the liberals alongside the French Quebecers, are guaranteed to win! You think about it," suggested the gangster closest to Jim.

Jim Clarity telephoned his boss' chauffeur and security detail and advised them to pick up their employer within the hour. The personal assistant then telephoned Mr. McArthur, but spoke with his wife who answered, and asked that 'she awakened him for an urgent unscheduled meeting'. The aspiring premier was awakened by his wife at 4:45 AM, after only closing his eyes for a meagre three and one-quarter hours. Mr. McArthur's wife handed him the phone with Jim, who advised him that his chauffeur and security detail were en-route to his home, as they'd entered a crucial phase of their campaign. Jim Clarity promised to debrief his boss in the privacy of their office, rather than have the minister endure the embarrassment at home around his wife.

The minister's bodyguard and chauffeur were surprised to arrive and find their client waiting at the front door. Before the chauffeur could exit the driver's cabin, to greet and open the door for his client, Mr. McArthur had entered and slammed the door himself. The fury and impatience demonstrated by Joseph McArthur was never witnessed by his personal detail, who had been in the aspiring premier's employ for more than four years. Monsieur McArthur travelled with the divider closed all the way to the office and refrained from uttering a word during the trip, which was unlike him. Once they'd arrived at the Liberals' Headquarters, Joseph stormed from the vehicle without his bodyguard's assistance and ran into the office.

Jim Clarity had everything prepared for his boss, who knew to expect the worst before arriving. The assistant assembled everything inside his boss' office and simply handed the minister the remote, before exiting the office. Mr. Clarity exited the office to find Matt the bodyguard pouring a cup of coffee, therefore he decided to join him during their final moments of peace. The coffee was hot and fresh, so Jim went over and fixed himself a cup, eased Matt's concerns about the minister ignoring him, and took three sips from the Styrofoam cup.

Suddenly a huge crash sounded inside the minister's office. Matt, as expected, went charging into the office to ensure his client's safety, while Jim continued nonchalantly sipping his cup of coffee. The bodyguard drew his weapon and busted through the door, to find that his boss had thrown a metallic ornament from his desk through the television screen, after watching an obviously bothersome program. The minister flung the remote across the room and smashed it against the wall, as he swore continuously, while ripping pamphlets of himself to shreds and littered the entire office.

"Are you okay, Mr. McArthur?"

"That fucking bitch! God damn it, let that fucking bitch die a horrible death! You fucking bitch! You bitch! You bitch! I could fucking strangle that bitch," the minister screamed!

Matt quickly closed the door behind himself and exited the office, once he realized the minister was throwing a tantrum. Monsieur McArthur stumped over to the DVD player, yanked it from the wall, and sent it sailing through a window. Once the minister realized he had tossed damaging evidence of himself through the window, Joseph ran out in search of the broken DVD player, to retrieve the disc.

The minister surprisingly returned with a different attitude and, the shattered DVD player underneath his arm, while his bodyguard, who never allowed him room to breathe, pursued. Minister McArthur threw the dismantled DVD machine on his secretary's desk and, instructed his bodyguard 'to remove the disc then give it only to him', before he signaled his assistant to follow him into his office.

"Okay, so which of my cock-sucking opponent's dicks do I have to suck to keep this bitch and this shit quiet," Joseph demanded?

"It looks like the French Quebecers, sir," replied the assistant.

"Of course! No one else has the power to scare Isabella into stooping to such immoral levels. And to think that bitch used to have class!... How long before she goes public? I mean, how much time do I have?"

The intellectual minister understood the railroad business side of politics and, had thought about what if his extra marital affair got out into the public. His sexual relationship at home wasn't anything in comparison to the freaky interactions he had with his side chick, therefore it had been difficult for him to terminate the affair.

"They said tomorrow at noon, sir."

"I expected that! Go for the kill when you got the shot," mumbled the minister.

Montreal's Liberal Party was the chief advocate for gay and lesbian rights across the province. The political party had been at the forefront of environmental issues, prompting major development and changes in many manufacturers across the country. The group supported marriages between the sexes and were the legislators of the act provided to Congress, mandating a law allowing gays to wed. The Honorable Sir Joseph McArthur III had been at the helm of the political party for over eight years and, have failed to win the provincial election three times.

The campaign trail for Chief Minister McArthur had him scheduled to participate in a number of fire drills, with the city's 27th district fire station in the Notre-Dame-De-Grace area, at 7:00 that morning. There were several internal primary components who contributed to the development and structure of the Liberal Political Party, who Joseph instructed his assistant to debrief in part, before his defection to the Devil's Court. To avoid an unimaginable fiasco that would guarantee his surrender of the provincial race, his removal from his current position at the helm of the Liberal Party, and possible divorce filings from his wife, who was slated to inherit millions from her ailing father, Minister McArthur took to his only possible solution. The notion that Minister Blanc plotted such a devious scheme infringed Joseph, who refrained from telephoning their new associates with the minister's decision. The aspiring premier chose instead to deliver his response during his message to the reporters and supporters, expected to cheer him on during his workout with the local firefighters.

An anonymous caller telephoned Montreal's largest news provider, the Gazette, at 6:42 AM and leaked information of the minister's intent to join forces with a group, which proclaimed themselves the healers of Quebec. Suspense and intrigue brought the entire news kingdom to the twenty-seventh district fire station, where liberal voters had camped out awaiting glorified moments to incite their support for the candidate, they envisioned becoming Quebec's premier.

Minister McArthur arrived at his scheduled appointment to an overwhelming crowd of supporters, who acted eager to catch a glimpse of or shake the hand of their commander and general. McArthur refused to comment on allegations being raised by reporters who stormed his transport, demanding his intent to merge with one of his party's three political nemeses. The professional lobbying for premier shook hands of supporters and neglected those determined to disrupt the cohesive ambiance between voters and their minister.

The training exercises between the brave men who placed their lives on the line daily to rescue victims and property from disaster, and the campaigning minister took place at the Fireman's Developmental Facility, located directly behind their twenty-seventh district fire station. Observers on hand believed their minister performed well throughout the event, which saw Joseph compete in fire hose carrying techniques, extinguishing fires, Jaws of Life rescue from a vehicle collision, and proper use of the breathing apparatus. An exuberant Joseph appeared ten years younger throughout the training regiment, as he laughed and joked with ordinary firefighters, who vowed to support his campaign.

Correspondence with the media was the candidate's main reason for accepting the challenge, therefore, Minister McArthur paused for questions after he had completed the exhibition workout with life's true heroes. With everyone vying to hear his decision, the politician thought gravely about his family and the seriousness of the situation. The question of the hour was answered by Joseph, who abstained from additional comments related to the issue of his political future. "My childhood dream was to one day become a fireman or the leader of this country. Thanks to wonderful friends like Colonel Dubury here, I've gotten the opportunity to see what it really feels like to be in one of those furnaces, rescuing trapped people and sometimes their pets. With the help of wonderful friends, I was able to live out one of my childhood dreams, and I am happy to inform you that come next election, with the assistance of Minister Blanc and the Française Quebecois Party, we will live out my second fantasy as rulers of the province!"

Part 18

The southern townships of Quebec such as Shawville, Aylmer, and the Gatineau areas across to Papineau, were territories that reported the most volatile acts against humanity, during a campaign dubbed by Rough Riders as, "the persuasion tour." The diverse scheme, intended to capture the voting interest of key activists against the Française Quebecois Party and, was handed to the gang leader with a "whatever required" directive. Members of the most dominant gang across Canada made house calls to neighborhood leaders, business owners, and clergymen, who were believed to carry a trusted voice among the voters of their communities.

In Hull, Quebec, eleven-year-old Adrian Lavoie awoke late for school and headed directly to the bathroom. While peeing, the thought of his mother awarding him additional time beneath the covers seemed abnormal to Adrian, who had always been taught to be assertive and prompt. The silence around the remainder of the house was unusual for a moderate day, where his parents always rushed him off to school, before tending to their own ambitions. Adrian flushed the toilet on the third tier of their house and ignored washing his hands or face, then walked down the hall toward his parents' domain. The young lad became frozen with fear, as he entered his parents' bedroom to find both parents hacked to death. The dismantled body parts around the room, along with the color of red blood splashed against the walls, hypnotized the young lad, who remained frozen for a few minutes. Although Adrian had never seen a corpse, the likelihood of anyone reviving without an attached head seemed farfetched, as much as he would like to have his parents back. With both eyes filled with tears, Adrian slowly walked back to his bedroom, from where he placed the critical phone call to emergency personnel.

At 1:29 that morning, Adriana Lavoie repositioned herself from the arches of her back to a kneeling position, while her husband maneuvered himself to enter from the rear. The lovers' sexual intimacy began with the stimulation efforts of Andrew Lavoie's tongue, fluttering across his beautiful wife's body, as she sucked and jerked his penis, while grinding on his mischievous index finger. Moments later came the moans and groans attributed to the passions of lovemaking between the pair, as Andrew sank his hardened penis into her vagina. Adriana Lavoie repeatedly reminded her egotistical husband to lower his outburst, as he grew increasingly loud due to her charismatic flattering, which overly stimulated him. Perspiration drained off Andrew's body like an open faucet, and thereby created a clapping sound each time their bodies contacted.

The compassionate husband caressed every tender curve of his wife's body, as he reached over and kissed her refined shoulder blades. The sexual escapade between the Lavoies' crept pass an hour, with both performers raging as if backed by Ecstasy or other performance enhancers. Adriana took hold of her husband's right hand and placed it beneath her crotch, instructing him to also caress the clitoris while stroking. Andrew followed instructions and gingerly massaged the tip of Adriana's clitoris, which sent his wife into a cosmic frenzy. Mister Lavoie found himself caught in the reverse role, where he became the sensible lovemaker reminding his partner of proper discretion.

Adriana and Andrew completed their ordeal and fell to the mattress like ducks shot from the sky. Andrew kissed his wife's tender lips, as he reached over her for the Du Maurier pack of cigarettes on the night table.

A deep voice from the frame of the door asked, "Want a light?"

"Ahhh," Adriana screamed, after being frightened by the male intruder!

A strange voice warned, "Shut the fuck up, bitch, before I come over there and slap the scream out of you!"

"Who the fuck is that? How did you get in my house," Andrew questioned, as both he and Adriana grabbed for the comforter that lingered by their feet?

"Don't worry about who we are, Mr. Lavoie. The important thing here is that we know exactly who you are!"

Two husky Caucasian men walked into the gloomy bedroom and stood on either side of the bed. The gentleman with the bass-toned voice, instructed their female accomplice who lingered behind in the dark, to bring a chair and station herself at Adrian's door. The instructor spoke as if he was instructing the female to shoot and kill the couple's son, if he accidentally heard the commotion and came out to investigate. The intruders knew the entire household by name, the layout of the residence, and key aspects that allowed them entry despite the security system.

The team of home invaders behaved and reasoned like professionals, although their hosts appeared far less confident that they would remain as such. Andrew held his wife tightly in his arms and felt the shivers and trembling of her naked body, as her concerns about being raped or molested grew. The nervous husband knew of his wife's personal demons, which included some molestation incidents by an uncle at the tender age of three. With such knowledge, Andrew was compelled to convene the negotiation talks, in hopes that their intruders were solely interested in monetary gains, rather than personal satisfaction.

"What is it you gentlemen want? Mind you, anything I have to keep my family safe is yours," negotiated Andrew!

The massive thug standing over Mr. Lavoie began removing a Manila envelope from beneath his jacket, as Andrew intensely watched both men's every move. The intruder tore open the envelope and removed an electoral ballot form from within, then slapped it square across Andrew's chest. Mr. Lavoie grimaced from the powerful hit, yet, pretended as if he wasn't fazed or in pain. Andrew lifted the ballot toward the gloomy nightlight plugged into the electrical outlet, to properly assess the contents of the document.

"Your support for your brother's political aspirations ends tonight! You're going to call our dear Minister Gerald Lavoie and inform him you'll be supporting General McArthur and friends from now on! You're also going to stir up some political friction between those you've already brought into your brother's fold and the remainder of his constituency! And don't worry—we've already removed his advertising plaques from your front yard. Now here, sign the fucking document," ordered the assigned spokesman!

"Associating myself with my brother's worst enemy would destroy everything we ever had. Nothing could ever heal our relationship after that. He would disown me publicly, and the rest of the family, too, if they ever sided with me. I-I-I-I-I can't sign this, I can't do all that," Andrew exclaimed, as he broke into tears!

"Click! Click!" The bullet selector of the thug's 9MM pistol, with an attached silencer sounded.

Andrew may have struggled seeing the fine print written on the electoral ballot; yet had absolutely no problem describing the model of the weapon, that was pressed against his head. Adriana became frantic, believing the intruder about to murder her husband and yelled out in reproach.

"Whack!" The slap across Adriana's face silenced her immediately.

"Didn't the man tell you to remain fucking quiet, bitch," said the intruder closest to the wife?

"As you can tell, we aren't patient people, so before something bad happens to your entire family that you love so much, sign the fucking document!"

"Please, please, I'm begging you! Consider my position," Andrew reasoned?

The second of the male intruders yelled, "Tracy, shoot the fucking kid!"

"No!" Adriana screamed, as she sat up and began moving toward her child.

In the blink of an eye, the intruder who held Mrs. Lavoie subdued, twirled around in a circle while he withdrew a Ken-Shin sword, which he used and removed his victim's head in one smooth motion. Adriana's decapitated head landed on her husband's lap, however the immediate shock protruded him from uttering a sound. The decapitator proceeded to hack away at his victim's stilled corpse, removing both her 38DD breasts from her chest, her arms, and every visible portion of the female. Andrew's reactions were held in check, by the Taurus 9mm with extended silencer, pressed against his head.

The homeowner was forced to watch as the decapitator transformed into a butcher. Liters of blood squirted at Andrew and splashed all throughout the room. However, the sight of his wife being carved up like a Thanksgiving turkey, drove the husband into a deranged, psychotic, and trance-like state. The mortified scream that refrained from erupting, exploded through Andrew's lungs though briefly, as the armed thug blew brain matter against the pillow that offered him comfort.

"What the fuck is it with you and these fucking swords? We're here to discuss business first, and then send a message should business fuck up! You just cancel business whenever you get fucking agitated, and we all know that doesn't take fucking much."

The bass-toned intruder removed the electoral document from Andrew's grasp and ignored both victims to his accomplice, who in turn left the mutilation that Adrian discovered the following morning.

In Saint Justine, Quebec, local farmer Jose Mercier was in the process of ploughing his cornfield, when in the distance he noticed an off-trail motorbike coming toward him through the grounds he'd already ploughed

"Who the hell is this damn dummy," thought Jose, as he brought his John Deere tractor to a halt.

The fifty-three-year-old father of five, who was a devoted Christian and community activist, supported the views and concepts of Minister Gerald Lavoie of the Party Quebecois, who fought for the rights and privileges of farmers. The areas surrounding Saint Justine, such as Saint Zachary, Montmagny off Interstate-132, Baie Johan Beetz, and Lac Frontier, were agricultural areas filled with farmers who all supported the campaign of Minister Lavoie.

Jose Mercier owned and operated the largest dairy, grain, and wheat farm of eastern Quebec. The highly respected farmer had four sons, who ranged in ages from seventeen to twenty-six, and a fourteen-year-old daughter, who people believed was conceived for the lone female inside the house. Jose had been a farmer all the days of his life, so was his father and grandfather before them. The dairy cattle from Mercier Farm's produced millions of liters of Quebec's most nutritious milk annually, while they cultivated the soil for award-winning produce.

The trail bike pulled alongside the tractor, while Jose continued bickering over the bike rider's route selection. Had the rider been one of Jose's sons, the angered farmer would've probably implanted his galoshes in the lad's rectum, but the stranger jammed a cork in his reaction.

"Didn't you notice that you've been riding on ploughed soil?"

"Whatever old man! Get down off the fucking tractor," ordered the bike rider, who motioned Jose down with his Springfield XD3 Sub-Compact 9mm pistol! The sight of the weapon immediately changed Jose's bitter tune, therefore he raised his hands and brought him quietly back to the earth.

"That's not necessary," declared Jose, pointing at the gun as his galoshes touched dirt.

The bike rider remained atop the trail bike with his gun aimed at Jose's stomach and handed the farmer a Manila envelope. Jose opened the envelope and withdrew an electoral ballot form, which brought a curious expression to his face. The scruffy-looking thug atop the trail bike used his free arm to point the farmer in the direction of his house, where four men armed with high-powered automatic rifles, had his entire family and staff knelt on the dirt, in preparation for an execution. Hysteria overcame Jose as he expelled a humongous sigh, before he brought his attention back toward the bike rider.

"You and family are all going to vote for Minister Blanc and company! We know you're a very influential man around these parts, so deterring anyone without a Minister Blanc's election plaque on their front lawn from voting for the opposition is also a job requirement. Sign the fucking documents and place them back inside the envelope, then our business is complete! And we know everything that goes on around these parts, so if you take your chances with your family by informing the local cops or not fulfilling your mission, I guarantee you'll see us again!"

Jose was signing the documents before the bike rider gave him the instructions to autograph the papers. The picture of everything he loved under duress, severed his connections to the Party Quebecois and landed him in the trenches of the devil.

In Salluit, northern Quebec, committee members for David Mc-

Neil's campaign orchestrated a strategy assembly, where they planned to reformat their slogan to involve native Indians, Eskimos, and immigrants who were qualified to participate in provincial elections. The meeting was scheduled after regular business hours, due to the heavy workload each member tackled during the peak hours of the day. The headquarters for The People of Quebec National Party, was located in an industrial area of town, where huge manufacturers of various products manufactured and exported their goods. Eighteen-wheelers, semi-trailers, production machinery, and hard laborer's, created a huge racket throughout business hours, leaving the nights more adequate for strategy developments.

The electoral candidate had a scheduled evening in Montreal, where he'd commence by mingling with important business tycoons, politicians, among others, at a gala held at the Queen Victoria Museum, slated to unveil historic artefacts from Canadian history. Minister McNeil and his wife, Francine, had a 7:00 PM dinner engagement at The Delta, which was a rotating restaurant, built on top of a five-star hotel. The minister and his wife were also being recognized by the Doctor's Association of Canada, for their continued zeal to raise funds in support of women with breast cancer. The awards celebration was scheduled for 9:00 PM at the Hilton Ballroom, located only seven blocks east of The Delta Hotel.

While the boss played, the workers work, as was evident by the group of eleven strategists, who met to strategizing formulas for victory in the upcoming elections. The team of five women and six men gathered around the huge conference table in the boardroom at McNeil's headquarters, to pitch recommendations and debate to find the best ideas. The conference table was littered with Tim Horton's coffee cups, fruit, stationery, and the boxes from devoured pizza, while the young geniuses devised solutions. Minister McNeil telephoned his election strategists shortly before 9:00 PM, to the response of playful workers shooting crumpled paper at each other around the room. A confident and joyous work force always pleased the boss, who expressed his gratitude, before continuing with his evening.

The roars from Harley engines outside the QAW building at such weird hour didn't unnerve the late-hour staff, which had become accustomed to high-octane engines passing on a regular basis. Outside the building, however, seven members of the Rough Riders gang dismounted their hogs, retrieved their semi-automatic weapons from the pouches attached to their bikes, and walked toward the office building. The men all wore German chopper helmets with black-and-white striped bandanas covering the remainder of their faces, black leather vests with patches of rank and gang insignias covering white T-shirts, black jeans, and cowboy-style leather boots.

There were three employees of Molly Maid Services assigned to clean the two-story office building, before the start of each new day. The lone male among the three cleaners was mopping the service entrance, when a member of the Rough Riders gang tapped the glass door with his automatic weapon, seeking entry. The sight of seven, heavily armed thugs wearing masks scared the man, who believed the four-inch glass separation between them thick enough to withstand bullets. The man dropped the mop and began running for a rear exit, before the spraying action of Uzis flung him to the concrete. One of the two females assigned to sanitation duties was busy sanitizing the bathrooms on the main floor, and nosily emerged to determine whether the blast was from a weapon or from something else. The female suffered the same fate as her co-worker, whose body was the first sight she came across after exiting the male toilet. The third female assigned to sanitation duties was busy cleansing Minister McNeil's office, with her iPod earplugs beating iTunes into her eardrums. Due to her loud music, the blast went completely unnoticed, as she continued with her assigned duties.

The eruption on the first floor had by then caught the attention of everyone inside the boardroom, and they also began frantically debating the type of sound they'd heard. The strategists were split on the exact action to take, as some were for alerting the police, while others believed such actions were premature without definite proof. Empty magazines were exchanged by the gangsters, who'd spat detrimental bullets at the civil workers, and the thugs all climbed the stairs leading to the second-story conference room.

One of the brave-hearted sceptics inside the boardroom quickly volunteered to settle the fears of doubters and, determined exactly what was happening. The strategist opened the huge mahogany door that lead to the hallway and froze in his tracks, after he came face to face with the death squad, sent to annihilate him and his peers. Bullets flung the brave soul halfway across the room, as the remainder of his crew began hysterically scattering for shelter, underneath the conference table, behind the leather sofa, or wherever possible. Many of the men inside the conference room screamed as loud, if not louder than the females, who were all screaming at the top of their lungs. One of the male strategists was attempting to open a second-story window in order to leap to safety, when plastering bullets hammered him through the thick pane of glass.

The mercenaries stormed into the conference room and immediately changed the décor inside the room. The masked thugs transformed the beige-colored walls to red in a matter of seconds, as bullets ripped through flesh and everything else inside the room. There were lonesome cries that silenced as the battalions exploded and, brought an end to the joyous laughter that once filled the room. Three of the mercenaries took a brisk walk around the room to make sure everyone was dead, by injecting additional bullets into their stilled corpses.

The third maid was cleaning Minister McNeil's office next door and narrowly escaped a scatter shot, which pierced through the gyprock wall and jammed inside the minister's laptop, on his desk. The sudden crash that occurred only inches from her while she wiped the desk, frightened the maid who fell to the ground, where she yanked the earplugs from her ears and gazed around the room. The maid threw her hands over her mouth to prevent herself from screaming, as she overheard the devastating screams of people being massacred in the room next door. Once everything silenced, the maid nervously began seeking somewhere to hide, fearing the killers may search around for additional targets. The terrified maid quickly ruled out the minister's personal bathroom and closet, before using her gymnastic talents to squeeze herself into a filing cupboard. From inside the cupboard, the woman listened as the death squad went from room to room in search of other victims, before total silence was had throughout. The maid, frightfully, waited an hour and eight minutes after the killers had gone, before she snuck a peek out the cupboard and informed the authorities.

In Poste-de-la-Baleine, Quebec, Pastor Guy-Francis Bouillon, who had been the lifelong clergy minister for Gerald Lavoie, held a memorial session for Andrew and Adriana Lavoie, who were also brought up in Pastor Bouillon's Anglican Church, before they relocated to Hull, Quebec. There was a stellar audience of family members, family supporters, well-wishers from miles around, voters, and government officials, who all turned out to commemorate the lives of two of their own. News reporters swarmed the festivities with press coverage, which generated from an incident that occurred over a hundred miles away. Citizens and friends created a shrine outside the main gate of the Lavoie's family home, where they laid seas of flowers, greeting cards, and teddy bears, to convey their heartfelt emotions toward their neighbors. The house of God, built to accommodate three hundred people, was over capacity by nearly two hundred, with patrons choosing to stand and mourn rather than return home.

Pastor Bouillon soothed the hearts of grievers, who were all still shocked by the horrific manner in which the couple had died. Preacher Bouillon uncharacteristically cursed the doers of the crime against the Lavoies, before rendering forgiveness unto the sinners, who terminated the lives of two wonderful human beings. The clergy leader believed it healing for the soul, to have personal friends conveyed their sentiments, and thus opened the floor for grievers to publicly express their thoughts. A line up of well-wishers slowly formed to the left of the altar, with many spokespersons being close relatives of the deceased. Each of the thirteen female speakers, who volunteered a kind word, broke down mid-speech and had to be aided from the podium, except for Adriana's sister, who brought everyone inside the church to tears, with a poem inspired by her personal reflections of the deceased.

There was a genuine expression of love, hurt, and regret throughout the ceremony, which lasted well over five hours. Patrons consoled each other, as the various speakers shared their personal memories of the murdered couple. Mourners joined in a prayer asking for justice and righteousness for the couple, before conveying their respects to the family inside the church. The night ended with Pastor Bouillon reminding his congregation to, "Hold firm and trust in God, for only He can truly take a life!"

Pastor Guy-Francis Bouillon had always maintained a none-political stance on the issues of voting, yet encouraged support of the Lavoies' political aspirations, through subtle messages during his sermon. The clergy leader loved the Lavoie family for their devotion, which stretched over thirty years and continued through three generations. Pastor Bouillon acquired flocks of supporters for the Party Quebecois, through his continued praise and glory about the magnificent work done by Lavoie family members, around the surrounding neighborhoods.

The pastor personally closed the doors to the church at 11:41 PM, before retreating to his domain only feet away from the house of God he governed. Pastor Bouillon partook of a spaghetti meal prepared by Sister Mary, the Sunday school teacher, who ensured the sixty-four-year-old celibate preacher had his daily meals. The pastor ate and, washed the utensils he'd dirtied, before retiring to his bedroom for the night. An upset stomach landed Pastor Bouillon on his toilet seat, reading his Bible at 12:43 AM, though stomach gripes offered him less time to read than he'd prefer. A sharp pain in his gut forced the pastor to cringe forward, as he muscled and tightened his buttocks in an attempt to expel the cause of his stomachache.

Two muscular intruders stormed into the bathroom, snatched the aching pastor from his toilet throne, and dragged him directly from the house. The unexpected bombardment shocked the defecation process into immediate termination, and frightened the old man, who experienced a mild heart attack. The scare and eventual heart attack rendered Pastor Bouillon unconscious, as the two men dragged him along his Varsity tiled floors and into the church, where he'd soothed the hearts of hundreds only hours before. The two assailants hoisted the unconscious man of God, up on the primary crucifix of Jesus Christ that hung inside the church, before they proceeded to douse the entire structure with gasoline. Pastor Bouillon regained consciousness by inhaling a huge gasp of oxygen, before the pain of his lower extremities being set ablaze, sent another sharp cramp to his heart. The sight of his congregation hall burning, along with the scent of burnt flesh seeping up his nostrils, brought on a second heart attack that immediately killed the Anglican pastor.

Part 19

Nicholas insisted on formally introducing Kadeem to Montreal's reggae dance hall scene, especially after receiving word that his favorite sound system was scheduled to perform that very weekend. Spice Promoters, along with Island Vibes Crew, presented, live in concert from Jamaica West Indies, the Mighty Stone Love, Metro Media, and Matteron Sound, at the spacious E&B restaurant. The line-up of selectors was not one to be missed by avid reggae adorers across the island, hence the boss had interest in attending. Nicholas rarely attended such venues with rowdy crowds, due to the probability that someone might succeed at assassinating him, yet he chose to throw caution to the wind, and party with the regulars.

With the decision made to attend the soiree came the daunting task of finding the perfect attire, elegant enough to express one's exquisite taste. The young gun hands, such as Damian, Tank, and the crew of shooters, all fancied the modern youth hip-hop generation style of throw-backs, jeans, sneakers, and baseball hats; while Nicholas and his red brothers opted for the elegant fashion designs by famous creators such as Kenneth Cole, Armani, and Chanel, just to name a few. Four top designers stacked with runways of creations were brought to Kevin's mansion, which was like an impenetrable fortress, heavily guarded twenty-four hours a day. Designers Ralph Lauren, Kenneth Cole, Armani, and local talent Carlton Daly, spent the majority of the morning of the soiree, fashioning their designs for a customer with whom they'd become quite familiar. The location for the showing of the designers' fashions was prepared inside Nicholas' humongous family room, before the proprietor decided to house the event on his stylish veranda, which stretched halfway around his mansion.

"Blood-clatt my youth, you do things with style and elegance! Kenneth Cole, Armani, Mr. Lauren, a chill and a beat Heineken, burn weed with the man them like is a family thing; a so man must live nice, respect my brethren," Killa said, as they relaxed on lawn chairs while enjoying the fashions being featured!

"Life nice all now even though we have a big war a go on, but things soon nicer man, as soon as we eliminate this pussy-hole yah," Nicholas commented, as he tossed a magazine that featured Martain on the cover on Killa's lap!

Killa stared deeply at the portrait of his friend's nemesis, hating and despising the man more with each passing second. The Title that highlighted the story said, "The Island's Most Revered Gangster," which prompted Killa to race to page thirty-eight for further details on the story. The article spoke of Martain's huge flock of followers, his many women, motorbikes, businesses, and leisure activities.

"So how you no manage to kill him yet," Killa asked?

"A just time mi boy, just a matter a time! That suit a fire," Nicholas said, as he pointed at the jacket suit ensemble being modelled!

"This is a nice piece," declared Danny, who quickly indicated to Esquire his interest in acquiring the garments.

Two of the four designers brought a few outfits for Nicholas' son to try on, which divided the proprietor's time between the adult fabrics and his son's personal fashion show. Junior, Kevin's son, would occasionally appear from the rear, wearing designer outfits for his father to choose from among. The young lad modelled the GQ assortment of exquisite linen with confidence and vigor, before appearing with tears in his eyes over an army fatigue outfit, he despised wearing. Junior walked out on his personal stage degenerate and slouchy, unhooked the buttons to his vest and tossed the vest at his father.

"I told them I don't like this suit," Junior complained, as he marched back into the changing room!

Everyone who witnessed the rage of the young lad broke out with laughter, over the manner with which the boy handled himself. Nicholas' arrogance was evident in his son, who, like his dad, accepted no form of bullshit or disrespect. With no motherly figure present, except for his personal nanny Miss Emma, Junior grew among the ratchet knife-wielding, ice pick-stabbing, gun-shooting maniacs his father embraced as family. Miss Emma was, in fact, responsible for maintaining discipline around the compound, thus, thugs were terrified of getting caught swearing or behaving unmannerly, around the seventy-four-year-old woman. The Mohawk maid, who was a devoted Catholic, tolerated the massive weaponry that was brandished by guards and gun hands around the compound, yet slapped gangsters across the head for making sexist remarks or speaking profanity in her presence. The maid, who watched over Kevin's only child, had protected and cared for the boy since he was the tender age of seven months. Without regard to the Esquada boys and Damian, Miss Emma had been in the trusted employment of Nicholas, longer than any other worker on his roster.

"Miss Emma, you know the boy don't wear them sort a clothes! See him a walk right out of them on his way to the back," Nicholas joked, while chuckling over his son's actions!

"What happened to Junior's mother," Killa asked?

Nicholas buckled over the first few words to leave his lips, which insinuated he still had emotional feeling. It was evident that the topic was one of personal affliction for the boss, who rarely allowed anything to affect his moods. Nicholas was considered "cool, calm, and collected" by his associates, and they had never seen him frown or murmur over any incident, regardless the magnitude.

"Martain…and his friends them…own a gentlemen's club downtown. When mi start, really hunt for the pussy hole…that spot was the first place we go look for him. He was somewhere else still, but one of the pussy-hole who did beat me into a coma, over some turf shit, was flossing on his birthday or some shit! From mi see the boy that was it, him had to pay back the piper right there and then, even though the club did full a bikers! But before mi step to him, a young lady I was rapping to, slip her phone number into mi pocket; and tell mi call her… Because me had to cancel the pussy hole who put him hands on mi, I didn't want call still, in case she decided to set me up for a little money. Still me give her a link and, it so happened that, was one a the best move me make in this country, cause she no stop give me info on where to find the pussy hole, Martain! Mi had the boy Martain a run round the city with no safe place to lay him head for weeks, every girlfriend, family member, any house him dock into a pure gunshot!"

Nicholas paused and took a sip from his glass with liquor, then lit his marijuana joint and took a huge toke before proceeding. "Me get message say the boy a hide out with some blonde chick in South Shore, directly in front them police station. Some tall building with about seven or eight floors and she lived on the fifth, so no chance for a drive-by and spray the place. But the boy, Martain, think him smart and set up an ambush with shooters on the fourth and sixth floor, plus the entire police station as backup! Anyways, me, Danny, and Tank drive go look for the pussy. Once we see the building location, we decide to leave Tank in the vehicle with the engine running by the southern exit, which was furthest exit from the police station. Danny and I walked into the building, a few seconds before an old lady stepped off the elevator, on her way out. We take the elevator up to the fifth floor and start walking toward apartment 509, before Danny's Indian senses start act up. To him, things seemed too easy for a man who no leave him heavy convoy nowhere. Same time, Tank notice three fresh replacements arriving for duty, and couldn't get in touch with me over the phone, so him decided to follow the replacements, in case them try get the drop on us. The replacement bodyguards walked up the stairs to the fourth floor and, enter some apartment up there. So, Tank wisely decided to lay low, and watch what happen," the boss took another toke!

"Knowing I was that close to Martain, after everything the pussy put me through clouded my judgment still. Anyways, mi shoot off the dead bolt lock and rushed into the apartment, spraying everything in sight! Is once we get into the apartment, I realize that Danny was right, it was a little too easy to get to that fucking biker! When we busted in, the blonde chick get scared and jump off the sofa with her TV remote in her hand, and frighten me, so I laid her ass out across the fucking coffee table! We spray up every room in search of that biker bitch, but couldn't find him! On our way out the front door, a pure gunshot greetings Danny and I get! We ran up in a roadblock in the hallway, where five heavily armed bikers decided we not exiting the apartment. Luckily, those five guys run up from the fourth floor, with Tank following them every move, or them would trap us there 'til the cops come and get we!"

Yow badman, them boys dumped a thunderstorm a bullets on us inside that apartment, but as we start thinking about alternative escape route, all we hear was shots being fired at the pussy them, from behind! Tank showed up right in the nick a time and give us a way to escape. Because if him never show up, the rest of guards from the sixth floor, plus them police friends who did a storm the building, would have definitely killed us that day! Martain revered me so much that, he'd only spend time with the young blond when him dick hard, and as soon as him buss, him would run right back to the guards apartment!"

"Apart from that, he made sure him bodyguards were around at every waking moment of the day! I believe the first time we actually talked was right after that incident… Martain called me crying, to inform me that, him personally took out a bounty on my head! I told that bitch that, unlike him, I will definitely be the one to send him back to his maker, and I didn't need anybody else to do the job!"

The boss man expressed a translucent smirk, though the memories of the incident were painful, and he paused for a couple of tokes off the marijuana joint. "After a few months, my little mole in the Rough Riders family got pregnant, and that was when some jealous gossipers found out, she was the one feeding me information. Between the strippers them gossiping about the little man's affairs, and the drunken bikers spilling more than them beer, I stayed knowing where to find that pussyhole. Martain took the betrayal by KJ's mother so serious, that he called mi and threatened mi that, 'he was going to kill her entire family, which he did', before he mutilated her… I kept her locked up at home, with guards galore whenever she decided to go out and do a little baby shopping. I thought knowing what Martain and his friends did to her mother and sister would scare her from wanting to leave the compound, but Stacey swore she was a gangster and refused to be intimidated by anybody!"

Nicholas took a drink. "The time for Junior's birth came and, we do the hospital thing, but his mom experienced some complications and had to stay over in the hospital for another few days. The doctors didn't like the idea, but I kept round the clock guards interrogating everything the nurses did pertaining to Stacey. Four days later, they evaluated her and decided that she was well enough to come home with Junior. Mi sign them out and tell Damian to push the wheelchair with Stacey so me can carry Junior in the little carriage, while Tank and the Rass go carry the vehicle 'round front. Walked through the huge sliding glass door from the lobby to the street, when three apprentices in a Chevy Trailblazer attempted a drive-by through the drop-off zone. Fucking idiots, trying to speed through somewhere where vehicles ahead of you are creeping at least five kilometers an hour. All I could do was lay low with Junior, but mi could hear Damian squeezing off rounds from his German Luger. The pussy them ran up into the back of a Mazda 6, crashed them vehicle, and then try shoot their way out to safety!"

"Don't tell me say them get away?"

"A police cruiser was parked right in the parking lot, with two on-duty officers, who claimed they brought some unconscious pedestrian to the hospital. But, sometimes I question whether them two officers were staking out the drive-by, to clean up the garbage after them assassins finished their work. Regardless of what I think, them cops shot the front passenger before him could get out the vehicle, and claimed that the driver got pinned by the airbag, before a stray bullet shot out the back of his head," added Nicholas!

"What happen to the third shooter?" Killa asked.

"Neither one of the police gave any chase, so him escape, and managed to accomplish his task still also; because after me get up off the floor, checked Junior, who did a scream his head off, me realize that Stacey did slumped over in the wheelchair. Damian rolled over off the ground and start scream her name, but the wheelchair prevented her from hitting the ground like everyone else and, she got shot twice in the chest. Junior lucky she was too weak to carry him, or mi would bury mi gal and mi son at the same time. Mi stand up over her while the doctors rush out to treat her, plus some other people who did injured, and is like me couldn't move, all them telling me to step to the side so they could help her! All I'm imagining was Martain, telling me by any means necessary, a message I've since then called him to relayed and will live to see come through," Nicholas relit his extinguished joint and inhaled a huge toke into his lungs, before slowly exhaling it through his nostrils!

"I know you like that suit, my boy, clean, can't stop grinning from ear to ear. Hah!" Nicholas shouted to his son, who walked out wearing a brown Armani trouser with a golden fabric shirt sporting Asian tigers. "Go tell Miss Emma to put that outfit among you choices!"

"Mi sorry to hear say is them tragic ways you lose your baby mother still, and knowing one a the pussy them who pull the trigger is still alive, must grieve you," Killa sympathized!

"I said the police were under the impression him get away because them didn't pursue, but the Rass and Tank were pulling in the drop-off zone, when the boy them pull off them stunt. Rass Ijah watched the police them move in on the Trailblazer, before deciding to pursue the batty boy attempting to escape. Fucking scared pussies got lucky, come to do assassination and end up running like bitches! After the beating me received at the boys them hands, that was the second-worst tragedy to hit me in this country, and all caused by the same motherfucker! Mi glad when Ijah check in and tell me him camp outside the pussy them hide-out, although me personally had to attend to my son's needs. The boys brought him over right after I put Junior down for a nap that evening, but I was so vexed, that I end up beating that boy stink, 'til the baby made a squeak through the monitor in my pocket! And, after all that, I still had to send Damian to attend to the baby, because I was drenched in blood by that time."

"Boss, the Africans them a wait for you inside your office," exclaimed a member of Nicholas' perimeter guards, who walked up.

"Yeah, tell them say I'll be right there! You boys continue enjoying the festivities. I've got some unexpected business that just turned up. I'll try to be as prompt as possible still," said Nicholas, who left to attend some personal matters!

The boss obliged all his guests by purchasing an array of garments for himself, the Esquada brothers, Junior, and Killa, whose eyes were altered from his typical thuggish look, once he observed the unique designs by some of the world's finest designers. Nicholas thanked his guests for their presence and bid them farewell should they depart before he'd concluded his other affairs. While leaving the boss instructed Kane to properly compensate their guests, for the thousands of dollars spent.

Nicholas and Danny shunned the festivities and began walking toward the boss' office, when KJ crept up in between the two men and held both their hands.

"Uncle Danny, are we still going to camp outside all night," KJ asked?

"Of course, Junior, and don't forget we got to set up our tents and fire equipment later this afternoon," said Danny!

"Are you coming camping with me and Uncle Danny tonight, Daddy?"

"Sorry, son, but I got a little jam to go to later, but I'm definitely in the next time! All right, bad boy! Now, can you please go harass some of your other uncles? Thank you," answered Nicholas!

"All right, Dad, I'll let you guys off the hook for now, but don't forget I'm in the shadows like Night Man," KJ exclaimed, as he scurried away!

There were two Nigerian descendants inside his office patiently awaiting Nicholas' presence, as he and Danny entered the chamber. Polite greetings of sturdy handshakes were shared among the men who gathered around Nicholas' desk to discuss business. The darker of the two black men placed a Hitachi briefcase atop Nicholas' desk, before gradually opening it to reveal the contents.

"The last time I was here, I talked with you about the problem I was having with this Officer Renick and his partner. I can't play soccer or do anything without these cops bothering me every minute of the day. You said fifty thousand to have them taken care of. There is that and enough money for three keys inside the case," exclaimed the apparent head boss.

"No problem, Hakeem! Danny, send for the products for them and tell Marcel them they got a green light," said Nicholas.

Executing Orders

Officer Renick and his partner, Doug Battier, were members of the Drug Squad Unit and the SWAT Division at the Thirty-First Police Precinct in Lachine, Montreal. The dynamic duo of crime busters was a constant thorn in the asses of drug dealers and crime offenders, within the perimeter of their patrol. The two officers had never participated in or orchestrated a raid on the public, without substantial arrests and seizures, which they dubbed as trophies throughout the local news programs. Their latest notable seizure was only a week prior, where they stormed and closed one of Hakeem's prized drug bases in Lachine. The officers raided the high-tech drug base, that was equipped with cameras, sensor equipment, and surveillance by paid neighbors, knowing they would not catch a dealer on the premises. The lawmen understood that any employee would be long gone by the time they reached the apartment, but they wanted to send a message that dealing drugs would not be tolerated around Lachine. Hakeem, however, chose to relocate his affairs from the third to the fifth floor of the same building, and reopened shop an hour after the drug squad left.

The ongoing feud between Hakeem and members of local law enforcement had brought the Nigerian to his final trump card, after which remained nothing less than surrender. The two officers in question were spotted in the alleyway behind Hakeem's prized drug base, which he refused to close despite opposition from activists and others. Officers Renick and Battier were gathering information on the number of known drug addicts to enter the premises at 11 Sacre-Coeur Street, from where Hakeem acquired 65% of his spoils. The unmarked cruiser from which the officers gathered their information was a turquoise Chevy Malibu, that had been seen around by offenders avoiding the long arms of the law.

The alleyway ran between rows of buildings inhabited by immigrants, welfare recipients and lesser fortunate patrons of society. A M&M produce delivery truck sneaked up behind the focused officers, before the driver abandoned the vehicle. Two minutes after the man abandoned the truck, a Greyhound tour bus pulled directly in front the officers' Malibu and blocked their vision of the building they were surveying.

"Partner, I'm telling you without a doubt, that's fifteen smokers in as many minutes," declared Officer Battier!

"Look who's running up into the hot spot! If it ain't our old friend, Twizler. We'll definitely get some answers about whatever we need to know now," said Officer Renick.

"Where did this fucking idiot come from, and why are there no windows in the frames," said Officer Battier, who started the engine to move and acquire a clearer view?

The officer's question got answered by eight, heavily armed mercenaries, who popped into the window frames and began plastering the Malibu with bullets. Both officers luckily ducked just in time from the unseeing eyes of bullets. Officer Battier yanked the gear shifter all the way down to D-1 and pressed the gas with his hand, to which the unmarked cruiser took off slowly. The coppers ran into the vehicle parked two car lengths ahead of them and crashed.

"We're under attack! We're taking serious fire! Help, officers need help! Location Sacre Coeur Street, oh, my God, I think they just shit my pants! Location Sacre Coeur," Officer Battier yelled through his two-way radio!

Two ignited torches sailed through the side windows of the Malibu and quickly lit the vehicle's occupants ablaze. The screams of men enduring torture could be heard blocks away, as the shooters' continued slamming copper into the cruiser. The entire ordeal, which horrified residents, lasted a mere two minutes, yet left the entire neighborhood infested with police, who combed through the aftermath for clues, on who orchestrated such an ambush. By the time help arrived, the shooters had already departed, and witnesses who watched from either their balconies or along the street, had vanished from sight. The locals from around the neighborhood knew who the shooters were, but nobody wanted to get involved in fear of the lives. Both victims died after receiving gunshot wounds and burns throughout their entire bodies, thus, the area smelt like burnt flesh before they removed the corpses.

The Party

Nicholas' Range Rover Sport SUVs sandwiched the Mercedes Benz 600 he was aboard, as they came to a halt in front the venue that hosted the dance hall event. There was a rolled out red carpet similar to the Oscar Awards, and numerous thugs evacuated the SUVs and immediately surrounded the boss' carriage. Nicholas' entourage treated him like an important dignitary, as they quickly scurried him into the building under tight security. Killa was aboard the boss' luxury chauffeured limousine, when the guards practically lifted Nicholas from his seat, yet the rude boy chose to remain aboard and accompanied the drivers on their valet duties. The drivers of the vehicles began circling the block in search of parking, before they decided to leave the vehicles directly in front a car dealership only a few yards away. As Killa and the remaining three drivers exited the carriages, Killa caught sight of a 323 BMW parked in the alleyway across the street. The black automobile could hardly be seen in the dark alleyway, except for the chrome insignia and lining details. Four men suspiciously exited the vehicle, and intensely checked out their surroundings, before they proceeded to conceal artefacts beneath their clothing.

"Yow, Tank, we a carry them things or what," enquired Killa?

"Don't watch no face man security a wi people! Wi well protected in these places," Tank answered, as he and the remaining drivers commenced grooming themselves, before they moved toward the dance hall.

Killa removed his Glock 9mm from the stash pot built into the rear armrest and shoved it into his waistband. The thought of guards with metal detectors and other devices in no way swayed the thug's decision, as he charismatically mingled with his associates as if all was well. The movements of the four suspicious men, who Killa positively believed armed themselves for a mission, prompted the wanted Jamaican to react cautiously.

"Boy, a tonight you a go see some big batty sexy gal, remember mi tell you," Tank exclaimed, as he playfully shoved Killa by the shoulder!

"A them things deah me used to king, nothing but the thickest," acknowledged Killa, whose attention momentarily swayed from the alley!

The gangster took a sneak peek over his left shoulder in the alley's direction, before their view got interrupted. Strangely enough, instead of the avid partygoers materializing from the dark alley, the men completely disappeared from radar, as the window to the alleyway closed.

Tank and the other two drivers were well greeted by the security personnel, who pointed out that the entrance fees had been taken care of and that, their associates awaited them at the top of the stairs. Killa slouched behind as the chauffeurs scurried up the stairs to the party zone, as he again attempted to see who the four secretive men were. Without catching a glimpse of the suspected men, Killa decided to join his friends and ran up the stairs. The remainder of troops had cleared security, and they began wondering where he might have run off to, before he materialized at the security check. Killa could see Tank pointing at him, indicating he was the final count as he walked toward the security personnel.

"Arms up so I can check you, please," said the security personnel?

"You don't need to check mi, mi can tell you straight, mi have mi gun on me," Killa declared without so much as a smirk, as he walked up toward the guard!

The man looked puzzled at first, as he thought about the consequences of trying to disarm this thug in front of him. The club's rules specifically forbid any form of alcohol, weapons, and illegal substances, and mandated they be confiscated before entry. However, the thug in question looked like a natural born killer and, the guard was not willing to sacrifice his life or get embarrassingly assaulted, for what he was getting paid. The security guard stepped to the side like Moses parting the Red Sea and allowed the stylish gangster entry without provocation.

Props and acknowledgments came from the DJ on the ones and twos, who spotted Damian and his entourage of thirteen. Nicholas remained constantly surrounded by his personal strike force, who allowed no one within three feet of the boss. The crew of fourteen hustlers took over the left corner inside the vicinity, before a small scouting team went off for refreshments.

Massive amounts of females of all makes and models paraded their attributes as they danced and enjoyed themselves. The music selector had the entire club ablaze, with certain male patrons dancing up a sweat with their energetic female partners, while others simply stood back and watched the provocative dancers exposed themselves. There was a smoking ordinance inside the club, which was difficult to believe considering of the huge clouds of marijuana smoke floating about the ceiling. Nicholas' scouting team, who went off in search of refreshments, soon returned with bottles of Hennessy, Cranberry juice, Guinness, Heineken, and a pack of Red Bull energy drinks.

The guards around Nicholas weren't only watching out for their boss' best interest, but they were also managing time for their personal desires. Not one female who passed by the dog pound went by without someone tugging on her arm or using some type of dialect to gain their attention. Ganja baseball bats began blazing all throughout Nicholas' minicamp, as the thugs began drinking, partying, and enjoying the festivities. Killa stood by Nicholas' side all night, while the boss and his associates enjoyed themselves freely. They were close to an emergency exit should they need to vacate the premises, but their location also allowed Killa a better view of the entrance.

West Indians from the Caribbean are overpowered by the musical creations of their islands, such as Salsa, Meringue, Calypso, Soca, and Reggae, to name a few. Trinidadians, Barbadians, Haitians, Saint Lucians, Grenadians, Jamaicans, and other Caribbean islands all celebrate their carnivals by declaring national holidays, for which their citizens are eligible to party for days on end. The travesties that occurred at such festivities are almost immoral, as patrons push the boundaries with sexually explicit behavior.

From among the crowd, Killa tried to pinpoint the four men from the BMW, although looking pass the females was incredibly difficult. While some of the females dressed flamboyantly in their evening gowns, others wore some of the skimpiest outfits, some of which were completely transparent. The female dancers who sought to exhibit their talents, took to the middle of the dancing floor and neglected any concerns for whatever they wore, as they performed maneuvers which in most cases exposed their privates. With each change of sound systems, the party enthusiasts grew more excited, as they partied into the night. There were ladies grinding on their male counterparts, whining while they balanced on the top of their heads, dancing on speaker boxes, and performing sexually enticing features, while the spectators cheered.

A number of hustlers came over to Nicholas throughout the night, to acknowledge the man most respected for his stance against the Rough Riders. Nicholas made it possible for any independent hustler to sell in the city, therefore he was very much revered by many. Huge quantities of liquor were sent over from the various high rollers inside the party, who all admittedly considered Nicholas "The One!"

"Yow mi have to let out some a this liquor from out a mi system," Nicholas declared, as he grabbed Killa around the neck! "Don't think I don't see you a watch that thing in the white all night!"

"You need to mind your own business," Killa joked, as he began walking alongside Nicholas!

Jasper, Damian, and Rass Ijah all broke ahead of Nicholas and Killa, as the remaining thugs held down the fort. Tank soon decided he also needed to empty his bladder and set off behind his peers, who'd gained a few paces on him. Killa and Nicholas continued their laughing ways across the huge dance floor, as they made their way to the men's facilities across the hall. There was a wall that hid the bathroom, which was opened on both sides, and offered patrons easy access from both directions. For the first time since they entered the hall, Killa caught sight of the four individuals whom he assured changed their minds about entering the soirée. The woman and three men were positioned at the opposite end of the wall, which Nicholas and company walked around. Killa pretended he was looking elsewhere and caught the female nudging her head at Nicholas, who they appeared surprised to see without numerous bodyguards. Kadeem was no Bill Gates, yet when it came to proficiency at one's job, he was as masterful at his craft as the Microsoft genius himself.

Kadeem believed something was afoot, and he decided not to enter the facilities should an ambush be forthcoming. The wanted Jamaican instead went around the wall and stood beside some strangers and inconspicuously watch the movements of his suspects, though visibility was indeed poor. With his focus aimed at the mischievous bunch, Killa felt someone jammed an open mouth iron in his rib, which felt like a weapon. The rude boy looked down at the weapon, before looking around into the eyes of the five-foot-four little man, who held him at gun point.

"Just relax yourself, brethren," said the Haitian man, who had a huge smirk on his face!

It was evident that his abductor didn't want the sound of gun fire to alert both Nicholas and his peers, as the other three assassins moved into position to sniper off anyone who exited the bathroom. Kadeem's eyes grew wider with each tick of the clock, knowing that at any second his friends would exit into a trap. With his eyes fixated on the door, Kadeem felt himself about to pull away from his captor, which would have resulted in a bullet to the rib, yet he was content to die if it meant saving his friends. Killa looked down at his captor, before making his move and realized the man was coughing up blood. Tank was on his way to the bathroom and realizing Killa's dilemma, therefore, he pierced his twelve-inch blade into the little man's abdomen. The Haitian assassin slithered to the ground and fell at the heels of a woman, who was enjoying herself with her girlfriends. The woman eventually stepped on the deceased assassin's hand, before she realized the pool of blood at her feet, then started screaming once she saw that he'd been killed.

The claps of gunfire erupted, as the frightful scream startled one of the assassins, whose twitchy fingers accidentally thumped two shells into the bathroom door. Once the assassin realized he'd possibly foiled the ambush, the man charged into the bathroom with the door quickly closing behind him. Following the initial sounds of the assassin's weapon being discharged, there were two huge blasts like that of a .357 Magnum, that flung the assassin back through the door he'd entered. Killa armed himself and used his weapon to blast continuously at the remaining pair. The second bullet to be discharged from his weapon laid out the male assassin across the party floor, as ruckus and hysteria ran rampant. The lone female assassin screamed in terror as she blasted bullets at Killa, who was forced to duck behind the wall for protection. Tank removed the deceased assassin's weapon from his grasp, as the onslaught by the female assassin kept them at bay. The female began moving toward a rear exit, as other members of Nicholas' party ran toward the gun battle. In an attempt to escape, the female assassin found herself erratically shooting at the hostile crowd, as her window to accomplish the slaying drastically diminished. The fright of suffering the same fate as her accomplices terrified the assassin, who attempted to clear the path through the exit with gunfire. Her attempt killed a pair of girlfriends fleeing the violence, as flares from other weapons around the hall terminated the assassin's hopes.

Part 20

Yves Buchard killed more of Nicholas' allies and Defenders since the beginning of the war, than any other soldier in Martain's arsenal. Since Nicholas murdered their close friend, Pierre "The Moose," Yves had waged a personal campaign against all who defied the Rough Riders' laws and vowed their termination. The Defenders gang had fought the Rough Riders for years over control of the distribution of recreational drugs around their West Island neighborhood. Before they got involved with Nicholas, they had to travel great distances to places like Niagara Falls, to acquire the products they trafficked. Their adversaries, on the other hand, would implement strategies to confiscate their shipments, in order to cripple their enemies' economic growth.

"Oui monsieur," Yves answered, as he spoke with someone over his cell phone!

The bikers' enforcer looked across the train coach, at the two men he'd been surveying, since the train departed the Bonaventure train station in Montreal. The Amtrak passenger train destined for Grand Central Station in New York City, had being used by the pair of Columbian runners for years, to smuggle large amounts of money into the United States. The two Spanish natives had absolutely no idea they were being followed, during their return trip to Miami, Florida via New York, after their two-day excursion at Nicholas' mansion.

"I will do exactly as you requested, sir," declared Yves, before the conversation was terminated!

The two Columbians were under the employment of one Ernesto Lopez, who handsomely rewarded both men for collecting his drug payments. The pair made a substantial number of trips during the year and retrieved well over a hundred million dollars in payment. The money was casually wrapped among clothing inside a huge traveler's pack, to avoid detection by the border patrol in search of various contrabands. Without a mandatory searching law of travelers' belongings at the border for railway cargo, intellectual smugglers transferred their black-market items, without the hassles of being scrutinized.

Yves watched the men place the money sack inside the overhead compartment, as casually as if they were taking the garbage to the corner. The men were conservative in their actions, despite the fact they were carrying ten million dollars in cash. For the first hour of the trip, Yves pondered over how he'd separate the sack from its handlers, who stood guard like centurions. Should a situation arise, however, Yves was prepared to dispense a bullet to the head and chest of each smuggler, before vanishing amidst the hysteria. The Frenchman carried an emergency compass and map inside his jacket pocket, in case he was forced to jump off the moving train and get back to Montreal. Whatever the requirements were to attain his goal, the biker assassin knew he'd have to accomplish his mission, between the train clearing Immigration and breaking at its first stop thereafter.

One of the smugglers, who had kept his head buried in the day's Gazette thus far, began scanning various faces around the coach and intently stared at Yves for a few seconds. The Columbian native believed the biker was a prominent businessman, due to his tailored business suit, his gelled back dark hair, his smoothly shaved face, his posture, his demeanor, and the laptop on the desk tray. Yves played the role to perfection and alleviated any false thoughts, hence neither smuggler suspected him to be a threat.

The smuggler seated toward the aisle soon arose from his seat and walked toward the restaurant and bar area. Yves asked the student traveler seated beside him, to watch over his belongings while he visited the onboard facilities. The biker assassin followed the smuggler to the bar, where the Columbian threw back two shots of Tanqueray, before purchasing himself a third and a single for his partner. The train attendant was passing out declaration forms for each passenger to fill out, to assist with the smooth transition through Customs. Those eating or partaking of the Happy Hour specials were told to complete the INS forms and return to their assigned seats, before the train pulled into the Custom's checkpoint.

By the time Yves returned to his seat, the train was in the process of halting to allow the Immigration inspectors time to board. A quick glance at his targets showed both men comfortably seated, with the empty liquor glasses before them. "Seemed like they needed those shots to settle their nerves," thought Yves, as he began preparing his documents for inspection. The Immigration officers who inspected the train were diligent, as they proficiently interrogated each passenger, while they ensured their travelling documents were in proper order. Two men and a female were removed from the company of those aboard, with zero dispute or quarrel about the claims. The Columbian travelers were barely questioned, which led Yves to speculate that the immigration officers might had been paid to ignore the smugglers. Following the Immigration officials' detainment, the train remained stationary for another few minutes, before the passengers of Amtrak 565 slated for New York City, were sent on their merry voyage.

With the only point of concern behind them, the Columbian smugglers believed they were successful and began their premature celebration. The same aisle seat guard who earlier visited the bar, seemed eager to gulp down a few more shots, as he bolted to the bar before regular transactions were announced. Yves followed the man, who had become totally complacent after the first few rounds, however, the Frenchman was unable to get within arm's reach of the smuggler. There was a young couple between Yves and the trafficker, with the female boasting about her young fiancé, taking her to Atlantic City to be wedded. The tight corridors along the train, offered enough space for two bodies at a time, which made it impossible for the biker to force the smuggler into a detour. Yves had selected his weapon of execution before leaving his seat, which was an eighteen-inch carving knife that he'd used to carve up a lot of his enemies.

The smuggler made it safely to the coach that housed the restaurant and bar, which was two cars behind the coach where their seats were assigned. The Columbian, who possessed that hazy look of an alcoholic, seemed furious to find he was not the first to arrive at the bar, as he jumped on one of the bar stools. An argument soon erupted over the purchase of an entire two-liter bottle of Tanqueray, with 40% alcohol content, which the vendors weren't at liberty to sell. The celebrating Columbian settled for a tray with as many shots of his favorite liquor as it could hold, then made his way back to his guard duty position. As the joyous smuggler passed the toilet facilities, Yves ambushed him by gagging him then, dragged him into a toilet compartment. The blade of his eighteen-inch butcher knife that had been smeared with garlic, sank deep into the smuggler's ribcage repeatedly, before a fatal stab wound pierced his heart. The Frenchman fixed the trafficker on the toilet seat, as if he'd fallen asleep, cleaned up the spilt liquor shots, and closed the door leaving him inside.

With his plot in motion, Yves moved to secure the package he'd come for, after he'd eliminated half the hostiles. Due to the late hour, the lights about the passenger cars were dimmed, to allow fatigued passengers the opportunity to rest. The biker assassin returned to the coach they were assigned and sat directly beside the second smuggler, who had begun dozing off from fatigue.

"What took you so long," demanded the smuggler in Spanish, as he turned to look at the goodies brought to him by his friend?

"Uh," groaned the smuggler, as Yves pierced a vital organ beneath the man's armpit. The biker assassin summoned the train attendant and demanded a blanket for his friend, whom he claimed fell ill along the journey. Once the attendant returned with the blanket, Yves covered the deceased smuggler, who had blood pouring down his arm, before he collected his trophy in preparation to depart the train. There were two bikers waiting for Yves, when he exited the train at the first stop in the United States. The chauffeurs allowed one of their top gunners to relax and snooze, while they drove him back across the Canadian border, following a successful operation.

Damian attended high school at James Lynn High in Montreal, where he met many of his close friends. One such friend was a Caucasian male named James Tea, who was a French-Canadian youth from Saint-Constant, Quebec. James joined the Canadian Armed Forces during his junior year as a cub cadet, and never wavered from the discipline acquired therein. Despite his bravery and his sacrifice to defend his country, James' upbringing taught him the value of a buck, and the hustling skills desired to acquire that buck. Hence, once confronted with the opportunity to earn some serious money dealing weapons to his old connections, James opened an offshore bank account and began supplying customers.

Nicholas had placed an order for some rather sophisticated, high-powered weaponry, that were modified to improve the American soldier's way of life. At the time the order was placed, the weapons, which ranged from long-range sniper rifles, capable of extinguishing one's target from a mile and a half away, to rifles that eliminated their targets around corners, were only available to the U.S. military. However, five months after the original order was placed, Damian received a confirmation phone call that, the order had been filled and was ready for pick-up.

The items ordered by Nicholas came to a grand total of $350 000.00 Can, which was handed to Damian to complete the transaction. Nicholas advised Damian to ride with Killa and two other shooters of his choice, to a prearranged address in Ottawa, Ontario. During their hour and a half trip to Ottawa, the thugs who were usually screw faced and unpleasant, joked around about women, social affairs, and guns. Some of the biggest laughter developed when two of the four men told stories, where they got caught having sex with either someone else's partner, or some father's daughter. The men joked about memories they possessed, where they were forced to either flee or stand and fight, during experiences such as gun battles. One of the men who hopped into the huge Chevy Suburban truck, was mocked for peeing on himself during a shoot-out, against Rough Riders representatives a few years prior.

Damian recounted the precise story; of why it was that certain individuals never journeyed away from their nests, unless they were detailed to a mission. "King man, an Italian brethren' of the family, opened a top-of-the-line clothing store downtown, right in the center of Rough Rider's city. These two idiots decided that, nobody naw stop them from going anywhere, even though there was a civil war going on, where one side of the town, a fight against the other half, so every man stayed strap!"

"You mean like now," joked Killa, who had rarely witnessed a day without the brandishing of firearms, since he began defending the cause!

The comment brought a slight chuckle from the vehicle's occupants, who all knew the statement to be one hundred percent true. "Fi real, still them Kloffie yah decided them going shopping with a bunch a chicks! Splurging and shit all over the place, like nobody don't know them! But you see how downtown is though—big enough to where you can shop in underground malls and above street level, but it's only a matter of time before somebody see you and word get out, and when that happen! I swear it's almost like the cops block off road, and you better have a few extra clips, because some sort a show down always possible! This fool walked out the Italian spot and, a biker boy put him big dutty Desert Eagle to his temple; and pulled the trigger. Them swear say Panta 'dead, cause is like everything freeze, the bags them in him hand drop, him legs get weak and him flatter to the ground, not to mention him bladder release an wet up himself! The biker boy 'til this day, in him grave a wonder how the gun stick, 'cause after that a pure gunshot for about half an hour. A channel-surfing cousin a do, when him call me and show me the big shoot-out, a happen live on the CFCF news station, that's why Nicholas always a watch the news fi see what a go on."

"You really piss up yourself, brethren'," Killa laughed and teased?

"Man, when I felt that blue steel next to my head, man, everything just went loose man! I couldn't hold nothing in man! I had to check my drawers after that, man, 'cause I swore I shit myself, man! Man, it was crazy. Laugh all you want, man, but that was real, man! I swore I was about to meet my maker, man," Panta confessed, and laughed at himself for his stupidity, before he jumped on Damian for revealing his most awkward moment!

"Your ass lucky you still alive to talk about it," stated the driver, who cruised along at a soothing 130 MPH!

As the gangsters neared the Castle Man's introduction sign on the 417, Trans-Canada Highway, the distance sign to Ottawa read fifty-eight miles to the capital. Damian telephoned his connection, who was stationed at the Royal Canadian Force Base, Petawawa, to advise him of his current ETA, which was an estimated twenty-five minutes at the speed they were travelling.

Once they arrived in Ottawa, the capital city of Canada, the men exited the 417, Trans-Canada Highway at the first sign, which read Walkley Road, and veered northbound. The location selected was an abandoned warehouse, which was once used by the premier shingle producer in Canada. The men had done prior dealings from this location, which was ideal for the soldiers whose temporary base was only a few miles away.

Sergeant James Tea had always included the same three officers of the Petawawa RCF base, in his illegal dealings, although there were a few higher-ranked officials whose pockets had to be greased, in order for such high-powered machinery to go unaccounted. The sergeant's allies were Private Doug Hayes, Private Lucien Harbour, and Gunnery Sergeant Matt Sikes. The higher-ranked officials involved in the scheme, were in on the deal since the debut, and their disassociation would be imminent should any accusations or actions be taken against the group. However, the constant flow of money kept the players' interest acute, and with secrecy paramount, nobody lodged their funds in Canadian institutions.

The soldiers arrived before their business counterparts and arranged the viewing of the products they had brought. It had gotten dark, so the soldiers knew they had to get back on base before "lights out". Within minutes, the buyers for the hardware entered the northeast hangar door and proceeded toward the arms dealers. The ambiance was perfect for the transaction and, both parties were eager to attain their portion of the deal, which benefited either sides. Damian first exited their SUV and, greeted their business counterparts, before introducing everyone else. Killa emerged from the 4x4, and inspected the surroundings throughout, before he joined his friends at the vehicle's bumper. After Killa got introduced to the soldiers, their relaxed nature calmed his nerves, while his associates inspected the weapons, which were laid out across a portable metal table.

"How the fuck come you in the army and you getting fat when, all that training is supposed to keep you slim and trim," Damian asked, Gunnery Sergeant Sikes?

"I can't speak for everybody else, but my training is eating and firing weapons, all day, all night," responded the sergeant, who found the comment slightly funny!

"Yeah, that's right, Sarge, we told you that exact same thing," said Private Harbour.

"Woo, me can't wait 'till them pussies in Montreal fuck with us," Panta hollered, as he keenly inspected the M-16 automatic rifle with the 40 MM grenade launcher attached!

"Killa, feel how nice and light this is," Damian said, as he tossed the Jamaican fugitive a M-203 compact grenade launcher!

Killa nonchalantly looked at the weapon, before he placed it on the table and picked up a M240B medium machine gun. There was an AS-50 sniper rifle that caught his attention across the table, but he had never fired a weapon that had to be belt-fed. The first thing the rude boy did was to insert a bullet-belt into the firing chamber, to test how easily the weapon loaded. The orchestrator of the deal was handed the briefcase containing the full payment. Sergeant James Tea opened the attaché case and began inspecting the deal sealer, when a loud shout came from across the warehouse.

"Nobody move! Hands in the air! Now!" A loud shout came from the southwest section of the warehouse.

Basic soldiers and Military Police began springing up from sewer covers, flying in through windowpanes, and charging in on foot, as the participants of the illegal transaction began looking around at each other. Killa removed the safety switch from the M240B machine gun and began emptying the belt at their antagonists. Young Panta needed no invitation to join the offence, as he moved to the front of the pack, believing his weapon sufficient enough to ward off their oppressors. Their initial outburst caused the invading forces to prematurely scatter, as bullets ripped through those who refused to seek shelter. The attacking soldiers returned fire once the opportunity was available, hence it became immediately evident who had undergone proper weapons training. Panta's brown eyes widened, after his M-16 automatic rifle indicated the bullet chamber had been emptied, though he quickly selected a grenade for launch as back-up. The sharpshooters of the army tattooed Panta, as he released a detrimental grenade that killed an additional five soldiers, before he succumbed to his injuries.

Gunnery Sergeant Matt Sikes had, like his assailants, taken a solid oath, to never bear arms against his countrymen and allies of war, which was a promise he intended to keep. The eighteen-year veteran of the armed forces threw his hands high in the air and fell to his knees, to gesture his peaceful surrender, while bullets sounded all around him. The gunnery sergeant could be seen shedding tears with his eyes tightly closed, as the thought of the humiliating procedures to come devastated him.

"I didn't mean to! I'm a true soldier, you hear me? A true soldier," Sikes exclaimed!

"Sarge, get your face in the cement before they put you there," James screamed from among Killa, Damian, and Tank, who were holding fast their position.

Killa caught sight of four army personnel attempting to flank them, by circling the warehouse and attacking from the rear. The men broke away from their platoon, which was being overpowered, despite their large numbers, by six armed and defiant men. The need to locate protection against the attacking Military Police, influenced Damian to overturn the table with weapons, although he misjudged the durability and thought it was bulletproof. Damian and his mates shot and killed many of their attackers, under the dominant force of Killa's M240B, until the bullet-belt ended.

Killa grabbed for the high-powered, fifty-caliber AS-50 sniper rifle and spun it toward the separated party, then illuminated the night scope to gain sight into the dark. Twenty feet away through a soiled pane of glass, Killa was able to catch sight of the men making their way to the furthest end of the warehouse. The gangster timed the men along the cement wall, then fired once he believed the platoon had reached a zinc-sheeting portion of the wall. The humongous blast tore out a twelve-inch gap from the wall and remarkably blasted two soldiers into Neverland. The remaining two soldiers became frightened and confused and decided to abandon the mission, fearing they would not be allowed to reach the specified coordinates.

Private Lucien Harbour and Private Doug Hayes were using the Hummer they rode in, as protection against the onslaught of bullets being spat at them. A bullet from the military police struck the gasoline tank and caused the vehicle to explode, which killed the evasive arms dealers. With their numbers dwindling against a determined force, Killa and the remaining deifiers began moving to the Chevy SUV, in an attempt to escape with their lives.

Tank was the first rude boy into the vehicle, therefore he started the engine while simultaneously laying cover fire through the window, for his friends to escape. Killa made sure he retrieved a few weapons despite the hostile environment; hence, he grabbed the lightweight M-203 compact grenade launcher, the AS-50 sniper rifle, the M240B machine gun, plus ammunition for them all. As he made his way to the SUV, he stumbled across the briefcase containing the payment, which he scooped up despite being unable to manage the load. Not everyone was able to move to the escape vehicle, but they continued administering suppressive fire against the MPs, which allowed Killa to run and dive into the SUV loaded with artillery and collateral.

James and Damian, who were the farthest from the SUV, began moving toward the escape vehicle, though the MPs were determined to stop them from leaving. Killa had never fired a grenade launcher, although the gangster did not need an instruction manual for any weaponry. The ghetto war veteran took the M-203 compact launcher and fired a grenade at three MPs, who held his friends suppressed and stopped them from reaching the vehicle. The grenade struck the barrier that protected the soldiers and blew everything sky-high.

The commanding officer for the Military Police grew furious at the notion that his intended targets could escape, despite his teams' superior training and skills. A few of the soldiers had positioned themselves behind supportive beams, to protect themselves from the gang of thugs, who'd managed to dominate despite their meagre numbers.

"Fuck," yelled the commander, as he and three of his squad members were forced to tuck their heads protectively beneath a barrier, that offered them protection against the crushing bullets.

One of the MPs posted atop a second-tier walkway, opened fire at Damian as he attempted the final sprint to the SUV. A bullet from the soldier's AK rifle, struck Damian in the right shoulder and flung him into a very compromising position. Tank caught sight of Damian going down and emptied the remainder of his automatic rifle's magazine, at the soldier who'd wounded his boss' cousin. The driver sought to award his brethren enough time to safely get aboard the SUV, thus while he hindered the soldier from striking at Damian, Tank yelled at the injured thug 'to get in the truck'!

Damian struggled to his feet and awkwardly drew his pistol with his left hand, then staggering to the rear truck door. The commanding officer for the Military Police rose to one knee and aligned Damian into his firing scope. Knowing he was about to kill one of the arms buyers; brought a slight smirk to the soldier's face as he squeezed the trigger. The commander tracked the bullet as it pierced through thin air en-route to its intended target. Damian's soldier friend noticed that he was about to get killed by the Military Police, and shoulder tackled him into the SUV.

"Get the fuck out of here," yelled James, as he returned fire through the open door at his estranged family!

"Don't let them get away," barked the frustrated commander, as the surviving soldiers fired bullets at the escaping SUV.

As the SUV sped through the huge hangar door, the commander in charge began sequestering the communications officer, in order to alert all public officials of the fleeing thugs. There were nine MPs unaccounted for, before further investigation revealed the communications officer and his equipment had been blown to smithereens, alongside other fellow soldiers. That disappointing discovery increased the commander's anxiety, as he stood over the kneeling gunnery sergeant, before putting his boot to the side of Sikes' face.

"Someone put this traitor in irons and get him out of my sight! Sergeant Docket, I want you to access the weapons and see to their transfer back to the base! The rest of you, gather the dead and the rest of the equipment! Let's go, gentlemen, today! I don't want to be out in this night dew longer than I have to," ordered the commander!

While the commander prepared the official documentation detailing what transpired for the Review Board, his squadron followed orders and retrieved their government's property, that was scattered throughout. Other officials from various organizations began arriving on the scene, such as the Royal Canadian Mounted Police, the base commander Admiral Tate, along with ambulances and mortuary vehicles.

Within three quarters of an hour, Admiral Tate, who vowed to find the salespersons behind the arms-deals, dispatched the vehicle assigned to transfer the stolen weapons back to base. The Ford Econoline 350 truck that was packed with the weapons which were slated for sale, was also used to transport the weapons and personal effects of the soldiers killed in the conflict earlier that night. Two senior privates were assigned the task of returning the truck's inventory to the local army base, which was only a few miles away, without added escorts for increased security.

The occupants of the Ford Econoline truck had no idea their skirmish with the weapons' buyers had piqued the interests of news reporters, who had to be held back by local police officers, at the abandoned warehouse's entrance. As the transport soldiers passed through the police barrier, a swarm of reporters corralled the truck, seeking confirmation about what they had heard. The soldiers, who'd lowered the windows of the Econoline truck for ventilation against the humidity, were forced to seal up the cab to avoid the intrusive questions. Once the soldiers cleared the reporters' checkpoint, they immediately reopened the windows and selected their favorite dial on the radio, as they cruised back to the base. Private Lee Chow brought the Ford Econoline 350 to a halt at the traffic light at Walkley Road and St. Laurent Boulevard. Very soon thereafter, a bike rider pulled up along the right side of the truck and waited for the light to change.

A Caucasian brunette out on an early morning jog caught the attention of the two soldiers, who keenly watched her jog from the right sidewalk, until she reached the front of their truck. The beautiful six-feet-two-inch female, who had a round cantaloupe ass in her exercise tights, wore an alter top that firmly secured her size twenty-eight breasts. As the female jogger passed by Lee Chow's window frame, the loud bang from a weapon frightened the private, whose companion fell on his right shoulder. The unmonitored bike rider shot and killed the passenger, whose focus was captured by the jogger. Before the surviving private turned and looked what happened to his associate, Lee wiped a slab of brain matter from the side of his face. The luscious female joggers walked to the driver's window and tapped the door with her firearm, then signaled him to exit the cabin. Private Chow shrugged the body from his shoulder and held up his hands, to signal his willingness to cooperate.

"Get out the vehicle, baby," softly instructed the female, as she evict-ed the private, confiscated his weapon, climbed into the truck, and drove away. The bike rider followed the truck, and they made a U-turn instead, then drove back toward the highway.

Part 21

The Gazette reported a story that originated in Montreal, Canada, though the actual events occurred halfway across the world in Shanghai, China. The economic trade arrangement between Canada and China, reported the discovery of a corpse, which was found hanging from a meat rack among exported beef, on a huge cargo ship slated for China. Inspector No. 374, Lee Han Sung, was checking the refrigerated container's supply, when he came across the nude and badly abused corpse of a man, strung up with a baseball bat lodged in his rectum. There was dried blood covering the entire body, with huge lacerations into the skin from head to toe. The discovery startled Inspector No. 374, who raced to his superiors and revealed his findings.

Although the discovery frightened Inspector Lee Han Sung, the corpse was not the first of such to be found. In fact, an open investigation was being pursued by a joint team of investigators from both countries, lobbying to terminate the human anatomies being sent to the butcher's market. The forensic report indicated the man had been killed and refrigerated in Montreal, before he was stacked among the frozen cattle, voyaging to the mainland China. An autopsy was done to determine the cause of death, as investigators compiled all the evidence, they possible could. Photos were taken of the man's face in order to properly identify him, although detectives had to first consult a sketch artist, to reconstruct the man's disfigured face. The sketch of the corpse was run through an international database, which provided investigators with the victim's real identity.

The Chinese authorities made evident the fact they had no wrongdoing in the tragic death of the Canadian male, so as to avoid any future disruptions between the two countries. The body was flown back to Canada at the country's expense, although Chinese officials saw to it that the corpse was given top priority. An insider at the Chinese international dock, who quickly jumped on an opportunity to pocket a few bucks, leaked word to the press, while the Agricultural Department contemplated whether they should release the story.

The frozen corpse, who was later identified after officials decided to release the story, was the eighth Canadian victim to be found overseas, packed into small crates or strung up inside containers. "Unsafe Meats & Contaminated Foods", was the headline for the story in the local press, which soon sparked an outcry from residents lobbying to terminate the free trade arrangement between the two countries. Certain officials of parliament began demanding that the shipment of beef be returned, after being exposed to a human corpse, that carried possible life-threatening bacteria.

Since the Defenders' originated, Brogan Alfonso who was the man credited for slaying Yves Lafleur, the former Rough Riders leader, had remained a constant thorn in the bikers' ass. Brogan headed the mighty Defenders crew, which competed strongly for their territory versus the Rough Riders' western division. Since the brutal slaying of one of the Rough Riders' most feared leaders, Brogan had survived nearly a dozen attempts on his life, ranging from sniper shots to bomb explosions. The lives of his family members had also been targeted, by biker extremists who believed that, "if you couldn't catch the prize, you fucked up the runners-up". The latest victim to fall to the Alfonso family curse was Brogan's youngest brother, Brandon, who was just in the wrong place at the wrong time.

Brandon was on his way to spend some time with a female he'd recently met at a party, when an altercation between he and some patrol officers, turned ugly. The twenty-year-old youngster had used public transportation to voyage from the West Island to the Atwater Metro

Station in Little Burgundy. The young man exited the Metro at Atwater Street and quickly hustled ahead of traffic to cross the road, although the traffic light wasn't on amber. There was a squad patrol parked halfway up the block, and the officers at first appeared uninterested in the jaywalker. The young Alfonso continued his journey to the female's house, with his headphones over his ears playing music. Before the young college student, who took no interest in his brother's choice of career, could walk the next block, the patrolling officers were on him.

The officers busted around the corner with their lights flashing, as if they had been summoned to an emergency, however, they drove directly onto the pedestrian pavement and stopped in front of Brandon. Both occupants leapt from the cruiser and withdrew their weapons, which startled the young man who only voyaged to that side of town, in hopes of getting some pussy.

"Get up against the fucking car and place your hands on the hood," ordered the passenger side officer!

"What the hell did I do," Brandon questioned?

"What? You didn't notice the red light when you ran across the road," argued the driver?

"Sorry, I was in a hurry," exclaimed the lad!

The officers grabbed Brandon and tossed him against the hood of their cruiser. With his hands on the hood of the car, young Brandon who had never been in such a predicament, twitched at the touch of the frisking officer. Before the officer proceeded with the body search, he enquired, "Now, you don't have any sharp objects in your pocket that might injure me, do you?"

"Not at all, sir," responded the nervous lad.

The officer checked Brandon's pockets and found nothing except for his bus pass, a few dollars, his wallet, and his keys. The young man had his school identification, which properly identified him among other documents that proved his eligibility to be in the country, yet one photo clip found of he and his elder sibling, brought his demise. Once the officers saw the photo clip, their nasty attitudes got nastier and the whole cycle flipped against Brandon.

"So you're a gangster," implied the frisking officer!

"Come on, man! I'm a student. It says so right there on my ID! You can even call the school if you don't believe me," said Brandon!

"You're posing big time with gangsters, you must be a part of the crew," suggested the driver, after sneaking a peek at the documents?

"It's not like that! He's my brother," Brandon answered.

The officer who searched Brandon, unexpectedly jammed the butt of his metallic flashlight into the student's lower spine. The young lad's limbs gave way, and he crumbled to the turf like fallen leaves come autumn.

The officer withdrew his restraints, then smacked the handcuff on and said, "You're under arrest for disobeying the traffic signal. You have the right to remain silent, anything you say can be used against you in a court of law. You have the right to an attorney of your choice if you so choose. If you can't afford one, one will be appointed to you by the courts. Do you understand these rights I've explained to you?"

The officers went through the motions of an actual arrest, due to the fact that a few bystanders had begun hovering around. Before witnesses could begin speculating, the officers scooped Brandon from off the turf and flung him into the rear of their car. That was the final time anybody saw Brandon alive.

Sofia Alfonso wept every night her youngest son was missing, while she mainly prayed for his body to be recovered, in order to properly commemorate the young man for his vast achievements. The fifty-seven-year-old widow had grown accustomed to the results of any family member going missing, after thus far losing two other members of the family to violence. Brandon was just the latest casualty of a war that had absolutely nothing to do with the future engineer, considering the family sustained the loss of one other brother, a cousin, and an uncle, who, like Brandon, lived a crime-free life. Once Brandon had been missing for the first six hours without a trace, Mrs. Alfonso was convinced that she'd seen the last of her son and went to church to pray.

There were two other members of the Alfonso clan, who also met their demise on the battlefield, skirmishing against their primary foe. Brogan's brother, Joey, and cousin, Todd, were killed defending their family away from home, and, as such, RIP West Island Defenders Syndicate, was painted on their murals in a local park, as a tribute toward their everlasting memory. Brother Joey, who was the third of five boys, was killed in one of the largest street shoot-outs in the city's history. On one side of the road were Rough Riders extremists, fully armed with automatic weapons, exchanging bullets with Defenders lynch men, who were trapped like fish out of water. Pedestrians fled for their lives in the center of downtown, while these two vigilante movements scattered shots heinously at each other. At the end of said battle, nine gangbangers, five Defenders, and four bikers were brought to the morgue, along with two officers, who should have followed the crowd and fled in the opposite direction of the spitting bullets.

Cousin Todd, or "Loco Extreme", as he was referred to by his gangbanging family, spent two weeks in Afghanistan as a Coalition force member. While battling the Taliban Insurgent Forces in the war-torn country, Private Alfonso was shot in the ribs and narrowly escaped death, after his convoy was ambushed in a small town outside Kandahar. The private was sent home after the incident and released from the army, and as such returned to Montreal to be among family.

The family motto, which was "Defend to the end your family and blood," plunged Todd into the middle of the war between his family and the Rough Riders, after he went to his cousin Mikey's assistance, one cold winter evening. A well-planned hit was arranged for Mikey, who had orchestrated the plot that destroyed a storage depot, that belonged to the Rough Riders organization. Espionage levels of intelligence were brought to Mikey's attention, which indicated that the storage facility was being used to store exquisite antique automobiles.

The automobiles had been stolen from their wealthy owners and sold to foreign businessmen, thus, they sat awaiting export in the storage facility. The stolen car industry made the bikers an annual $500 million, which, like most of their fundraisers, went to "The Society" as payment for their judgment as overseers. The shipment of cars contained twelve rare collectibles, that were all stolen from targeted owners, mainly, eccentric millionaires who simply spent their money buying items the general population couldn't afford. Mikey and one of his bandit friends broke into the storage facility, stole a 1964 Aston Martin, and set fire to the remaining structure. Every vehicle inside that warehouse went up in flames, while the bandits drove away laughing. Non-distribution of the vehicles in turn cost the bikers, respectability, money, and public inquiry into their business affairs.

News reporters flocked to the U-Haul storage and rental facility, located close to the pier on Old Notre Dame Street, after word leaked that the unsolved mystery behind the disappearance of countless millionaires' toys had been solved. Even though the evidence pointed at the Rough Riders gang as the only culprits, nobody dared mentioned them in connection with the theft. Investigators concluded after checking the VIN numbers of each vehicle found, that "the vehicles were indeed being sought after, and further investigations were on the way"!

There was no way for the biker organization to legally discredit the theft charges lobbied against them, by the insurance companies which were held liable for the stolen vehicles. The Rough Rider's lawyers made a deal with the attorneys for all the insurance companies involved, which sent the operator of the storage facility to prison for eight months and, steered the blame away from the bikers. When emergency officials arrived at the burning storage facility, there was nobody on sight to question or arrest, so instead of prosecuting the biker crew, officials decided to remove the gang from all involvement. Rough Rider members understood that they could be called upon anytime for small sacrifices, that were vital to the success of the club. Unfortunately, the storage facility was Yves Bouchard's legal source of business, therefore the mercenary turned himself in following the attorneys' arrangement.

Days after the arson ordeal, reports reached the Rough Riders captain that Mikey had been spotted parading the town in the re-stolen, '64 Aston Martin. The order was immediately given to locate and assassinate Mikey and everyone who aided in the exposure of one of the bikers' major enterprises. With Yves imprisoned for a few months and members of "The Society" calling for unification, Martain felt even more empowered to erase his enemies, rather than embrace them.

Cousin Todd received his honorable discharge for bravery from the army and sought to join the police cadets, before discovering that the criminal histories of certain individuals in his family prevented those dreams from becoming a reality. The ex-soldier of the 39th Battalion located in Surey, Quebec, believed in hard, honest work, and devoted himself to working construction while attending college. Todd was returning home from classes one evening, when he stumbled upon three uniformed officers harassing Mikey, behind the Lola's confectionary store on Sources Boulevard. The officers lay awaiting Mikey and two of his partners, after they'd entered the convenient store to purchase cigarettes and soda. The officers preferred confronting the men in a situation where they had the upper hand, and thus waited for all three men to enter the vehicle, before swooping down on them.

"The cops," yelled Ryan, who, along with Johnny, bailed from the front section of his automobile and took off running!

The lone rear passenger was caught attempting to flee the vehicle and soon found himself trapped in a den of lions. A search of the detained thug revealed a Glock 40 shoved into Mikey's waistband, with two extra clips in the adjacent pocket. The uniforms and badges disclosed the officers' ambition, but none of the disloyal civil servants aboard cruiser 5-16, were afraid to exhibit their Rough Riders insignia tattoos. All the West Island Defenders knew of these officers and would attempt to avoid them at all cost. The arresting formalities where adhere to, considering a few locals had stopped to watch what was taking place.

Matters grew worse for Mikey once he was placed in the rear of the cruiser, with both hands handcuffed behind his back. The officer seated in the rear could barely wait for the cruiser to go into motion, before he started repeatedly rammed his metallic baton/flashlight into Mikey's ribs. The long ride to the Cop Shop that Mikey expected was short and decisive, as the coppers simply circled the building and parked in the rear, which was allocated for delivery trucks.

After fracturing two of Mikey's ribs, the rear officer demanded, "You fuckers like to take things that are not yours? I'm going to ask you one time only—where's the fucking car?"

Mikey could feel a distinctive change in the amounts of oxygen he was allowed to inhale, and he crouched over in an attempt to protect his ribs. The groans he muffled were difficult to transform into words, and every muscle in his body tightened for what might transpire. The officer came down in the center of his back with a thundering blow, which prompted Mikey to sit upright, with pain gushing to the tips of his toes. All at once, the cruiser came to a halt, as the punishers' friends decided to join the party.

All Mikey could hear being yelled by one of the front passengers was,

"Get his ass out the back of my cruiser, before he starts bleeding his shit all over my seats!"

The door opened and a boot to the right arm pitched Mikey directly from the seat, out onto the pavement. Todd came by after the officers had had their way with Mikey, who could only manage to crouch in order to protect himself. The student was taking the shortcut through a hole in the fence behind the confectionary store, when he caught a glimpse of the winter jacket the assaulted man was wearing. With all three officers putting a clubbing on Mikey, they had no inkling that they were being watched, and Todd began looking around for means to equalize the injustice.

There was a garbage container across from the Subways, where Todd noticed a few empty soda bottles and bricks, stacked in the corner. Despite all that could have gone wrong, the young man hid behind the container and began flinging items. From the glooms and shadows of the dark came a soda bottle, which opened a huge laceration above the driver's left eye. The officer grabbed for his face, as if a flash fire had burned off the skin.

"We got you cops on camera," Todd shouted!

Some joggers passing by the mouth of the alleyway noticed the commotion and began moving toward the officers. Todd used his combat training to maneuver himself, before he hurled his second article at the frightened policemen. By the time the brick collided with the head of the shotgun-riding officer, the decision had already been made to abandon their detainee and flee. The coppers released a few scattered shots, aimed at convincing their antagonists to remain at bay, while they hastily made their escape.

After personally witnessing the evil, that those who had sworn to defend so mindfully committed, Todd changed his perspective on life and joined the vigilante movement. "Loco Extreme" soon changed the tactical approach to dealing with the enemy, as he inaugurated the art of bomb explosions. Within the coming weeks, Todd became one of the most infamous men in the Defenders' history, after levelling the Rough Riders' clubhouse with a bomb that drew national attention. The bomb prompted government officials to question, "whether it was related to overseas terrorist activities or if bombs were now a part of the daily lives of Canadians?" Todd made their enemies cower with fear, which prompted more phone conferences between bikers than ever before registered throughout their history.

Todd was assassinated, along with a hooker he'd only recently acquired, by an officer of the law who pulled him over, claiming he'd run a red light. The officer collected Todd's driver's license, car registration, and proof of insurance, returned to his cruiser and pretended to be issuing a ticket, before he returned with his side arm cocked and ready to fire. The officer shot and killed Todd before turning the gun at the lone female, who had her index finger shot clean off, after attempting to block the shots fired at her with both of her hands. The officer checked Todd's vital signs to be sure that he'd died and tossed the weapon used to kill both victims onto Todd's lap, before returning to his vehicle. The copper cancelled the flashing lights and slowly left the scene, without so much as a call to emergency assistance to report the incident.

Part 22

Miss Samantha Tea made her living by cleaning office buildings after hours for Molly Maid Services. The morning following her son's altercation with his fellow brothers in arms, Samantha returned home completely unaware of the developments. There was a huge commotion with members from the press, law enforcement personnel, and emergency handlers parading in front of the maid's apartment building. At first glance, the fear of a disaster such as fire devastating her building went through her mind, as her asthmatic condition forced her to gasp for additional oxygen. The single mother of three was bombarded with reporters immediately after exiting her co-worker's vehicle, a few feet away from the pile of emergency wagons. Neither of the janitorial employees thought the huge crowd they speculated about while approaching the building, was awaiting one of them, thereby, an array of questions fluttered in from the many reporters who were scattered across the walkway.

"Are you hiding your son the traitor inside your apartment, Ms. Tea?"

"Can you tell us, why are there MPs searching your apartment?"

"Have you been in contact with your son?"

"Do you know where or did you instruct your son to hide from authorities?"

Samantha held her coat tightly closed and kept her purse tucked underneath her arm, while she walked briskly ahead and ignored all the questions. There were also parents of a couple of the young men who'd lost their lives in the shoot-out, among the vultures scavenging for something to report. Those grieving parents were sure to voice their anger, at a parent who had struggled to provide for her children and had taught them wrong from right since Day One.

An angry father yelled, "What kind of a fucking parent are you? They should try you instead of your butcher son!"

A grieving mother cried, "Your animal murdered my son! I want you to always remember that! Murderer, murderer, murderer!"

Another female shouted, "I pray they find your son and give him the same opportunity he gave my boy!"

The accused maid's coworker watched with awe, until some of the reporters began moving toward her asking questions, at which she pressed gas and drove away. Samantha's entire focus was on her youngest son of thirteen years, who was her sole responsibility, because he was still a minor. The maid hastened her pace to the front entrance, having to use force to clear a path through the hounding reporters and hecklers. Once inside the building that prohibited loiterers and solicitors from entering, Samantha rode the elevator to her tenth-story apartment, hesitant to find out if her premises were, "being searched by law officials".

There were law officials from the Canadian Army [Military Police], the Ottawa Police Department, Royal Canadian Mounted Police, gentlemen in suits and other personnel in green uniforms, strolling all over her hallway whose job classifications Samantha did not acquire. An officer, who was stationed at the end of the hall, stopped Samantha as she stepped from the elevator. The maid frantically identified herself, before she was allowed to proceed onward. The fatigued female, who'd been toiling since 10:30 the previous evening, hastily found her son, who'd received the fright of his life when the SWAT team barged into their home.

"For God's sake, what the hell is going on around here," Samantha screamed, once she'd gained a hold of her son?

"Mom, they're looking for James! They said they thought he ran off here after some shoot-out last night! But they scared the Jesus out of me when they broke into the apartment!"

"Thank God you weren't shot!"

An officer in a green suit walked over to Samantha and her boy and introduced himself. The officer was placed in charge of apprehending Sergeant James Tea, for the AWOLed soldier to be court-martialed and sentenced.

"Hello, madam. My name is Christophe Lavoie. I am with Army Corrections Division, and I have been put in charge of capturing your son. I would very much appreciate your cooperation with this matter, so we can apprehend James without any further altercations," began the French native officer.

"Did you boys find James anywhere on the premises," Samantha asked?

"I'm afraid we didn't, madam!"

"Okay, then! You and your gun-wielding buddies tore my door off, ran up into my apartment, scared the shit out of my boy, nobody removed their shoes and so now my house is filthy, I gotta clean it, and you're trying to get me to snitch on one of my other boys!? After a bunch of know-it-all reporters, just tarnished the shit out of me! I came home to relax, take a pee, have a cup of tea, and get some rest, but you and your evidence-collecting friends won't let that happen. So, I want everybody out of my house right now, before I catch a case for fucking up one of you! Get out, get all your shit and get the fuck out," Samantha angrily yelled!

"Here is my card in case you decide to assist us in this matter madam," Monsieur Lavoie indicated, as he scampered out behind his peers.

The officers were in the process of evacuating the premises, when Samantha's home phone rang. Speculations of it being the man they sought, hindered a few members of the Military Police, who awaited confirmation of who the caller was. Samantha walked over to the phone in the hallway and answered it. The caller was her girlfriend from work who had brought her home, and sought to uplift her co-worker's spirit, after receiving the full disclosure of what occurred.

"Lord have mercy! Are you okay, baby? Those vultures wouldn't even allow you to get into your building. You know I had to get home to the baby, or I would have kicked a hole through them reporters for you," Samantha's co-worker exclaimed!

"Grace, I feel like I'm a criminal in my own home. All sorts of police all over the house, in my panty drawers and Lord knows where else!"

The officers exited Samantha's domain once they became satisfied the caller was not the man they sought. Samantha's friend, Grace, who had been watching the morning's newscast, suggested she tuned in to CBC for further details on the story. While the confused mother watched the news highlights, her youngest son grabbed his school bag and yelled, "bye mom", before he left through the door. The references about James on the news immediately overwhelmed Samantha, whose attention was not focused on the fact, her high school pupil had declared 'he was leaving for school'. Moments after the clack of the door sounded, Samantha realized her teenaged son had unknowingly departed for the parade of vultures, before she could warn him to stay home from school for a few days.

"Oh my God, Gracie! My baby left for school," Samantha exclaimed, as she flung the phone onto the sofa and ran out the front door!

Samantha ran down the stairs instead of waiting for the elevator, opened the main entrance to the building, and found her son being gang-rushed by the slew of reporters, who were camping out in front her apartment building. The frustrations of the morning brought the vicious protective mother to the forefront, as Samantha began slandering the reporters, who had earlier taken advantage of her.

"You parasites stay away from my boy, and if any of you have any problem with any of my children, you bitches know where I live. As a parent, I raised my children knowing right from wrong, and if later in life they decide to mess up, I can't guide them forever! When my boy was throwing his life on the line for this country, he was something to you then! Now a little mishap occurs and he's public enemy number one! Stay away from me and my family and that is all I have to report!"

James Tea sat with a bottle of Canadian Club whiskey while watching the skit of his mother against the media. There were muscled guards racing around him, as the voice of a doctor in an adjoining room yelled for additional support. The loud murmurs of Damian could be heard throughout the house, as a physician attempted to save his arm, which was almost severed from his body. The physician could be heard barking instructions at the apprentices who aided him, due to their inability to stabilize the patient. Damian scratched, punched, and kicked those attempting to subdue him, as the unbearable pain that had rendered him unconscious twice before, threatened his existence due to the huge amount of blood lost.

James was a twelve-year veteran of the army, who knew and understood the penalties and consequences of his actions. The sergeant expected to be named the principal conspirator behind the mishap that occurred, and would welcome an eternal life sentence behind bars, although he knew the contrary was imminent. There was such a stir inside the guest house/guard quarters attached to Kevin's mansion that morning, that it led to the soldier believing he was still on base, with the family he'd gone to war with. Several well-dressed men came marching down the stairs from the third level, as the intoxicated soldier raised his bottle of liquor in appreciation of his mother's valor, before reacquiring the taste of the Canadian Club whiskey.

"That's right, Mom, tell them motherfuckers like it is! Fuck them all, anyways! I don't need them," James yelled!

The men walked to the main house and entered the premises from the side door that led to the grounds. They met with Kevin and went over a few details regarding their tasks, before exiting through the main entrance. The men surrounded and ushered their client into an awaiting SUV, before they divided their sum between the two vehicles. The identical SUVs speed off along the half-mile property driveway, before they reached the main guard's gate, which was always tightly guarded by a number of well-armed men, who also patrolled the terrain surrounding the house. After clearing the main guard's shed, the men had to drive another quarter mile down a private road, that was built with hidden metal spikes that ran across the roadway, which was their first line of defense against intruding vehicles. The SUVs entered the main roadway at Oliver West road, which was a few minutes away from the highway. St. Jean Baptist Boulevard was one of the two frequently used routes into Chateauguay, with the next being Pont Champlain, which was over thirty miles away. There was the St. Lawrence River separating the island of Montreal from its Chateauguay neighbors, with the all-important Pont Mercier Bridge being the sole means of crossing for miles.

Kevin received a phone call from his prized nemesis, Martain Lafleur, who called to offer his condolences on the retirement of his archrival. Martain had organized a demonstration of force that, was practically a page torn from Kevin's war doctrines. The overzealous Frenchman had in his possession, the very same long-range cannons that Kevin had speculated would terminate the war, with an ingenious plot to gain victory over a foe he'd rendered as formidable.

"Genius, genius, genius! I have turned things around, but I must give you credit on a plot well planned! I've got you now, you son of a bitch! Let's see you get out of this one, you black piece of shit," Martain lamented, believing Nicholas was aboard his convoy!

Earlier that morning before daybreak, a model Bell-206 helicopter hovered above the Pont Mercier Bridge, at which two men disembarked and slid down on ropes. The men were dressed in black, with black masks and carried two huge automatic rifles. Once they slid down onto the overhead framework of the bridge, Martain had his people anchored two of the stolen AS-50 automatic sniper rifles atop the metal frame. Both weapons were prepared by two sharpshooters, capable of centering a penny from a thousand yards away.

The phone call Martain made was synchronized by the Rough Riders' captain, who had to inject his farewell comment at the thorn, who had ached him for far too long. Directly following his threat, an onslaught of bullets opened up on the travelling SUVs, from a standpoint ahead that was indefensible. The sharpshooters aiming through the AS-50 precision scopes, waited until both vehicles were two hundred yards away, before they opened fire. Fifty-caliber armor-piercing bullets completely ripped through the SUVs, and tore away windshield, severed heads from their shoulders, ripped open chest cavity and detached other limbs. The bullets also destroyed the leather seats, interior upholstery, busted tires, deactivated the engine, before striking and erupting the fuselage, which caused them to explosions.

Once it became evident that the vehicles had been destroyed, the shooters armed two timers that were attached to explosive devices on the weapons. The helicopter returned and sent down the extraction ropes, therefore the shooters attached themselves then signaled their readiness. With both men securely fastened the helicopter flew away but, travelled westbound along the Saint Laurence River until it vanished from sight.

The weapons used to deliver the tyranny that obstructed thousands of morning commuters, were destroyed as the C-4 explosive blasted aspects of the weapons into the Saint Lawrence River and onto the roadways below.

Kevin knew his opponent well enough to take him at his very word, hence, he assumed his aides aboard the SUVs were possibly in danger. Once the threat had been administered, Kevin's also feared for his son's safety, therefore he immediately disconnected the link between Martain and himself, in order to alert those in charge of his son at home. The decoy, which was meant to trick suspected informants, featured a Rastafarian attired as Kevin, along with his usual two-vehicle entourage. The boss' reduced security force was equally as deadly as any twelve-men protection force, considering they were armed to the teeth with guns, bombs, and more guns.

"Killa, link up Crazy Indian and the convoy and tell them to watch out," Kevin exclaimed, as he nervously awaited a response on his home phone line!

The telephone was answered by one of Kevin's Indian maids named Hyacinth, who relieved the gangster's mind with her mild and relaxed tone. The maid calmly followed her employer's orders, which were to notify all security personnel of a possible breach and ensured his son's safety. Kevin had developed a fascination in safety chambers, after watching a film where the essential concept saved a family from invaders, who'd broken in with evil intentions. The gangster insisted his son be placed inside the chamber, with adequate help and support to protect him fully.

"Mi can't get no signal from the phone in the van," alerted Killa, after attempting the call a few times.

"Boss, I was just talking to Leo, and his cell went dead, too," said the chauffeur, after Killa's provoking revelation!

A silent calm fell over the four occupants inside the dark, limousine-tinted Mercedes 500 Benz, after the final judgment on who had been attacked became evident. Kevin withered away into the soft leather contours of his seat, as he puffed the fumes from his marijuana joint through the rear sunroof. It wasn't long before a conniving smirk grew on Kevin's face, which was generally the indication of a brainstorm plot by the boss.

Killa whispered to his long-time associate, "Why you pull for a decoy today of all days? Something you never did before?"

"Knowledge come through all sources, mi boy," began Kevin, as he inhaled a cloud of toxins into his lungs, before slowly blowing it through the open vent. "You see the shipment me send you fellows to pick up? After the altercation between you all and the batty boy them, someone walked right in and snatch them up the shipment, while on its way back to the base! With this important meeting this morning, mi had to make sure 'bout some speculations mi had! Everything else is just elementary!"

The longer ride along Interstate-30 to the Champlain Bridge took an extra hour, yet safely brought Kevin and company into the city. The Honorable Sir Joseph McArthur had personally contacted the only man he believed capable of disrupting the plots of a secret organization, intent on dominating once again the ruling and handling of the Quebec government. The politician invited Kevin to his personal home in order to avoid the prying eyes of the public. Minister McArthur had a fully scheduled day ahead of him, and so, he chose the early portion of the morning, since it was his only grace period that day.

The AK assault rifle that Apache had lying across his lap was so huge that, they wondered if the guards assigned to the counsellor would allow them free entry. The 500 Benz came to a halt at the guard's gate, only for the guard to pinpoint where their host awaited them. As the vehicle pulled up to the main house, the minister's wife walked out to greet her husband's guests. Kevin and his entourage with their big guns and all marched behind the main lady up to their million-dollar house.

Should this intended meeting be a hoax, Kevin and company, after their morning's loss, were not willing to take any further chances. Proper introductions were made once the French doors were closed behind those involved, as the minister personally invited his honored guests into his luscious home. Tank chose to remain near the front door and maintained a constant visual of their vehicle, to ensure that no one tampered with the ride. Killa and Apache joined the minister's wife for a cup of tea, inside the day room as she watched her favorite morning program, The View.

"Suzy? Tea for everyone, please," the lady of the house commanded? "So, you gentlemen are those thugs I've been reading about from the south side?"

"That would be correct," Apache answered, with his rough Indian tone!

"Huh, you are quite the wild one now, aren't you!"

The Honorable Joseph McArthur and his esteemed guest both retreated to his office for the business of the day. The minister went right to the business he'd invited Kevin over for, as he began with confidential tales from ancient history. Kevin refused the beverage offered and went right to the chairs and their conversation, with business always the first selection on his plate.

"This country was founded, and then retained, by a bunch of men who owned three-quarters of this city and 60% of this province! These men have placed into one of the highest offices in the land, a mayor who has left the office in more disarray, after ripping off the economy and small businesses around the province! The laws they've made are purely for their advancements, and now—"

"You've joined their den of lions! Why exactly is that, Minister? Because Richard Blanc is obviously the devil you're addressing," Kevin argued!

It became apparent to the minister that he was consulting with an intellectual of the handlings of government affairs. "My case is difficult in the sense that, I have a family, and may I just say that my extra activities after work, are not ones I'd want my wife and kids to hear about!"

"So, they've got you, but you refuse to go down without a fight?"

"I'm a fighter, which is why I'm a liberal. Those pussies like Lafleur and Trudard and friends aren't about to win like that! I already told my wife, and our little conversation here has given me the strength I needed to face my public! I may cost my party and followers an election and probably have to resign the post, but I won't give another party my voters like that!"

The name "Lafleur" was the minister's trump card, and he played it like a true politician. With government's backing, the already ruthless gang of thugs known as the Rough Riders, would eventually possess God-like capabilities and the means to govern fully.

"Lafleur? You wouldn't be referring to Martain Lafleur's dad, Michel?"

"He's one of the heads of their covenant, as they so like to call their little gang of billionaires. They've bled this province from the bottom up since the beginning of time and, are still as greedy as ever for more wealth, with their 'govern from the underground to the senate' bullshit moto! Michel Lafleur is the only man in this country's history, to find himself being chased by an entire police force, doing two hundred and fifty miles per hour on the 401 Highway! And I swear if he didn't have to stop for gas in that Lamborghini Diablo, they never would have caught up to him! You would expect handcuffs or detention or something, but nah, the officers simply returned his documents and apologized for interfering with the man's stroll!"

"So, what exactly do you need me to do, sir?"

"That son of a bitch Blanc has been using the Rough Riders' power to influence key voters around this province. I know it for a fact, but I just can't prove any of it! What I'd love for you to do, because it's obvious I found the right man, is to find out whatever you can about these home invasions and shitty tactics they're using, so we can shut them down before the final votes are tallied!"

"I have been hearing a buzz about something like that. Don't worry, I'll get to the bottom of all this and find that information for you!"

They both stared into each other's eyes, then nodded and shook hands to confirm their secretive arrangement, before Kevin and his associates departed.

Part 23

Martain Lafleur sat back and watched the events which occurred earlier that morning on the hourly news updates, courtesy of the special footage he awarded the CTV news station. The entire household surrounded the boss, celebrating as the flick played continuously on the huge Panasonic seventy-two-inch LCD flat screen television inside Martain's living room. The video was shot from angles that made it impossible to identify the shooters or the exact hardware used to mash the demolition. Liquor was being consumed in large quantities, as the Rough Riders partied early into the morning, way before the sun actually appeared in the skies. The snipers who demolished the SUVs and their contents', were being praised and placed on high pedestals, as Martain happily paid the bounty to the assumed winners of the prize. After paying the snipers, Martain continued partying with his crew, and he vowed a city-wide party for all Rough Riders.

For the first time in years, Martain, who could not dance to save his life, jubilantly danced around like a little kid in a candy store. The liquor coupled with humongous marijuana joints that were laced with cocaine, the ambiance, the belief that his prized nemesis was to be placed beneath the soil, and a sense of freeness to party with the female after years of abstinence, all combined and influenced Martain to contact his accountant, Luc Savage. The two had secretly discussed the biker leader's intentions, after he got rid of the primary distraction against his affairs, thus, Martain felt invigorated enough to invoke those plans.

Luc had his girlfriend in a compromising position with his head planted deep between her thighs. You could hear the moans and groans of his girlfriend throughout his apartment, as she grabbed the bulk of his hair and tried to pull him up on top of her. All her attempts to remove her lover from his clitoris licking fetish failed, even though she craved the sensation from him thumping her in any position instead. The personal ringtone Luc assigned for Martain's calls, brought the accountant from beneath the sheets faster than the speed of light, hence, the bewildered female stormed off into the bathroom.

"You fucking asshole! You can't even fuck me right! You seem better off fucking Lafleur than me, because you're always available every second he calls," The female cursed, then slammed the bathroom door behind her!

The accountant quickly covered the speaker portion of the phone, while praying his gangbanger client, who alone furnished Luc's lavish lifestyle, hadn't heard the disrespectful comment. "Morning, Monsieur Lafleur! How are you this fine morning?"

"You mean you haven't seen the news broadcast all morning? Half the city is over here partying! As a matter a fact, that's exactly why I called you! Remember that little business we spoke about regarding the celebrations, after my guaranteed victory?"

"Are you referring to the center town affair?"

"Exactly! I want it announced immediately that this weekend we're bringing back the block party in the center of town! Get the particulars together and come party with me and the boys afterwards!"

The accountant ensured the call was disconnected, before he reconvened the argument with his girlfriend. He tossed the cellular phone atop his bed, then first attempted to enlighten his girlfriend on the errors of her actions.

"I'm tired of telling you, these people aren't the type of people you fuck around with! I swear, I'd throw your ass to the wolves if he ever overheard your comments and sent someone to deal with the disrespect," Luc threatened!

The beautiful young lady the accountant had in bed came storming from the bathroom, fully dressed and fiery as ever. The female shoved her lover from her path with such brutal force, that the accountant tumbled atop the bed, as she collected her personal belongings and headed for the exit.

"You don't have to worry about giving me up, because I won't be here for you to give up, you thirty seconds fucking asshole!"

"Come on, baby, you know that's why I have to lick it a little longer! Don't leave, baby! I'll get some pills or something to lengthen the time, baby! I'm an asshole, baby, I know, but please come back," Luc begged, as he stood in the middle of the open doorframe, naked as the day he entered the world!

While members of the Rough Riders gang partied in anticipation of the glorious times to come, Martain found he'd gotten an erection from watching the destruction of his nemesis' SUVs. The Rough Riders' point guard, therefore summoned one the biker club's groupies inside his residence, and simply whispered his desire in her ear. While the boss hypnotically remained in front of his massive television, the groupie bent down on her knees, then withdrew his penis and began performing oral sex, as the tilt of the SUVs played continuously.

The original sounds of hogs or Harley Davidson motorbikes, which disappeared with the years of war, once again became a passion the bikers could freely enjoy, without fears of being easily ambushed. Word had spread, 'that the glory years of the Rough Riders were back, following the slaughter of the only person to ever impede the club's sovereign rule, over the underground. Rough Rider foremen from across the province and beyond, all rode the distance to convey their sentiments to the biker don, after years of battling the same foe. Lanes of bikes spread across Martain's lawn, with many more entering the property through his huge, well-guarded metal gates.

"Yow, boss, it's like Christmas all over the city! Everybody is watching this video with complete belief! I saw some of our Aryan and skinhead brothers showing homage, by beating the crap out of a bunch of small-time Haitian hustlers downtown! The news hit this city like mad, now everyone is trying to show good faith, before you start regulating shit again, and inflicting our brand of martial law," Ivan announced, as he walked into the day room and gave his boss a fist pump! "I see you celebrating in fine style!" Martain's long-time friend and gunner added, after seeing the groupie on her knees.

"Only way we do it, bro, after almost a decade fighting that black fuck! Roll me up one of your specialties, because today we party, but tomorrow we remind everybody of the way it was, before our sovereign rulership was questioned," Martain stated, then slapped the groupie on the right side of her head and signaled her to exit the room! "That was nice, girlfriend! Make sure that I can find you when I'm ready!"

"No problem, Mr. Lafleur," the very lovely blonde answered!

"It appears the Feds are going to head the investigation into the stolen military weapons, but there is also supposed to be some special detective for the army, who apparently is on some related case. Find out what exactly this detective is searching for; maybe we can help him with it, so he doesn't need to unpack his luggage. I'm waiting on Luc to bring my passport, stamped and showing I was in the states throughout all this shit, because this is one multiple homicide certain prosecutors would love to hear my name mentioned with," Martain instructed!

"So, when do we start going after the rest of Nicholas' bunch?"

"Let these so-called investigators do their work and go home satisfied, then after the election when we're rulers of this entire province again, we massacre them wherever we catch them! Before all that, I want you to get me a copy of the autopsy report! I must see the fucking name Nicholas Henry on that list! I must see that final assurance! And one more thing, Luc has a big-mouthed bitch he's fucking! I don't want to ever hear that voice again. She knows a little too much!"

"You still the most thorough person I know! Even though the newscast said that Nicholas is dead, you still got to have your hard evidence! Anyways, you got a lifetime to watch this video as much as you want, so let's take the full party outside, because you know it's never a real party unless you're present!"

Martain hated the idea of being drawn from in front his Emmy Award skit, but he had to admit that it had been ages since he'd been himself. The biker don had remained hidden thus far from most of his party attendants, who all attended to celebrate with Martain, just as they had bled and suffered losses with him. However, the don had no inkling that, the handful of gangsters he celebrated with earlier, had grown to such a massive crowd. The sun had made its morning debut in the sky, to a crowd of bikers who all intended on partying the day away.

The atmosphere at Nicholas' estate was somewhat different, following the loss of eight veteran fighters who were all devoted to eliminating the corrupt system of the Rough Riders gang. This was the single deadliest attack against Nicholas' coalition forces, considering they had never before experienced such a high mortality rate. Nicholas returned home to an estate in mourning, with teary-eyed guards grinding their teeth, in anticipation of a retaliation attack against their nemesis. Each security guard had bloodshot eyes, from a combination of the alcohol, heavy tears, and marijuana. The guards at the first checkpoint informed Nicholas that, 'he had a few long-distant guests awaiting him at the mansion'.

There was a Lincoln Town car limousine parked along the guests' parking spots, that was so long it commanded three car slots. Nicholas, despite the morning's horrific ordeal, showed a pleasant gesture for the first time that day, as he developed great skepticism for who his guests might be, due to the flare and extravagance of the limousine. The daily sounds of dominos clashing against tables, or thugs threatening to kill their opponents' players in Ludie, or arguments from cheaters hiding cards in Poker, or dice smashing against the wall while patrons' wagered, were all replaced by cultural music from reggae artists, while those in mourning grieved their loss.

Nicholas' demeanor never swayed, whether he was enraged at the world, staring down the barrel of a gun, or having sex with one of his many concubines. In fact, the only person to totally alter his emotions was his son, Junior, who always managed to brighten his father's gloomy days. Before attending to his guests, Nicholas made a pit stop at the guards' house to settle a matter of extreme importance. The boss walked into the unit assigned to his guards and gun hands, went directly up the stairs to the sleeping quarters, and dragged a gun hand from the comforts of his bed. The young man was whacked across the head with a police yardstick, which immediately opened a huge gash across the gun hand's head. The young man was still groggy from being unexpectedly awakened, before he was made discombobulated by the whack across his head.

"Ouch! What did I do wrong, please, please," the gun hand begged, as he staggered to the bedroom door, with licks falling like rain?

Killa had chosen to remain on the main floor, not knowing his boss' intent, as Kevin marched up the stairs without hesitation. The loud screams from Zebb getting the shit kicked out of him, alerted everyone to the situation, before the bloodied body of the person whom Nicholas blamed for the ambush, came toppling down the stairs. Zebb's body fell head-over-heels down the long staircase and landed lifelessly on the living room floor. Nicholas pursued, while he instructed people on the main floor, 'to raise Zebb to his feet'!

"Please, boss, don't kill me! I didn't have a choice! They were going to---ahh," the gun hand screamed, as another guard put his Timberland boot to his ribs.

"You went from doing no wrong to apologizing for the wrong you did," Nicholas declared, as he planted the yardstick into Zebb's ribs! The boss proceeded to credit their loss, to the false allegiance of the traitor in their midst and the Rough Riders' mercenaries who carried out the hit. Nicholas vowed to avenge the deaths of the men lost, before he left the traitor to his band of misfits and, tended to his guests.

Nicholas and Killa walked into the entertainment lounge, where his primary guest was being served a glass of Napoleon Brandy on the rocks. The waitress had just handed Nicholas' guest his drink and was about to return to the maids' quarters, when she observed her boss and confidante. The waitress turned back to inform the guest that his sandwich would be ready momentarily, when she observed the guest removing his pistol from the holster beneath his jacket. The glass of brandy had been released from the guest's grasp, and it shattered against the floor, while moist liquid spat from the frightened waitress' vagina. The woman found herself staring down the barrel of the guest's pistol, with absolutely no capability of expelling a sound.

The shocking revelation of who Nicholas' guest was, terminated with all three men aiming their weapons at each other, with the waitress in the middle terrified to death. Ernesto Lopez saw a face that had haunted his dreams for many years, and was a split second from blasting a hole through Killa, when he saw the fear he'd lived with for years in the eyes of the young Indian, beauty. Killa instantly remembered the man he'd held hostage and robbed, although he assumed Nicholas had sold him to the hyenas and thought of cancelling his mentor, with his weapon pointed at his childhood acquaintance. The notion of Ernesto killing Killa frightened Nicholas, who simply aimed at Ernesto to challenge his decision and negotiate.

"E, what are you doing? This is my friend I told you about from Jamaica," Nicholas yelled!

"I know him, all right," Ernesto replied!

"Then put the gun down, before one of us shoots accidentally," Nicholas reasoned!

"Sir, I know I've done you wrong, but give me the chance and I'll make things right some way or the other," Killa commented?

Ernesto took a few seconds, before he completely removed his eyes off Kadeem. As the guns slowly descended, the maid's feeble legs succumbed to the pressure, which caused her to tumble to the ground. The three men rushed to the woman's side, as she fell only inches away from the broken liquor glass. The tense situation between the three men was averted, due in part to conscious reasoning, the trust factor, and their capability to move forward, despite the disagreements life threw at them. Each man apologized to the other as they attended to the maid, but moreover, it became evident to Killa the level of love and respect Ernesto had for his long-time associate.

The doctor who attended to Damian was lounging out by the pool with a small group of thugs, drinking, smoking and carrying on before, he was summoned to help with the fainted female. Once the doctor saw Nicholas, he immediately began offering his diagnosis on his young cousin's recovery prognosis, which was quite positive and upbeat. The doctor quickly relieved the fears of the three men, who had run to the Indian woman's side, and acknowledged that the maid had simply fainted.

Killa helped the doctor to lift and move the maid to a more comfortable resting area, while Nicholas and Ernesto went for a walk. The two ancient friends hugged and complimented each other, Nicholas on the esteemed gut which Ernesto had developed, and Ernesto on the luscious dreadlocks cascading down Nicholas' back. Nicholas owed his long-time mentor, boss, and friend for all he'd been able to attain and accomplish, after being forced to flee the United States in order to escape captivity.

"It's really good seeing you, my boy! For years, I've been saying, 'One day, I'm going to come and visit you!' It might be a little late, but I'm here. I brought a surprise for you with me, but I have absolutely no idea where it went!"

"Where did all this grey hair come from? I must admit it fits you—gives you that distinguished millionaire look! How you like that new Rolls Royce I sent you for your birthday last week?"

"Kevin, I love it, my boy! I don't even allow my chauffeur, Rahoul, to drive it, because that came from you, so I drive it myself," Ernesto exclaimed, as he looked around for the surprise he'd promised!

"How is business running?"

"Those federal boys stay knocking at my door! If it wasn't for my legitimate affairs, I would be rotting away in some federal institution somewhere. Remember that detective boy, Carbonelli? Blond hair, tall, with some dark blue eyes, who swore he'd lock us all up?"

"Yeah!"

"That's one white boy who stays determined to find you, and lock me away no matter what, according to him! Apart from my problems with the Feds, who are the only disrespectful bastards on the continent, you know respect is due right across the country. I presently got no quarrels, enemies beneath ground and, business always fair. Still enough about me. We can finally discuss permanent solutions to your problems!"

"I received some important information this morning that is going to put things into proper prospective real soon! Tell me something: who is the highest-ranked person you know?"

The two men walked like brothers, arms around shoulders, as they travelled throughout sections of the house. Their stroll took them along the maids' corridor on the first floor, as they discussed matters of 'personal security'. Kevin's cellular phone kept sounding every few seconds, with concerned friends seeking confirmation on the latest rumors. With Nicholas assumed dead, the movement against the Rough Riders would hardly be considered viable by the other key participants involved. Eventually, each drug kingpin from the Africans, Indians, and the Defenders would either have to resign from drug trafficking or team with the devil, in order to retain that guaranteed retailer.

Nicholas had devised a plan he believed adequate to defeat Martain and his band of marauders, although the finer details weren't exactly hammered out. Hence, given the opportunity, Nicholas confided in his mentor, boss, and friend, who was also a veteran of multiple drug cartel wars, and could offer suggestions on how to attack a force, almost twice the size of their outfit. Ernesto, regardless of insurmountable odds, always believed in his once, Chief of Business Administrator, especially regarding matters involving firearms. The Floridian drug boss promised Nicholas, 'all the men available to travel across the Canadian border he could find', to assist in the final judgment his long-time understudy so passionately spoke of. In fact, Ernesto was amid donating as many mercenaries as possible to the cause, when both men became conscious of a rather strange sound. At first, the faint muffles sounded in the distance, yet gradually increased the closer both men got to young Junior's nanny's quarters.

Junior's nanny was a seventy-four-year-old widow, whose husband drank himself to death at the tender age of thirty-six. The old Indian nanny had been in Nicholas' employ since Junior was seven months old and had become a staple inside Nicholas' home, after vowing never to return to the horrors she endured inside the house, she had shared with her husband. Nicholas was sure the woman had taken a life of celibacy and curiously pushed her door ajar, to investigate the cause of the mysterious sounds. The door swung open and revealed Nicholas' long-time mate, who'd spent his last eight years in federal prison, the one and only Swarty.

Although at first glance the massive human before Ernesto and Nicholas stood completely naked with his back to the door, the Roman letters strutting across his back pronounced his name loud and clear.

"Swarty," Nicholas yelled at his friend, who had the grandmother of eight in a rather precarious position!

It became evident by his lack of clothing, and the manner in which the big man physically rotated his waistline, that Swarty was engaged in sexual activity, although his partner could not initially be seen, due to their size disparity. The sound of his ancient partner's voice excited Swarty, who withdrew himself from his partner and spun around without consideration. Swarty reacted as if he wanted to run over and hug his friend, who disgracefully turned his head away, with Ernesto.

"Kevin," Swarty yelled!

"Miss Emma," Nicholas murmured!

"Excuse me, boss, but I send out big boy in few minutes," insisted the nanny, as she pulled the straying Swarty back onto her.

Part 24

Kane became a different man after their father passed away. Without Eagle's constant supervision, the young native Indian began trafficking drugs throughout the reservation. Eagle was never against the sort of work Nicholas did for a living, yet he stood fast against the distribution of drugs among his people, who he believed suffered enough turmoil and poverty without the detriment of such a destructive product.

"The white man brought my people alcohol, and all the vile things of this earth, to wipe us off God's planet! Look at us today, nobody wants to do anything, just sit around and wash down the poison they brought us. No way: bring that stuff across the bridge where they can afford the high it brings, but not to my people," warned Eagle, the day the mention of the unconquered market was first brought up! Nicholas had always respected Eagle's wishes, even after he'd moved on to the spirit world. However, the youth in Kane detached all sense of humanity and compassion, after seeing his father's mutilated corpse.

Kane had been drinking and smoking heavily, while partying the day away with several of his warriors, at the annual neighborhood multicultural barbeque. The event was, sponsored entirely by the Defenders and held in the Pierrefond district of West Island. The party was a yearly event, where members of the community, gang members, and specially invited guests gathered, to commemorate the multicultural society they'd achieved. There was a certain young señorita belonging to one of the prominent gangsters in Brogan's army, who managed to captivate the intoxicated Indian, who seldom found time for any female not of the Nubian complexion. Kane was captivated by the female the instant she stepped from her BMW coupe, with her expensive Coach handbag, which she tossed over her shoulder to create room for the box of liquor she carried in her arms. The young native Indian sent one of his posse members to assist the female, who politely refused the offer. Kane watched the female intensely as she made her way to the gate of the soiree, where fellow girlfriends surrounded and aided her with the box of liquor.

There was a huge sound system strung up with humongous speaker boxes around the children's and the adults' pool sides, with local DJs playing the latest in hip-hop. Kane entered the pool area to the arousing accolades from fellow thugs, who all welcomed both he and his entourage, who were among the honored guests. The organizers of the event orchestrated matters to cater for the children in a completely separate portion of the pool, which gave the adults more freedom to do as they wished. During the greetings process between the Indians and fellow Defenders, Kane sneaked a peek over Chico's shoulder and caught the young damsel sneaking off to play with the children, who were all enjoying the pool and various activities.

The peaceful atmosphere was an opportunity to witness a tranquility never before observed, by certain roughneck shooters within Brogan's elite. The thugs laughed and joked among themselves, as if they were of the same household since birth. Regardless of the peaceful assembly brought about by the gala, each and every thug stood ready to defend his home turf, with their pistols concealed in their waistband and heavier firepower inside their vehicles around the parking area. Despite their era of warfare, it was beautiful to witness men openly enjoyed the company of friends, as they played dominos, gambled cards, and celebrated among themselves.

Brogan chose not to attend the festivities following the recent occurrence between his friend Nicholas and the Rough Riders. The Defenders' boss chose safety and remained at home under heavy guard, not knowing if similar weapons used to create the tarnish along Interstate-10, were still in the possession of Martain and company. The news inserts on the deadly attack were repeatedly broadcasted, although the reports on those deceased remained unclear. Nicholas himself had decided to go underground and remained dead until his grand resurrection, where he hoped to land his nemesis a crushing blow.

The multicultural festival went on regardless, as the theme of "Community First" brought hundreds out to enjoy the festivities. The kids had spent the majority of the day eating various foods and treats, while having the time of their lives without their parents. The parents, on the other hand, were all engaged in some illicit or candid affair, with farfetched thoughts of their children. The young teenage boys who weren't attempting to score a date with the young señoritas, were off either getting high on chemicals of their choice or, shooting hoops on the basketball court next to the pool. There were a lot more physical activities occurring in and around the children's pool area, with only a few adults vying for a dip in the warm waters. Most of the men chose to drink, converse among themselves, or play social games, while watching the ladies tour about in their sexy swimsuit outfits. The women, on the other hand, did as ladies in groups, which was to gossip about everything from their Gucci purses, to who their favorite actor was sleeping with.

Khai, Samuel, Malki, and Kevan from Kane's rebel Indians, struck up a challenge against members of the Defenders, after Khai suggested that 'the Defenders had no skill or flair atop a high-powered motorcycle'! A large number of spectators soon gathered around the parking area, to witness bone-chilling antics atop motorcycles, as gangsters illustrated their control over their monster bikes.

Once they had regathered out in the parking lot, an ace shooter named Juan Sanchez said, "All right, who's putting up what? I got a hundred here that says Defenders all the way!"

"You boys poor around here or what? I got five bills that says Indians taking it all! Now who's got balls to take my money," wagered Jericho of the Sioux tribe?

"Easiest money I'll make all week! I got my boys' back, get ready to pay me, Jerry," Carmichael yelled!

Khai began the stunt show with a rear-wheel wheelie, which he maintained from one end of the parking lot to the other. Such an amazing feat was topped by Eddie, who began with a rear-wheel wheelie, before he switched to the front wheel for his grand finale. The Hurricane bike Eddie rode held him hunched over the handlebars, as he rode the front wheel for almost a hundred yards. The surrounding crowd cheered for Khai's spectacular antics, but instead screamed for the grand theatrics Eddie performed.

Malki positioned himself over the front fender of his motorbike and took off on that lone wheel down the long parking aisle. Once the ponytail-wearing Indian got to the end of the parking lot, he immediately switched atop the bike and, with the same wheel aloft high into the air, rode back to the starting point. The crowd may have chosen to render a biased decision against Khai but, were impressed to the extent they shouted at the antics of young Malki, atop his Ninja.

Carlos Alvarez, who was the lone child to Felix and Maria Alvarez, went against his parents' wishes by joining the neighborhood gang of thugs, instead of acquiring a trade and working. The twenty-year-old attempted the same difficult maneuver his counterpart had succeeded, and crashed his bike after it tossed him a good twenty yards. Friends of the young daredevil rushed to his side, as he was a bit slow getting to his feet. However, once the wooziness cleared from Carlos' head, he immediately pounced to his feet and indicated he was okay.

Kevan had those in attendance in awe, as he handled his Suzuki like a piece of paper, by standing basically on the side of the bike and riding with the motorcycle almost touching the ground. He brought the bike to a standstill, before he began bouncing off either wheel like a bouncing ball. The skilled bike handler, then balanced the motorcycle on the front wheel, released the brake and allowed it to run about six feet, before he flipped the rear of his bike completely around, after he came to a pin stop on the same tire. Samuel joined in on the act during Kevan's performance and brought the house down, as both men exchanged handlings of their bike in mid-pass. Both men began at separate ends of the parking lot and charged at each other. A third of the way along, both men leapt onto their seats and stood on their bikes, then slowed down slightly to switch bikes. When they completed the tactic, everybody looked at each other with disbelief and amazement. The crowd went ballistic, as both men returned to the point from which they started, before they swapped the bikes again with the same amazing maneuver.

The competition seemed finalized; however, Young Jit of the Defenders had one maneuver he simply had to perform. With everyone dramatically cheering the Indians, it took a few minutes to clear the track and allowed the last rider to showcase his skills. The youngest of the Defenders' shooters began with an ordinary ride down the lot, before he flipped himself upside down onto his head, and rode the length of the parking area. With the crowd once again invigorated and, in a frenzy, Khai came back with his second stunt, which brought the noise decibels to its all-time high. Khai began by lifting his front tire off the ground, before he brought himself to a handstand while operating the motorbike.

"Give it to the Indians! They killed that shit," yelled one spectator!

Another spectator added, "Oh, shit! Did you see that shit? That shit was tight! Indians! Indians! Indians!"

"Indians! Indians! Indians," everyone who enjoyed the competitive demonstrations shouted!

Two teenage kids from the West Island territories rode their BMX bicycles into the center of the action and began dazzling everyone with their style and pizzazz. The teens were jumping onto parked cars, doing donuts, and summersaults, and flying off structures fearlessly, yet always landed safely on two tires. The young men twirled, twisted, and flipped their way into the good graces of the crowd, who were previously completely blown away by the thugs on the metal horses. The youngsters took over the show after a few gimmick tricks and impressed those who chose to remain, while most of the crowd returned to party by the pool area.

While the youth of the future dazzled friends and neighbors, the contestants who participated in the bike skills contest, high-fived and congratulated each other as they boasted about their individual accomplishments. Bets were paid by satisfied betters, who joked about matters as they walked back toward the pool area. Those who participated in the motorbike contest, who had given close associates their weapons for safe keeping, were given back their firearms, once the gimmicks were concluded.

As the gangsters returned to the pool area, an old Hyundai went by on the main road a few yards away, with a loud bang caused by the engine backfiring. Some of the brave-hearted thugs reacted as if they were a Canadian platoon inside a war-torn country, as they all but scattered for safety. Several of the gangsters performed evasive maneuver, as they withdrew their weapons and, sought cover by either running to some objects or somersaulting at it, before any of them checked to verify the cause of the noise. The Indians and others who didn't even flinch, began teasing the less confident in the group, who they assessed would abandon their comrades, should they see danger forthcoming.

The entire high-powered bike contest transpired without Kane watching a single stunt, to determine how his boys took the bragging-rights trophy. Instead of morally supporting his allies, Kane's intrigue had not wavered from the delightful beauty he beheld in the parking area, hence he sought the perfect opportunity to insert a phrase. The white Bikini Village swimsuit the señorita wore, made it impossible not to stare at her unique physique, that was undoubtedly carved out by the Almighty Himself. While the Indian waited for a chance to ask the female's name among other questions, Kane phoned Kevin and gave him an update on the proceedings. To avoid being noticed while staring at the female, the Mohawk warrior kept on his full-frame Armani sunshades, which made it impossible to tell where he was looking.

Kane watched the female as she entertained a bunch of girls between the ages of nine and fifteen. The radiant señorita, who appeared to be in her mid-twenties, genuinely cared about the children enough, to where she spent the duration of her time entertaining them. The Indian bad boy leader from Kahnawake, was in dire need of information about the woman he'd spent the entire time admiring yet, remained a bit skeptical about whom to interrogate for the information. Once the gentlemen who participated in the bike rally returned from the parking lot, the perfect opportunity presented itself, when Kane motioned Chavo to join him.

As luck would have it, the female was a cousin to Chavo, who volunteered every bit of information possible. Chavo was delighted to hear a man of Kane's stature was actually interested in his cousin, Alyiah, especially since he hated her boyfriend, who was one of Brogan's personal bodyguard. Kane discovered that her love for the children came long before she became a social worker, who worked with displaced and abandoned children. The more Kane learned about the beautiful señorita, Alyiah, the more intrigued he grew, and he removed his American Express card from his wallet and informed Chavo to pass it on directly to his cousin.

Khai and the other victorious stunt performers began debriefing Kane on what tricks they performed, in order to claim the entire winning pot and trophy. The Indian boss could all but get excited for his victorious riders, whom he knew endured countless scratches, bumps, and broken bones, in order to perfect their craft. Kane's associate Jerrico went to each of their comrades with the bottle of Silver Patron they'd been abusing and refreshed every man's plastic cup, as the boss toasted and congratulated his troops on a victory well earned. During the congratulation speech, Chavo dragged his cousin Maria Sarapuncho, aka Alyiah over to introduce to Kane. Although Chavo was the one tugging on his cousin's arm, Alyiah resembled the enforcer, as she squeezed his humongous earlobe, while pretending she had no interest in accompanying him.

A long, black-tinted limousine sandwiched between two General Motors Tahoe SUVs, pulled in front of the gate before coming to an abrupt stop. Almost everyone with interest looked to see who the client was aboard the limousine, with the latest rumors circulating that Brogan and Nicholas were absent, because they were both mutilated inside the vehicles on I-10. Brogan had speculatively sent a messenger to declare he would not be in attendance, while the highlighted footage of Nicholas' motorcade being annihilated ignited the curiosity from associates of both men. The men from the rear Tahoe climbed from their vehicle and positioned themselves around the limousine to ensure the client's security. Once the security personnel from the Tahoe were revealed, everyone looked in astonishment because they expected Nicholas to emerge from the limousine.

Killa stood at the door to the limousine and awaited confirmation, from his client tapping on the window to suggest he was ready to exit the vehicle. James Tea, Ernesto's personal bodyguard, and one of Nicholas' gun hands, all stood guard around the vehicle, while spectators gathered for a look at the occupant. It wasn't long before the crowd disappointingly returned to whatever activity held their attention previously, after their intrigue subsided when the Columbian stepped from the limousine. While the unaffected locals returned to the fiesta, the gangbangers of the Defenders sought to learn more about this mystery person, who commanded the respect and honor of Nicholas' most proficient shooter, Killa.

The limousine and front Tahoe sped off once the occupants who bailed from the vehicles, had gotten safely into the pool area. Once inside the actual grounds of the cultural event, Ernesto opted to tread about without being closely followed by his security detail. The Floridian drug boss wanted to lessen the stares and discomfort of the local patrons, in addition to casually enjoying himself, like he did before the wealth and popularity. Ernesto remarkably chose Killa as his walking partner, over his personal bodyguard, who rarely left the boss' side.

"I know you Jamaicans have a pride about you that can never be disputed! I also saw that Kevin trusts and knows you, to the point where he was willing to bet his last dollar on you! I want to know, if this is the life you saw for yourself, and are you happy about your choice," Ernesto asked?

"I believe we're all dealt a deck a cards, and it is up to you how you play the game of life, because, like it or not, until God come for his world, we all go dead out like the roses! Cancer, wicked people, gunshots—all amounts to the same thing Mister Lopez! As long as you enjoy the ride, don't complain," Killa answered, as they stopped to watch a dance recital by a Latina female group!

"I see myself in you more than any other man on this earth! Like you, I come from the ghetto, ambitious and hungry to make a better life, for myself and my younger brothers and sisters. The first time I gripped a pistol was off a dead drug dealer's chest, after some padres filled him up with lead and left him to die! I took that pistol and brought my family their first steak meal ever! Never before had my mother eaten a T-bone steak, and I swore to have her eating like that every day. I got caught stealing purses at seventeen and they were going lock me up and teach me a lesson. Luckily for me, the drug cartel wanted to destroy the local police station and, sent a hit squad out to cancel the twenty-six officers on the force. I was beaten for nearly an eternity, before the eruptions of gunfire sounded in the station. The hit squad went through and killed eighteen officers, including the three who were inches from breaking my arm. One of the killers for the hit squad, invited me to join these militia drug traffickers, since them my life has changed, and the rest, like they say, is history," Ernesto revealed!

Following the performance, both men walked over to a vendor's stand to purchase beverages and nutrition, from a lady of Spanish persuasion. Ernesto had asked Killa, who he referred to by his given name, "whether he'd ever eaten a taco or a burrito", to which Killa responded, "Them things there is not on the Jamaican menu Mister Lopez!" The big boss chuckled to himself after Killa responded and walked up to place an order, before the vendor froze him in mid-order.

"Oh, my God, no! El Chacha, is it really you," the vendor said, as she covered her mouth in amazement?

Brogan was camped out inside the dungeon of his mansion, when Nicholas arrived with his rugged entourage. The black-tinted limousine accompanied by the Tahoes entered from the rear to Brogan's mansion, in order to remain under the radar. Following the morning's debacle, where key military personnel of Camp Nicholas were brutally ambushed and killed, nobody expected the man himself to be among the day's commuters. However, Nicholas had important matters to discuss and came in person, which symbolized the integrity of his message.

Tensions reigned throughout the city, as the rumors of Nicholas' slaying provoked racial clashes, between minorities and Caucasian French Canadians. There were guards in numbers around the property brandishing humongous weapons, as if they had been placed on military high alert. Once Nicholas' entourage identified themselves at the rear gate, they were permitted to enter and drive to the rear door, where Brogan's female partner awaited them.

"Hi, Nick! Brogan asked me to escort you to his office," said the half-drunk female, wearing a dark see-through lace robe, over her two-piece bikini swimsuit!

The female showed Nicholas' entourage the section provided for gun hands and bodyguards, where a few of the security helpers were participating in a boxing challenge, courtesy of their Nintendo, Wii console. The two men with the controls were perspiring as if they were actually engaged in a battle of monumental proportions, as they slugged each other across a huge, seventy-inch LCD screen, mounted on the wall. The three-minute rounds went like a regular boxing exhibitions, with both combatants exhausted to the point where, they actually sat down between rounds to conserve energy, while jawing off at each other about what they were going to do to the following round. The excitement had even the onlookers in attendance fanning the flames, as one corner manager was overheard accusing the other, 'of being enraged for not being at the multicultural gala, while some amateur grinned on his girlfriend'. The other corner responded by insinuating, that 'no man could ever take their claim, and it was the other side that needed to worry about their women'.

"What the hell is going on in there," Nicholas thought to himself, as he went by and proceeded onto the boss' office?

Brogan's lady quickly eased the boss' fears, as she explained, "Oh, that's just one of the guard's favorite pastime event!"

Nicholas' associates settled in and began participating in the drinking and social activities, while their boss followed the female to the office, to handle the business for which he'd visited. Brogan was extremely happy to see Nicholas, and to know that he hadn't perished in the demolition, which left the crime scene scattered along a wide distance of Highway-10.

Nicholas believed that Martain and the Rough Riders' cockiness, had enabled them the opportunity of a lifetime. The bikers were so eager to attain the eradication of their most prominent nemesis, that they callously announced the reinstatement of their blockbuster event, which had been cancelled since the beginning of the war. The Rough Riders sought to revive an event of huge proportion, that involved the closing of the entire Montreal downtown core, from Atwater Avenue to St. Denis Street. Their city party, that primarily traveled along St. Catherine Street, was one of the biggest free outdoor summer gathering across Canada. The event was first introduced to the city by Martain's late uncle and ex-leader of the Rough Riders, who rocked the entire town with the biggest free concert downtown Montreal had ever hosted. From Martain's late uncle's biker party, where countless musicians and art performers showcased their talents, came the idea to host jazz festival and other events on an annual basis. Contrary to every other live show, Martain intended on engineering a day of bonanzas, which would set his bikers' spectacle apart.

Nicholas envisioned total annihilation of his enemies, should his plot be executed to perfection. The blueprints demanded precision for the plan to work, therefore, there were three phases, which required three groups working simultaneously, none of which could fail, or they were all doomed. The importance of Nicholas' visit was to hammer out strategic maneuvers, before the individual tasks were administered.

There were certain unresolved aspects of the plan, therefore the meeting between both headmen was progressive, and even provided a solution on how to manage the hundreds of police officers expected. Further discussions were had on what duties to offer to whom, though it was agreed that their absent comrades would tackle the final and easiest leg of the operation. The two bosses sat and talked for hours and were only interrupted once by Killa, who telephoned to assure Nicholas that they needed not return to pick them up from the multicultural affair.

Part 25

The parking attendant parked the Tahoe and handed Killa a parking tag, the moment they pulled in front the fabulous, five-star Queen Elizabeth Hotel, on Rene Leveque Boulevard. The concierge opened the rear doors for the passengers seated in the rear, and Killa quickly ushered his four passengers inside the hotel. The choice of hotel spoke resoundingly for the men who made the choice, as merely entering such lavish facilities, moistened the crotches of their female companions. The financially endowed guests walked to the reservation counter and requested two separate penthouse suites, with adequate amenities to suit both men.

Ernesto Lopez had the honor of reuniting with one of the only women he ever truly loved, although they'd been separated for nearly sixty years. As a young ambitious thug growing up in Columbia, Ernesto was ruthless after poverty showed him little in the means of survival. Carmen came with the best of times, during the early days of a child's innocence, when a young boy ran the school playgrounds careless and free, before the proper distinction of having nothing sunk in. An era where young Ernesto learned that, unlike him, a great multitude of children brought money for lunch. Back in those harsh, early years, his mother would send him to school with empty pockets, and the government assistance programs were what allowed him the opportunity to fill his stomach. Carmen was the light toward which Ernesto strived, though she, too, came from a poor and broken home. They shared a youthful love for the short period when, Ernesto attended La Matador Junior High school, before he dropped out to support his family. It wasn't long after Ernesto's departure, before Carmen was sent to reside in Canada with close family members. Circumstances prevented the two from continuing any formal means of communicating, as even a mere phone call was somewhat of a delicacy to Ernesto.

The Floridian drug boss rented a double-room suite on the penthouse floor for three nights, at a rate of twenty-two hundred dollars a night, and he insisted the receptionist keep his credit information handy, as he might be telephoning to lengthen his stay. The big boss then motioned Killa over and sneaked five, one-hundred-dollar bills into the palm of his hand, and insisted that he find a partner, to serve as his honored guest during his stay at the lavished hotel. Killa immediately withdrew his cellular phone and telephoned his long-time girlfriend, whom he rarely saw on account of his lengthy hours at Nicholas' estate.

After the receptionist finished registering Mr. Lopez, the bilingual female who spoke with more of a French accent, graciously welcomed their guest and his female companion, to the majestic Queen Elizabeth Hotel. Kane Esquada tossed his Platinum Visa card atop the counter, along with his driver's license, as the female proceeded to register both he and his date. While registering Kane, who also opted for the same length of stay at the hotel, the receptionist handed out brochures, that highlighted the different amenities provided for their honored guests. The pamphlet featured their massage therapy session, the health and fitness gym, pool facilities, sauna, deluxe bar, and a five-star kitchen, which were all hospitably offered to guests at the hotel. The receptionist also proceeded to inform the group, that each room came with a hospitality kit, featuring a hot bar, free robes, and comfort slippers, along with several other offers they'd find appealing.

Kane felt at conflict within, knowing a Mohawk Indian should be more economical, but his interest barely shifted from the magnificent creature he'd captured, from the multicultural gala in the West Islands. The thought that Alyiah belonged to another man, who frankly wasn't aware of the new developments, didn't matter to the Indian warrior in the slightest, as he drooled over her every action. There was a concerned glare in the beautiful señorita's eyes, that Kane intended to transform, and very little else mattered from that point on.

The Indian warrior had successfully swept the beautiful señorita off her feet, from the moment he acquired the opportunity for them to converse. Alyiah later revealed that she had taken notice of Kane, but it was not until 'he begged her to marry him', which was the first statement he made to her, that she felt the genuine sincerity of his actions. Kane's finesse stunned the gorgeous Spanish heritage señorita, who was silently searching for an escape from the nightmare of a relationship she was already in.

"Oh, my fucking God! Is this guy for real? Wow; look at this fancy fucking hotel! I got this handsome, genuine man standing in front of me, who is capable of protecting me both physically and financially! I really don't want to lose something special, so I'm going to fuck the shit out of him! Huh, fuck Eddie, he's a loser anyways," were some of the thoughts floating through Alyiah's head!

Even though Kane's date was already confident she chose a good companion, he proceeded to strengthen his relationship argument, by tossing his motorbike keys at one of his troops and, insisted 'she became his chauffeur'.

The Queen Elizabeth Hotel was second to none throughout the province of Quebec, with its Eighteenth-Century English decor style hallways, chambers, and suites. The hotel provided exquisite services, and had a knowledgeable staff, with first-class chefs who were trained to prepare any cuisine from around the globe. The hotel was a favorite stay over location for several National Hockey League teams, whose members would often highlight their trips to the monumental hotel, in their social media posts. While Kane submitted his information to the receptionist, Ernesto continued waving his magic wand, by summoning the concierge and bribing the man, with three one-hundred-dollar bills in the palm of his hand. The proud Quebecois, whose job was to assist the guests, became Ernesto's do-boy from that moment until he departed. Ernesto ordered three bottles of the hotel's finest champagne for his suite, plus a complimentary bottle for Kane and his lady friend, along with Caviar, a fruit platter, a full course meal and other hors-d'oeuvres.

Before they all separated to their individual suites, Ernesto welcomed his companions into his penthouse for a quick drink. The double-room suite that Ernesto rented was described as "divine," according to Carmen, once she entered the rental and saw the size. Poverty throughout his early years, had fueled Ernesto's crave to experience personally, the magnificence and splendor produced by countries from continents around the globe, as he travelled to places, he only dreamed of as a child. The hotel suite was far more spectacular than regular apartments, with a living room, full kitchen, and two bedrooms with individual bathrooms. The concierge was at the front door with the items Ernesto requested, before either of them could have removed their shoes, or surveyed in its entirety the luxurious penthouse suite.

Killa's date had not yet arrived, but that did not hinder the party spirit of everyone else present, as Ernesto immediately popped the cork of one of the three bottles of Dom Perignon delivered to him. The concierge had a maître-d' assemble the cutlery and essentials prior, to the arrival of the feast, that Ernesto pre-ordered from the lobby. Carmen was still in awe, as she walked around the suite and admired the exquisite, handcrafted furniture, that was all imported from England. A sense of royalty surrounded Carmen, who looked out the windows at the magnificent penthouse view, which overlooked the beautiful city of Montreal.

Ernesto asked everyone to raise their glasses as he proposed a toast. The elderly, yet jubilant Floridian, threw his arm around Carmen's shoulder, and looked out into the night sky, at the outstretched streetlights across the city. "First of all, I must thank you all for this day, it has been years since I was able to do anything so free! To friends of old, who are reunited with the joys of the present, I salute you, and feel blessed being in your presence, this wonderful evening!"

"Salute," Killa acknowledged!

Alyiah and Kane raised their glasses high, before they drank to the well formatted toast. Carmen rested her head on the shoulder, of the man whom she'd considered her first crush.

The annoying rings of the lodgment's telephone could not disturb the seventy-seven-year-old Ernesto, and his seventy-six-years-young female companion, both of whom wandered off, as they admired the enchanting city view. Kane who could barely wait to seduce the beautiful senorita he envisioned spending his life with, bided everyone 'a good evening', after they consumed their drinks. Killa raced to the telephone in anticipation of it being the receptionist, calling to announce that his date had arrived. Once it became clear that the call was indeed to announce the female's arrival, Killa waited by the door, for his date to exit the elevator.

Mocha had completed her studies at Concord University and was looking forward to returning home to Brazil, to begin her illustrious career as a doctor. Killa had attempted to change her mind from returning home, by offering to finance her own personal private clinic, which she graciously refused. The reasons for Killa's objection to Mocha's lifelong dream, soon emerged from the elevator, wearing a pair of Gucci jeans, a fitted T-shirt, leather boots, her Gucci purse hanging off the shoulder, and an evening sweater tossed over the left arm. The five feet seven inch, one-hundred-and-twenty-pound delight, may have been adorned in moderate attire, but her sensational curves and eternal beauty, made it impossible not to stare at the South American bombshell.

"Kadeem," Mocha yelled, as she ran toward her boyfriend, whom she hadn't seen for almost two weeks!

"Shhh!" Killa remarked, as he placed his index finger over his lips.

The two embraced and French-kissed in the doorway, before they joined their hosts in the lavish apartment. Killa had grown accustomed to, although he had long outgrown, the hails of people who referred to him by his actual name. For that one evening, Kadeem Kite was a mere mortal, without the qualities that terrified people in some instances. Mocha was very well received by Carmen and Ernesto, who both indulged in a conversation in Spanish, with the young graduate. Kadeem did his best to make Mocha feel comfortable, by fetching her a glass of the bubbly, and serenaded her with a toast to congratulate her on successfully completing her studies.

Both Carmen and Ernesto were utterly impressed by Mocha's decision to put the needs of her people first before all else and, return home with the knowledge and capability to help the poor and needy sufferers of the slums. Ernesto insisted on footing the bill for the facilities, from where she would offer the assistance, to the lesser fortunate people of whom she so passionately spoke.

"Any cause, which is aimed at bettering the lives of the less fortunate, is a cause I'll happily support, as long as I still have life," promised Ernesto, who was always a man of his word!

The feast that Ernesto requested arrived moments later, hence, they all sat down and dined like long-lost friends and lovers.

Across the hall from Ernesto's penthouse, Kane and Alyiah were already making out before they entered their single suite. Without the unscrupulous eyes of the public, Alyiah began passionately undressing her partner from the door entrance, while he behaved like a sex famished animal. Kane began licking the captivating señorita from her lips, until he was engulfed in vagina, moments after the door closed behind them. Unlike some of his Jamaican associates, Kane enjoyed performing fellatio, therefore he fell to his knees and immediately began tickling her clit.

The Indian warrior had his proposed fiancée draped against the door, as he licked every inch of her pelvic area. Alyiah ripped the hair band from Kane's long hair and twirled her fingers around in his hair, as she cringed under the erotic tingles flowing through her body. There were immense groans and murmurs by Alyiah, who made no attempt to deviate from the pleasures she experienced.

"Ai, si pappy! Oh my God! Oh my God! Right there, baby! Don't stop, I love it! I love you," Alyiah yelled!

The extravagant exhibition of pleasure portrayed by Alyiah, froze the concierge, who had walked to the door and was about to knock and announce, "the complimentary bottle of Dom Perignon that was sent over by Ernesto!"

The interruption by the concierge, offered key insight about the woman, Kane had all but decided to marry. When the raptor sounded at the door, Alyiah had Kane attend to the visitor, as she scampered off to "freshen up for her future husband," according to the female! The mention of champagne delivery tickled Alyiah's ears, thus she promised Kane an alter-ego performance once intoxicated. Without further emphasis, Kane opened the door and collected the bottle from the concierge, then quickly filled two glasses to the brim. In his haste to experience the transformation described, Kane almost tripped and spilled the bubbly, he was rushing to bring his fiancée.

By the time Maria returned from the bathroom, Kane was comfortably seated on the edge of the bed, surfing through television channels.

She walked over with her outstretched empty glass, to which he poured in more bubblies. They embraced and snuggled in each other's arms, while they drank a few more glasses of champagne. Halfway through the bottle, Alyiah was as drunk as a skunk. With her intoxication, however, came a totally different woman from the more conservative version of herself. Alyiah became somewhat of a sex-crazed maniac, who attacked Kane and ripped the remaining pieces of clothing from his body. Kane, in response, quite frankly surrendered and offered himself as a sacrifice, while Alyiah made him an offering which, only increased her chances to become the future Mrs. Kane Esquada.

The Indian assumed that he was the king of foreplay, until Maria flipped him over and did things to him with her tongue, he never thought possible. The sensuous senorita placed ice cubes in her mouth from the champagne bucket, and sent chills through Kane's very core, before she climbed onto him and did as she had intended, from they stepped into the luxurious hotel. Their first sexual interaction was extremely passionate and memorable, thus, the warrior Indian wanted to relive that experience on a regular basis.

Immediately after sex, Kane who would later declare that "he'd been dumbstruck by love and, knew he had to put that ring on her finger," contacted the hotel's receptionist and asked her to locate a priest, who would perform their wedding ceremony. Within fifteen minutes, the female phoned back and gave the Mohawk the number for a church, that offered the homeless meals and shelter, and provided many other services, twenty-four hours a day, seven days a week. The Indian warrior solicited a priest from the Catholic church, located two blocks away, to tie the knot between Alyiah and himself. The couple had to include a sizable donation and lie about how long they had been engaged, to get the priest to even consider performing the ceremony, without the pre-Cana consultation. Although the priest eventually agreed, he first advised the couple that, their marriage was not conclusive until the legal documents were filed.

Kane didn't wish to be scrutinized and, believed the odds weren't in his favor, as he tapped on the door to Ernesto's penthouse, in an attempt to conjure up a best man for his wedding. Ernesto and Carmen had partaken of supper with their honored guests, who were busy banging the headboard through the wall, inside their bedroom. The romantic attraction, between the two elderly lovers, was more symbolic of the times missed, therefore they emotionally hugged and waltzed to the soothing romantic sounds of Jazz. Ernesto answered the door, after he looked through the peephole to ensure who the visitor was. Both he and Carmen became elated at the honor, to stand with a friend on his most important day.

Alyiah contacted her biological sister and asked if she would be her bride's maid, but her disapproving sibling remorsefully declined, and falsely stated "she had no one to babysit her three children." When Carmen heard the disappointing news, she politely offered her services, that was graciously accepted. Therefore, dressed in formal attire, provided by the Gentlemen and Ladies Apparels Department inside the Queen Elizabeth Hotel, the Esquada wedding party stood before Pastor Forbes, in holy matrimony. The Catholic pastor was happily compensated, for even considering the ceremony at the unprecedented hour of 2:40 AM, plus his church received a healthy donation.

Pastor Forbes performed the ceremony, although the wedded couple would have to return to sign the documents. Mr. and Mrs. Esquada were treated to the grandest of gifts, as the Queen Elizabeth Hotel opened their grand ballroom and popped a romantic CD into the disc player, for the wedded couple to dance the night away. Both Carman and Ernesto joined the newlyweds on the dance floor for a short time, and continued their reunification affair, before they returned to the privacy of their own suite.

Eddie got word that his girlfriend Alyiah left the multicultural festival with Kane; and went ballistic at the disclosure. Once the news was received, Eddie left Brogan's estate with two of his closest friends and went in search of his 'so-called property'. Eddie was a prominent soldier for the Defenders, who often hustled throughout their territory, as a drug mule for the products they trafficked. As they cruised around the city, reluctant to cross the Pont Mercier Bridge and continue their search on Indian soil, Eddie received a phone call from an informant, who disclosed the church where Alyiah was to marry.

Eddie was late disrupting the wedding proceedings, as he arrived after the wedding party had returned to the hotel. Pastor Forbes rarely found himself awoken at those hours and, decided to prepare a few items for early morning mass, before he returned to the comforts of his bed. Eddie and his cheerleading squad broke into the Catholic church and attacked the pastor, who was assessing the amount of choir magazines across each aisle. The disappointment of not catching his supposed girlfriend, who had neglected to mention her intentions to part ways and move on, infuriated Eddie, who simply walked up and began pistol-whipping the pastor.

"Where did the couple you married tonight go, pastor" Eddie asked, before the clergy member slipped into a state of unconsciousness?

The pastor was beaten for almost three minutes before he even got an inclination of what the intruders wanted. The bloodied clergyman, despite his antagonist's hideous actions, blessed and forgave Eddie, as he lost consciousness. Eddie's accomplices weren't as comfortable assaulting a priest, as they would have been had it been a Rough Rider's member, therefore, they bolted for the exit, before Eddie got through with his interrogation. While walking back toward their parked vehicle, the two Defenders members who accompanied Eddie looked puzzlingly at each other, as a single shot sounded back inside the church.

An irate Eddie telephoned the informant, who had disclosed Alyiah's supposed location the first time, and insisted the person find her present coordinates. The informant advised Eddie that, 'they'd get back to him as soon as some information became available', before the person began telephoning others. Within minutes, the informant responded with the correct information, although the actual suite number was unknown.

The busboy, who worked the graveyard shift at the Queen Elizabeth Hotel, was toking on a marijuana joint behind his workplace, when Eddie and his two misfits crept up on him. Eddie behaved like some rich aristocrat, as he began threatening to have the busboy fired or arrested and charged for possession, should he not respond to a few questions. The busboy confirmed, that a couple from the hotel had indeed gotten married and were loaned the ballroom, where they were currently partying the night away. The disrespected boyfriend noticed the slightly ajar service door and, motioned his companions to subdue the young busboy. The young hotel employee believed they were making progress, and hoped to discourage the person he perceived important, from informing his supervisor. The only reward the busboy received was a knife to the abdomen, which paralyzed him immediately and sent him crashing to the ground.

Eddie and his accomplices covered their faces with ski masks and barged into the hotel, in search of Alyiah and her new husband, Kane. The Defenders interrogators forgot to request the precise route to the ballroom, during their question-and-response session with the deceased busboy. The service entrance led to the employees' lounge, across from the kitchen and managerial services, but the ballroom was located to the very end of that corridor. As Eddie snuck close to the managerial services office, a female employee stepped from the bathroom next door, and frightened all three men. One of the intruders who had a very sensitive 9mm Barretta trigger, frantically blasted the woman right back into the bathroom.

That initial gunshot echoed through the empty hallways and alerted the small staff within the vicinity. Kane had heard enough gunshots through his lifetime, to mistakenly diagnose the sound he heard, thus he was confident something wasn't right. The superstitious Indian warrior had begun moving his wife toward the alternative entrance, when the three masked marauders busted into the ballroom. Protecting his wife was his first priority, therefore Kane shoved Maria behind a building column, withdrew his Hellcat 9mm semi auto hand pistol and blasted two shots at the intruders, who all dove and hit the turf, before they returned fire.

The masked intruders intended to cause their targets obvious bodily harm, as they punctured bullet holes into the beautiful architecture. Kane noticed the ski masks covering the faces of their assassins, and thus ordered Alyiah 'to exit through the door and run for her life'. As soon as Kane instructed his wife of the plan, he fired several shots at their antagonists, before they busted through the entrance and ran. When Eddie and his associates rushed into the ballroom shooting callously, one of the masked marauders got shot in the gut by Kane, which somewhat compromised their mission. The Defender who got shot, began hollering and screaming for them 'to get the fuck out of there', although Eddie impulsively wanted to pursue their targets.

The masked intruders could not afford to leave their ally to die inside the hotel, nor could they leave him to the authorities, for fear of him being identified and triggering a full-scale war. Therefore, the two other Defenders aided their friend to his feet and escaped through the nearest exit door. As for Kane and his bride, the Indian warrior immediately chartered a local taxi in front the hotel, to carry them to familiar grounds, across the bridge on the Kahnawake reservation.

Part 26

Martain awoke from a nightmare, where he was surfing on huge waves. There were lots of ladies wearing sexy swimsuits along the beach, cheering him on, as he cut across the waves, while balancing himself on his surfboard.

"Look at him, he is so handsome and sexy!"

"Oh, he is the perfect bad boy!"

"There is nobody cooler or sexier," were some the remarks being uttered by the females, who were all in awe over him.

Suddenly a huge wave appeared ahead of him, and Nicholas' face popped into the overhanging water.

"Mi did warn you, don't fuck with badman pussy," Nicholas lamented!

The waves transformed into a huge scary mouth, with razor sharp teeth, and was about to bite him in half, when he jumped up from the dream and frightfully looked around the room. There were two females on either side of him fast asleep, the room was dark, and the television on the wall, was on the news station.

The news anchor began talking about a memorial service, to be held on behalf of Nicholas and the other men killed in the horrible bridge tragedy. Martain watched the broadcast in its entirety, before he climbed out of bed and lit himself a cigarette. The biker boss walked over to the window, stood there naked while he stared out at his yard, and puffed away on the cigarette.

The shock of being shot at had Alyiah's entire body shivering, as if she was suffering from pneumonia. The thought that she could have been wiped clear off the face of the earth terrified her, and she clung tightly to her new husband's arm. Kane gripped his new bride tight, as he threw both hands around her and apologized continuously, for exposing her to the graphic reality of his life. The warrior Indian hopped into the first taxi he saw after the ballroom incident and headed directly to the sanctity provided across the bridge.

Once over the Pont Mercier Bridge, Kane instructed the taxi driver to find the closest Tim Horton's, for him to soothe his wife's tense nerves with a cup of warm beverage. As they travelled along Saint Jean de Baptist Boulevard, the driver observed that Alyiah appeared a bit ill and offered humor as a remedy. The driver insinuated that the vast number of cigarette and cigar huts, significantly outnumbered the Tim Horton's, fast food restaurants and delis, around the entire Indian reservation. There was a vast difference in the quality of tobacco, produced by the government of Canada and those of the Indians! Hence, a grave number of cigarette-puffing Quebec taxpayers, were inclined to make the short journey in order to purchase the cheaper generic brand, produced by the Indians. As such, there was an array of cigar and cigarette shacks, along the main roads throughout the reservation. The couple in the rear of his taxi chuckled over the statement, although it was evident that the female was still quite shaken from her ordeal.

Despite his recent brush with death, Kane appeared unflappable as he ran into the Tim Horton's restaurant, to fetch the items he deemed vital to strengthening his wife. As soon as Kane exited the taxi, Alyiah began confessing to the driver, as if he were her priest from church. The frightened young señorita, told the driver she had just recently tied the knot, but questioned whether she'd made the right decision. The female neglected to mention the incident that brought her to her dilemma, although her gibberish at times made her sound at bit nostalgic. During her flapping-at-the-mouth session, Alyiah suddenly thought of a piece of evidence vital to solving the masked intruders' identities, and she went racing from the taxi into the restaurant.

Kane collected the beverages, a few doughnuts, and his change from the servicer, and was about to exit the restaurant, when Alyiah rushed him as if she'd discovered the cure for mortality. The Indian warrior's new wife disclosed her suspicions about whom she perceived their attackers were, that attempted to snuff out their life forces on this their most memorable day. Alyiah had caught a glimpse of their attackers, as Kane fought to preserve their lives, but in all the confusion and the ruckus, her jittered nerves protruded her from processing certain information. Given the time and ability to reflect, Alyiah analyzed the entire evening as she recalled it, before she determined and rendered her final judgment on who exactly attacked them.

"Honey, I know exactly who tried to kill us tonight," Alyiah began, before stressfully collapsing in Kane's arms at the thought of the implication she was about to disclose!

Kane guided his wife out the restaurant, before she caught the attention of those eavesdroppers seeking a wisp of gossip. The pair of Esquadas stood in front the restaurant, where Kane made sure his wife wasn't delusional, before curiously deciphering her information.

"Baby, I… know the bullets and stuff startled me to where… I screamed in fear of losing my life, but before I turned to run, I saw something familiar that… identifies who the shooters were," Alyiah commented!

"How can you be so sure about who it was," Kane asked?

"Because… I personally bought one of the shooters… the Triple B T-shirt he had on," chuckled Alyiah over her words.

"You're fucking kidding me! You mean that was your ex," demanded Kane?

"Yes, and… I guess the other two were his little stoolies," Alyiah said insightfully.

"It's all right, baby! The Saint Laurence River is not one that many people cross over, in fear of us crazy Indians in Chateauguay. But I guarantee… they won't get that chance again! I promise," Kane soothingly declared!

The Indian warrior was about to re-enter the taxi, when four Kawasaki motorbikes roared into the parking lot and drove toward the yellow cab. Almost instantaneously, Kane began walking toward the men, who were all fully decked out in cyclist gear, as if he knew exactly who they were. The Indian warrior was a few paces ahead of the four riders, when he suddenly dipped, made a one-hundred-and-eighty-degree turn, and began bolting toward the awaiting taxi. Two teenage high school seniors had just exited the Tim Horton's and, were heading to their vehicle in the parking lot, when Kane scurried by the inattentive lads. Before the actual eruption of bullets was heard, Kane felt positive he'd been struck, as he lay directly in the path of the oncoming riders. The two senior students went flying, as if they'd gone skydiving from twenty thousand feet in the air. Once Kane made it into the taxi, he knew the youngsters he'd run past had saved his life, although they paid the ultimate price.

With his patented 9mm barking cover fire at his antagonists, Kane crashed on the rear seat and immediately yelled to the taxi driver, "Hit the gas!" Following Kane's order to flee the scene, he returned to dousing their attackers with lead, after he opened the rear window and snuck his hand through, while he discharged his weapon.

Kane managed to separate one of his attackers from his iron horse, as the taxi went screeching out onto the main roadway. The heavier firepower from his antagonists, who were armed with Uzis, forced Kane to protect himself and his wife by shielding them on the rear seat, while bullets shattered the rear glass, other side windows and ripped into the leather seats.

"Are you fucking crazy? You could have been killed! Why would you possibly walk toward people who are trying to kill you," Alyiah angrily demanded?

"Two of those guys are wearing Mohawk riding gear. I thought I knew them," Kane answered!

Reports of the incident were made to the different agencies of law, which scrambled police and emergency technicians to the scene. There was an Indian police officer parked three miles from the incident, with his radar speed analyzer surveying the traffic, although his interest was primarily captured by his girlfriend on his cell phone. The taxi and pursuing motorbikes sped by the monitoring cop at speeds exceeding one hundred and fifty miles per hour, with a significant amount of ammunition being dumped on the taxi. Officer Yukon Geronimo ended his phone sex chat and threw on his sirens, as he engaged the disruptive vehicles wreaking havoc along the roadways. The repeated announcement informing all emergency personnel about the murders at the Tim Horton's, blasted over the air waves the moment Officer Geronimo turned up the volume on his transistor radio. The officer listened to the report and the description of the assailants, before informing the dispatcher that he was, in fact, giving chase to the shooters. As the convoy of victims, mercenaries, and police sped by Anjou Boulevard, a provincial police officer joined the chase alongside Officer Geronimo, who was also being doused with bullets by the bike riders.

The provincial cruiser, unlike the reservation patrols, was equipped with two officers to combat the tough situations on the reservation. The provincial officers joined the chase and immediately turned the tables, as the bikers faced turmoil for the first time, with officers taking aim and returning fire. The barrage of bullets fired at the riders eventually decreased their numbers, when two of the mercenaries went crashing along the roadside. Kane squeezed his pistol's trigger until the hammer cocked back, which signified he had run out of bullets. The Indian warrior held his newlywed tightly, while they crouched on the back seat of the taxi, hoping the police would rid them of their antagonists. A detrimental bullet from one of the bikers, shattered the taxi driver's skull against the dashboard, at which the speeding taxi abruptly turned, then went spiraling in midair, before it crashed against a huge pine tree. The bikers, who devoted themselves to eliminating the Warrior's leader, had to flee the scene, as more police cruisers began converging from all coordinates. All but one police cruiser continued chasing the speedy bikers, hence the vast number of officers stopped and ran to assist the victims inside the crashed taxi.

There was utter chaos aboard the vehicle that transported Eddie Cortez and his crew of mercenaries. The shooter, who was shot in the stomach, was twenty-year-old Miguel Torres, a high school dropout who lived for the thrill and excitement, brought about through hustling. The driver, Marquez Dominguez, like his counterparts, was grass-rooted in the west end and rarely visited the center of town. Hence, the directions to the closest or any hospital was to them, like finding the nearest police station. The Toyota Camry they utilized drove about the center town region, as they searched for signs or indications of a hospital. With bloodstains throughout the car, and on everyone's clothing, Eddie thought it best they refrain from asking anyone for directions to a hospital and, completed the search themselves.

Miguel exclaimed, "Oh come on, Eddie! Fuck! Just pull over and ask someone for the fucking hospital! I'm bleeding to death here, can't you see?"

"He don't look too good, Eddie! I think, we should pull over and get some directions," Marquez added!

"Are you both stupid? Don't you think they got the entire downtown searching for us right now? If it wasn't for your stupid ass, we would be on that highway back to the West Island right now! Instead, we gotta be riding around this stinking town searching for a hospital," Eddie declared!

"Don't let me die, Eddie? I don't want die! Please don't let me die? Drop me off by an ambulance or something, but don't let me die, please?"

"Just hold on, M-Ten! We gonna find a hospital real soon," Eddie advised!

The driver looked back through the rearview mirror at his allies and shook his head, as Eddie ripped open Miguel's shirt, exposing his horrific wound. The bullet struck at the very base of the chest and slightly above his stomach, which caused the victim severe pain as blood gushed from the wound. Marquez knew that without immediate attention, his friend would certainly succumb to his injury and die, yet there still remained no sign of a hospital. As the driver returned his focus to the roadway, a blue, square sign with a giant "H", which indicated the route to a hospital, flashed by attached to a light post.

The driver said, "I just seen a hospital sign! We'll be there in a few minutes, M-Ten!"

"Hold on, my boy, you can't die yet! Nobody else I know, rolls an L like you," Eddie confessed! "You remember the time we met those sisters? The old and young one from Laval, who we sent to Columbia for business? Remember what happened the first night we took them back to their house? You rolled a couple Ls… and got them fucked up out their minds, before they started sucking our dicks and shit! Yow, Marq-Five, this fool fucking this chick in the living room up the ass, and her father comes home, Fam! The man walks in and sees this fool piping this chick, walks over, and taps him on the shoulder! You know what this fool says to this chick's father, who was probably having a heart attack? 'This ass too sweet! If you want to switch, you go have to give me a few minutes to finish busting up this ass'!"

Everyone inside the vehicle laughed at the amusement, before Eddie continued his story. "Marq-Five, the man couldn't handle it! He raced up stairs for his revolver and would have blasted this fool, who until now, didn't even turn around to make sure I wasn't tapping him on the shoulder! Luckily for him, the father walked in on me and his older daughter on the parents' bed! That chick would have given me the world, and I chose this bitch over her! Before I got down to tearing that ass up, though, that chick gave me her daddy's gun, a box of bullets, and all the cash out the safe! I had to push that man's own revolver down his throat, in order for us to get up out there that day! You have never seen a father before, who sits back and allows his daughters to pack their shit and leave, with no arguments!"

"Hospital two blocks ahead! How we gonna do this, Pump E? We might as well drop him off at the emergency entrance. Someone is guaranteed to wheel him inside, once they find him in the state he's is," Marquez suggested!

Miguel began convulsing and grabbed on tightly to Eddie's hand, as if grasping for added strength to help combat the pain. The wounded gangster's eyes expanded as if they were about to pop out of the sockets, as Miguel attempted to communicate with his peers. Instead of words, a vomit of blood spewed from the injured thug's mouth, and his body began trembling, before the life force exited his body.

"M-Ten! M-Ten, wake the fuck up," Eddie yelled, as the final breath exited the Young Gangster's body! Eddie pounded the young thug's chest in order to jumpstart his heart, yet all his efforts went in vain, and Miguel's blank stare professed to what he'd succumbed.

Marquez pulled to the curb and stopped the vehicle, two street blocks away from Montreal General Hospital. The lifeless corpse of his ally was slumped across Eddie's legs, and Eddie began vowing to avenge his death. The survivors aboard the Toyota Camry immediately headed for the safety of the west, and along the way, they drove to a familiar dumpsite to destroy the evidence. There was an old chop shop on the border of Lachine and Pierrefond, across from the Old Garmin Steel Factory, where the Defenders typically dumped vehicles, they wished to hide from law enforcements.

The old Frenchman who controlled the Slater's Junk Yard and Chop Shop, had done a lot of business with the mischievous bunch, who supplied 85% of the stolen vehicles dismantled inside the shop. Hence, for a meagre fee, extra services, such as total annihilation of property by explosions, chemicals, or fire, could easily be arranged. The proprietor at the junk yard charged the vigilantes one hundred dollars, before providing the essentials such as gasoline and a ride home after the ordeal. The bloodied and enraged gangsters drove the Camry to the furthest region of the yard, doused it thoroughly with the fuel, and set it ablaze, with the corpse of their fallen comrade inside.

The Press Conference

The media coverage of the Rough Riders' free event celebration for the public was ridiculous. Numerous news agencies from around the world, flocked to the conference room at the Bell Centre, home of the Montreal Canadiens. The promotional event was opened purely to media, in order for the celebrities and important officials to respond to questions regarding the event. There were thousands of fans around the Bell Centre, awaiting a slight glimpse of their favorite artists, who all arrived in flare and style. The strictly Canadian performances event had humongous stars performing on the same show, for the public in the center of town. At the announcement of the scheduled performances, sceptics declared that such a line-up would be impossible to achieve, with such little advanced notice. Therefore, as superstars such Celine Dion, Nickelback, and Wolf Parade, stepped from their limousines to enter the media affair, it was no surprise to witness those same sceptics snapping photos.

The ambiance was somewhat inappropriate for someone seeking the top position in Quebec politics, yet Councilman McArthur sought every means necessary to gain a leg up on his opponents. Mr. McArthur excused his presence, by suggesting that his thirteen and fifteen-years-old children, requested to join the festivities, in order for them to get the opportunity to experience their favorite performers live. Thus, the councilmember was center stage, praising the secret contributors to his campaign, while he magnified his personal status in the polls, especially among the younger voters.

"Good day to everyone present! I'm here to help kick off this spectacle of magnificent music for the citizens of Montreal, Quebec, Canada!" The councilmember paused for the huge cheers and applause from around the room. "Before we proceed with the questions, I'm told that each performer will be available for questions, so please be patient; you will be able to get your questions in. This event was once an annual affair, that was started by a late high school friend of mine, Mr. Yves Lafleur, who passed away a few years ago! Today, I'm here with my children, whom I've been telling about this show since they were babies. I've told them about the glamour and finesse of times past, where people couldn't wait till the next year to experience this spectacle again. I pray this festive engagement returns to its annual form, because I'm looking forward to standing right here next year as your host and your premier of this province! Long live Quebec and its sovereign father, Canada," Councilman McArthur proclaimed!

The cameras belonging to the paparazzi and freelance photographers snapped furiously, as reporters dove into questions pertaining to the rumors surrounding the campaign trail. Councilman McArthur shunned all references to politics, as he insisted the event remained paramount for discussion. Monsieur McArthur was sure to advise the public that a security team would be in place at the venue, for precautionary measures only, as they expected very limited incidents of violence. When asked whether he believed an attack was inevitable, Councilman McArthur responded, "I'll certainly be there with my kids!"

Minister Richard Blanc's wife, Francine Belle Blanc, was devastated to find out her husband had a secret mistress, who he confessed to fondling more times than he'd sexually appeased her in almost three years. The political celebrity, whose grace and mannerism had always disdained her husband's foes, decided, like most supportive wives, to remain encouraging and vigilant by her man's side. The Blancs discussed the effects and turmoil of Richard's decision, which was to confirm the slutty gossip in the tabloids, instead of subletting their party's priorities for power-seekers. Following their decision on how to proceed, the minister informed his personal liaison of his decision to remain an independent political party.

Minister Blanc was not booted from his family home for his promiscuous affair, because Francine chose to save face, instead of awarding the media more ammunition for their newspapers. The minister, however, was tossed his pillow and a comforter and sent to the guest chambers, until further notice. At 11:47 that evening, while Richard watched the day's news, Francine walked into the room with her eyes filled with tears and handed him the telephone.

The minister, who appeared to be dozing off to sleep, asked, "Who is it?"

Francine remained quiet as the tears ran down her face. The minister had been with his wife long enough to know her boiling point, which was quite evident by her breathing like a fatigued horse.

"Hello, Minister Blanc, how can I help you," the minister asked in French, the language of his forefathers?

"Daddy! Daddy, I'm sorry," the voice over the phone broke down crying!

"Guinevere? What's wrong, honey," Richard demanded of his twenty-two-year-old daughter, who was away attending University in Vancouver, British Columbia?

"Daddy," cried the female, who was obviously under some sort of duress!

The phone was snatched from the female, who sounded like her mouth was being tampered with by someone. Mrs. Blanc covered her mouth in order to avoid from screaming, as she fell to her knees beside the bed. The voice of a French-accented male came over the phone, as the minister sat up in curiosity and concern for his daughter.

"Good evening, Minister! I'm not going to beat around the bush! It has recently come to my attention that you've changed your mind regarding the offer made to you! I personally believe young Guinevere here is a beautiful young woman. I'd like to get to know her under different circumstances, but for now that's all up to you!"

"What is it you want? Please don't hurt her!"

"Like I said, that's all up to you and how well you take directions!"

"Whatever you want, he'll do it," Mrs. Blanc shouted in the background!

"Nice! Just what I want to hear! Now, if you and your wife ever want to see this pretty young lady again, I suggest you be a good candidate, and illustrate the great team player you are," the caller threatened!

There were so many visitors who went out to show their love, respect and support for Nicholas, and the rest of the shottas suspected to have perished with him, that officers had to be called in to control the traffic. The memorial service was held at a quiet little church in N.D.G, located on the corner of Sherbrooke Street and Marcil Avenue. There were so many mourners present, that the crowd could not fit inside the huge church hall, thus there were people playing reggae music, beating pans and singing praises, from Oxford Avenue all the way up to Avenue-de-Melrose. A number of police officers were visibly present, observing the crowd without interacting with the grieving mourners, some of whom shouted vulgar comments at the coppers and wanted them to leave.

Despite the predominately black crowd, there were people from many nations present, such as Mohawk Indians, Latin Canadians, Chinese, Africans, Europeans, Inuit's and many others. Damian, Tank, Kane, and the majority of Nicholas' shottas gathered inside the church, where Pastor Simone Luther commemorated the spirits of those killed. There were females weeping in sorrow, while the preacher spoke of the eight men, some of whom had family members inside the hall. Kane and most of the gangsters exited the church before the service ended, and walked out to a different ceremony, where the crowd celebrated the men's lives in true Caribbean terms. Large posters of Nicholas were being paraded by several patrons among the crowd, who hailed the rude boy like a national hero.

As the gangsters stood on the top steps of the church listening to the crowd, the overpowering sounds from nearly twenty Harley Davidson's pulled up across the street. The officers who had been rushing other motorists along, neglected the bikers, who stopped their bikes and sat atop their mounts, while they looked at the gathering. Martain, who lead the group, wore his German style biker helmet, black jeans, leather boots and his Rough Rider's club jacket, with the huge biker insignia on the back. The Rough Rider boss engaged in an intense stare-down with Kane, Brogan, Damian and others, before he threatened them all by slashing his right index finger across his throat. That single moment was the most intense time of the entire ceremony, considering the crowd was on edge, not knowing if gunshots was about to start ringing out.

Following the threatening gesture, the Rough Riders fired back up their engines, then slowly rode away through the red light, which forced the traffic officer to abruptly stop the vehicles that had priority. Even the news reporters who had been recording one of the largest memorial services they had ever seen, could not believe the audacity of Martain Lafleur, who used his visit to demonstrate his dominance. Immediately after the bikers departed, the crowd turned back up the volume, and continued celebrating the memories of those murdered. The Alliance members who knew otherwise, looked at each other and smiled, as the crowd chanted Nicholas' name. Kane dialed Nicholas' phone, to give him a sense of the vibrant energy and the outpour of love in his honor.

The phone rang twice, before Nicholas answered, "Yow brother, what a gwan?"

"Your man, Martain, was just here!"

"I know... they just showed it on the news."

"I don't know if they showing this on TV, but listen, it's crazy out here brother," Kane stopped talking and casually held the phone, but crossed both his arms to conceal his actions!

Part 27

Martain had a viable concern whether Nicholas was deceased or alive, after the autopsy technicians reported, "Inconclusive evidence, regarding the positive identification of his most potent nemesis." The biker boss' corporate analyst advised him, that he believed 'politics played a role in the proper disclosure being released and, as such, a concrete summary of the findings would not be possible'. The analysis proceeded to argue that, 'because they were so close to Election Day, every party leader would rather bury a topic such as Nicholas Henry, than lose grounds in the election polls.' The explosion and dismantlement of both SUV vehicles, disfigured the anatomies of all eight men, leaving only those with Canadian dental or medical history, with the possibility of being identified. After days of repeated nightmares that included Nicholas, Martain had to seek the advice of his most trusted analyst, before wholeheartedly agreeing to proceed with the momentous event.

Downtown Parade

Police officers from the downtown precinct began sealing off adjacent roads to St. Catherine Street at 10:00 on the morning of the Rough Riders' grand celebration. Roadblocks prevented motorists from occupying the busy commercial and tourist portions of town, which were the areas that operated twenty-four hours a day, seven days a week. A number of semi-tractor trailers with volunteers, began dropping off and installing musical equipment along the highlighted route, directly after the officers secured and safeguarded the venue. There were huge sound systems set up every four blocks, with one main stage set up inside the industrial park, across from La Baie shopping center. While various infamous DJs excited the crowds throughout the highlighted route, the main stage would showcase some of Canada's most famous superstars, such as Nickelback, Arcade Fire, Wolf Parade and others.

There were a few events scheduled by the organizers, that catered mainly for the children and their biker peers. Ronald McDonald would be at and around the McDonald's, at the corner of McGill Boulevard and St. Catherine Street, from 11:30 AM until 6:00 PM, taking pictures with kids, while he collected and lobbied for donations to help the sick children of the Ronald McDonald House. There were artists along the highlighted route, who would paint patterns on the children's faces for free, as well as magicians who thrilled the crowds with glorious magic, all of which began at 11:00 AM. Hamburgers and hot dogs were offered to the children under the age of thirteen, at more than twenty food stands along the route. Free beer was only offered to members with the patch or insignia of the Rough Riders on their jackets, as it was their day to feast, celebrate, and fully enjoy the atmosphere.

Nicholas' ambush plot went into action the moment the green light was given to proceed with the Rough Rider's spectacle. Many of the officers who stood guard at the road blockages, were actual members of the Defenders posse or Nicholas' mob in disguise. While a crew of police officers, swept the venue area, which was a customary security measure before important delegates or persons of stature visited an area, twenty-four mercenaries outfitted like officers, branched off into higher level buildings and businesses along Saint Catherine Street. Before they sat out, Nicholas made it known that 'there would be no glory if they didn't work together, and thus every crew member involved was given equal share of the duties.' While some of the mercenaries who dressed like Montreal constables found higher grounds, a large number still mingled in the crowd, and served as decoys for the event slated to transpire.

Kane and twenty of his Indian Warriors were outfitted like the merciless Rough Rider bikers. The Indian Warriors astoundingly resembled their hated nemesis, wearing their patented leather jackets, decorated with patches of various valours, plain denim jeans, leather cowboy boots, and the Harley Davidson hogs they rode. Aside from their means of transportation and attire, some of the Indians also wore fake beards, tattoos and mustaches, which undoubtedly molded the bikers' characteristics. The Warriors awaited their cue to join the battle, which was to come during the grand introduction of the host and all his merry men. Nicholas planned to have his imposter bike riders, integrate with the last group of Rough Riders to enter the festive celebration, then flanked their enemies, like many victorious war generals have done through history.

Scores of people, from all walks of nations, poured off each Metro station from Atwater to St. Laurent, in anticipation of seeing their favorite rock bands for free. Busloads of out-of-towners, and local transit takers, also descended into center town, but most vehicle owners were forced to find parking, great distances from the event. The streets, which were semi-tranquil during the early morning's road blockages, security protocol and other setups, were remarkably transformed to the vibrant atmosphere, by 10:40 AM. The trans-continental highway, I-20, had been backed up with traffic since 9:00 that morning, with impatient motorists attempting to enter the downtown area. The pedestrian ambushers, drawn up in Nicholas' plan, took basic transportation like the metro and city buses to the gala. Theirs was a mixture of men and women involved in Nicholas' plot, as the Alliance forces came out in full, to annihilate their prized enemy.

Nicholas had met with both generals from his Alliance force only once to discuss the plan, which would have been practically foolproof, had not their opponent been Martain Lafleur. The biker leader expected an attack from the remaining rebel forces, who he knew cared deeply about Nicholas and had to avenge him however possible. Moreover, Martain expected the political party they endorsed to jog away with the election, and thereby hand over, 'a "do as you wish" license', to help his rebel movement extinguish the remaining Alliance insurgents. Martain had implanted a few insurance policies in the crowd, to mainly serve, as backups should his combatants be unable to weather the storm.

Five minutes into the spectacle, the Rough Riders' event was already being heralded as, the greatest event in Montreal's history. For a single day, the poor and less fortunate, felt as important as the financially secured, and they partied side by side with everyone. Nicholas sat inside the Starbucks on the corner of St. Catherine and Atwater Boulevard, indulging in a cup of mint tea with Killa, as the roaring engines of Harley Davidsons sounded in the distance. Both men, like many others of the ambushers' group, had to disguise themselves in order to not give themselves away, to their opponents, who knew them quite well.

"What's this rumor mi a hear, 'bout Kane get shot after two time the other night," Nicholas asked, as he sipped a bit of hot tea from his cup?

"We did so busy with Boss E leaving and thing, that mi forget totally to mention it! But you know say the man come check we, way after mi lock down with my gal, to get a witness in his marriage," Killa commented!

"Marriage? Kane married somebody," Nicholas asked?

"Yah, man! Some shorty from the West Island who him thief from one a them Defenders boys. I must admit, that gal was thick like a mudfish," Killa implied!

"Yeah, mi get a text from him wha night, I guess that's his urgent message. Mi have to talk to him 'bout that still, cause at a time like this, them things there can divide we, when we need the unity," Nicholas conveyed! "I wonder which man gal him take away?"

"When Kane called us and mention that 'we need to leave the hotel', him did say the man them who rush him a wear ski masks, to hide them identity," Killa announced.

"Hold on, hold on, tell the gal behind the counter fi turn up the TV?" Nicholas said, after glimpsing news footage of the Honorable Minister Richard Blanc, who was holding a press conference to disclose his and his political party's future intents.

"We've embarked on a historic journey, which will without a doubt, empower us to make those changes we've always preached about. As was rumored, my electoral party has joined forces with Minister McArthur and the Liberal Party!" The minister paused in mid-speech, to accommodate the cheers and applause generated by loyal supporters of the party, who were willing to follow their leader to the ends of the earth.

"Once a politician, always a politician," declared Nicholas, who wasn't surprised to witness the minister rescinding his pledge!

"That's why mi did tell yu, you can't trust them politicians for nothing! From mi live a Jamaica, mi no fuck with them, cause come election time is the only time them know ghetto youths. Is them bring the most big guns in the ghetto, then turn 'round and send soldiers fi go kill off the same youths them, who them did give the guns them to! That's way from me make a money to buy my things, mi just buy mine, cause me will never make some boy come talk 'bout, carry back him things! You crazy," Killa declared!

The roars of what sounded like a million Harleys, began showboating in front the restaurant, as the Rough Rider bikers paraded by. Neither Nicholas nor Killa had any concerns of being spotted, considering they were dressed like females, wearing make-up, long brunette weaves, skirts, tank tops with fake breasts, women's sneakers, huge gold earrings, and designer glasses. Both men arose from their table and grabbed their full-sized Louis Vuitton purses, from off the floor as they went out to view the bikers' spectacle. The gangsters in drag, depending on who you asked, made awful-looking women, although a few men either tooted their horns, or tried to acquire their contact information. As Killa and Nicholas stood in front the coffee house, watching the exhibition of Rough Riders parading through the center of downtown, a few riders offered to take the ladies for a bike ride, but they were declined.

Nicholas had analysts posted at each entry point into downtown, to determine the number of transports and bikers involved in the parade. After the final numbers were tallied, an analyst telephoned the boss with the information he had them obtain. The caller was unable to provide a exact number of riders, but she had ascertained that they were scattered across a six city blocks radius, therefore, they had an army with which to contend. The female watchdog also reported, that 'the senior advisors were scattered between the fourth and fifth blocks, with their Commander-in-Chief well protected among members of the fourth block. Nicholas desired such prudent information, for the finalization of his tactical strategy, as he sought to invoke his toughest firepower especially at those key areas.

Nicholas contacted Brogan, who was relaxing in the serenity of a luxury suite at The Business Suite hotel, located at 2866 St. Catherine Street West. Brogan was camped out as a sniper, at a vantage point from where he expected to massacre as many Rough Riders members as possible. The chief for the Defenders misfits had just finished his oversight on the positioning of his troops, who were scattered from edifices to the streets, all along the highlighted route.

"Yow, Brogan, come in," Nicholas requested over their two-way radio, as he adjusted the volume so his conversation could not be overheard.

"Go ahead, partner, I'm right here," Brogan answered.

"The fishes them, entering the pond as we speak! Mi just receive the clarification, that the head groupie a swim around the fourth and fifth pond, but overall, them stretch out over six ponds' length. So, inform the fisherman dem, no fishing until the captain give the go-ahead, cause we definitely a catch some big fish today," Nicholas instructed, as he spoke using their broken English code talk!

A male pedestrian, was walking by the gangsters dressed in drag and, caught the final instructions on Nicholas' tactical update. The white male had set out, like everyone else, to listen to the delectable lyrics, of their favorite rock bands. The thirty-five-year-old bachelor could not ignore what sounded to him, like the desperate plea of an attractive filly, whom he perceived was somewhat sex-starved. The indulging heterosexual male, diverted from his path, along the St. Catherine Street sidewalks, and rudely took Nicholas' left hand into his palms.

"Let me spend the—," began the intolerable male, before Nicholas formed a fist with the phone in his right hand, and clobbered the man, who was knocked out cold, and fell to the ground.

"Copy that, General," responded Brogan, as static sounded through the radio, from Nicholas' TKO punch, which broke their communication device.

Almost everyone who witnessed the TKO of the woman-heckler, particularly the females travelling along, cheered and applauded the valiant effort of the assumed female gender. Through all his ignorance, Nicholas neglected to consider the importance of the radio, which he desperately needed to dispatch the troops. As Nicholas pondered over solutions to reacquiring certain numbers, that weren't embedded into his memory, but simply stored on his SIM card, a little girl, who was skipping along the sidewalk in front of her parents, stopped and bent to her knees, in order to retrieve the many broken sections of his phone. As Nicholas stared at the little eight-year-old girl, he began envisioning his son, whom he hoped would grow up to become a productive member of society. The thought of innocent children being wounded bothered Nicholas, who had devoted his life to the extinction of the greater evil. The generosity of a child, who handed him the broken device, momentarily weakened Nicholas, who for the first time had second thoughts about their plan. For her troubles, the mastermind behind what was secretly dubbed, 'The Extinction Project', gave her ten dollars for her pocket.

"Thank you, miss! That was a hell of a right hand," stated the young girl, who went right back to skipping down the sidewalk!

"Pass me yu Cellie," Nicholas asked of Killa, who was sizing up the competition?

"Hold this," Killa responded, as he immediately passed over his phone!

Nicholas telephoned Danny Esquada, whose number he'd dialed more often than anyone else's inside the country, that it was imprinted into his memory. The phone numbers belonging to Kane and Brogan, were given to Nicholas by his personal advisor, who oversaw dispatching their personal troops, at the safest and at the most volatile areas. Killa tapped Nicholas on the shoulder and pointed to the convoy surrounding Martain, which consisted of twelve riders wearing tailored Icon Leather suits, specially designed to harbor heavy weaponry, and to protect the wearer with its bullet-proofing capabilities. The personal security surrounding Martain, was expected by Nicholas and his constituents, but there were also six uniformed police officers assigned to the detail, who weren't foreseen in the planning. Martain appeared cocky and dismissive, as he briskly sat up in the saddle of his Harley, while onlookers fought to capture a photo of one of Canada's most notorious mobsters.

"Let's walk," Nicholas directed, and they began strolling through the huge crowds, gathered along both walkways within the entertainment zone! Nicholas then telephoned Kane and his band of pretenders, who were mainly supposed to flank the enemy, before engaging the battle and giving chase to the fleeing cowards.

"Yow, Kane, congratulations, mi buoy! Later we buss some juice, but right now, creep and come in, 'cause everything set," Nicholas exclaimed!

"This the day we waiting for a long time! Say no more, Chief, we en route," Kane answered!

Kane and his band of Warriors looked similar to their Rough Rider counterparts, with their multiple tattoos, fake beards, and wigs gushing through the air, as they cruised along Atwater Boulevard. The graciousness of the biker gang enthroned them as royalty for the day, thus, patrons heading to the soiree, cheered Kane and his portrayers as they rode by. The Warriors rode up the hill and turned left two lights before they reached St. Catherine Street, travelled three blocks west along that road, then headed back north toward St. Catherine.

By the time the Indians reached their designated location, the real bikers were two blocks ahead of them, with another block to complete before they entered the festive area. Saint-Catherine-Street was Montreal's downtown core, which ran in one direction from west to east for several blocks, yet sections of the street allowed for two-way traffic. There was a slew of high-rise buildings along both sides of the road, with the city's largest economic underground connections. The Warriors, who didn't want to interact with their nemesis, before they'd gotten within inches of the event, shortened the distance between them, yet maintained separation.

The royally majestic treatment, being showered at members of the infamous gang, lessened their fears that any attacker would proceed with his intents, after witnessing the godly love being flung at them. Therefore, the centurions, who toiled at the rear of the convoy of bikes, found more interest in gawking at beautiful women, than ensuring their rear was actually secure. Kane and his Warriors sneaked ever closer, as the train of Harley Davidsons entered the highlighted route. There was a huge banner that hung across the road, which advertised the event, along with ear-blasting hip-hop, echoing through huge speakers, by the first sound system along the route. DJ Mes, a well-known music personality across the country, rocked a crowd of young hip-hop generation students, who'd gathered around the trailer that was provided to each DJ.

A single shot erupted at a distance, although it sounded to observers as if it originated from the northwest, rather than along the trail. Those who actually heard the shot paused and waited to see the reactions of others, before deciding how to respond to the disturbing sound. Several spectators in the crowd grew somewhat nervous, out of fear of retaliation against their hosts, by members of Nicholas' cabinet, who were believed to have lost their leader. Contrary to the sceptics and the chatter, on the streets and over radio talk shows, prior to the event, fans of the performers would rather to get caught in a tornado, than miss their favorite artists for free. There were thousands of attendants, who also thought the Rough Riders were revered by all, thus, no one would dare challenge their superiority, even though the event was being held at the perfect setting for a mass slaying.

The horrific screams from females, were almost as loud as what sounded like a cannon, which blasted the biker at the helm of the parade, completely off his Harley Davidson chopper. The pursuing bikers drew their arms and immediately looked to the buildings, as separate incidents began transpiring among patrons in the crowd. All at once, windowpanes along several edifices from Atwater Boulevard to Guy Street began breaking, as the ambushing forces rained down showers of bullets. A few bikers attempted to utilize the banks of the sidewalks as cover, before discovering first-hand, that some of their so-called police security, were actually enemies in disguise.

Pure chaos erupted, with what seemed like police killing police, civilians killing bikers, and bikers killing randomly, while the innocent became causalities of war, as they attempted to flee the battleground area. Civilians began breaking through windows, in order to escape the bullets at their backs, hence, they broke into businesses either closed or opened. Inconsiderate escapees were seen pushing aside children, elderly folks, physically impaired, the handicapped in wheelchairs, and even trampling over patrons who fell, while they attempted to flee the massacre. Ronald McDonald was greeting people along the route, before he was forced to kick off those humongous clown boots, in order to run for his life once the fighting began. There were the tragic sights of a few parents' corpses, protectively cradling their infants, while their children either suffered the same fate or cried uncontrollably.

Rough Riders were falling like ducks during hunting season, as bullets dislodged many of them from their Harleys. Kane and his Rough

Riders' mimicking Warriors began opening fire at the riders in front of them, who were fast realizing the severity of what they'd gotten into. The surrounding buildings echoed the sounds of gunshots and magnified the decibels, which sounded similar to humongous cannons being blasted from the decks of war ships. Those who were fortunate enough to escape during the initial surge, kept their backs to the bullets and, in most cases, ran directly to the serenity of their homes.

The leading pack of bikers never made it to the event center, as bodies littered the downtown streets from McGill Boulevard back to Atwater. There was an exchange of gunfire along every street block of the gala, as chaos and anarchy bewildered the security officers, who became as ignorant as the public they were tasked to protect. Police officers soon became uncertain with whom to engage, as the Alliance vigilantes who pretended to be cops, began targeting the corrupt officers they recognized, in addition to their biker targets. The first infringement against Montreal's protective forces, occurred at Metcalfe and St. Catherine, where two Jamaicans disguised as police officers, bushwhacked a group of four officers and killed them all. The disguised Jamaicans pretended, they were assisting a young lady who had sprained her ankle, and waited until their targets walked by, then shot them dead from close range. The reports into 911 dispatch of police killing police changed law enforcement's prime directive, as the real Defenders of Montreal became confused about who their actual predators were. Along the street block between Stanley Street and Drummond Street, two sexy-ass females attired in skimpy outfits, opened fire at another bunch of five officers, who were all slayed instantly.

Reports of disrespect against Montreal police officers were being transmitted across the band waves, at an unrelenting volume. Where it wasn't reported that officers were killing officers, it was said that civilians were partaking in the deed, of eliminating the security obstacles. Hence, the protection that should have been awarded the host of the event, found that they needed protection from the entire city, which had obviously gone mental. Nicholas' plot on how to puppeteer the officers at the event worked brilliantly, as soon, similar altercations provoked officers into killing biker members, who were merely trying to protect themselves from the assassins decimating their population. Remarkable amateur video footage made by a number of fleeing civilians, captured actual police officers, who normally run toward disaster, racing the pack and out in the lead, as they fled for their own safety.

The street block between Côte-des-Neiges-Boulevard and Guy Avenue, was one of the two blocks entrusted into the defense contract of the Defenders. Eddie Cortez chose the best vantage point along that route, which was inside the tallest edifice on that block; the fifteen-story welfare building. The overall strategy devised by Nicholas was relatively simple and, required each sector to only: 'eliminate all foes in your vicinity, especially the chief commanders who oversaw their business interests across Montreal'. Should the ambush strategy pay gross dividends, those who survived would be much easier handled, and the eradication mission would persist, until the last Rough Rider was killed.

Nicholas and Danny Esquada were flowing through the crowds along the right side of St. Catherine Street like hot metal through butter, while they slew every enemy counterpart they encountered. The two men killed swiftly in poetic harmony, as if they'd perfected their art of Indian Warrior silent assassination. Armed with eight-inch daggers in one hand and their Mohawk axes in the other, both men were more equipped to tackle their foes in close combat situations. The automatic weapons that rained bullets from above, aided drastically the Warriors' advancements as they inched ever closer to Martain's motorcade, which had firmly held off all mediocre attacks thus far. Killa, on the other hand, found it tougher to maneuver through the crowds along the left side of the road, as his convoy that consisted of four of Nicholas' loyalists, trailed their boss by a few feet.

There were areas along the trail, where huge bullet exchanges rumbled on continuously, with either sides unwilling to compromise or surrender. The Barrett automatic weapons stolen from the military, held all attackers at bay, with their capability of piercing cement walls and various sheets of metal. However, the limited number acquired by the bikers, did not completely discourage their ambushers, who believed they still could have annihilated their foes, and thus continued their assault.

By the time it became clear to the biker leader, that the bullets sound they heard weren't firecrackers, the crowd had scattered, and was in a frantic frenzy to get off St. Catherine Street. The officers assigned to the detail, began hearing the disturbing reports, of 'officers killing officers', over their headsets and were uncertain what to do. Surprisingly, two imposter police officer stepped from the crowd, with Uzi automatic rifles and began extinguishing several of Martain's guards. Some of the elite guards returned fire and killed both imposters, who were dressed like the officers they had killed.

The rest of Martain's entourage was forced to dismount their Harleys, but members of the opposing forces found it difficult to overpower them, with their superior high-teck weaponry. The Rough Riders' head honcho was tossed from his Harley Davidson, yet instead of immediately acquiring shelter, Martain, coupled with members of his security force, and began shooting at everything that moved. The group of bikers stood in the middle of the street and, began disbursing bullets at every police officer, Defender, members of Nicholas' personal strike force, musicians, vendors and pedestrians. The full body armor cycling suits the bikers' wore, were fitted with matching bulletproof boots, and helmets; hence, while bullets practically bounced off of them, they kept all challengers at a distance with their devastating firepower.

Eddie Cortez had an alternative plan that, purely called for the demise of his newest nemesis, Kane. The vengeful Defender assured Brogan and others he would, "Kill every biker he saw", before the battle began, yet chose to stand and watch his comrades get slaughtered, instead of ensuring them the advantage. As the battle raged on between Martain's defensive forces and their ambushers, Eddie glanced out the window at the fearless biker boss, as he yelled furiously and dared his attackers to kill him.

After subduing the immediate threat, Martain angrily shouted at his attackers, "You fuckers dare to ruin my shit? I'll kill all of you bitches! Come on, come on!" The AS-50 caliber, high-powered rifle braced against Eddie's shoulder, could have ended it all for Martain with one shot, yet, instead of accomplishing their primary objective, Eddie chose to settle his personal grudge. The largest slaughter of activists against Martain's Rough Riders occurred beneath Eddie's watchful eyes, as he conspired and waited patiently for a glimpse of one specific target.

Without sticking your head through the office windows, there was no means of viewing more than ten feet in either direction. As such, it was impossible for Eddie to calculate the exact moment Kane would be passing, in order to acquire the single shot, he'd waited for. Eddie placed his lookout, Marquez, outside the building along the northern section, behind the huge garbage containers filled with rubbish. Marquez was supposed to phone Eddie the moment he saw Kane and his band of pretenders, instead of reporting the discovery in person. Following their conflict at the hotel, Kane knew Eddie would be seeking some sort of revenge, therefore, he found out exactly where the Defender's gunner was stationed along the route and, implemented his own strategy. Marquez the lookout, was smoking a cigarette and looking up St. Catherine Street, when the Mohawk he was checking for, jammed a 9mm Taurus in the pit of his back. When the startling knock sounded at the door, Eddie grumbled as he walked over to unlock the barrier.

"I told your dumb ass, to call me the moment you see those redskin freaks! Don't tell me, you lost your damn cell phone again," Eddie argued, as he opened the door?

The indignant sniper's hands fell lifelessly, when a chrome .357 Magnum was thrust directly against his head. "I—I—I," Eddie mumbled, before, "Boom"! The pistol exploded and lifted Eddie from his Timberland boots and flung him halfway across the room.

Kane tossed Marquez, whom he'd held securely in a choke hold, into the office where the Defenders' sniper had set up operations. Marquez, who was a bit woozy from a blow to the head, had a massive amount of blood gushing from the wound, as he went tumbling over chairs that were prearranged for customers. "Keep an eye on our little friend," Kane instructed his companion, Big Bear, who was a massive six-feet-eight-inch, four-hundred-and-thirty-two-pounds beast.

The sounds of emergency sirens could be heard forming a perimeter around the entire area. The Montreal police were delicate in their handling of the situation, after confirming reports that members of their family, turned their weapons against their very own. Barricades were set up to prevent anyone dumb enough to enter the war zone, from actually attempting the suicide. News reporters from every media possible, waited by the safety barriers installed by police, for word on when it was safe to proceed onto St. Catherine Street.

When Nicholas and his posse came along, both sides again exchanged gunfire the instant they saw each other, thus everyone was forced to scramble for protection. While moving for cover along the cement wall of a resident building entrance, Nicholas fired several shots at Martain and another male, who resembled the third man on his hit list. Even dressed in drag, Martain had no problem identifying Nicholas, whose face he'd dreamt in nearly a thousand dreams. The collision between Martain and Nicholas had finally transpired, and neither gangster sought to retreat. Martain had full confidence in the protection of his armor, as well as his superior firepower, and he aimed to finally rid himself of the one itch, he couldn't have previously scratch.

The two crime bosses, trash-talked for a few ticks, which led many to believe they were fueling each other's rage, when in fact, they were! There was finally a moment's calm along that stretch of St. Catherine Street, thus Killa, who advanced along the opposite side of the road, looked back and realized his personal associates had all been terminated. Despite the calm among Nicholas' entourage, gunshots rang out in abundance along other city blocks, as the gangsters and bikers continued their showdown.

"You ready to die, you, black piece of shit," Martain yelled!?

"I'm not here to talk and make bombo-clatt friends, pussyhole," Nicholas answered!

"Then push your big fucking watermelon head out and show me, you fake Rasta," cursed Martain!

"Right after you push out your suck pussy mouth! Batty-boy," responded Nicholas!

The middle of St. Catherine Street, of all places, became like Tombstone with Wyatt Earp and his brothers, blasting against the Clancy pose. Before a single shot could be squeezed off by either team, Danny fired an arrow directly into the throat of one of Martain's centurions. The frightened guard dropped his weapon and grabbed for his throat, as he began gasping and sucking for oxygen. Martain and company responded by opening fire at Nicholas' entourage, which was forced to hunker down behind whatever offered them protection, knowing the damage capability of the bikers' armament.

Kane observed the perils his associates were facing down on the street level and, took over the job awarded to Eddie. The Mohawk Indian braced the 50-caliber rifle against his shoulder and, centered one of the bikers assaulting his friends in the telescope, then squeezed the trigger. The fifty-caliber bullet struck the guard who Nicholas confused for the third male that assaulted him, and thus, plastered the biker against the Roots store wall. That massacre was all the demonstration Martain's peers needed to see, before they grabbed their boss and forced him to retreat through any alleyway, that lead over onto Boulevard Du-Maisonneuve.

When the Rough Riders who, were just ahead of the leaderless Mohawk Warriors, heard the onslaught of bullets rippling towards them like a tidal wave, they tried to make U-turns, to avoid the upcoming danger. The original plan had called for the ambush to begin after the fourth street block, once the bikers had fully entered the killing zone. But, following Nicholas' mishap, they were left without a director, hence, the well-organized ambush began before the appropriate time.

With panic setting in, the Indian Warriors opened fire at the retreating bikers, and began slaying everyone ahead of them. The Rough Riders who were out to enjoy a fun and memorable parade and stage show, found themselves in a bit of a pickle, riding into a boiling lava, with a heated furnace directly behind them. The rear bikers developed the same confused mentality as the police officers, who found themselves in conflicts with each other, due to the implanted imposters.

Part 28

The wealthy billionaires of the secret society, called an emergency meeting to discuss the atrocious events, that occurred during the Rough Riders' day of celebration. Each member of the covenant received his summons through an ancient method, which was simply a note tied to the foot of a pigeon. The members would all read the note, before properly burning the evidence, in order to prevent the material from being acquired by infiltrators. Whenever there were matters of importance to be discussed, each member would be awakened between 4:15 AM and 4:20 AM, by a courier pigeon, which carried a note. Once the pigeon reached its destination, the bird would ring a bell placed outside the recipient's window, to announce its arrival.

The location of the chambers of the covenant was known only to the members, who'd been attending secret assemblies, since their induction into the secret committee. Each member had his personal entrance, from the limited number of secret accesses built around the city. There was a short distance to travel between the entrances and the assembly hall, considering you had the knowledge of where to find an entrance and how to open it. A typical voyage to the covenant was like sifting through a maze, where the different corridors and open spaces were enough to discourage any explorer. The quarters of the assembly hall were built beneath the city, by French King Louis X1V, who sought an escape route, should any attacks occur. The secret chambers were not merely lavished quarters, but were instead a mixture of grace and horror, considering the dungeons and jails integrated into the architecture.

There were jail cells and a dungeon, that provided evidence of the horrors, that transpired in the year's past. Inside the cells were heavy chains and shackles hanging from the ceilings, with the skeletons of the humans who suffered the ordeals, still laying in their unrestful graves. There were whips and multiple weapons of torture, inside one chamber that was obviously an interrogation room. Here, deep beneath the Metro system and the underground pipes, was where the rulers of all evils and kindness throughout Quebec, convened their assemblies.

One of the secret entrances to the domains of the covenant, was inside Lloyd's Barbershop, located at 6666 Sherbrooke Street West. The location was known only to Michel Lafleur and three other members, each of which arrived at separate times on assembly days. Monsieur Lafleur would visit his barber and sit for a trim and a shave, until the precise time for his departure. After he received his two-hundred-dollar pampering, the billionaire would disappear into the restroom, where he'd enter a specific stall, that had a private entrance to the secret cabinet. Michel would enter the bathroom facility and ensured there was no one else present, before he went into the stall, closed the door and, pushed in three specific tiles, which would open the access door to the assembly hall.

On the day of the assembly, Michel arrived at his barber for his 6:00 PM appointment. There was a man awaiting his haircut, from the barber who worked for Lloyd, but he first had to wait until his son got his hair styled. Lloyd Bathurst had been a barber for forty years, and he personally trimmed Michel's golden locks for thirty-seven of those years. 'The Montreal Business Mogul', as described by the Wall Street Journal in a post, had never once been asked to wait for his haircut, and Lloyd's barber chair was always cleaned and awaiting, the owner's most valued customer. As Michel entered and went directly for his barber's chair, the kid getting his haircut shouted to his father as if some humongous hockey star walked into the shop, "Look, Dad! It's Monsieur Michel Lafleur!"

The young lad frantically persisted to gab about, "the most magnificent car race he had ever seen," which involved an SAAQ highway patrol chase, between the boys in khaki uniforms and Michel. Apparently, for his sixty-fifth birthday, Michel received a Lamborghini Diablo as a present, from his deceased brother, Yves Lafleur. On the night of his birthday gala, Michel was caught by his ex-wife, Theresa, having sex with a female from the guest list. Theresa, despite the festive affair, vulgarly assaulted her husband for the disrespect, before she jumped into her Porsche Carrera and drove away.

Michel wasn't fazed by his wife's reaction to his demeaning stunt. In fact, he and his new-found beauty hopped into his most expensive present that year and, abandoned his guests to continue their private celebration. For five days, Michel and his sex partner toured the local regions of the northeast, where French-speakers dominated the countryside. The pair awoke the first morning in Quebec City and found a separate town to awake in every morning thereafter.

On their journey home, Michel decided to exercise his newest toy and set a new record, for the fastest time to Montreal from the provincial border, near the Laurentians. The Lamborghini sports car roared as it massacred Interstate 30, at speeds described by the Highway Commission, as "dangerous" and "suicidal." Michel's lady friend readjusted her seat and reclined to a more comfortable position, before she selected her favorite radio station, for tunes to jam to. Instead of mentioning her jitters, the female relaxed and as she put it, "You gotta allow boys to be boys!" Pedal was far from metal, yet Michel's Diablo was screeching by commuters as if they were crawling along like ants. The music system inside the well-tuned machine, sounded with absolute clarity, and the Solo 11 laser detector Yves had installed, beeped every so often to indicate it had obstructed the speed assessing of another highway trooper.

There was a police helicopter on its way into the mountains, to search for illegally grown marijuana, which is a yearly battle fought by the Royal Canadian Mounted Police and outlaw producers throughout Canada. The Lamborghini was spotted by the pilot of the helicopter, who alerted his astonished crew aboard and began recording the event, before radioing his allies on the ground. The pilot gave the vehicle's description and requested troopers prepare, from as far away as fifty miles ahead, because it would be impossible for any trailing vehicle to catch the speeding Lamborghini.

Michel raced along Interstate 30 at speeds that exceeded two hundred miles-per-hour. There was an unmarked police cruiser travelling along discreetly, behind an armored Brinks Security truck destined for Montreal, and Michel sped by the two vehicles as if they were motionless statues. The undercover officer immediately engaged in the chase, but not wanting to embarrass himself, chose not to activate his siren and speakers. Michel noticed the increased speed of the brown Chevrolet Impala, yet paid it no attention as it quickly became a dot in his rearview mirror.

The billionaire was flying by exits so quickly that, they simply began identifying each off-ramp by the more recognizable numbers. As they approached Exit 238 south of Quebec City, Michel noticed four cruisers preparing to enter the Interstate. The Lamborghini Diablo flew by the police cruisers, which were aligned behind a tractor-trailer that was slowly entering the highway, by use of the onramp. By the time the cruisers got onto the highway, the Lamborghini was nowhere in sight, so the officers activated their lights and sirens, before attempting to catch the speedster. The undercover officer, who had secretly begun chasing the Lamborghini, joined the flock of predators' intent on catching and prosecuting to the fullest, the reckless driver and his passenger.

Commandant Danzel was seated behind his desk at the Surette Du Quebec Headquarters, when a roadblock demand came into the dispatcher. A ranking official's authorization was needed, for such a tactical maneuver to unfold, considering it required the closure of a main highway. The dispatcher was somewhat amused, that the officers seeking the roadblock were reportedly chasing a ghost, they believed was still mutilating the highway! The officer who made the request sold his reasoning to the commandant, by implying 'the Lamborghini was travelling erratically on the highway, while exceeding speed of up to two hundred and fifty miles-per-hour'! Directly after receiving such a report from the field officer, Commandant Danzel ordered a blockage of Interstate 30, between Exits 221 and 220.

The Royal Canadian Mounted Police who answered the direct order to place a barricade across the extremely busy Interstate 30, responded as professionals who had been properly trained, considering they'd simulated the incident during training many times. Four police cruisers stretched across the width of highway and, allowed a single lane pathway for traffic to slide through. The officers were given information about the situation, including the possible make of the speeding vehicle and its color, without an actual number to distinguish a license plate.

Michel could see in a distance, the flashing lights of sirens attached to the roofs of four police cruisers, that were as tiny as little flies, flickering around in the dark. Without alerting his guest, Michel smirked to himself, as he reached for a cigarette in the glove compartment of the vehicle. The thrill of lightning speed, energized by a fingernail pinch of cocaine, empowered the female to express her jubilance, thus, she unbuckled Michel's trousers and began administering fellatio. Michel rambunctiously muzzled his head across the seat's headrest, as the stimulating sensations of her tongue electrified his senses. The billionaire moaned and closed his eyes for an instant with pleasure, before he reopened them to their pending predicament.

There were six vehicles attempting to arrange themselves in order to pass through the police barricade, when Michel came blasting around the corner. With his limbs showing signs of paralysis, from the shock treatment being awarded to his genitals, Michel rammed the brakes and gripped the steering wheel tightly, as the road beast came screeching to a halt, inches from a Ford F-150 truck.

RCMP officers quickly surrounded the Lamborghini Diablo faster than Usain Bolt winning the one-hundred meters sprint. There were weapons drawn and pointed at the driver, while officers uttered threats and instructions, before the fellatio-performing passenger came up for air, and frightened the law enforcement professionals, who believed the driver was the lone occupant.

"Oops," exclaimed the female, before throwing her hands in the air, to comply with the orders being dictated to her!

Despite the weary officers threatening to shoot and maim the driver, Michel picked up his cardholder from the armrest console, and slightly lowered his window, before handing a Mountie his license, registration, and proof of insurance. By then, the trailing group of RCMP officers had joined the traffic stop and, began assisting by offering protective cover for their allies. Motorists became concerned after the traffic was altered, by what seemed like a police station of officers, engaging two motorists. People were seen attempting to capture the video on their cell phones, while others settled for still portraits with their cameras. It did not, however, take long for officers to resume the flow of traffic, and the entire incident transpired as if it was a staged performance.

The officer who collected Michel's driver's license, was not at all amused by the billionaire's cockiness, and "insisted the driver open the door and step out of the car"! Michel, under the pressures of blue steel packed with lead casings, refused to obey the orders given, despite the officer's threat to "blow his head off". Once the officers realized that Michel was not about to corporate, they went after his passenger in order to terrify the woman into allowing them entry.

"Lady, open the door and I promise you won't go to jail with this guy, because he is definitely going to jail, and we are, going to impound the car!"

The speeds at which Michel was travelling, were punishable with jail time, immediate seizure of one's vehicle, and a first offense suspension of the driver's privileges for three months. While other officers attempt to negotiate with Michel, whom they perceived was on his way to jail, one way or the other, the Mountie who'd collected the driver's license, returned to his cruiser to insert the offender's information into their system. The officer entered Michel's information into the cruiser's computer terminal and was about to impose several fines, when Commandant Danzel radioed in with executive orders, which counteracted the Mounties intent.

Commandant Danzel declared, "Listen to me very carefully, Mounty Androusy! The man you gentlemen are trying to detain cannot under any circumstances be arrested! You gentlemen are to release Monsieur Lafleur immediately, and I suggest if any of you have offended him in any way, shape, or form, be sure to apologize or find another occupation! That's an order! Am I clear?"

"But sir, the regulations specify that we seize Mr. Lafleur's vehicle and suspend his license, for his antics and recklessness!"

"Did I ask you about the man's antics? I said return his documents and send him on his way immediately!"

"Understood, sir," exclaimed the Mountie Androusy, who immediately went and informed his comrades.

Once Mounty Androusy translated the Commandant's orders, the

RCMP elites who were inches away from using firemen, with their Jaws of Life tool to pry the car door open, changed their tune, to that of a more respectful and submissive bunch. The Mountie, after denouncing his allies' actions, walked over to the Lamborghini and offered his apologies, before returning the billionaire's license and other information. The recorded version of the entire incident was uploaded to YouTube by Frank Riley, and it caught nearly ten million hits after the first day. Audiences around the world, could not believe that someone who defied more than two dozen officers, scattered among eleven vehicles and a helicopter, would just simply speed away, after he exceeded the speed limit by more than one hundred and fifty clicks.

The young lad brought a smile to the mogul's face, but Michel left thereafter and went to the gathering with his secret brotherhood. Twenty minutes after the old man disappeared into the restroom, the kid grew curious and went in to check if he was OK. There was no sign of the old man, who the kid concluded had some sort of superpowers, considering there was only one entrance into the bathroom. Michel's disappearance puzzled the lad, who felt certain that he had not passed by, and exited through the front door.

There was no assembly of the brotherhood prior to the covenant being called to order, as members would typically arrive inside their quadrants, don the sacred black robe, be seated in their assembly glory, and await their time to be hailed, which brought the Chair into the Hall of Conference. Each member was brought into the Hall of Conference in sequence, as the chairs would mechanically maneuver into the dim slots, designated for each participant. The gloomy lighting, dark quarters and, mysterious outfits, made it impossible to see the members across the aisle, who were also shielded by walls on either side. Each member was given the opportunity to vote on amendments, and votes were made with one of two colored chips—one for and the other against. There was a mediator, whose voice was always heard on topics, although he was never visible. Members could argue their case, once awarded the floor by the mediator, but proper etiquette and respect for peers, were laws never to be violated by members of the covenant.

The Meeting

"Gentlemen, our beloved city has been attacked, our way of life challenged, and our very existence questioned. Our very rulership over this province, has been mocked and degraded by a foe, which we've for far too long allowed to thrive! These vagabonds who've killed innocent women and children, along with our selected police officials, must be dealt with accordingly. Our continued partnership, with the various syndicates who govern this country, depends upon our ridding this province of these lowlifes! As members of the sacred covenant, and the core of this nation, you've all basked in the glories and accolades awarded this cabinet. Today, we've entered a new age and a new era, where our might and vigilance will once more shine, as the beacon for all Quebecers and Canadians! As is evident by the numbers in the political polls, this nation cries for leadership, that only comes from true leaders, and we will give it to them! Here today, we've installed a graphic image transponder, that will offer everyone, a clear and precise picture, of this Nicholas Henry," said the mediator!

There was an octagonal platform placed in the center of the floor, with three humongous cables, attached to a computer monitor in a separate room. A perfect image of Nicholas was transmitted to the platform, where everyone could visibly see the outlaw standing with both hands by his side, as the imagery rotated above the platform. The cabinet members around the chamber, who were all seated inside their cubicles, saw first-hand the vigilante, blamed for the massacre that transpired in center town.

"Make sure you all take a good look, because as it's a new day, with new times, I throw the first hundred thousand in the pot, for whomever brings the head of that man on a platter!"

Someone rudely began clapping their hands and laughing out loud, which startled the cabinet members, who detected an unfamiliar accent.

"Blood-clatt! Make me get in on some of that gambling action!? Let me check my figures, there is eighteen of you in here, at a hundred thousand a piece, so that's 1.8 million, just for my head! Don't be alarmed; you old forts looking at the real thing now, not some imagery, so make sure you take a good fucking look," Nicholas mocked, as he walked into the center of the chamber, with two 9mm Glock-19 pistols at hand!

The mediator, after leaping to his feet in order to highlight his protest, insisted, "Sir, I don't believe you were ever awarded the floor!"

Nicholas found the outburst disrespectful and grew ferociously annoyed, so he raised his left hand and hammered two rounds into the man's chest. The loud blast from the weapon indicated to everyone the severity of the moment, yet none of the billionaires reacted as if they were scared.

"Have you any idea who we are," Michel Lafleur demanded?

"Actually, if I don't everyone else inside here, I'm positive about who you are, Michel Lafleur," Nicholas retorted, before he turned his weapons on Martain's father and awarded him a permanent sleep!

The blatant murder of their brethren agitated members of the secret cult, who all began voicing their complaints, despite having an enraged murderer in their midst. Nicholas walked over to Michel, and stared at the French mogul for a few seconds, before, he hammered two more shells into his corpse.

"See, I believe it is unpatriotic for any country, province, or what have you, to have an undermining government, while the heads of state, who were voted in by the people, forcibly have to submit to some high-powered, greedy forts, who will go to any means to achieve whatever they want! The rest of the country may be duped by the suave means through which you gentleman do business, like kill all who oppose and, buy out whoever can be bought, as long as the end result provides whatever you seek! You men don't give a fuck! You all have a hand in almost every money, equipment, legal, and illegal transaction, that happens in this city. But all that isn't enough, is it? Now you want to take it one step further again, by stealing the provincial premier's job!"

One of the members demanded, "What exactly do you want, boy? A seat on this counsel?"

Another member in his native French tongue interjected, "Holster your tongue, Monsieur Raymond! We are the leaders of this great nation, not some fraternity you became a part of in school! We are lords whose veins pump pure French blood! White is the color of our skin, and we will never integrate anyone of lesser stature!"

"I wouldn't sit with you pathetic invalids to save my life! See, understand this—it is a new era, like the little man said, but this is one era, you gentlemen won't get the opportunity to experience," Nicholas said, and he exited the chamber's center, before six shooters ran in to finish the job!

A senior counsellor argued, "We are the advisers to the government of this nation, there will be anarchy throughout this country without our oversight! You can't treat us like second-class citizens! I'm talking to you, boy! Don't walk away when I'm talking—!"

The explosive sounds of high-powered automatic rifles sounded throughout the chamber, as the shooters went around and killed everyone. Nicholas thereafter entered Monsieur Lafleur's compartment from the rear entrance, with a razor-sharp machete at hand. The corpse of his enemy's father was slumped across the table inside the compartment, therefore, Nicholas positioned himself accordingly and beheaded Michel with one clean swipe. The drug boss picked up the head and placed it into a black plastic bag, then handed the bag to Killa.

"Mi surprise the information from that politician boy was legit," Killa stated!

Several men who wore plastic coverings over their clothing and shoes, along with gloves, hair nets and masks, entered the Hall of Conference and began handling the corpses. While his companions assembled the dead bodies for transport, Nicholas went into the cult's library, which was filled with secretive files and information about the group's documented history. The fugitive was eager to learn about the construction of the cult and its members, so he locked himself inside the library and, started studying their dark and corrupt past.

Part 29

There was a nightly vigil held for the victims murdered prior to the bikers' concert. Thousands of Montrealers showed their respects and brought flowers, teddy bears, and wreaths to a makeshift memorial, at the corner of Rue-du-Fort and Sainte-Catherine Street, where the youngest victim was killed. Residents throughout the city were furious and wanted drastic actions taken, against the gangs and hustlers across the island. To make their voices heard, activists organized several peaceful rallies, where protestors marched with signs demanding change.

The city held an elaborate ceremony for its civil servants killed in what was described in the Gazette as, "The day Montrealers' mourn." The prime minister of Canada attended the ceremony, where he laid a wreath at the designated commemoration location, before he addressed the large crowd of mourners. Various dignitaries such as Montreal's mayor, the premiers, preachers, family, and friends poured out their emotional grievances, while those in attendance and millions around the country, mourned along with them.

The event aired on local and international news stations, which also highlighted footage from the talks between the prime minister and law enforcement superiors, for the province of Quebec. Prime Minister Daniel Couture, who was scheduled to leave office within months, after losing the general election to Mathew Layton, was adamant in mentioning drastic changes in leadership, should those responsible for the debacle not be brought to justice. The number of lawmen killed, according to the prime minister, 'was unacceptable', as was the number of civilians who also lost their lives, that tragic afternoon.

When the gunshots finally ended, 734 bodies laid scattered about the downtown streets. A lot of those killed were innocent bystanders, who only wanted to see their favorite artists perform. Concert tickets would have cost hundreds, to see the lineup of artists the bikers' booked, therefore, people were quite excited to attend the show.

"I can't believe this is downtown Montreal! I swear, it's more like a battleground after a clash between two armies," remarked one reporter, after personally seeing the carnage!

There were more than three hundred Rough Riders killed, over a hundred Metropolitan police, more than two hundred innocent victims, and seventy-six coalition members. The entire city was left incensed by the vile and wicked actions of hateful men, who were insistent on settling their differences wherever they encountered each other. The news agencies that featured the story, were all puzzled about the motive behind the numerous officers killed, although the slayings eventually brought merit, to a news report filed by the W-Five News program, some two and a half years prior.

In the report, the accusations of metropolitan officers accepting bribes, performing assassinations for the bikers, and transporting illegal items were just the tip of the iceberg. The implications, although proven accurate by investigators, were expelled as being inconclusive, due to the sources from which the accusations originated. When questioned about his officers' conduct, the ex-captain of the police force, refrained from directly answering the question, and instead chose 'to demerit the drug addicts and criminals', who allegedly testified against his lawmen.

Several of Nicholas' coalition troops attended the parade event, to settle past grievances versus officers, who had violated their civil rights in the past. There were officers, who were more hated than the true foes of Alliance members, and thus, many were placed on the extermination list, and marked for death. On many occasions during the attack, there were circumstances where Nicholas' coalition members, broke away from their engagements versus the Rough Riders, to settle personal conflicts with the police instead. The stigma used against blacks and other ethnic groups, for the first time in history, got reversed against the inflictors of such treatment. Throughout the conflict, what grieved law officials more than anything, was exactly how precise and keen the attackers were in their endeavors, to massacre all friends, acquaintances, business associates, and members of the infamous gang. After the forensic investigators tallied up their initial body count, officers discovered that nine of the uniformed deceased officers, were coalition members dressed like the police.

An extended length of, 'Police line do not cross' yellow tape, stretched along several street blocks, with at least two cruisers parked at each intersection. Forensic investigators blocked off a significant percentage of downtown for more than sixty hours, before any agencies or businesses were permitted to reopen their doors. Investigators combed through every section of the crime scene, collecting items from spent shells to bloodied knives, as they retrieved precious evidence, to help find the killers and, for prosecution usage. The determinations of who fired what weapons were made by the forensic investigators, along with the information desired to seal perspective convictions.

The guarantee made be Minister McArthur, was severely scrutinized by one local reporter, who was among the few allowed to film the disaster area. The reporter suggested that the minister who stated that, 'he would be jamming with his fellow Montrealers', undergo a lie detector test, as he believed McArthur had first-hand information about the ambush, which was the perceived reason for his silence. The minister declined to comment on the allegations, but his spokesperson stated the comment had been debunked, and described the theory as, "ridiculous and reprehensible!" Minister McArthur chose instead, to stand alongside the top brass behind the municipal police of Quebec, business owners, and neighborhood activists, who held a news conference to stipulate what injunctions would be imposed against the organizers. Law officials also scrolled through hours of video footage, from several cameras throughout the downtown core, to positively identify the shooters, they believed must be brought to justice.

The weeks following the horrific downtown incident, saw police changed their tactics and increased their resolve, to bring closure for thousands of residents, who pled for justice and the citywide violence to end. Officers combed and searched the streets, for all the patriotic gangsters caught on video, exercising their rights to bear arms, and arrested them all. For the first time in their existence, police officers raided several institutions that belonged to the Rough Riders club. The police seized drugs, weapons, ammunition, and took several bikers into custody, who were wanted for multiple crimes, that ranged from drug trafficking to bench warrants.

Royal Canadian Mounties went to Martain Lafleur's establishment, to bring the biker boss into custody, for weapons violations after his arrogant proclamations in the center of town. The Mounties, after sounding the buzzer for a few minutes, forced their way inside, and found the mansion had been recently vacated, which was evident by the cigarette butts still burning in the ashtray.

Several minutes before the Mounties arrived to arrest Mr. Martain Lafleur, a Fed-Ex deliveryman was announced at the front gate, with a package labelled "DAD." Martain had his guards bring the deliveryman, along with the package, up to the main house, which was like an armed fortress with over fifty heavily armed bikers. Due to his recent misfortunes, the biker boss was extremely short-tempered, hence, he sat around a plate of pure-uncut cocaine, that he had been snorting in excess. The Fed-Ex deliveryman nervously walked into the den of lions, where even the lionesses appeared thirsty for a kill.

"What the fuck do you have that is so fucking important, you feel you had to disturb me," Martain questioned?

"Bring that shit over to him," instructed a guard, who shoved the man in Martain's direction!

"I-I-I-I got a package for you," declared the delivery man!

"Who the fuck is it from," Martain demanded?

"There—there is no sender's name, sir!"

"Then you open the shit, and you'd better hope it's not a fucking bomb," joked Martain, whose head bobbled around his shoulder, as if he was suffering from fatigue and a lack of sleep!

The deliveryman reached into his pocket and withdrew a small pocketknife, which was barely capable of cutting a tiny hair. The man opened the knife and was about to cut open the box, when all around the room cartridge selectors started loading, as the armed bikers prepared their weapons to disburse. The deliveryman was so terrified that he released a loud fort, that stunk up the entire room, and forced the bikers to cover their nostrils. Following his embarrassing accident, the Fed-Ex dude apologized to everyone, then tried to steady his trembling hand and cut open the box. Even though the deliveryman slowly opened the package, the sight of what was inside frightened him enough, to where he dropped the box atop the center-table and dashed out of the room, with his hands squeezed tightly over his mouth.

Curiosity brought Martian to his feet, hence, he peeked over inside the box, that rested at the other end of the table. At the sight of his father's head inside the box, Martain's mouth fell wide open, and he fell back onto the chair behind him. The biker boss threw his right hand over his face to cover his eyes, as he began weeping over the loss of his dad. Inquisitive bikers around the room gathered to observe what frustrated their leader, who had his face covered and the handle of his pistol tightly gripped. The telephone atop Martain's desk began ringing, and after he removed his hand from his face to answer the call, everyone else realized that he had been crying.

"I know you dream about killing mi, as much as I dream about burying yu, blood-clatt! And I still remember what you and your two goons did to me that cold day in the tailor's shop! You make me even had to bring your father in our private affairs," Nicholas calmly threatened!

"You're dead! You hear me? This world isn't big enough for you to hide! You think you and a couple of punks can cripple an entity like the Rough Riders? You think you got clout, because you bumped off a few of my riders and killed my father? I got almost a million warriors at my disposal! You want to fuck with us, all right! All right!" Martain definitively warned.

"Calm your blood-clatt down, because I want you to understand that there is a shift in power taking place here! Ain't going to be no more laws from your old regime! Yu feel me? We're going to regulate this business properly," Nicholas assured!

"Ha-ha-ha-ha!" Martain laughed, "You aren't the first to challenge the only imperial entity in Canada, and you won't be the last fake dread! This is French-Canadian territory, and the French-Canadians will forever rule it, regardless of what you think! Frankly, you're right; all I dream about is killing you, and the time has definitely come!"

"Is that a challenge? 'Cause we can meet anywhere and settle our private differences quick," Nicholas asked!?

"It's time for the better man to run this shit once again," Martain remarked!

"You have ten minutes before some Mounties arrive with a warrant for your arrest! Them about to lock up yu blood-clatt, for that amateur stunt you pulled downtown! Next time wear a disguise, you dumb fuck! Personally, I believe locking you up is a slap on the wrist, 'cause where I'm going to send you, is no fucking bed of roses! Meet me on Saint Helen Island at eight o'clock tomorrow morning; we settle this fuckery once and for all," Nicholas instructed!

"I'll be there, you can bet your life on it! I'll be there, you fucking coward," Martain agreed!

The metropolitan police service of Montreal received a report, from a female who indicated there was a foul stench like dead bodies, emanating from deep inside the sewer system, next to her place of employment. An investigator followed maintenance engineers deep into the sewers, from which the reports were heralded, in order to dismiss the claims, and find the cause of the stench to reassure public confidence. City officials had been drenched with reports of missing individuals, especially since the bikers' parade, where many families and friends were forced to scatter, in order to avoid being slain. There were individuals reported missing, who were either found in hospitals, at police stations or were wandering the streets confused. Such was the case with four of the many survivors, who were believed killed, yet found days later wondering about senselessly, after they either had someone's brain matter splattered over them, that constant image of bodies being decapitated or, the memory of a loved one's final facial expression. Retrieving individuals reported missing, practically became a matter of national security, following the reports filed by sixteen billionaire wives of the members of the secret society, who'd exhausted all means of finding their husbands, before they alerted police officials.

Investigators were skeptical, that ridiculously wealthy men, such as those being reported missing, would have vanished off the face of the earth, without at least one bodyguard squeezing off a few rounds. With all their skepticism about where they believed the husbands had run off to, investigators were compelled to begin an investigation, after the men had indeed failed to respond to their various communications devices and, had exceeded the maximum time allowed for any human, to disappear without justification.

The sewer technicians believed they were experts in deciphering the maze of tunnels beneath the city, that were built centuries prior, but they were surprised to come across a secret entrance, hidden since the creation of Quebec's greatest city. Neither of the technicians had ever before seen hidden passages, around the tunnels they had maintained for decades. There was no disputing the source of the odor the female had reported, as the scent of rotting decay grew ever stronger, the closer they got. The entry led directly to a secret passage, which eventually brought them to a dead end, where the bodies of the missing billionaires were found.

The exclusive list of men found inside the sewers, included industry owners, as well as presidents and CEOs of major franchises, which were relevant to the daily operations of the entire province. Most of those deceased were third and fourth generation members, whose ancestors established the private cult. Some of the gentlemen killed were, Sir Marcus Herrera, the retired president of the Water and Sewage Department; General Donald Drummonds, the former chief of Canada's National Security and, Sir Ronald Bell, the first head of the Canadian Espionage Division.

Other victims found were, Sir Joseph Artours, the first president of the Tobacco & Alcohol Federation of Canada; Monsieur Christophe Langelier, the first headman of the Rifle & Gaming Association and, Jean-Guy Macdonald, a business tycoons, who was a descendant of Canada's first prime minister. There was also Michel Lafleur of Lafleur Enterprises, Steve Harding of the National Banking Association, Leonard Miller of the Miller products of beers, Gerald Severe, the former president of Boeing Air Dynamics, oil tycoon Lloyd Roberts, who was voted the richest man in Canada, plus other former members of the government and businessmen.

Director Paul Carbonelli, who had justifiably achieved awards of splendor, for his years of dedication and service to his country, was watching CNN news footage describing the second national funeral event, to be held in Montreal, Canada, in less than a week. There were many departments within the Canadian government that were affected, which created a trickle-down effect that wavered down to the U.S. FBI Director's, "Code Yellow" threat alert status. The slaying of such high-profile businessmen, especially Sir Gerald Severe, who was paid handsomely by the United States, for the valuable information he'd provided, warranted an investigation according to the U.S. Secretary of State. Executive orders were handed to the FBI director, "to form a team in order to assist the Canadian Mounties, who were being overwhelmed by the two rival gangs, that were constantly bucking horns".

The extravagant funeral events in Montreal, overshadowed other major developments of importance, such as the victor of the provincial election. The front pages, of every mainstream newspaper, featured some grieving, emotional individual, who had been deeply saddened by the death of one of their icons. The news of the combination duo winning the coveted job of premier, wasn't even printed on the front page of certain local newspapers, since the historic drama, which shook the city-maintained precedence. The newly appointed co-premier, Minister Richard Blanc, secretively arranged for the assistance of the FBI special agents, whom he believed would provide better results, against the different divisions of gangsters, without the political interference of the secret chamber. Minister Blanc had a few dark secrets he'd rather never resurfaced, since they'd destroy him publicly, even to the extent of a prison sentence.

An undercover RCMP agent was sent from Quebec City to Miami, Florida, to brief U.S. agents on the turmoil, between Nicholas Henry and Martain Lafleur. The RCMP agent brought mug shots of both Nicholas Henry, which stemmed from the incident at Carlton's tailor shop, and Martain Lafleur, who was arraigned some years prior, after an ex-girlfriend reported to police, that he'd sexually molested her with his Smith and Weston pistol. Canadian officials acquired the identities of key players, in the war between the Alliance and the Rough Riders, by scrolling through the different surveillance cameras around center town.

There were distinctive video footages of Martain, Brogan and several known gun hands, who were callously disbursing their weapons, like soldiers on a battlefield.

The importance in using the Americans, was because they had the technology to distinctively identify the shooters, who were disguised as women. The new premier was eager to get rid of criminals like Nicholas, who could have blackmailed him, or exposed him, for revealing the secrets about the billionaire cult. Premier Blanc also knew that certain law representatives, would shy away from arresting members of the biker club, in fear of reprisals from the vindictive bunch. Even law officials knew that everything and everyone, related to those who offended the Rough Riders, were fair game during war, and for officers with families, that was too great a price to pay. While the Americans could easily flee to the sanctity of their borders, the same could not be said for their Canadian counterpart, who in many cases supported the biker crew.

An example of the levels of intimidation came after police investigators reviewed taped footage, that caught Martain in the act of murdering a few hysterical youngsters, who were merely attempting to flee the violence. Martain was clearly seen, although he was covered with bullet-resistant armor, incapacitating both ambushers and fleeing spectators alike, who were trying to get out of harm's way. Regardless of the airtight case, lawyers inside the prosecution office shied away from the glories of imprisoning one of Canada's most infamous gangsters, because they knew, should they be fortunate enough to survive the trial, death would be imminent. The case was eventually snagged by a rookie prosecutor named Sarah Finch, who craved the opportunity to display her talents, while polishing her resume and impressing the superiors.

The RCMP agent stood before the six men assigned to the detail, along with Director Carbonelli who joined in simply to show his moral support. The Canadian agent was using the CNN network, as a means of illustrating the activities presently inside Canada, where the actions of one of the men spoken about, caused the city to close down, in order to commit some well-known figure to the grave. The agent soon dimmed the lights and began showing still shots of the two gangsters, on a projector machine.

Once Nicholas Henry's face popped up on the screen, Director

Carbonelli briskly walked from the briefing room. The director of the Miami division of the FBI, walked directly to his office and instructed his secretary to follow suit. Once inside his office, Director Carbonelli began instructing his secretary on a number of matters, as he planned on being away from the office for a few days.

"Mary, I want you to cancel those six U.S. Airways tickets to Montreal, and call Jim over at the Air Force base and tell him to fire up the private jet! I'll personally be going back into the field, which means I'm joining this little escapade. I'm leaving Colonel Brittle in charge, but you already know how to handle that issue. Call me if anything arises, bring those treasury forms in here for me to sign, and get the Secretary of Defense on the phone for me," Carbonelli instructed!

"Right away, boss!"

Part 30

There was a gathering held at Nicholas' estate to commemorate the soldiers who had fallen in battle, as well as those who were about to sacrifice their lives. Nicholas had made arrangements for young Junior to be sent to the only person he truly trusted, which was Ernesto Lopez, in case the unforeseen should occur. Prior to such lifestyle changes, Junior was transported to Killa's girlfriend, whose three months pregnant stomach was just beginning to form an arch under her clothes. Killa had convinced Nicholas that, should anything unfortunate happen to them both, the desire for him to secure his loved ones was as grave for him as it was for his boss. Hence, Junior was brought to lay low with Mocha while the heavy female hitters in the crew protected them.

    Killa connected Junior's Nintendo Wii video game to Mocha's living room television, in order for the young lad to enjoy himself while he awaited his father's return. Junior's nanny, who also made the trip, sat and challenged the young gamer to a boxing match, which seemed for the moment to settle the nervous youngster's anxiety. Junior was terrified he would never again have the chance to hug his father, who he knew was going off to war as soldiers have done since the beginning of time. Nicholas may had involved his young son in matters well beyond his years, but as a patriot and a realist, the gangster lived by a strict code of conduct, which was to "put God the Almighty first, respect and love your fellow man, don't disrespect no woman, and never leave home without your gun!"

Mocha was so nervous that her bowels would not allow her to leave the toilet. The expectant mother summoned Killa into the bathroom, where she poured out her heart in an attempt to alter his plans. As a first-time mother, Mocha expected her child's father to play a commanding role in the child's life, yet there he sat, weakened by the fact he may never hold his own child. Killa empathically sat on the ledge of the bathtub and listened to Mocha's outcry, although he'd rather walk through Hell's lava pits, than miss a gun battle of such magnitude. Mocha went from reasoning with him, to exploiting her love for her boyfriend, as she furiously tried to channel her needs into him. Tears poured from Mocha's eyes, as she cleansed herself and crawled on feet and arms over to her baby's father. The expectant mother, after realizing the determination in Killa's eyes, grabbed onto her boyfriend and began instructing him, 'to return home to his family'.

Killa passionately kissed the lips of the only female he'd laid with on Canadian soil. The gangster lovingly rubbed the tummy bearing his unborn child, before slowly reaching down and kissing Mocha's navel. Killa paused by the stomach and whispered, "Daddy will always love you," before he continued to kiss upwards, until he landed a breast in his mouth.

Mocha instantly began breathing heavily, while her body temperature elevated, hence she grabbed for Killa's crotch and began unbuckling his pants. As their passion intensified, Mocha yanked Killa on top of her, then guided his penis into her vagina, after she slid her French cut panties to the side. There was absolutely no lack of passion between the expectant parents, who growled and grabbed for each other as if they were wild wolves mating. Two hours later, after the Kevin Junior's nanny had retired from playing and was passed out beside the lad, the lovebirds exited the steamy bathroom, like whales leaping from the ocean for oxygen. The female guards were cooking food, smoking Marijuana, and enjoying themselves, like it was their personal residence. As Killa exited the premises, the tough security females ganged up on him and pinned him against a corner.

"You a listen me, rude buoy! You have a decent young lady who love you very much! Make sure you come back to her, I'm sorry—I mean them," Gwen exclaimed!

"It a go be a boy, eh. I just know," Joan commented, before being rudely interrupted by Eva!

"Shut you pussy, 'bout you know! You don't shit, you obeah working bitch!"

"Don't hate, bitch, you know I have the gift," Joan argued!

"Must your man thieving gift, you a talk 'bout," Gwen commented!

"Bitch, I don't need to thief no man, cause them already a run leave them woman, for this goody-goody tight hole mi have," Joan replied!

Killa sneaked out the back door the moment the ladies spurned up one of their legendary arguments, which were always a compound of foul dialect aimed at toppling each other's insults. As Killa raced down the stairs toward an awaiting SUV, Eva called to him and stopped him in his tracks.

"I love you! Y'all my family, so make sure y'all come back home safe," encouraged Eva!

"Yah man, not even a scratch," Killa boasted, before he hopped into the vehicle!

Nicholas' estate was like a pool party at the Playboy Mansion, with countless females partying about the grounds, wearing the skimpiest of bikinis. The table, which was generally stacked with the complimentary marijuana and alcohol for invited guests, had an array of very potent drugs, such as cocaine and Ecstasy, for the special visitors at that celebrative affair. The main mansion was always off limits to basic visitors, and Nicholas had always been careful as to whom he allowed, within such close proximity of his son. The gathering was a means for the troops, who had orchestrated a brilliant ambush attack against the Rough Riders, to regroup, collect their thoughts, party a little, and prepare for the upcoming battle. Their scheduled confrontation would determine whether the regime of sanctions remained, or would free enterprise thrive across the island. Even though they celebrated for a while, Nicholas had never been one to leave matters to chance, and such was his motivation in creating an attack strategy, guaranteed to bring forth victory.

The complete association of Defenders, Indian Warriors, and Nicholas' Rude Buoys, all celebrated what they had accomplished, with the killings of several high profiled bikers. After witnessing the deaths of many of the bodyguards and shooters, who had committed serious violations against his peers over the years, Nicholas was not content, until he had completely dismantled the biker organization. There was one major piece to the entire puzzle that, Nicholas was intent on configuring as his life's masterpiece, the moment he was able to wrap his hands around Martain Lafleur's neck and, made him ceased breathing. While everyone enjoyed the festivities around him, Nicholas sat watching the news, as he oiled and cleaned his pistols and, reminisced on how close he came to either killing Martain, or being killed by the biker boss.

The jubilant screams of ladies being pestered by drunk, disorderly, and horny men, were heard throughout the party grounds, as patrons danced around the pool, while others simply sat with their feet dipped in the water. A Defender gangbanger who'd gotten drunk off Petròn Tequila, and high off Ecstasy, was told by a peer to "find a bathroom or something," after the man was interrupted attempting to engage in sexual affairs with a female, on a lawn chair. There were a few thugs inside the pool, who weren't about to reassess their achieved advances any other place, after softening up their victims enough for nature to take its course. Those who had sweethearts or were partners in longstanding relationships, were either seen yapping away on their phones with their loved ones or, gambling games of poker with others.

The music was loud, and combined with the screaming females, it was impossible for anybody to hear the three approaching Huey helicopters, until they began raining fifty-caliber bullets and laser-guided rockets on Nicholas' estate. One helicopter approached from the west and came up behind the mansion, while the others came up from the east, spitting bullets at everything that moved. The timing of the attack by the pilots, couldn't have been more perfect, considering that the outpost guards capable of eliminating such threats, were all relieved of duty in order to attend the function. A few armed centurions returned fire at the non-relinquishing hovercrafts, that maintained their altitude and distance, while annihilating everything within their paths. The military fugitive James Tea used his combat training to survive the attack, as he sheltered himself and the female he was with, by hiding behind one of a few support columns, built to hold and stabilize the huge building structure.

The screams of ladies and frightened gangsters sounded about the grounds, as people attempting to outrun bullets, found out quickly the task was easier thought of, than accomplished. People attempting to leap from the pool, met similar fates as those standing forthright against such lethal firepower. Even the rude boys who believed the automatic rifles they had at hand, could challenge the hovering ammunition-spitting beasts, discovered instantly that they were of no significance. The entire pool and its surrounding areas were painted red with the blood of Alliance members, and a vast number of their honored guests.

Nicholas was pinned behind one of the huge columns, while bullets skipped overhead and collided into the cement barrier, that shielded him from the onslaught. Thoughts of there being another traitor in their midst, grieved the Jamaican rude buoy, who sought to bring the fire-breathing dragons crashing to the ground. There was a bazooka rocket launcher inside the weapons depot, that was approximately twenty feet across the room. The attack formation of the helicopters, suggested to Nicholas that the informant must still be among them, because their attackers knew precisely how, where and when to strike. A huge explosion erupted at the mansion, after Nicholas' gas tank was struck by rockets, meant to level the humongous home.

Killa saw the huge fireball shoot into the air, as he turned off the main road onto the private driveway, which led up to Nicholas' estate. The Jamaican-Bad-Man immediately turned off his CD player that, pounded some Caribbean dancehall tunes, in order to listen to the destruction that was taking place. Killa stopped the SUV at the guard's station and ran into the checkpoint, as if the solution to his problems could be found within. Inside the guard house, the concerned thug withdrew his Beretta M9 and, shattered the padlock used to secure the weapons. The rude buoy affiliate then exited with a ground-to-air rocket launcher, while he puffed with rage as if he was experiencing a heart attack. The furious gangster moved to a clear vantage point, from where he could launch his retaliation of destruction.

The two hovering Huey choppers that attacked from the east, had laid waste to many of the party hicks, while the other chopper stabilized some eight feet off the ground, prepared to disembark the six bikers aboard. The objective of the bikers, who exited the chopper, was to seek out, find, and assassinate any survivors found, without interference from intruding local police. Killa shoved his handgun into his pocket, threw his personal Barrett automatic rifle over his shoulder, positioned himself, adjusted the scope, aimed the bazooka at one of the two eastern choppers, and blew the helicopter right out of the sky. The pilot, who flew alongside the annihilated aircraft, panicked and took off, before Killa could reload his weapon, and destroyed both aircrafts.

Experience taught the veteran pilot to elude the situation, regain the vantage point, and reengage the enemy after you've secured the above. Killa, however, began moving to another sniper's kill point, immediately after dousing his first helicopter, as the art of war had taught him that camouflage and confusion protected soldiers. By the time the Huey got through its maneuvers, Killa had vanished from sight, which left the existing pilots nervous, not knowing from where exactly the threat emanated. The pilot, who was forced to change his positioning, began randomly firing rockets, at areas he believed possible for the sniper to hide. A second rocket was fired from the guards' housing unit, which struck the paranoid pilot's helicopter, the moment it skimmed above the six advancing bikers' heads. Nicholas, who was given the time to collect the bazooka, had timed perfectly his direct hit, which destroyed the chopper and sent debris flying. The bikers were forced to scatter in order to avoid the crashing helicopter, which unfortunately dismantled in a manner, which inflicted catastrophic wounds to three of six men.

The latest revelation frightened the third pilot, who immediately reported the situation back to base. Before the pilot could finish his report, the surviving three bikers who were flung to the ground, were being attacked and beaten by the very survivors they were sent to kill. Five survivors were bashing in the skulls of the bikers with baseball bats, rifle handles, lead pipes, and any other destructive material they could possibly get their hands on, as huge flames lit up the evening skies. The pilot moved to intercept the angry mob, but then noticed what felt like acid burning his shoulder, when rifle shots began piercing the skin of the helicopter.

On the ground beneath the pilot and the "Systems Failure" alert, flashing across his monitor inside the aircraft's cockpit, were Bad Boys Damian, Tank, Brogan, and Kane, emptying rifle magazines into the skin of the helicopter. The systems alert warning forced the pilot to veer off to the south and attempt an escape, which seemed less likely with each passing second. The Huey's engine began smoking and sounded like a vehicle stalling, thus the pilot, who'd been shot in the right shoulder, muscled the failing aircraft in an attempt to return to base. Everyone who survived the ordeal gathered on the lawn and watched as the helicopter swayed and dipped, until it went down and crashed in some thick brush, a few miles away.

There were no words to describe the sorrow Nicholas felt, as he looked over the field of bodies, scattered across his football field-sized lawn. Other survivors began moving to help their injured allies, which, in most cases, was an unfortunate waste of time. Those who yelled for help, all clung to life by a mere thread, as their bodily injuries were so severe that, a priest may have been a better choice, than to call 911. Killa stood frozen at the sight of the massacre, as men he'd had the privilege of knowing, and more importantly battling alongside, laid lifeless across the lawn. Bodies were dismantled and chopped up, as if someone had taken a dull and rusty machete and butchered them like ground beef.

"No," Kane screamed, as he checked around for his brother, only to find Danny had suffered the same fate, as many of their allies!

Nicholas ran to his friend's side, regardless of the fact he had to step on corpses and body parts, in order to get to him. Danny was one of those unfortunate victims, who managed to stubbornly still be breathing, despite the fact he'd been completely chopped in half, by a fifty-caliber shell. The boss' eyes immediately filled with tears, at the sight of his friend with his internal organs lying callously on the grass. Both men bumped foreheads together and held each other behind the back of the head, as they said goodbyes secretly to each other, in an appreciative manner. Nicholas held his friend until the final breath exited his body, at which time he rose to his feet, looked around at the survivors, and pulled his cell phone from his pocket.

"I'm sure you can appreciate me returning the favor, though I didn't expect you to still be alive," Martain boasted!

"Would that be with this hit on me, or the countless failures in the past," Nicholas cynically answered?

"I don't want you dead yet! That's my job, and tomorrow I'm going to make sure I finish the job properly," Martain threatened!

"You couldn't kill me if I lay down helplessly across a train track! Your informants finally ran out, just like your coward-ass followers! They didn't do a blood-clatt thing, tomorrow you a go still haffi answer to my nine," Nicholas warned!

"All's well, that little nigger, Nigel, already out served his purpose, anyways! Everything else is only technicality," Martain assured!

Nicholas looked over at the Defenders' gun hand to whom Martain referred, as the young lad stood nervously over some of his deceased allies, while sucking the air out of a cigarette. If body language foretold guilt, then young Nigel was definitely guilty of a thousand sins, as he fidgeted about the grounds.

"Oh, and one more thing: I don't think you're going to want to stick around there until the U.S. Marshalls arrive. Shit could get sticky," Martain warned!

The Alliance Army of one hundred and eighty-seven Defenders, fifty-nine Indian Warriors from the Chateauguay area, and thirty-one Rude Boys were reduced to thirteen, like Jesus and his twelve disciples. Nicholas instructed his survivors to gather the necessary items, while he gathered with his chief personnel, to discuss their strategic options. Brogan had lost a great deal and saw no reason to "commit suicide", as he perceived an attack against the Rough Riders was, at that junctions. The Jamaican drug boss understood his general's concerns, and thus he began telling a story, about the type of city he originally believed Montreal to be, and the type of city it had become, which was a far cry from the communist laws of the Rough Riders. The man who had led them to where they were, reassured his troops that they would be victorious, despite the peril they faced, before he departed and sat out on a mission of immense importance.

The entire helicopter attack happened in less than four minutes, therefore the mans them weren't taking any checks from law enforcement officer thereafter. Despite the festive times they were having, everyone felt regret abandoning their weapons while they enjoyed the function, thus, they rode around heavily armed with high powered rifles. Within six minutes after the massacre occurred, everyone fled the scene and found somewhere to lay low until they heard from Nicholas. It took eight minutes for the police, firemen and ambulance to reach the scene, where all they found were dead bodies and a mansion engulfed in flames.

News of the destruction of Nicholas' estate, sent an overwhelming joyful reaction through Martain's camp. The bikers who were around the leader, all began cheering and jumping around, as if they had won the war. Martain was in way less of a celebrative mood, knowing that his helicopter strike had failed to exterminate the one person he intended to assassinate. He instead sat miserably watching the highlights of the destruction on television, with a glass of Cognac in his left hand, a burning cigarette between his lips, and his Glock-19 9mm automatic in the other hand. Contrary to Nicholas' estate, where the thugs celebrated because they felt like they had personally accomplished something, the bikers had made no such drastic dents, thus, Martain made them refrained from going overboard with their celebration, until their enemies were all deceased! While watching the highlights, Martain received a collect call from Yves Buchard, who was still serving time in prison. Both men hadn't spoken since Yves' conviction, but that was typically how things went whenever any biker went to prison. During his incarceration in the detention facility in Rivière-des-Prairies, Montreal, where the government housed a large group of bikers, Yves was treated like a king due of his status in the gang. The call from his long-time friend was the only time Martain smiled since their center town debacle, where the biker crew suffered their biggest single day loss ever. Yves had recently watched the news highlights about Nicholas' estate and sounded excited over the phone.
"Hey my brother! We seen your handy work all over the news," Yves declared in French!
Martain giggled, "It's been hell out here without you my friend! But things changing, I guarantee it!
"My sincerest condolences for the loss of your father!"
"I thank you brother! Revenge is only hours away!"
"It has been difficult for us in here, watching our brothers get killed and we could do nothing!"
"These fucking Jamaicans and Mohawks have cost me my respect, all across this country! Our affiliates from Vancouver to Nova Scotia, believe that I've gotten weak! But in a few hours, I aim to show them, who

alone controls this fucking province!"

"Sorry I won't get out of here in time to fight by your side brother!"

"I would love to have you there beside me, but that won't be necessary, because with less than twenty fighters, we going to bury those bastards!"

"Yeah! That is what I love to hear brother! Can't wait to celebrate with my biker brothers!"

"So, when they letting you out that rat hole?"

"In ten days, brother! Booze, bitches, drugs, and my Harley!"

"Then I see you at the gate!"

"Ride or die brother! Rough Rider for life!"

It was 12:00 midnight on the morning of the battle at: an old warehouse in Ville St. Pierre, Montreal. There was a singular Mercedes Benz parked in the middle of the warehouse, until a Maserati slowly rolled in, followed by several other high-end cars and trucks. The vehicles that arrived all formed a circle around the Mercedes, before the front passenger door opened and Nicholas stepped out.

Nicholas used his influence to orchestrate a general meeting with all minority ethnic group leaders, who'd suffered under the tyranny of the Rough Riders, yet tasted success through the defiance of the Alliance. The secret meeting was called so abruptly that no entity had the services available to infiltrate it; thus Kevin invited everyone exactly an hour before the event, gave them the area in which the meeting was to be held, and then texted the exact address an half hour prior. The meeting was an all-star event, where the bosses chauffeured themselves and drove into the warehouse, parked, and listened to the speaker, before they exited at the termination of the speech. Nicholas centered the many vehicles that belonged to prominent businessmen in the city, who were all faced with the same dilemma he battled against.

"Ladies and gentlemen, I want to thank you all for coming tonight, because here tonight is our final opportunity to rid ourselves of this band of misfits, you've been forced to honor and strengthen with your hard earned dollars all those years! Tomorrow, a handful of warriors and I are going up against this immovable force that believes it can never be altered or destroyed. Until the final breath is blown from my body, I refuse to believe that! Through matters beyond my control… fuck it, I had an army well prepared to kill every one of those sons of bitches, before them ambush us a few hours ago, and killed off most of my brave fighters! In a few hours we can change this whole island, or we can just go back to the way things were and accept it as the way it is," Nicholas exclaimed, before stepping into his vehicle and departing the scene, while everyone else followed thereafter!

Part 31

Ile Ste. Helene, as the French referred to the small island, was easily accessible by the Metro, which had a special route dug underneath the St. Lawrence River, to get there. The route along which the metro had two stops, before it turned back around and returned to the primary boarding location, which was the Berri-UQAM Station. Visitors could also commute onto the island or take the city bus, which also provided service for their clients. There wasn't anything significant about the island, such as population or dwelling, but it hosted one of the biggest annual events in Canada, which was the Formula-1 Racing. There was historic significance and major reasons visitors flocked to the island, one of such being the Montreal Casino, where gamblers went to entertain themselves. The amusement park, La Ronde, was filled with roller coaster rides, games, and excitement during the summer, while visitors partook of ice skating and tobogganing-type sports, during the winter.

Nicholas' scouts reported that Martain had confidently boarded the metro, for transportation of his troops onto the island at 7:00 AM. The report given to Nicholas stated that Martain had up to two hundred troops, which was a staggering number considering the number of bikers killed during their parade. The Jamaican drug boss hoped the biker tally would have been well beneath that quote, still he had courage to tackle the entire bunch even if he had to go alone.

Nicholas arrived at Berri-UQAM Metro Station at 7:08 AM, with his army of twelve fighters, prepared to tackle their primary nemesis, for the final confrontation. The underground Metro trains to the Island of St. Helene, were running on schedule by the transit operators, who had the least number of service stops compared to the other service lines. Nicholas waited for a surprise he promised his troops until 7:47 AM, before they moved to an awaiting train, to make their scheduled showdown. When it appeared that the surprise he promised would not arrive, it prompted his fighters to wonder if their leader, was stalling because he was afraid. In time, Nicholas accepted his fate and boarded the Metro with his allies, who believed in the cause for which they fought, and would gladly give their lives for it.

When they reached Jean-Drapeau station, all thirteen men exited the Metro and walked outside. There were two kids by the station entrance, doing flips with his skateboards, who pointed the gangsters toward the public park, which was where the bikers awaited them. Instead of any further hesitations, Nicholas briskly walked directly to the site, to reencourage his fighters' morals and beliefs, that they could be victorious. Martain could be heard boasting, 'how he knew Nicholas and his posse would never show up', as the thugs approached the park. The bikers' faces lit up with delight, at the sight of the small number of challengers approaching. Instead of cowering or showing any fear, the thugs walked directly up to the bikers and, stood approximately twenty feet away from them.

There wasn't any prearranged format how the confrontation between the two Canadian gangs was supposed to transpire. Nevertheless, it was expected that both armies would face each other, exchanged whatever salutations or degrading comments they desired, until the charge was sounded, at which time, both groups would attack each other and fought to the death. A clash between two Canadian gangs hadn't occurred since the 1800s, where British Columbia orchestrated the barbaric event. The only rule agreed to, was that the battle would last until the last man or team was left standing, at which time said entity would be crowned, "Montreal's Underground Rulers."

There wasn't a sole to be seen anywhere in the park, because once all joggers, nature watchers, and hikers, saw the intimidating group of bikers, they made immediate U-turns and scurried away in the opposite direction. While the Alliance members moved toward their nemesis, they began removing their individual weapon from bags and elsewhere, as they prepared themselves for battle. The single line of thirteen allies resembled a stone being dropped into a pail of water, yet they stood before the much larger army, unfazed and unafraid. Nicholas, along with his troops, walked up to the massive bully and stopped some twenty yards shy of their combatants, while both sides began sizing up each other. The grin on Martain's face was the first noticeable reaction by his army, as Nicholas and company approached while they surveyed everyone. The grin only managed to widen the closer Nicholas came, hence Martain sensed victory and paraded about accordingly.

"I'm glad to see you found the balls to show up, and brought the rest of your clown show to their funerals, because you're all definitely going to die here today," Martain insinuated, with a huge smile on his face!

"You fucking coward, you send some helicopters to do your dirty work," Brogan shouted!

"Of course, it worked, didn't it!? Ask Nicholas here, or should I say Kevin, if he wouldn't have done the exact same thing," Martain boasted!

"You know I bombo-clatt would, but we way past that now! It's time for us to settle this issue once and for all," Nicholas stated!

"Everyone is always in such a rush! Why you boys in such a rush to die? Eh! Take a minute and savor that last breath of fresh air, and you all might as well tell me what you want me to tell your girlfriends and family members, because I'm going to visit them all real soon! You can guarantee that! Pop a couple caps in those snotty-nosed rug rats of yours, some dick in those juicy black bitches of yours, and those old folks, y'all get the idea! People won't even remember none of you ever existed, once I'm done eliminating your past and future! Must admit, I never thought it would be this easy to kill the Dream Team, but here y'all are, about to quit breathing for the rest of your lives," rambled on the biker boss!

Martain walked around behind the protective shield of his much taller bikers while he spoke, knowing how deadly accurate the Indian Warriors' were with their bow and arrows. During Martain's speech, a train arrived in the Jean-Drapeau station, where 240 Africans and other blacks, Chinese, Indians, Lebanese, South Americans, and many other nationalities of people, descended from the underground train. The gang of multi-ethnic men stormed out of the metro uncertain where to go, before the astonished skateboarders pointed them toward the park. The late arrivals took off racing to the park, where the killing was yet to begin.

When the reinforcements who got sent by the people Nicholas spoke with reached the conflict, they all joined the revolutionary group, which was transformed into an army. Martain was at the height of his speech and refused to be interrupted, despite several of his bikers' clearing their throats, to inform him of the developments.

"… Such stupid bravery, and all easily avoided had you fools just simply paid homage to rulers of this fucking game in this city! Now look at the pathetic crumbs I've reduced you to! No man is above my law! You've all witnessed that before, and you're all going to witness that permanently," continued Martain!

"Shut the fuck up, bitch! Like I promised you, brethren', you a dead motherfucker, today," Nicholas declared!

"Who the fuck you ta—," began Martain, who couldn't believe the audacity of someone whom his bikers outnumbered?

The biker leader stood on the tips on his toes to look over one of his six-foot-four giant's shoulder, as the original thirteen dramatically increased to hundreds. Members of the Rough Riders, who primarily attended the clash to act as intimidators, began reversing to the rear of pack, as their opponents' numbers surpassed theirs.

The format of the battle had changed, to where individuals sought to exchange blows in physical combat, rather than simply massacring each other in a horrific gun shoot-out. Nicholas had spent the greater part of the evening speaking with tribal leaders of every nation throughout Montreal, in an attempt to convince them about the importance of supporting his cause against the Rough Riders. The revolution was one that affected every nationality, considering the Rough Riders had their laws implemented throughout the land.

"That over there is you talking, as usual! This over here is the communities of Montreal all standing up to tell you, to go fuck yourself! Enough of the Rough Riders' laws! From now on, it's all about free trade! Whoever want to sell whatever them want, go right ahead! We also go replace them retired secret covenant judges, 'cause real gangsters need to handle real gangsters' shit! You feel me? Now a war mi come, so let's war, pussyhole! Attack," Nicholas yelled, with a resounding charge that invigorated his followers!

Once the battle cry sounded, the representatives of free trade released the fury that was brought on from the years of suppression. Most of the new arrivals were hustlers from various parts of town, who had suffered beneath the reign of the bikers, yet made great strides through Nicholas' revolution. The loud roars, of the attacking Alliance forces, appeared to frighten some members of the bikers, who weren't sure if they should attack or turn and run. Martain raised the Mini-14 automatic weapon he'd paraded around with and sprayed several bullets directly at Nicholas. The scattered bullets bore a hole through Nicholas' right shoulder and shredded the front of his Versace shirt, exposing the bulletproof vest, which protected his chest. The single giant among the Alliance forces, was a scrawny six-foot-six-inch Nigerian, who perished and toppled onto his face, when a single stray bullet struck him in the head.

"Kevlar, motherfucker! It won't be so bombo-clatt easy this time, pussy," Nicholas warned, despite the fact not everyone came similarly equipped!

A few fighters from both sides went down during the shooting exchange, but within the squint of an eye, both sides were within arms' reach of each other. Thugs wielded axes, machetes, knives, baseball-bats, swords, pipe irons, chain saws, guns, scissors, shanks, self-altered weapons, fists, and feet at each other, as they fought like barbarians scrapping for wealth. Most fighters were eventually covered in their own blood, the blood of friends, or that of an antagonist who they had mauled to death, with either their bare hands or some foreign object.

Killa used a machete for close confrontation, that he swung like a countryman farmer reaping his sugar cane harvest. The Jamaican Rude Boy had five Glock 9mm pistols, shoved all throughout his waistline and pockets, which he sparingly used to ward off the threats, that he believed were costing them victory. The battlefield was nothing pretty, nor were the men engaging in war, as both sides carved, decimated, and disfigured each other, in an excruciating manner, which left most of those deceased, adequate only for closed casket funerals. The screams of men being brutally murdered sounded across the board, as the combatants fought for their very survival.

Nicholas, Kane, and five Warriors, fought like men with proper training, while they made the art of killing look simple. Kane had his tribunal dagger, which he creatively maneuvered like an extension of his arm. The rigorous training by Eagle, had prepared his pupils for many ranges of tactical battles, and motivated them enough to the point, that failure wasn't option. Nicholas had a dagger he'd bought on a fishing expedition to the Sioux Land, along with a Manchurian Axe, that was made in Alberta by the Navajo Indians. The pioneer against the Rough Riders, had trained extensively at the advice of Eagle, who believed a man should be capable of protecting himself against his enemies. Eagle taught Nicholas how to feel his way around a battlefield, which was a trait that, if properly maneuvered, became somewhat of a sixth sense. At one point during the battle, Nicholas felt the spiritual forces of his deceased friends, Danny and Eagle, while he fought two bikers simultaneously. The spirit forces encouraged Nicholas to peek over his shoulder, while engaged with the first biker, at which he caught sight of the second male rushing in to stab him. To avoid being stabbed, Nicholas swung his hand holding the axe at the biker, who was forced stop suddenly or get his head bashed in. The Alliance leader had to use his defensive skills to fend off both bikers, until Killa noticed their boss' plight and, shot and killed one of the attackers. With one of the two bikers' dead, Nicholas stood his ground and baited his opponent into lunging at him, at which he severed the man's arm with his axe, then shoved his knife into the attacker's gut.

Martain had enrolled in self-protection courses, since he was old enough to kick a soccer ball. The biker boss had studied various disciplines of martial arts, such as Karate and Taekwondo, and he was quite capable of protecting himself. Those who fought alongside the Rough Riders' boss', were always cognizant of his well-being, since he meant a great deal to the continued existence of the club. A representative from almost every culture that formed the Alliance group, attempted to kill, or injured the reigning ruler of the biker club. The name Martain Lafleur, was legendary throughout the underground; hence, whoever was credited with killing him, knew his name would be guaranteed to be written in history books. For such an honor, many men threw away their lives recklessly, as they shunned their responsibilities to strike a blow at Martain.

The battle raged on for more than an hour, but it wasn't until the fiftieth minute, before the sound of an intruding helicopter was heard in the skies. The RDS Broadcasting Station received information of a brutal battle and sent their traffic update helicopter to investigate the claims. The footage captured by the helicopter, which wasn't allowed to hover over the fight zone, due to gangsters shooting away at the hull, was disturbing to viewers, who thought they were watching the taping of a motion film. There were bodies scattered across the plains, but only a few anatomies were left intact, as the majority suffered severed limbs, scalped hairlines, and cut open wounds, which exposed their intestines. The scent of death made vultures gather and circled around the battle-field, like they had appointments for a free feast.

Martain glared over at Nicholas, as the field of over five-hundred fighters, shrunk to forty plus men. The two warring factions had surrendered a great deal of their soldiers to the cause, but the Alliance mob still maintaining a slight edge in numbers. Following the warriors first assault, the helicopter pilot circled to another location, where they again tried to record the battle. The helicopter distraction gave both parties the opportunity to re-evaluate their stance, after the armed combatants shot at the hovering metal bird, then retreated to their individual quadrants. The eighteen remaining bikers, along with the twenty-three Alliance members, were all tired beyond comprehension, and yet their genuine hatred for each other fueled their fighting spirits. Martain and Killa were the only combatants, who, although covered with blood, were not actually injured, or wounded.

Kane, Tank, and Brogan, among others, slumped forward or fell to one knee, as they grabbed or attended to their wounds. Nicholas, despite the bullet that went directly through his shoulder, appeared physically stealthy, although his breathing demonstrated his fatigue. The Alliance forerunner stood tall in front his troops, as those who redirected the helicopter, dropped the weapons they used to do the job. Martain also stood vast before his troops, with words of encouragements, while the two leaders stared at each other like raging bulls, priming to attack.

The unspoken fury that transcended from both men, soon brought their remaining faculty members to their sides, as both gangs stood fifteen feet apart, soliciting the other to attack. Suddenly, without any warning, both groups collided with each other, in what only could be described as a catastrophic masterpiece. Killa found himself submerged in a battle against an opponent, who had an actual Chinese sword that, he'd used to carve his way through the first round of the battle. For the first few minutes, Killa was forced into a defensive posture, as the Asian-Canadian wielding the sword was quite skilled and, swore to "decapitate the Jamaican's head"! The Asian born Canadian had Killa in reverse mode, as he bobbed and weaved his body to avoid the chops being swung at him. While backing up, Killa tripped over the corpse of a slain Nigerian and fell flat on his ass. The fall caused Killa to lose his machete, which went flying as he collided with the ground, thus, his opponent moved in for the kill. The reluctant Jamaican's eyes opened wide, as he anticipated the blade piercing his skin, therefore he grabbed for the first object within arm's reach. The Asian-Canadian biker was poised to run his sword through Killa, when the rude boy gripped tightly onto the deceased African's spear, and thrusted it into his attacker's belly. The biker froze with astonishment, then looked down at the blade and grunted like a bear, before he expelled his final breath. Killa tossed the biker to the side, collected his machete, then charged back into the raging battle.

There were bikers' intent on slaying the leader of the opposition, as was evident by the two separate stab wounds, which Brogan received from cowardly opponents, who attacked him from behind. The Defender boss was engaged with the Rough Riders' west division captain, when a biker private who killed his opponent, began moving in from behind, to pierce his fifteen-inch blade into Brogan's back. The attacking biker was inches from killing the Defenders' leader, when Killa chopped his arm off from an angle, which sent the knife holding hand twirling in the air, before they landed a few feet away. The surprised biker's mouth fell wide open, as he watched in slow motion, his arm leave the base from which it was attached, before it went airborne like a bird, then crashed. Before the biker's arm and knife could hit the ground, Killa decapitated the man's head with one clean swipe, thus, the head fell with the same astonished expression. The rude boy then proceeded to assist Brogan, who wasn't one hundred percent, nevertheless together they disfigured the Rough Riders' west division captain. All across the battlefield, the Alliance members had begun to take full control, therefore, those who had won their challenges, helped their struggling companions achieved victory.

Nicholas and Martain engaged in a classical battle the moment they clashed into each other, as they vowed to physically rip each other's head off. The two men were drastically improved in skill from their original encounter, which was actually a show of power by the Rough Riders. The memory of everything Martain and his goons did to him, replayed continuously in Nicholas' head, as he sought to slice and dice the biker boss. Martain had armed himself with a dagger and a meat hacker, to complement the dagger and axe of his opponent. The 'cling-cling' sounds of metal colliding, echoed for nearly five minutes, as both leaders went back and forth at each other. The battlefield had decisively been conquered by the Alliance, who defied all odds fighting with rookies.

The six surviving Alliance members gathered to watch the battle between Nicholas and Martain that, had been raging on for thirteen agonizing minutes, in a seesaw affair. Killa thought back to his days on the playground in Jamaica, where his battles against future friends and foes occurred. The Jamaican Rude Boy, thought of a maneuver that was done to him by Stamma, which, had the altercation not been interrupted, may had won him the match.

"Remember the slide-and-pop move that Stamma lick I with? Put it pan the buoy," Killa instructed, after observing the proper opening for the technique!

Martain had Nicholas in a chokehold, while he attempted to plunge his dagger into his throat. Nicholas had been disarmed of both his axe and his dagger, after the biker boss smacked him with a three-punch combination, directly after catching him with a stunning kick to the side of the head. Martain faked as if he was leading with his blade, before he delivered that colossal kick, to the side of Nicholas' temple. The combination of blows staggered Nicholas, who only managed to remain conscious, through the cheers and encouragements of his friends. Martain fought valiantly and attempted to end the battle by piercing his blade into Nicholas, who was on the verge of being killed by the only man he truly despised.

Nicholas, from the standing position, folded his legs like a Muslim crouching to pray, which released him from Martain's secured grip. As he fell to the ground, Nicholas grabbed the blade from Martain's grip with his countered weight, against Martain's one-handed grip. The maneuver by Nicholas was so smooth, that it caught Martain complete by surprise, because he doubted the Jamaican knew such a technique. Nicholas knew that Martain wore a vest beneath his clothing that might, interfere with him puncturing one of his main arteries. The Rude Boy leader, therefore rammed the blade directly up the crotch of his revered enemy and left it stuck directly between his testicles and buttocks. The jolt of electricity that shocked up Martain's intestines, froze the biker boss in position, thus, he fell to his knees and grabbed the blade's handle, unsure of what removing it might do. Nicholas arose to his feet, looked around and grabbed the closest pistol in his vicinity.

Three Black Hawks and a Huey military helicopter approached from all four directions, as Nicholas held his weapon aimed at Martain's head. The tall trees around the park made it somewhat difficult for the helicopters' crews to see everything happening on the ground. There was a mixture of officers from both the U.S and Canada, aboard each of the helicopters, which hovered above the park. Chief Carbonelli, of the Federal Bureau of Investigation, grabbed the loudspeaker aboard his chopper and announced who they were.

"This is Agent Carbonelli of the Federal Bureau of Investigation! Drop all your weapons! I repeat; drop all your weapons! I need to see everybody's hands in the air! I have an Immigration Deportation Order and a Federal Warrant for the arrest of Kevin Walsh—," barked Agent Carbonelli over the loudspeaker!

"Shoot him! Shoot him and shut the fuck up! For Christ sakes, he's got a gun pointed at my head! Somebody shoot his ass! I need help! Shut the fuck up and shoot him," Martain begged, as the loud sounds of the helicopters muffled his voice!

"Good-bye, Martain," Nicholas stated!

'Boom! Boom! Boom!' The Glock 9mm pistol in Nicholas' grasp fired.

Part 32

Nicholas and his surviving cast were all taken to the Patinè Central Jail for processing, prior to their early morning rendez-vous with the presiding judge. The Alliance members were transferred to the central holding facility, by the largest prisoner convoy ever formulated, as law officials took all precautions with their high-profile prisoners. The Patinè Central Jail was located to the east of downtown, inside a twenty-story edifice, of which the top five floors were used to house prisoners. The facility mainly held prisoners who were being transferred, court-appointed individuals, and prisoners who had been sentenced to serve six months or less. Each prisoner's level of offense, was used to determine what floor they were assigned to; therefore, the most violent offenders were held on the top two floors. Nicholas was the first person processed, then taken to the top floor, where many of the prisoners cheered him. With the arrival of each member of Nicholas' coalition on the range, came humongous cheers and applause, after it was rumored that they were triumph versus the Rough Riders. Despite the cheers, many prisoners had hoped the Alliance would have been defeated, thus, not everyone was as celebrative.

Patinè Central Jail did not offer the housing amenities of permanent holding institutions such as Bordeaux, where inmates were permitted to walk from one activity to another. The transition jail kept its inmates confined for twenty-four hours a day, with an hour of exercise only offered to those who remained for more than a week. The institution's exercise area was a large room, with four thirty-foot walls, that was covered with a chain-linked wire, where the inmates could only walk around. Patine's entire operation was different from regular prisons, where more freedom was given to inmates. The cells held two men reasonably comfortably, inmates received three meals daily, and showers were given on Mondays and Thursdays. Nicholas and company were not, however, treated to any of the fine hospitalities provided by the jail, as they were summoned with the morning court appointees, and transferred to the courthouse for arraignment.

The elaborate motorcade that transferred Nicholas and company to Montreal's Palais-De-Justice courthouse, resembled that of the United States' president, with its vast amount of police detail and armored vehicles. The posse that defeated the great Rough Riders crew was reunited in the Bull Pen, which was in the basement of the Palais De Justice building. None of the victorious fighters were housed together, therefore they high-fived, fist-pumped, and hugged each other, like lost friends. Despite their enthusiasm to see each other, Nicholas understood that they were all fearful of the court system, so he spoke with them and assured them that 'none of them would spend a moment in prison'. The late helpers who survived still maintained that level of fear, but Killa, Kane and even Brogan, knew Nicholas was the type of person who covered all angles.

"Where is James," asked Tank, who noticed that the AWOLed soldier was missing?

"His army buddies most likely came and picked him up! Remember, he ain't no regular civilian like us," Kane answered.

At 8:45 the on-duty sergeant walked over with a list of names, which only included Nicholas and his Alliance team, who were scheduled for a private hearing before the Honorable Judge Antoine Bryere. Every defendant who had passed before a magistrate, had developed some sort of nervous feeling, knowing the judge had the power to reprimand them, or grant them their freedom. Following their discussion, the Alliance members began exhibiting a more positive outlook on their situation, which enlightened the other inmates who were scheduled to see the judge. The guards handcuffed all the crew members and brought them by elevator up to the third floor, where, instead of a locking them in the holding cells again, they were rushed directly into Judge Bryere's courtroom.

The courtroom was nearly barren, with only Judge Bryere, the prosecuting attorney, Agent Carbonelli, and Nicholas' high-priced attorney present. The guards, who led the accused into the courtroom, remained for a moment, before the judge instructed them to vacate his chambers, as the matter was one of extreme confidentiality. News media personnel packed the hallway outside Court Room #305, desperate to capture the photos of the men who'd become infamous across Canada. Discovery disclosures were often sent to media relations, in high-profile cases such as, 'The Canadian Government vs. The Alliance'. However, Judge Bryere issued a gag order, which prevented any leaks of information pertaining to the case. All entries to the courtroom were prevented by two correctional officers, who allowed no one within six-foot of the entrance.

Inside the courtroom, Judge Bryere politely asked the gangsters before him to, "take a seat," as he read over a letter that was handed to him, moments before they entered. The judge also held a cellular phone to his ear, which was unusual for a presiding judge, while seated on his bench. Nicholas' lawyer signaled his clients that everything was proceeding accordingly, as he confidently stood behind the defense table. Judge Bryere terminated his phone conversation, and then summoned both legal counsels to approach his bench. The judge was incensed, as he grimaced at the members of the Alliance, who sat serenely awaiting his decision.

"Chief Prosecutor Ramous, I trust you've spoken with your superiors and understand the critical junction we've come to in this case," demanded the judge!

The prosecutor exclaimed, "Yes, sir, I most certainly understand!"

"Okay. Mr. Paventrum, I guess your clients are free to go pending proper documentation," ruled Judge Bryere! "You gentlemen have been struck with the hand of the Almighty, because I don't believe any trial would be necessary to convict you men of all these charges here before me, especially premeditated murders! I guarantee, should I ever catch one of you back in my courtroom, it will be the last time you freely see the light of day! You gentlemen are all free to go!"

"Wait a minute, Your Honor! I'm Agent Carbonelli, of the Federal Bureau of Investigation, and I have here a warrant and a deportation order for Mr. Kevin Walsh, aka Nicholas Henry, in connection to the deaths of U.S. Marshalls on American soil. Mr. Walsh's extradition has been signed and approved by the Attorney General of the United States, and I have every intention of honoring this warrant," Agent Carbonelli argued!

Judge Bryere requested the documents and took them from Carbonelli, who maintained a vacant stare at Nicholas, as if he was attempting to intimidate the Rude Boy. Nicholas smiled at Carbonelli before raising his handcuffed hands and applauding the agent for his years of dedication. Carbonelli was content with seeing Nicholas confined, and he envisioned removing the third most wanted fugitive's name, from the infamous FBI's Most Wanted list.

"These documents appear to be in order. He's all yours, Agent Carbonelli," Judge Bryere disclosed!

"What the fuck? What kind of shit is all this, Judge," yelled Damian, who leaped to his feet the moment the judge gave his ruling?

"Your Honor, I don't believe you have the power to sign an extradition order for Mr. Henry! Furthermore, this is all new to Mr. Henry's defense team, so we request the necessary time to file an injunction in this case," Nicholas' attorney protested!

"Are you attempting to lecture me on the requirements of my job, Mr. Paventrum," Judge Bryere asked?

"No, sir! I'm simply unaware of these charges against my client and need time to formulate a defense," Mr. Paventrum explained.

"This case has not provided your typical pre-trial hearing. I personally believe our taxpayers deserve more accountability from their government, but then again, in the long run, what difference am I making? You may state your grievance with the committee, but I'm releasing Mr. Henry into the custody of the U.S. Marshalls! Thank you and, have a nice day," Judge Bryere stated, before he stormed from the bench for his personal chamber!

The corrections officers who led the men into the courtroom, returned and brough them back to the holding facilities, pending their release documents by the Bureau of Corrections. Nicholas was in Killa's ear the moment the judge rendered his final verdict regarding his deportation, hence, the outlaw issued his desires and wishes pertaining to his son. Killa vowed to protect and raise young Junior according to his friend's wishes, while he continued the growth of Nicholas' empire, during his absence.

Following the provincial and general elections, Canadians elected Mathew Layton, from Almont, Ontario, to the post of prime minister. The new prime minister was the person with whom the judge spoke, when Nicholas and his associates, entered the courtroom. Prime Minister Layton hung up the phone with Judge Bryere, after he instructed the judge on how to proceed with the surviving Alliance members. The prime minister was at home, where he had summoned his entire cabinet, for a viewing of a private DVD he received via Fed-Ex courier. The DVD disclosed years of political manipulations by the secret covenant, assassinations orchestrated and performed, business affiliations where political figures accepted bribes and payoffs, personal favors that involved building contracts, real estate developmental contracts from the days of our founding fathers, and many more illegal transactions. However, the most compelling disclosure of all, was the revelation of all the former appointees to political offices, who were elected through the vigilance and roughhouse tactics of the secret covenant.

There was incriminating evidence, documented and filed, which proved the Rough Riders were the puppets at the end of the string, who were controlled and manipulated by a bunch of old geezers. Throughout the entire history lesson, everyone who watched thought the most detrimental disclosure, was the secret cult's affiliation with the man whose picture graced the Canadian hundred-dollar bill. The entire DVD, which would have been a political nightmare for any regime had it been publicized, came with specific instructions that stated, "DVDs will be sent to all news media should the Alliance survivors not be released!" The embarrassment that loomed, especially after the recent slayings downtown Montreal, was believed to be too stressful for Canadians, by a prime minister who sought immediate closure to the entire ordeal.

The governing cabinet weighed its options and decided to release without restrictions, the accused gang members who were caught red handed, on the field of battle. Despite their assumed guilt, none of the survivors felt any remorse for killing the bikers and, were proud to admit it. The floods of the heavens would have poured, had the prime minister not accepted the deal, after he watched the powerful bargaining chip, that was in the hands of mysterious foreigners. The prime minister was cognizant of the reprisals against the newest appointed officials in Quebec, who were also mentioned on the DVD, with those illegally appointed into office, since the beginning of Canadian democracy.

Prime Minister Layton telephoned Premier Richard Blanc, whom he believed might be the sole voice of reason, to which French Quebecers were willing to listen. The Canadian prime minister withheld mention of the scandalous DVD, as he encouraged half of the first joint premier team, to take the lead on the arising issue. When asked by Premier Blanc, "Why were video-recorded killers being set free?" The prime minister soberly explained, "Our hands were tied behind our backs, Richard! God damned in-house affairs!"

The premier refrained from any further enquiry, as he intellectually deciphered that Pandora's box had been opened, which, if exposed, brought the possibility of impeachment charges. With that, Premier Blanc issued a press conference, where he, along with Police Chief Arnold Dubois, Montreal's mayor and the RCMP Commander Lucien Lapierre, answered tough questions from the media, regarding the decision to release the Alliance members, without restrictions.

Police intervention was necessary for Brogan and his liberated friends, who exited the courthouse to a huge mixed crowd of protestors and admirers, who anointed them or believed they should be locked away with the grimiest of criminals. The police officers had to form a pathway from the front entrance of the Palais De Justice Building, down the long steps along St. Antoine Boulevard, to four Chevy Suburban's, being driven by the ragamuffin ladies of the Alliance. The loud roars of a thundering Porsche Phantom came to a screeching halt in front the awaiting SUVs, before the luscious, long-legged Alyiah pranced from the conductor door. Kane smiled at his wife, before he fist-bumped his mates and assured them 'that he'd be in touch', then he hobbled down to his awaiting chauffeur. Killa, Damian, Tank, and the rest of the crew all climbed aboard the identical SUVs, and completely ignored the crowd and media personnel asking questions. The vehicles all sped off down St. Antoine Boulevard, before they veered west onto the Ville Marie Express Way.

The moment Killa hopped into the SUV, he began checking for young Junior, but believed the female left him secured due to the hectic pressures they'd face. It wasn't until the SUVs were speeding along Interstate 20, that Killa asked about the young lad of whom he had been placed in charge. The female driver apologized for the news she was about to deliver, before she recounted an incident that had occurred only moments before, where they were ambushed and hijacked by a bunch of females, who took young Junior hostage. Killa's entire mood changed the instant he heard the news, however, before he went in search of Kevin Junior, his first priority was to spend time with Mocha.

Commander Carbonelli and his strike force drove into Hangar #11, where their private charter awaited them at Dorval International Airport. The commander was jubilant after apprehending a suspect he'd chased for more than a decade, and he advised his central command that "they were returning with the package!" The commander came off the phone and looked back at Nicholas, who appeared tranquil for someone about to get buried.

"I'm going to make sure they put you in a hole so far underground that if you ever come up for light, you're either dead or getting transferred to an even deeper hole! I told you I was going to get you, didn't I," Carbonelli bragged!?

Nicholas remained quiet and smirked at Carbonelli, as if he still had an ace card up his sleeve. Once they entered the hangar, Carbonelli's men took up positions around the area, which was standard procedure to ensure the perimeter was secured. Carbonelli waited for the 'area secured confirmation', before, he attempted to transfer Nicholas from their vehicle to the airplane. The Jamaican rude boy was shackled at the ankles, and wore handcuffs, which were both attached to a chain around his waist.

While Nicholas shuffled along across the hangar floor, two black Hummers pulled up in front the huge doors, at which several armed, uniformed men dismounted. Carbonelli's special forces personnel surrounded their prisoner, and removed the safety clips from their automatic weapons, in preparation for any forms of aggression. The armed men who dismounted from the Hummers all wore dark, lime green uniforms, which was the standard color for Canadian special force members.

The Americans were under strict, "Shoot only when shot after" orders, which prevented them from just opening fire at the approaching figures, regardless of the huge weapons they carried. The armed Canadians walked directly up to Commander Carbonelli and handed him a letter. Carbonelli opened and read the letter, and said, "No fucking way," before he withdrew his side pistol and jammed it directly against the head of the Canadian, who handed him the paper. The sounds of hammers being cocked echoed inside the hangar, as both sides prepared for an altercation.

"Sir, may I remind you that you're still on Canadian soil, and I doubt you guys have enough ammunition to hold off my boys, and whatever reinforcements respond to our SOS?"

Commander Carbonelli was furious that he was about to lose the man he had searched for years to find, but he agreed to the terms, nevertheless. A confrontation with their next-door neighbors and allies, would not be in the best interest for their public relations, so Carbonelli tossed the restraint keys to Nicholas' confines at the agent, and boarded the plane with his peers. The Canadian special force soldiers who negotiated Nicholas from the Americans, removed the thug's bondages, before they ushered him into the dignitary cabinet of the vehicle. The Hummers sped off with Nicholas comfortably relaxing, as he laughed to himself, then sparked up a huge cigar, that was given to him by the negotiator.

"Excuse me, Mr. Henry, but the prime minister would like to have a word with you over the phone," said the shotgun rider.

Yves Buchard exited the Riviere-des-Prairies Detention Facility empty handed and began walking toward the bus stop. As he walked across the parking lot, he noticed a white stretch limousine coming around ahead of him. The tinted glasses made it impossible to see who was inside the vehicle, therefore, Yves' heartrate increased slightly due to fright. The biker feared that the occupants might had been Alliance members sent to assassinate him, therefore, he prepared himself to race back to the prison, if necessary. The limousine drove up next to Yves and the rear window slowly rolled down, with White Widow, of the Pigeons of The Order, as the lone occupant.

"Get in the car! The Old Man wants to see you! He is fucking pissed," White Widow declared!

Yves opened the door and climbed into the limousine, which slowly drove away.

The End

Acknowledgement

Cover By: Clyde Williams www.graphiquemezza.com
Andrene Bryan
Book Layout By: www.bookdesign.ca